Travellers' Nature Guides

Greece

Travellers' Nature Guides

Series editor: Martin Walters

This series is designed for anyone with an interest in the natural history of the places they visit. Essentially practical, each book first introduces the ecology, geology, and wildlife of the country or countries it covers, then goes on to describe where to see the natural history at its best. The entries are the personal choice of the individual authors and are based on intensive travel and research in their areas. Sites range in size from a few to thousands of hectares, be they National Parks, nature reserves, or simply common land, but all are open to the public and accessible to the ordinary visitor. The books are designed to complement each other and to build into a nature library, together giving an introduction to the natural history of Europe.

Britain: *Travellers' Nature Guide*
France: *Travellers' Nature Guide*
Greece: *Travellers' Nature Guide*
Spain: *Travellers' Nature Guide*
Portugal: *Travellers' Nature Guide* (forthcoming)

Travellers' Nature Guides
Greece

Bob Gibbons

Photographs
Natural Image

Maps, animal drawings, and panoramas
Michael Wood

Plant drawings
Stella Tranah

OXFORD
UNIVERSITY PRESS

OXFORD
UNIVERSITY PRESS

Great Clarendon Street, Oxford OX2 6DP

Oxford University Press is a department of the University of Oxford.
It furthers the University's objective of excellence in research, scholarship,
and education by publishing worldwide in

Oxford New York

Auckland Bangkok Buenos Aires Cape Town Chennai
Dar es Salaam Delhi Hong Kong Istanbul Karachi Kolkata
Kuala Lumpur Madrid Melbourne Mexico City Mumbai Nairobi
São Paulo Shanghai Singapore Taipei Tokyo Toronto

and an associated company in Berlin

Oxford is a registered trade mark of Oxford University Press
in the UK and in certain other countries

Published in the United States
by Oxford University Press Inc., New York

First published 2003

A catalogue record for this book is available from the British Library

Library of Congress Cataloging in Publication Data

Data available

ISBN 0-19-850437-3
10 9 8 7 6 5 4 3 2 1

Typeset by Pantek Arts Ltd, Maidstone, Kent
Printed by Giunti Industrie Grafiche, Prato, Italy

Foreword

The primary aim of this series is to act as a guide and a stimulus to holidaymakers, be they specialist naturalist or interested amateur, and to teach them something of the wealth of wildlife that is to be found in the countryside around them, whether at home or abroad.

Despite the continued encroachment of housing and intensive farmland, and the disappearance of so much natural and semi-natural habitat over many decades, the wildlife of Europe is still remarkably varied and rewarding.

One of the major developments of recent years has been the rise of so-called 'ecotourism', which has combined the interests of the naturalist and the holidaymaker. Such tourism ranges from specialist guided tours for small groups of keen birdwatchers or botanists (often both) to more leisurely holidays that involve perhaps a sprinkling of nature study along with the more traditional goals of the tourist, such as visits to famous buildings or architectural sites. At the same time, the general traveller on a private holiday to a hotel, villa, *gîte*, or campsite is frequently keen to learn more about the landscape and countryside of the region he or she is visiting, and such knowledge can considerably enrich and increase the enjoyment of a holiday.

Throughout the books there is a strong emphasis on conservation and the need to ensure that a representative range of habitats remains long into the future for coming generations of naturalists and nature-sensitive tourists to enjoy.

Each book begins with an overview. This is in essence a background sketch of the country – mainly in terms of its ecology and wildlife – with a look at the major habitat types and their importance. The overview also contains some details about the state of nature conservation, and considers the various types of reserve, conservation laws, and related matters.

The overview is followed by a systematic gazetteer of selected sites, grouped by regions, of particular natural history importance. Of course, with so many fascinating areas – not all of them protected – in addition to the large numbers of reserves, our coverage cannot be comprehensive. Nevertheless, we have chosen sites that are generally not too difficult to access and which together give a full picture of the richness of each country. The choice aims to give a representative range of visitable sites, encompassing all the important habitats. The sites vary widely in status and size, but all have something special to offer the visitor, and repay a visit.

The books in this series are highly visual, and are enlivened by the use of colour photographs of landscapes, habitats, species, and locations, many showing the actual sites described. The photographs were provided by the Natural Image photograph agency. The photographer was Bob Gibbons except where otherwise indicated in the caption. In addition, selected animals and plants are also illustrated by black and white line drawings, accompanying the relevant text. Maps of the country, regions, and selected sites enable each site to be quickly located and placed in the context of the country as a whole.

A special feature of these *Travellers' Nature Guides* is the composite painting, painted by wildlife artist Michael Wood, depicting a range of classic habitats for each country, and illustrating a number of characteristic species. This will help to give a flavour of the richness of the wildlife awaiting the informed naturalist traveller.

Martin Walters
Series Editor
Cambridge, 2002

Contents

An index to scientific and English species names used in all the
books in this series can be found at
www.oup.com/uk/travellersnatureguides

Overview

Introduction

For most people, Greece conjures up visions of beaches, sunshine, and ancient sites, but little else. In practice, it is a wonderfully varied and exciting country, with unspoilt scenery, from hot, barren, sun-baked rocky wastes to snow-capped mountains, forests, abundant natural lakes, many of the deepest gorges in Europe, and vast areas of saltmarsh and coastal lagoons, all relatively undiscovered, in addition to those sandy beaches, classical sites, and sunshine. It is quite possible to spend a week in summer in north-west Greece, in the Vikos National Park for example,

amongst extraordinarily dramatic gorge and mountain scenery, constantly surrounded by butterflies, seeing eagles, choughs, and many other exciting birds, and an endless variety of flowers – and meet very few other tourists. Anywhere comparable in western Europe would be overrun with people.

The natural life of Greece is quite exceptional. There are almost 6000 species of native flowers (about 750 of which, depending on how you define a species, occur nowhere else), 422 species of birds recorded at some time or other, 232 species of butterflies, and about 70 rep-

Opposite page: **The semi-desert eastern coast of Crete, near Zakros**

tiles and amphibians. For the naturalist, it is a rewarding country to visit, with much to see in every season, and something new around every corner, as we hope the following pages will demonstrate.

Geography

Greece is by no means a large country. With a total surface area of about 132 000 square kilometres (c. 51 000 square miles), including all the islands, it is only about a quarter the size of France or Spain, and not much more than half the size of Britain. Out of this area, about 106 000 square kilometres are on the mainland, with the remainder spread amongst the islands. Its particularly indented coastline, and vast number of islands, means that it has an extraordinarily long coastline – some 15 021 km, of which about 11 000 is around the islands. The bulk of Greece is in the form of a peninsula jutting southwards from the Balkans, where it borders on (from west to east) Albania, Macedonia, and Bulgaria. It shares a relatively short land border with Turkey in the far north-east, though of course the border between the two countries also meanders through the Aegean Sea. No islands are split between the two countries, and the great bulk of the Aegean islands belong to Greece, even to within a few kilometres of Turkey at some points, such as Samos. The southernmost parts of Greece, especially Crete and its offshore islands, lie only 200 km from Africa, so Greece effectively forms a meeting point between Europe, Asia, and Africa, and this is evident both ecologically and culturally. In fact, the southernmost parts of Greece lie well south of parts of the north-African mainland, so its warm climate is hardly surprising, though it is also heavily influenced by the proximity of the Balkans in winter.

Greece is a surprisingly mountainous country, with significant high ground in all parts, including on many of the islands, and substantial ranges in the north. The average altitude of the country

Summit of Mt. Taigetos

is about 500 m above sea level, with about one-third of the country lying above 500 m. A total of almost 4000 square kilometres lies above 1500 m (= 4920 feet), which is higher than the highest mountain in Britain. This is a substantial area of high-altitude country, and many of Greece's special plants and animals occur here. The main mountain ranges split effectively into two broad areas; the Pindos mountains, which are a southwards extension of the Dinaric Alps, run in a broad swathe south-eastwards through mainland Greece, continuing into the Peloponnese via the high peaks of the Giona–Parnassus area. The Peloponnese is almost equally mountainous, with Chelmos and Killini dominating the north, and a range extending southwards through Taigetos, down the Mani Peninsula, and ultimately curving around into the high mountains of Crete. The other main range runs roughly east–west along the Macedonian and Bulgarian borders, where it is known mainly as the Rhodopi range. There are other mountains which do not quite fit into this pattern, noticeably the highest mountain in the country – Mt. Olympus (2917 m) – which lies in the eastern part of Thessaly, as well as Mt. Pilion, the mountains of Evvia, and the many isolated peaks on islands. This vast extent of relatively high mountains is a very important strand in Greece's ecology: many of its endemic plants have evolved in isolation on high mountains, many of its special birds find a degree of sanctuary here, and it is on the middle and lower slopes of such mountains that very large areas of forests occur, home to all manner of species. As a general rule, mountains have escaped more of the changes wrought by humans, as they are less suitable for residential land, intensive agriculture, and tourism development. Greece has not been subject to the mass pressures of general tourism in summer and skiing in winter that has affected the Alps and Pyrenees, though this is beginning to change as a number of ski stations have been established recently, and general tourism is increasing. A very high proportion of the sites that we have selected in this book are mountains or land associated with mountains – an indication of their importance for wildlife in general.

Between the high points of the mountains, there are valleys, including gorges, and some relatively flat areas. Gorges are a great feature of Greece, largely because there are so many limestone mountains, and these are wonderful places for wildlife.

Each gorge is unique, but virtually all of them support a rich flora and fauna, especially the larger ones, and the major ones, such as the Samaria Gorge on Crete, and the Vikos Gorge in north-west Greece, have an international reputation. Indeed the Vikos Gorge (900m deep and 12km long) is claimed to be the deepest gorge in the world, though this must depend on your definition of a gorge, and others would undoubtedly dispute this claim! Be that as it may, it is an exceptionally spectacular place, as are many of the gorges.

Another key feature of the more mountainous areas of Greece are the curious internally draining valleys, sometimes known as *poljes*. These occur in limestone country, where the water falling on the range does not form into an overground river, and therefore does not erode a valley; it collects into gradually enlarging basins and sinks into the ground. In winter, or during wet periods, a lake may form that sometimes remains all year, become marshy for part of the year, or dry out. Inevitably, large quanti-

Parnassus in winter

Ancient amphitheatre at Dodoni, north-west Greece

ties of silt are deposited, so the floor of the polje gradually becomes flattened out. Such features can be found throughout the country; most are now cultivated, though some – such as the Omalos Plain in Crete, or the plain on the south-west side of Parnassus, still retain features of interest.

There are about 20 main rivers in Greece, though they do not all rise within the country. None is particularly long or large, and most share the feature of draining a relatively large catchment within quite a

short distance of their mouth. Because the range of Mediterranean tides is noticeably small, and the currents and wave action are generally weak, the silt brought down by the rivers tends to be deposited as deltas, rather than forming estuaries which are typical of more oceanic river mouths. Such deltas, especially for the larger rivers such as the Evros, can become extremely large and complex areas as more and more silt is deposited; the pattern of river flow constantly shifts, producing a mosaic of river channels, salt-marsh, lagoons, and mudflats, often edged with sand dunes, together with more stable vegetation such as reedbeds and riverine woodland. The many Greek deltas must have been extraordinary areas once (and many certainly were until quite recently), but they have been prime targets for agricultural and industrial expansion and other exploitation, and all are now but shadows of their former selves. At least a number of them have been recognized for their international importance, even in their impoverished states, and are being partially protected as such (see p. 24).

Saltmarsh at Pylos, on the west coast of the Peloponnese – an internationally important site

The slopes of Mount Lepetimnos on the north coast of Lesvos

There are a surprising number of natural lakes in Greece; surprising, because the fate of most lakes in a warm climate is to fill with vegetation and peat, then disappear, usually to become cultivated. There are, indeed, many areas of Greece which were quite clearly lakes in the not very distant past, but which are now intensively cultivated, with just lines of reeds and a few *eutrophicated* (excessively rich in nutrients) ditches to indicate their past. However, many remain, especially in the north where the rainfall is higher and temperatures (and therefore evaporation rate) are lower. A whole series of beautiful natural lakes is strung across north Greece, from Lake Volvi, north-east of Thessaloniki, to the Prespa Lakes National Park on the Macedonian and Albanian borders. These are in various stages of change, and some are now largely filled with peat and aquatic vegetation such as reeds, but all are important wildlife resources. In some cases, such as Lake Ioannina and Lake Kastoria, an important town has developed on the lake margin. Although this inevitably increases the pollution of the lake, it also makes for a very attractive interface between water and town, which often provides an ideal place from which to view the wildlife of the lake without effort.

Islands form a particularly important part of Greece. Without them it would still be an interesting country, but their presence extends and enhances its interest considerably. As we have already seen, about 70% of the coast of Greece is around the islands (so their importance to the holiday industry is obvious). There are said to be 9838 islands and islets in Greece, of which over 8000 are in the Aegean Sea – an extraordinary area, and a true archipelago. Of this vast number of islands, only about 200 are inhabited, so the possibilities for birds which need to escape the effects of human settlement – such as shearwaters and Eleonora's falcons – are obvious. In fact, the largest concentration of Eleonora's falcons in the world is to be found in the uninhabited islands of the Aegean. The Aegean islands are mostly the tops of mountains that have progressively sunk and become submerged, and some still reach considerable heights, such as on Samos, where they reach 1433 m.

The population of Greece is currently about 10 426 000, giving a density of 79 people per square kilometre; this compares with 239 per square kilometre in Britain, 227 per square kilometre in Germany, or 106 per square kilometre in France. In other words, the population density is relatively low, by European standards, and there are large areas of little-used land. About 72% of the population is urban or semi-urban. Most towns and industry in Greece lie on or close to the coast, and this clearly has a considerable effect on the ecology of the coast.

Climate

The climate of Greece can generally be described as Mediterranean – that is, having hot, dry summers, and mild, damp or wet winters. However, Greece covers such a range, from the near semi-desert conditions of coastal southern Crete to the high mountains of north-western Greece, that it is impossible to generalize adequately, and some more detailed explanation is necessary. There is, of course, a general cline of decreasing warmth from south to north, and the mountain areas are mostly decidedly cooler and wetter than the lowlands; however, the picture is made more complex by Greece's position, squeezed between the Balkans, Africa, and the Middle East.

In summer, things are relatively straightforward. The intense heat of the Middle East causes dry continental air to be sucked in over the eastern Mediterranean, including Greece, almost entirely from the north. Summers are characterized by endless warm or hot sunny days, with a steady northerly wind, known commonly as the *meltemi*, though naturally there are many local variations according to topography. It is particularly strong over the Aegean region. In many lowland and eastern parts of Greece, there are 6 months when barely any rain falls.

In winter, however, the situation is more complex. The Siberian anticyclone (or 'high') extends to the northern Balkans, and the Azores anticyclone extends towards Greece from the south-west. Between the two, the Mediterranean acts as a low pressure funnel. So depressions, which come mainly from the Atlantic to the west but also originate within the Mediterranean, speed across Greece, bringing rain and wind, and because the pressure and temperature gradients are so sharp, there can be intensely strong winds at this time, particularly in the Aegean and Libyan seas. Some depressions pass across the mainland of Greece, while others veer to the south, and they may pull in warm or cool air, depending on their path.

The changeover period between the two main seasons is by no means clear-cut, and varies from year to year. Winters are extremely varied in their weather anyway – there can be long periods of warm, settled weather, and it is not uncommon for southern areas to have better weather in November or February than in April. Late March in Crete sometimes brings violent gales and heavy rain. But within a couple of days the wind may drop, the sun come out, and the temperature climb steadily to 30°C. In other years, the warm weather and cooler, damper weather continue to alternate, and April can often be quite a cool month. By late April or early May, the weather has usually become settled over most of the southern lowland areas.

The extensive mountain ranges of Greece complicate things further, as they

The east coast of Crete near Zakros

do almost anywhere except in the driest air flows. The westerly mountains of Greece receive the highest precipitation in the country, with up to 200 cm recorded in the Pindos and mountains of Crete, for example. In the north, this precipitation is spread pretty much through the year, though in Crete it is more seasonal. The northern parts of Greece may be affected by the edge of depressions moving across central Europe, and the temperature can drop sharply and the rainfall increase. Thus, although different parts of Greece may receive broadly similar amounts of rainfall, they can look quite different in appearance: those that receive most of their rain in winter can look remarkably barren after 5 months of hot sun, while those that receive rain throughout the year tend to remain green and more forested.

Natural Greek fir forest, Pindos mountains

Much of the precipitation falls as snow in the mountains and the north. A visit to Greece in March or early April gives a good idea of the relief of the country, as almost all ground above about 1500 m is snow-covered. In the north, especially the north-west, quite deep snow may lie lower down for several months. Frosts are frequent in the north and the mountains, though many southern lowland areas are normally frost free. A visit to, for example, the Prespa Lakes National Park in winter may be severely hampered by snow, and temperatures are likely to be low well into April. It has an eastern European feel to it, rather than a Greek feel.

When planning a visit to Greece, if weather is important, then all these factors need to be borne in mind. The weather is only really predictable in the south between late April and early October, when you can expect it to be mainly warm and sunny. In the north, you can predict that it will be cold from November to April, and probably snowy, especially in the west.

Vegetation and habitats

As the land warmed after the last ice age, the present-day land area of Greece became almost wholly forested, with the exception of the highest mountain areas, open waters, and some coastal areas. Since about Neolithic times, humans have gradually cleared the forest, initially for grazing animals, then for cultivation, then latterly for a whole range of activities. The natural vegetation cover of Greece was heavily influenced by climate (including the effects of altitude), geology and soil, and aspect, and many different woodland types developed in accordance with these influences. Nowadays, it is much harder to make the straightforward connection between natural conditions and vegetation, as the bulk of the country's vegetation has been human-influenced, to a greater or lesser degree, and only a small percentage of the original post-glacial forest exists. The precise figure for the percentage of original vegetation remaining is not known; it is not the same as the percentage of forest cover remaining, since this includes planted woodlands, woods that have regenerated on formerly cleared land, and heavily-modified woodland. Apart from the obvious effects of climate, it is still worth noting whether the underlying rock is of limestone or

Gorge: ❶ Griffon vultures *Gyps fulvus* ❷ Crag martin *Plyonoprogne rupestris* ❸ Caper *Capparis spinosa* ❹ *Onosma echioides* ❺ *Petromarula pinnata* ❻ Blue rock thrush *Monticola solitarius* (male) ❼ Aubretia *Aubrieta deltoidea*

High mountain slope: ❶ Golden eagle *Aquila chrysaetos* ❷ Choughs *Pyrrhocorax pyrrhocorax* ❸ Shore lark *Eremophila alpestris* (male) ❹ *Iris attica* ❺ Balkan green lizard *Lacerta trilineata* ❻ *Crocus veluchensis* ❼ *Anemone blanda*

Garrigue: ❶ Western rock nuthatch *Sitta neumayer* **❷** Spiny broom *Calicotome villosa* **❸** Hermann's tortoise *Testudo hermanni* **❹** *Orchis italica* **❺** *Cistus creticus* **❻** Painted lady *Vanessa cardui*

Coastal saltmarsh and reedbeds: ❶ Emperor dragonfly *Anax imperator* **❷** Collared pratincole *Glareola pratincola* **❸** Black-winged stilt *Himantopus himantopus* **❹** Kentish plover *Charadrius alexandrinus* **❺** Ruddy darter *Sympetrum sanguineum (male)* **❻** Sea aster *Aster tripolium*

Old olive grove on Lesvos, with masses of
Barbary nut and other wildflowers

some other rock, such as schists (coarse-grained metamorphic rocks that consist of layers of different minerals and can be split into thin irregular plates) or serpentine (dark green mineral consisting of hydrated magnesium silicate, sometimes mottled or spotted like a snake's skin), as this continues to affect the present-day vegetation and landforms. Limestone is porous, so water soaks into it. This has many effects, including an absence of surface streams and lakes, very limited soil formation, except where water collects because it cannot drain as fast as it arrives (such as in the poljes – see p. 3), and a different topography. Gorges, caves, and poljes, with an abundance of bare rock are key features of hard limestone country. The presence of high amounts of calcium in the soil can also be particularly important for some plants; for example, orchids tend to do best on limestone, and most orchid-hunters will seek out limestone areas if they have no other information. Other rocks, which are almost invariably more acid than limestones, are largely impervious, so they support streams and lakes, greater soil formation, and a generally different topography with fewer gorges and more

V-shaped valleys, and they often have far more extensive and denser forests, at least in hill areas. Two almost adjacent mountains that can be usefully compared are the limestone peaks of Parnassus and the acid, more rounded mountains of Mt. Iti (see pp. 139 and 143). Iti has rounded peaks, no high cliffs, running water everywhere, and extensive lush forests, while Parnassus has vast areas of dry limestone slopes, no surface water, and limited, rather open forest. Both of course have been influenced subsequently by people, but the later differences are a product of the original geological differences. Serpentine, which outcrops in the north Pindus, on Evvia and in other places, has some of the characters of the more acid rocks, but it breaks down into such a specific soil type, particularly high in heavy metals, that it supports its own vegetation, and many flowers are confined to serpentine.

The main significant vegetation types in Greece today are the forests, scrub of various sorts including *garrigue*, alpine areas, wetlands, coastal habitats and agricultural land of various kinds, and minor habitats such as gorges, cliffs, and screes.

Forests

It has recently been estimated that forest covers about 25% of Greece, a marked increase on the 19.6% estimate made in the early 1960s. Assuming that it is roughly correct (and much depends on the definition of forest, aside from other variables), then this is a remarkably high percentage, and much higher than most visitors to Greece might expect. Much the highest proportion of the forest lies in the north and in mountain areas, where the climate is cooler and damper, and agricultural, residential, and tourism pressures are less. These are the very places least visited by tourists in Greece at present, so the perception of a bare, largely unforested landscape is not surprising.

The forest is very varied in character, containing a wide range of trees in different proportions, accompanied by an even wider range of shrubs and sub-canopy trees. About 57% of the forest area can be characterized as deciduous (i.e. dominated by deciduous trees such as oak, though evergreens may occur in small proportions), with the remaining 43% dominated by coniferous trees.

In the deciduous group, about 75% is dominated by oak (genus *Quercus*) of some sort or other. There are 12 species of oak in Greece, of which the most frequent, dominant, canopy-forming species are sessile, downy, Hungarian, Turkey, and Valonia, though others such as *Q. dalechampii* can dominate occasionally. The oaks are particularly common and dominant (except for Valonia) in the north, where they can be quite difficult to identify with certainty. Common beech forms extensive forests too, again mainly in the north, and most often at middle altitudes; eastern beech and the natural hybrid between the two *Fagus moesiaca* may also be dominant in a few places, and in total the beeches dominate about 18% of the deciduous forest. Although all the old forests are of interest, beech woods are particularly notable for the range of special flowers which most often occur in them, such as the wintergreens, red and narrow-leaved helleborines, greater butterfly orchid, bird's-nest orchid, and a bittercress *Cardamine bulbifera*. They also have a good range of breeding birds, especially where old trees are present, such as the semi-collared flycatcher.

Of the remaining deciduous forests, Oriental planes dominate about 2%, forming forests along the river valleys, where they can stand considerable flooding and are often pollarded, and sweet chestnut and birches make up the small remaining amounts.

In general, the old deciduous forests, such as along the Rhodopi Mountains (see North-east Greece), in the Cholomondas Mountains (North-east Greece), and at certain altitudes on Mt. Olympus (North Greece) are exceptional places, particularly rich in birds and flowers, with abundant butterflies wherever there are clearings, and additional species such as fire salamanders, deer, and even brown bears in places along the Bulgarian border.

Oriental planes along the course of the river, Vikos gorge

It is estimated that forests are the main habitat for 41 of Greece's butterfly species.

Amongst the conifers, Aleppo pine covers the greatest extent at almost 40%. This includes both Aleppo pine and *Pinus brutia*, two closely related species, often hard to separate. Pine woodland formed by these two species is often open in character, in quite dry areas, and is not infrequently of secondary origin – that is, following on from clearance of the original forest, or fire. It often supports many sun-loving species which can acquire enough warmth through the open canopy, yet benefit from the increased shelter, humidity, and protection from the hottest sun. Fir-dominated woodlands make up just under 40% of the coniferous woodlands. Greek fir is the most frequent dominant, as on Mt. Ainos on Cephalonia, or Mt. Parnassus; silver fir and the hybrid *Abies borisii-regis* are more local. They tend to grow at higher altitudes than the Aleppo pine woods, and are usually denser (where allowed to be), with many more old trees. Where they do occur, they are almost certainly normally the original post-glacial forest, or at least a modified version of it, and are usually particularly good for specialist woodland birds such as white-backed woodpeckers, Tengmalm's owl (which is rare in Greece), crested tits, firecrests, and goshawks. There are also much smaller areas of coniferous woodland dominated by Scots pine, Bosnian pine, black pine, Norway spruce, umbrella pine (in lowland areas, such as the Strofilia forest – see p. 250), and mixed coniferous woods.

Scrub, including *garrigue*, *maquis*, and *phrygana*

The term 'scrub' means vegetation dominated by bushes. This is rarely a natural climax vegetation, as it would proceed towards woodland if allowed. In Greece, as in many countries, it is a transitional vegetation, heavily influenced by people, that may come about as a result of fires, abandonment of agricultural land (in both these cases it will eventually succeed to woodland unless there is some intervention), or – most commonly here – as a result of grazing pressure. On good quality land, sustained grazing pressure will normally produce grassland, especially if the activity is accompanied by some clearance. In Greece, however, as in many countries bordering the Mediterranean, the grazing is very extensive in character and takes place on land that is considered unfit for other agricultural activities. Normally the soil is shallow, there may be little rainfall for half the year, and the ground will almost certainly be covered with rocks of various sizes. Little additional management takes place, with the possible exception of burning, because each grazier covers vast areas with mobile flocks, and often has no exclusive right to the land and so may not directly benefit from any additional work. The result of this system in the Mediterranean climate has been the spread of extensive scrub in areas which were once forest (and would eventually become so again in the absence of grazing). Such habitats are dominated by low, often spiny, shrubs that can partially resist grazing, a selection of unpalatable perennial herbs such as asphodels, and a wide range of other plants which take their chances as they can, surviving in the shelter of bushes, by setting seed only occasionally, or by adopting various other strategies.

There are different types of scrub according to the underlying geology, the amount of surface rock, the intensity of grazing, the

Black pines *Pinus nigra*

A lone Greek fir close to the tree-line on Mount Parnassus

frequency of fires, the climate, and other factors. Because this vegetation is so widespread around the Mediterranean, it has acquired specific names in different countries, some of which have come into use in English, causing a degree of confusion. The French term *garrigue* describes an open type of scrub, rarely exceeding about 50 cm high, with a good deal of bare ground and rock, and dominated by sub-shrubs such as sun-roses *Cistus* species, heathers, spiny burnet, spiny spurge, thymes such as *Coridothymus capitatus* and various others. It tends to develop where the soil is very poor and rocky, or where there are frequent fires or very intensive grazing. *Maquis* (another French term) is taller, 1–2 m, denser, and tends to include more typical bushes and small trees such as strawberry-tree, kermes oak, spiny broom, junipers, lentisk, myrtle, and many more. It develops in more favourable conditions, where fires are less frequent, the soil is deeper, or grazing less intense, and may naturally soon proceed towards woodland if grazing animals become excluded. The Greek word *phrygana* is a useful term

which equates roughly to *garrigue* but extends into *maquis*, so it covers a wider range of conditions.

Garrigue or *phrygana* grades into *pseudosteppe*, which is similar but tends to contain a higher proportion of grasses, and perennial herbs such as asphodel. It occurs most frequently in dry, grazed sites, particularly in rain-shadow areas in the north of the country.

Collectively, these scrub habitats are extremely widespread and make up a very important part of the Mediterranean vegetation. Not surprisingly, many plants and animals have become closely associated with them. These are good areas for tortoises, snakes, lizards, birds such as short-toed eagles, black-eared wheatear, Sardinian and subalpine warblers and stonechats, many butterflies (about 100 species of butterfly in Greece use *garrigue* and related habitats as their main home area), and a wide range of flowers. The plant life is actually highly diverse, but with few species (except the grazing-resistant ones) occurring in any quantity. They are excellent places to search for

Phrygana in full flower in spring, on Rhodes

orchids, bulbs such as crocuses, and little herbs such as flaxes, mallows, or crane's-bills. One often hears complaints about the overgrazing of all these areas preventing the orchids and other plants from flowering, but in the absence of grazing the flowers would very quickly disappear. It is a fine balance which can easily stray in either direction. In general, extensive grazing of the *garrigue*, etc. is decreasing as this solitary and financially unrewarding way of life becomes less appealing, and many areas of *garrigue* are converting to the less flowery maquis.

Alpine areas

The alpine zone is that part of the mountain area which is at too high an altitude (and therefore has too unfavourable a climate) for forest growth, so there is a natural scrub area that grades into grassland and other open habitats. It is probable that the natural tree-line would lie at about 2000–2200 m in Greece, though in practice it is normally much lower than this. It is believed that the upper levels of the tree-line were one of the first targets for active clearance (and passive clearance by heavy grazing) by

Toadflax *Linaria peloponnesiaca* on the slopes of Mount Olympus

early settlers, because this was the easy place to start. There was natural summer grazing nearby, and relatively open scrub and woodland which could easily be grazed into. This practice continues in Greece, either where the high areas are within reach of pastoral villages, or in some cases as a result of transhumance, where flocks are moved wholesale to the high pastures for the summer, and the shepherds stay with them. This practice has declined, but still occurs. The overall result is that the natural alpine zone has generally been extended downwards, and the intriguing transition zone between forest and alpine grassland has largely gone. Mt. Olympus is a good place to see a more natural alpine zone, as mixed forests give way to open forest dominated by Bosnian pine, which gradually becomes more gnarled, smaller, lightning-struck, and scattered, before yielding to open habitats at over 2000 m.

On limestone mountains, these alpine habitats are usually rocky and dominated by small shrubs, rather like high-altitude

Sheep grazing in the volcanic landscape of west Lesvos

garrigue, though there are likely to be many other flowers of interest scattered amongst the shrubs. They tend to be dominated by spiny shrubs such as *Astragalus angustifolius* or *Berberis cretica*, with unpalatable species such as *Daphne oleoides* and junipers. Very large numbers of flowers occur in such situations, including many of the special Greek endemics which may often be confined to just one mountain or group of mountains. On more acid mountains, or where the rainfall is higher, there is a more distinct turf dominated by grasses and sedges, often with damp flushed areas and pools, perhaps where snow has recently melted. This equates more closely with the alpine zone of many other European mountains. The wet areas in particular often have special flowers such as snowbells, rare sedges and rushes, louseworts, and many more.

The mountain areas, excluding montane forests, provide the main habitats for

Ancient gnarled Bosnian pines, near the tree line on Mount Olympus

Mt. Falakro

Juniper (*Juniperus foetidissima*) forest, Mt. Astraka

87 species of butterfly, including many beautiful species such as Apollo, clouded Apollo, Greek clouded yellow, and fiery copper. They also have special birds such as shore-lark, which is found in high-altitude plateaux, alpine choughs, alpine accentors, snowfinches, wallcreepers, and golden eagles. Mountains frequently act as last refuges in our overused world, and it may often be the case that species are confined to mountains without being really specialized for them. They have simply retreated from other more favoured habitats that have become unsuitable. Whatever the reasons, these high alpine zones in Greece are extremely attractive and exciting places for the naturalist, and well worth the effort of getting there. Unlike in the Alps (fortunately), there are very few cable cars or high altitude passes to make access to these highest areas easy, which has had the advantage of keeping them less spoilt.

Wetlands

The range of freshwater wetland vegetation in Greece is not as great as in north European countries with higher rainfall or lower evaporation rates; for example, it lacks extensive rich fens, bogs, or other unspoilt peatlands. However, there are numerous rivers with pools and wet areas, a number of natural lakes with associated habitats such as reedbeds, and other minor wetland habitats associated with springs.

Rivers vary enormously, both between rivers and along the length of specific rivers, as they change from highly oxygenated upland streams to slow-flowing lowland rivers moving sluggishly towards the sea (though this section tends to be rather short in most Greek rivers). Within the rivers, there are often abundant pondweeds *Potamogeton* species, water-crowfoots *Ranunculus* species, and other aquatics such as fool's-water-cress, whilst towards the mouth there may be species tolerant of slightly saline conditions such as the pondweeds *Zannichellia* and *Ruppia*. Mayflies, stoneflies, and a few dragonflies such as golden-ringed, club-tailed (e.g. *Gomphus schneideri*), and the agrions *Calopteryx* species all breed in the rivers, and birds such as grey wagtail

Ancient pollarded oriental plane in floodplain woodland, north Greece

marking out a river course from a distance. Once there were extensive riverine 'gallery' forests in the lower reaches and throughout the deltas, made up of willows, narrow-leaved ash, elms, alders, and black and white poplars, with hops, vines, and other climbers below. These were almost certainly superb havens for wildlife, but now they are reduced to a few scattered remnants and often grazed, so they have little natural structure. The best examples occur at Amvrakikos, in the Nestos Delta, and associated with the Prespa lakes.

Most of the natural Greek lakes are relatively shallow and eutrophic (rich in nutrients), with a general trend to become more so as silt and peat fill them up, and agricultural and industrial chemicals drain into them. In most cases, there are belts of reeds or giant reeds around their margins, providing a degree of protection, and excellent habitat for birds such as water rail, little bittern, great reed warbler, and marsh harrier, as well as a wealth of other life. In deeper water, there are often extensive areas of white or

and dipper are directly associated with them. Oriental planes are almost always found along river courses, even where there is virtually no flood plain, and they turn a glorious golden-red in autumn,

Brackish pools, with flowering tamarisk, on the Gulf of Kalloni, Lesvos

yellow water lilies, water chestnut, and several pondweeds *Potamogeton* species. While some lakes still have large areas of open water, many others, such as Himaditis, Stymfalia, and Distos are well on the way to becoming dry land, and many more have long since been converted to fertile agricultural land. Those that remain are superb areas for wildlife, especially birds, amphibians such as tree frogs, marsh frogs, and green toads, reptiles such as two species of terrapins and dice-snakes, dragonflies, and many other invertebrates. A few, such as the Prespa lakes, are protected, but most are not, and all are vital strands in the wealth of Greek wildlife.

Freshwater marshes or wet meadows are extremely rare in Greece now, though there are still low-lying, often coastal areas which flood in winter and are grazed in summer, but which are not normally fertilized or ploughed. There are good examples in the Cape Araxos complex (p. 249), and associated with some of the deltas. They have flowers such as yellow iris, galingale, flowering-rush, reeds and reed-mace, water-plantain, and a variety of sedges and rushes. Elsewhere, there are often small wet areas associated with springs or wet flushes, varying from the picturesque springs of Louros, which is something of a tourist site (p. 166), to endless little wet areas on banks in the mountains, where there are marsh-orchids, loosestrifes, marsh bird's-foot trefoil, mints, and a wealth of other attractive flowers.

Coastal vegetation

As already mentioned, Greece has an extraordinarily long coastline. This is made up of a variety of habitats, particularly rocky shores and cliffs, sandy beaches, dunes where the sand becomes piled up and partially stabilized above the high tide mark, saltmarshes, brackish lagoons, mudflats, and a series of habitats such as damp grassland. One might think that, with a coastline of over 15 000 km, there would be many of all these habitats left, but unfortunately, certain coastal habitats are much more favourable targets for development and exploitation than others. Sandy beaches and associated sand dunes have mostly disappeared under tourist-related developments; other flat coastal areas, including coastal marshes, are prime targets for industrial

Part of the vast area of saltmarsh in the Gulf of Kalloni, Lesvos

and residential development, and for airstrips. Saltmarshes, brackish lagoons, and other typical delta habitats have been steadily brought into cultivation, and sometimes other uses, especially at the upper edges of the deltas, and those that are left are often heavily exploited for fishing, shooting, boating, or other environmentally unfriendly uses. So, there are plenty of rocky coasts and cliffs, but relatively few of the other habitats, though there are encouraging signs that the protection of a number of coastal sites is being taken seriously now, thanks to encouragement and funds from the EU.

All these coastal habitats are important. Sandy beaches are vital for loggerhead turtles, breeding and feeding birds such as little terns and Kentish plovers, a few special flowers such as purple spurge and sea knot-grass, and a wealth of intertidal life. Sand dunes support a range of specialized flowers such as sea daffodil, sea-holly, sea medick, campions (including a number of endemic ones), and insects such as tiger beetles, ant-lions, and the pretty *Nemoptera* species, with their long tail-like wings. Chameleons have their only Greek sites on dunes (at least, they need the dunes for breeding). Saltmarshes, mudflats, and associated areas are important winter feeding resources for large numbers of birds, especially waders and wildfowl, and they provide breeding sites for collared pratincoles, black-winged stilts, fan-tailed warblers, common terns, and others. Coastal lagoons are feeding areas and safe roosts for abundant birds, many species nest around them, and they can be the ecological centrepoint in a complex of coastal habitats.

The rocky coastlines, of which there is still an abundance, are much less productive and support far fewer species. They have their value, though. Where there is a level rocky beach, there are likely to be abundant marine algae (seaweeds), sea anemones, and a range of marine invertebrates which provide good feeding for waders, egrets, kingfishers, and other

The Gulf of Amvrakikos (or Gulf of Arta) at sunset

birds. Flowers such as sea-lavenders, including some rare ones, can grow here. Drier rocky coasts have limited vegetation, though species such as the little campion *Silene sedoides*, and the yellow-flowered *Anthemis rigida* seem to specialize in such places. Higher cliffs often support some of the same vegetation as gorges, with plants such as bellflowers, red valerian, tree spurge, and many more, and there are a number of Greek endemic flowers that are confined to sea cliffs. More isolated cliffs provide secure nesting sites for Eleonora's falcon and peregrines, lesser kestrels, blue rock thrushes, crag martins and other birds.

Other habitats

Greece has a particularly large number of gorges, thanks largely to its mountain topography and limestone geology. These are amongst the most interesting of its habitats for the naturalist, and each one is different and special. They provide several special features not found in the general countryside: large areas free from grazing by domestic animals, a low-competition environment, and a range of aspects and humidities varying from extremely hot and sunny to cool and damp on overhanging north-facing slopes. They vary enormously according to their structure (the amount of cliffs, the angle of the slopes, their width and depth) their alignment (whether they run east-west, north-south, or curve and meander to give all possible aspects), their geology, the character of the surrounding land, and the climatic area within which they lie. Many of the deeper gorges have special flowers, some of which may be endemic to just the one gorge or to gorges in one area. Crete is especially noted for its gorge flowers, such as Cretan sainfoin, the white-flowered *Coronilla globosa*, the beautiful purple-flowered *Origanum dictamnus*, several shrubby St. John's-worts such as *Hypericum amblicalyx* and many more, and the same pattern is repeated throughout the mainland and on other islands. These special gorge plants are known as chasmophytes.

Gorges can be good places for trees, especially where the slopes are not too steep, because genuine mixed woodlands can develop in the absence of grazing of palatable species (such as the limes or elms) or selective management of useful species. The Vikos Gorge in north-west Greece for example, has some wonderful forests with almost all the possible species in them. Gorges can also be exceptionally good places for breeding birds such as griffon and Egyptian vultures, lesser kestrels, choughs, crag martins, eagles, eagle owls, blue rock thrushes, wallcreepers, and many others. Some of the larger more wooded gorges are good for mammals, too, as large areas are so inaccessible. They can provide sites for an extraordinary variety of snails, including a number of endemic species, and a good range of other invertebrates.

Other cliffs, not part of a gorge, occur widely in mountains and on the coast. They have many of the elements of gorge cliffs but are usually not quite so rich because the subtleties of aspect and humidity are not present.

Much of Greece is covered by agricultural land of one sort or another (though the figure of roughly 30% is lower than for most European countries). This includes olive groves, vineyards, apple orchards, almond orchards, wheat fields, cotton fields, and many other uses, but excludes extensively grazed, unenclosed areas. In

A waterfall in a side valley off the Aoós Gorge

general, these habitats are not of especial importance for wildlife, though of course they support a good number of more common species, and many birds depend on the by-products at some time or other. Olive groves, however, hold a special place in Greek culture and wildlife. They cover enormous areas, especially in the south and on the islands (for example, there are said to be 11 million olive trees on Lesbos). They can be very dull places, if the trees are quite young and the ground beneath is fertilized, regularly ploughed, and possibly irrigated, and this type of olive grove is becoming commoner as agricultural intensity increases. At the opposite extreme, though, they can be marvellous places, with ancient, hole-ridden trees and flowery turf below, blending in with the natural topography so that rocky areas, sheltered corners, springs, and other small-scale variations remain undisturbed. Such olive groves can still be found on Lesbos, on the Mani Peninsula, in Evvia, and elsewhere. In places they have something of the character of the Spanish cork oak *dehesa* that has received so much attention recently as an important and declining habitat. Old olive trees become particularly gnarled and full of holes, and they provide excellent nesting sites for tits including sombre tit, masked shrikes (in the east of the country), spotted flycatchers, Scops owls, and numerous other birds. The ground underneath may either be ancient grazed turf, full of flowers such as orchids, grape hyacinths, alkanets, mandrake, arums and other perennials, or it may be occasionally ploughed to keep it clear; if it is left unsprayed and unplanted, it becomes a riot of colourful annual flowers such as crown daisies, poppies, corn marigolds, and many more. Along banks, there are often giant and naked man orchids, one or more species of dutchman's pipes *Aristolochia* species, providing larval food-plants for eastern and southern festoon butterflies, and much else of interest. Any old walls will be full of lizards, geckos, snails, and a variety of invertebrates, and such walls are a favourite nesting site for

The striking conglomerate cliffs at Meteora, north Greece

hoopoes. Collectively, olive groves make up a marvellous wildlife resource.

Apart from this, arable fields in Greece can still be of interest for their weeds, especially in areas where agriculture is still on a small scale. In many hilly limestone areas, there are only cultivated fields in areas where there is a little more soil, and these are often too remote and small to warrant much attention. Cornfield weeds in such places can include tulips (including the endemic *Tulipa doerfleri* on Crete), tassel hyacinth, anemones, celandines, the striking yellow pyramids of *Leontice leontopetalum*, blue woodruff, fluellens, ground-pine, and many more. Any such field is usually worth a look, and it is a fair bet to assume that there will be more food for birds in such sites.

Natural history

In most respects Greece has a remarkably rich diversity of natural life, thanks to its variety of climate and landform and its relatively unspoilt nature.

Botanically, it is particularly special. Precise estimates of the number of native flowers in Greece vary, partly because there are always more being discovered, but also because opinions often vary as to whether a given plant is a different species from another, a subspecies, or simply a variant. The native flora consists of at least 5000 species of higher plants (i.e. flowering plants and ferns), of which over 700 are endemic to Greece (i.e. they occur nowhere else in the world). This level of endemism (14% of the flora) is not matched anywhere in Europe, and only southern Spain comes at all close. Although Greece does not have quite the highest number of species for any country in Europe (Italy and Spain each having somewhat more), the few countries that exceed it have a much greater surface area. It would be fair to say that Greece has more species of flower for its area than any other country in Europe. However you look at the statistics, it has an extremely rich flora, and almost any excursion will turn up something new.

Greece also has a particularly abundant bird fauna. About 425 species of birds are accepted as having been recorded in Greece. Greece lies on an important migration route, and a large number of birds pass through in spring and/or autumn, but do not breed or spend long here. More significant is the fact that about 243 species regularly breed in the country, with a further 15 or so occasionally or possibly doing so. This is an extremely large number for a relatively small country – slightly more than Italy, for example, which is well over twice as large a country. Out of this total number of breeding species, 141 are considered to be species of European conservation concern, and four are globally threatened: Dalmatian pelican, ferruginous duck, lesser kestrel, and Audouin's gull, and four more are close to this category: pygmy cormorant, black vulture, cinereous bunting, and white-

Hoopoe *Upupa epops*

tailed eagle. Greece also holds globally important breeding populations of two species: Dalmatian pelican (the largest population outside the former USSR) and Eleonora's falcon, of which about two-thirds of the world population breed in Greece. So, by any European standard, Greece is important for breeding and migrating birds.

It is also important for wintering birds, mainly because of the generally mild climate and availability of frost-free areas, which contribute to a continuing supply of various types of food. Apart from the resident birds (of which there are about 154 species), there are a further 55 or so which regularly pass the winter here.

Greece cannot be considered to be quite so important for its mammals. Although 116 species have been recorded, many of them are rare or occur at very low densities, and it is certainly not a good place to watch mammals. Species of interest include the brown bear, which occurs in small numbers in the northern border areas, especially in the Rhodopi Mountains; the golden jackal, which has its main European population here, though it is currently thought to be declining; the Cretan wild goat, or kri-kri, which is virtually confined to Crete; the monk seal, which has its main European populations in the Aegean; and the Cretan spiny mouse which, as its name suggests, is confined to Crete.

Greece has particularly rich populations of butterflies: 232 species are regularly recorded, with a number of others possible or occasional, which is well over half the total number of species known to occur in Europe. Eleven species are considered to be endemic to Greece. Butterflies are a constant feature of excursions in Greece, and the density of butterflies in some of the mountain areas is quite extraordinary. The same sort of information is not available for many other groups of invertebrates, but there is little doubt that Greece is an excellent area in which to look for insects and other invertebrates of virtually all types.

Greece also has a rich and varied herpetofauna (a useful composite word for reptiles and amphibians), with 68 species recorded so far, and possibly more to come. This is more than the total recorded for either France or Spain, which are both about four times as large as Greece. Greece has especially important populations of loggerhead turtles (with much the largest breeding population in the European Mediterranean), and two endemic species: the Milos viper, which only occurs in the western Cyclades on

four islands, and the Milos wall lizard, with a roughly similar distribution.

Apart from all this, Greece has an interesting and varied range of lichens, fungi, bryophytes, and seashore life.

Nature conservation in Greece

Looking at nature in Greece provokes a curious blend of exhilaration and depression! The extensive areas of habitat and the enormous range of species, combined with the beautiful landscape and generally good weather are all causes for elation. Unfortunately, there is a much more difficult side to the Greek environment.

It would be fair to say that conservation in Greece is in its infancy compared to most European countries, and there are many obstacles to be overcome before it advances far. There are currently 10 National Parks, spread fairly generally through the country (except for the Peloponnese, which has none), though they are very poorly resourced and generally barely protected. In some cases, it is

Olive grove

virtually impossible to detect that one has entered a National Park, and there is clearly little control on grazing, timber-cutting, and even cultivation. There is normally no interpretation of the environment for visitors, and certainly no concentrated conservation management. More National Parks are said to be 'in the pipeline', though there is little obvious progress in this respect, and the protective umbrella that they can provide needs to be strengthened before they will carry much authority.

Until very recently, there was no network of state nature reserves at all in Greece. In the last few years, essentially as a result of pressure and funds from the EU, all the Ramsar Sites (sites designated as internationally important wetlands) in the country have been surveyed and recognized, and clear attempts are being made to delineate and protect them, with the additional benefit of some potentially useful interpretative centres, too. Ramsar Sites are internationally important wetlands, designated as a result of an original conference in Iran, but which now have a

momentum of their own and a permanent secretariat in Switzerland. Greece has 11 Ramsar Sites, covering a total area of about 107 400 ha (though a recent Greek government publication indicates a total area of 163 500 ha within Ramsar Sites). These include all the important coastal wetlands such as the Evros Delta and the Messolongi Lagoons, as well as inland sites such as the Prespa lakes and Lake Kerkini (all the Ramsar Sites are covered in the site guide), and if they are genuinely protected *and* managed for conservation, this will be an enormous step forward. There are other sites that are being protected, or scheduled to be protected, under the EU Natura 2000 scheme, which provides for a network of protected sites under habitat and wild bird protection legislation. The lagoon at Pylos, and the Evrotas Delta, both in the Peloponnese, are two such sites where active protection is proceeding. It remains to be seen how well such commitments will be implemented – it is a long and complex path from governmental agree-

Mass of spring flowers including pink hawksbeard and purple bugloss

ment to continuing action on the ground. Greece is currently a party to the Ramsar Convention, World Heritage Convention, Bern Convention, and the Barcelona Convention, and is necessarily bound by some of the protective legislation of the EU. On the ground, however, such agreements are not always entirely apparent!

There are other statutory protected sites within Greece. Internationally designated sites include two biosphere reserves (part of Mt. Olympus, and the Samaria Gorge, Crete), 16 special protection areas under EU legislation, primarily for the protection of birds, 8 Mediterranean special protection areas, and one biogenetic reserve. As yet, there are no world heritage sites, though several possible candidates spring to mind. Nationally designated sites include the protected 'Monuments of Nature', which vary from individual ancient plane trees to quite large forests (for example the 550 ha Zagradenia Forest in the Rhodopi Mountains). There are also 19 'Aesthetic Forests', defined under national legislation as having, amongst other things, 'characteristics that demand the protection of their fauna, flora and natural beauty'. These vary enormously in character and in the degree of their protection, though in general they are treated more as recreation areas than nature reserves. There is also a network of no-hunting reserves, though at present these are very loosely controlled.

In addition to the designation and protection of sites by the state, which has considerable limitations, there is also a very limited amount of reserve tenure and management by voluntary organizations, of which the most significant is WWF Greece, who manage the Dadia Forest (see p. 112) and part of the turtle breeding site on Zakynthos (p. 267), amongst other sites, and who are very active in promoting general nature conservation awareness in Greece. The Society for the Study and protection of the Mediterranean monk seal is closely connected with certain sites, especially the Sporades Marine Park; the Hellenic Society for the Protection of Nature is involved with many aspects of

Butterflies, including scarce swallowtail *Iphiclides podalirius*, in mountains south of Karpenisi

nature conservation in Greece, though it does not run reserves itself. The Hellenic Ornithological Society (HOS) is engaged in protection plans for sites such as the Evrotas Delta (see p. 229), and the Sea Turtle Protection Society of Greece is heavily involved in all turtle issues, particularly those affecting breeding beaches. Sadly, the vast network of nature reserves run by voluntary societies, such as those found in Britain or Germany, is almost totally lacking.

Scops owl *Otus scops*

Other conservation issues in Greece that are not readily tackled by the 'protected sites' policies include the endless dumping of rubbish along virtually all roads, the continuing intensification of agriculture, the apparently uncontrolled extension of tourism developments along the coasts, the vastly expanded network of forest tracks that has allowed logging, poaching, grazing, and burning into formerly pristine areas, and excessive hunting.

Greece is a wonderful place for the naturalist, and things are undoubtedly changing. One is constantly left with the feeling that it could be so much better if only there was a serious attitude towards conservation and environmental matters on the part of the government, translated into ongoing action on the ground.

Access and route-finding

Access in Greece is generally straightforward. There are very few restrictions on entering land that is unfenced and not clearly private, such as a garden. At the moment, the great majority of the countryside remains unfenced, though this is changing slowly, and more areas are becoming distinctly demarcated. The downside is that there are relatively few marked footpaths, and it can sometimes be difficult to follow a route as a result. In the more popular mountain areas and gorges, there are often waymarked routes with paint on the rocks, and these

Nemopteran Nemopteridae

are easy enough to follow (though you may not always know where they are leading, without the benefit of a leaflet or book). Elsewhere, there are virtually no marked paths.

Maps in Greece are another matter. Until recently, there were no generally available, accurate, large-scale maps, though it was possible to get military-based maps at a few outlets in Athens. However, the Athens-based 'Road Editions' company have brought out a series of maps, with more appearing regularly, that have improved matters considerably. There is a series of six 1: 250 000 maps (in reddish-brown covers) covering the whole country (except some of the islands), which are very useful for route-planning and general road use, though not for walking. They claim to be wholly accurate and to cover the unsurfaced roads, though this is not quite true. The same company also produces maps in green or blue covers of most islands and selected mountain and tourist areas at 1:50 000 or sometimes 1:70 000. These are extremely useful, and pretty accurate. For addresses, see p. 310 .

North-west Greece

North-west Greece

North-west Greece

Introduction

North-west Greece is a quite remarkable area, which in almost any other European country would be a major tourist region, buzzing with visitors. Apart from its obvious attractions of generally good weather and a string of Adriatic beaches, it boasts some really exceptional mountain scenery, extensive forests, some of the finest gorges in Europe, and many unspoilt mountain villages with a long history and fascinating architecture. However, because it lies far from the main population centres of Greece, it has relatively few visitors, and because of the encircling protective shell of Albania, Macedonia, and the other states of former Yugoslavia, there is really no direct road access from the rest of the populous EU states. It is possible that potential visitors may also be put off by its proximity to these unknown and slightly daunting countries, though in practice it is a friendly and crime-free area. Things are changing, of course, and there is some tourist-related development in hot spots such as the villages around the Vikos Gorge, and along the coastal strip, though these are few and far between. Ioannina is directly accessible by air from Athens, though perhaps more significant is the increasing use of Preveza (just south of this region) as an airport for direct flights from north Europe, though most visitors head directly for the coast and stay there.

For the naturalist, it is an exceptionally rewarding area, whatever group of plants or animals interests you. Although it lacks some of the more warmth-demanding species of southern Greece, this is amply repaid by the presence of a mixture of Greek, Balkan, eastern, and central European species. Brown bears are still thought to occur in the more remote woods, for example; snow finches, alpine choughs, alpine accentors, and other typically alpine birds are common in the higher mountains, and flowers such as snow gentians and snowbells are much more redolent of the Alps than of Greece, though they grow right next to Greek endemics, and are visited by Greek clouded yellows. Indeed, the scenery is quite alpine in character, albeit without the visitors and endless roads, ski-lifts, and developments. For example, on several consecutive days of walking in the mountains around Timfi and Astraka (see p. 39) in mid-June – probably the best time to be there – I met one small English group, a few shepherds, and no one else, and this is probably the best-known, most-accessible, and one of the most spectacular areas. As long as you are prepared for the lack of facilities (and it is worth bearing in mind that even though refuges are often present in the mountains, they are frequently only open to key-holders), this is one of the most enriching mountain areas in Europe for the naturalist-walker.

Ancient monastery in the lower Vikos gorge

Previous page: **Early summer, high on the slopes of Mount Astraka**

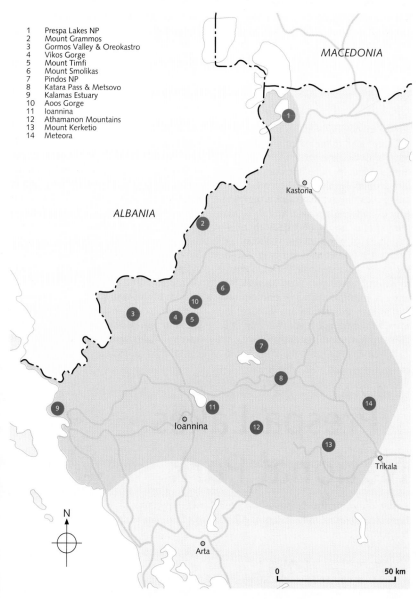

1   Prespa Lakes NP
2   Mount Grammos
3   Gormos Valley & Oreokastro
4   Vikos Gorge
5   Mount Timfi
6   Mount Smolikas
7   Pindos NP
8   Katara Pass & Metsovo
9   Kalamas Estuary
10 Aoos Gorge
11 Ioannina
12 Athamanon Mountains
13 Mount Kerketio
14 Meteora

MACEDONIA

ALBANIA

Kastoria

Ioannina

Trikala

N

Arta

0   50 km

Although there were once good coastal wetlands in this region, those that remain are poor shadows of their former selves, and there are no coastal Ramsar Sites (internationally important wetlands) in the region (though there is one just into the next region, in central Greece). You need to look inland to find good wetlands, most notably Lake Pamvotida at Ioannina, or the extraordinary Prespa Lakes National Park tucked right up against the borders with Albania and Macedonia (FYROM) (and extending over both borders in one of the first cross-border conservation initiatives in this area). This is one of the best inland wetlands in Europe, though again

North-west Greece

it is little-visited and very quiet at almost all times.

There are three National Parks in this area, more than in any other region of Greece: Vikos-Aoós, Pindos, and Prespa Lakes, and these are the sites that catch the eye. However, one of the great features of this wild part of Greece is that almost anywhere is of interest. We have selected a number of mountains and other sites that are particularly noted for their wildlife in some form or other, but they are simply the tip of the iceberg here. Apart from the fact that there is undoubtedly still a lot to discover, and these may not prove to be the best sites, there is a vast area of good-quality habitat. For example, if you travel north-eastwards on the main N20 which runs from Ioannina to Kozani, once you pass Konitsa you enter a wonderful area of endless hills and forests, with hardly any villages, and many tempting side roads into this virtually unknown and unvisited area. In autumn (late October to mid-November here), the colours of the trees are quite splendid, with probably the best autumn colours in Europe (together with the rest of north Greece and adjacent areas).

When considering a visit to this part of the world, you need to bear in mind that the weather is distinctly different from that of southern Greece. It suffers from Balkan winters, even on the coast to some extent, with much lower temperatures and higher rainfall or snowfall than most other parts of Greece. In addition, many areas are well above sea level (for example, the Prespa lakes lie at 850 m altitude, with the surrounding hills going much higher). So, April is still winter here, though it can almost seem like summer in the south. Probably the best time for a visit, depending on whether you plan to go high in the mountains or not, is from late April to early May in the coastal lowlands to mid-June and into July, or even later, for higher areas.

SITE 1 Prespa Lakes National Park

A superbly unspoilt area of lakes amongst remote mountains, tucked up against the borders of Albania and Macedonia (FYROM).

Tozzia alpina

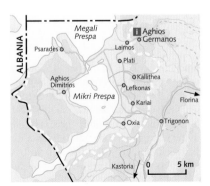

The Prespa Lakes National Park covers about 19 500 ha, and the wider area of interest covers at least 30 000 ha. Part of the area is a Ramsar Site, and it is at last receiving the protection and attention that it deserves. It is one of the most important ornithological sites in Europe,

White pelicans *Pelecanus onocrotalus* (Mike Lane)

with many features of interest, yet as recently as the mid-1980s (despite declaration as a National Park in 1974) it was the subject of an EU-financed agricultural and picicultural improvement scheme which resulted in considerable damage, some of it irreversible. Nevertheless, it remains a remarkably beautiful, unspoilt, and valuable site. If it were somewhere less remote, it would be crammed with visitors coming for the scenery as much as the birds; in fact, it is remarkably quiet, and one may see no one all day other than a few resident farmers and reed-cutters.

The park consists essentially of the Greek parts of two large lakes, together with surrounding mountain areas, though the area of general interest extends much more widely in this remarkably unspoilt corner of Greece. The smaller lake – Mikri Prespa – forms the core of the park; it lies almost entirely within Greece, with just the south-western tip lying in Albania. The northern lake – Megalo Prespa – is much larger, separated from Mikri Prespa by a narrow bar. Less than a quarter of this lake lies within Greece, with the remainder split between Macedonia and Albania. Just recently, a three-country agreement has been reached to protect all parts of

the lakes as a cross-border National Park. From the Greek side, Mikri Prespa is much the more interesting lake, with its extensive reedbeds and shallow areas. The lake surface is about 850 m above sea level, with considerably higher mountains around, so the lakes fall decidedly into the montane zone, with long, cold winters and relatively unsettled summers.

Ornithologically, the park area is outstanding. Over 260 species of birds have been recorded, of which at least 60 are rare or threatened. It is the only place in Europe, apart from the Danube Delta, where both European species of pelican breed, and in recent years both have been doing well here, with a significant proportion of the world population of the Dalmatian pelican breeding. Pygmy cormorants have a strong breeding population here, together with

Eastern spadefoot *Pelobates syriacus*

Euphorbia myrsinites

common cormorants, from which they can be easily distinguished by their small size. All the European herons occur here (though not all of them breed); little bitterns and squacco herons are both surprisingly common, with large breeding colonies. Great white egrets are a common sight in winter and spring, and a few stay on to breed, though numbers have decreased in recent years. Both purple and grey herons are frequent, with the latter staying all year. White storks are a pleasantly common sight around the marshes and shallows, breeding mainly in the surrounding villages, where they are welcome. Both black tern and whiskered tern breed sporadically here, though there are no reliable colonies. Water rail, Cetti's warbler, and great reed warbler can all be heard in the reedbeds. Greylag geese are frequent in the more open parts of the reedbeds – they are rare and local in Greece as a breeding bird, and this is probably their largest population, with up to 60 pairs.

Not surprisingly, birds of prey are a key feature: booted, short-toed, golden, white-tailed and lesser spotted eagles, peregrine and lanner falcons, and lesser kestrels in villages such as Aghios Germanos. Marsh harriers are common, and pallid harriers pass through, especially in spring. Many of the birds of prey breed in the surrounding wooded hills, and there are also barred warblers here (a rare breeding bird in Greece), and perhaps still a few hazel grouse, though their present status is unknown. This is still a remarkably

unknown area, especially outside the National Park boundary, and there is undoubtedly much to be discovered. It has more in common ecologically with the countries to the north than with most of Greece, and new records for Greece are likely to continue to be made here.

Passage periods can be excellent times here, depending on the weather, with abundant waders, wildfowl, and birds of prey. Spotted, little, and Baillon's crakes all occur, of which only little crake breeds. Winters tend to be rather quiet as the lakes usually freeze, though not every year.

About 40 species of mammal have been recorded in the Prespa area, though many of the larger ones are declining. Brown bears still occur in small numbers, with a few wolves, and the occasional lynx comes over the border from the wild mountainous country to the north. Otters are resident around the lake, and wild cats can be seen occasionally in the hills. In addition, there are at least 5 species of bats and 14 rodents, with probably more of both still to be recorded.

Reptiles and amphibians have been well-recorded here, with over 30 species seen. Around the lake, there are marsh and agile frogs, green, common, and yellow-bellied toads, and several newts. Common tree frogs call harshly from the reeds, and stream frogs are common in the streams around the lakes. Fire salamanders are quite common (though rarely seen) in the surrounding woods, and eastern spade-foot toads can be found here and there.

Hermann's tortoises are common in dry areas and European pond terrapins occur in the marshes. There are nine species of snakes, including grass snake and dice snake around the lakes, with Aesculapian snake, nose-horned viper, and Balkan whip snake in drier habitats. Amongst the nine species of lizards, there are Balkan green lizards and the very similar green lizard, wall lizards, Erhard's wall lizard, and Balkan wall lizards.

Although not so well-known as a botanical site, it is actually rich and varied, with several interesting species, some of which only just creep into Greece at this point. The dominant plants in and around the lakes are common reeds, lesser and common reed-mace, yellow iris, purple-loosestrife, and hemp-agrimony, with white and yellow water-lilies further into deep water. The pink-flowered flowering-rush is common along the margins. In drier wooded areas, there are appealing plants such as scarlet avens, pencilled crane's-bill, a leopard's-bane *Doronicum hungaricum*, foetid meadow-rue, the curious little semi-parasite *Tozzia alpina*, and yellow gentian. There is an endemic knapweed *Centaurea prespana* (though this is a particularly difficult group to identify in this area, and most books don't mention this species), and a number of plants that are rare elsewhere in Greece such as the lily *Lilium jankae*, a house-leek *Jovibarba hirta*, a periwinkle *Vinca balcanica*, white false helleborine in its *flavum* form and many others – a decidedly central European or alpine list rather than Greek. Other flowers of interest in the area include the lovely white-flowered sage *Salvia candidissima*, the large blue-flowered flax *Linum hirsutum*, two tall yellow toadflaxes, *Linaria pelopon-*

nesiaca with spike-like inflorescences, and *L. genistifolia* with fewer, larger flowers, the prostrate spurge *Euphorbia myrsinites*, and several juniper species including Greek and foetid junipers.

It should perhaps also be mentioned that the lakes are noted for their interesting and varied fish populations, which include a number of endemic species, subspecies, and variants.

Access to the site is easy, except in winter. A good road (the N15) from Florina winds its way into the park, via some interesting mountain scenery, passing along the east shore of Mikri Prespa then across the causeway between the two lakes. From here, one can go north to Psarades on Megali Prespa, or southwards along the western shore of Mikri Prespa, from where there are excellent views over the reedbeds and across to the island of Ag. Achillos. There is a small information centre in Ag. Germanos, and a few tower hides. The Society for the Protection of Prespa, based in Ag. Germanos, which draws on many organizations for support, is trying to work with local people to protect the park.

Mikri Prespa lake in spring, surrounded by snow-capped mountains

SITE
2 Mt. Grammos

High mountainous area on the Albanian border. Grid reference:
40°20'N 20°50'E, which is particularly good for birds.

The Mt. Grammos massif, straddling the border with Albania, is one of the least-known and least-visited parts of Greece. The mountains rise to 2520 m on the Greek side, high enough to hold snow well into the summer, and to have a fine zonation of deciduous and coniferous forest, with alpine grazing pastures, screes, and occasional cliffs above. The deciduous forests are dominated by common beech, with Bosnian pine in the coniferous zone.

It is considered to be an important bird site, though currently largely unprotected and subject to grazing pressure and forestry. It is particularly good for birds of prey, with breeding griffon and Egyptian vultures, honey buzzard, and golden and short-toed eagles, together with rock partridge, common chough, tawny pipit, rock thrush, grey-headed and middle-spotted woodpeckers, and many other birds of interest. Semi-collared flycatchers breed in the woods – we are out of the range of pied and collared flycatchers here, which makes identification quicker and easier! Red-breasted flycatchers have also been recently recorded as a breeding species, and there are reported sightings of both capercaillie and willow grouse. It is such a remote and largely trackless area, that many more species could be discovered.

Botanically it is of interest, with some unusual orchids such as the special marsh-orchids *Dactylorhiza baumanniana* and *D. pindica*, both confined to this part of the world, together with frog orchid and other more widespread species. There are other rare plants such as the sandwort *Minuartia graminifolia* and the alpine stitchwort *Stellaria nemorum* subspecies *glochidisperma*. The rare

borage relative *Solenanthus albanicus* was recently re-discovered here.

Access is difficult. The E90 passes relatively close, to the south. From this, minor roads lead northwards onto the slopes, through the villages of Plikati or Aetomilitsa, or there is a more tortuous route from the east and north to the village of Grammos. The mountain straddles the Kastoria/Ioannina state boundary, as well as the Albanian border.

Minuartia graminifolia

SITE 3 Gormos Valley and Oreokastro

A large area of unspoilt countryside on the Albanian border.
Grid reference: 39°56'N 20°30'E.

North-westwards from the village of Kalpaki, on the main E90 north of Ioannina where the road to Albania branches off westwards, there is a large area of hilly wooded country extending up to the village of Meropi, and beyond to the Albanian border. It is not spectacular country, either for its scenery or wildlife, and it is not worth making a long trip for, but it is pleasantly varied and unspoilt. The density of habitation is low, and there are no tourists at all.

Among the habitats within the area is extensive oak woodland, including some wood pasture, scrub, bare stony hills,

Praying mantis *Iris oratoria*

small gorges, and cliffs, and an attractive reed-fringed lake by the main road to Albania. It is a good area for breeding and resident birds of prey, including Egyptian vulture, honey buzzard, golden, lesser

Gormos Valley

spotted, and booted eagles, and Levant sparrowhawk, and no doubt others could be found with more detailed study. Smaller birds such as red-backed and woodchat shrikes, cirl bunting, woodlark, and middle-spotted woodpecker are all frequent.

The lake is an oasis in an otherwise dry area. Great reed warblers and other waterside birds are common here, together with marsh frogs and other amphibians. The loose-flowered orchid grows in the marshy fields, together with yellow iris and purple-loosestrife. Tortoises are common throughout, and butterflies and other insects abound. On a recent trip, I recorded 25 species of butterflies in a brief visit, numerous bush-crickets, several longhorn beetles, and found the extraordinary larvae of the puss moth searching for a pupation site.

There is easy road access into the area via the villages of Geroplatanos, Kefalovriso, and Meropi, though there is a huge area without roads.

SITE 4 Vikos Gorge

One of the most spectacular gorges in Europe, with marvellous flowers, butterflies, and other natural history. It lies within the Vikos-Aoós National Park.

The Vikos Gorge lies north of Ioannina, not far from the Albanian border, though there are no problems of restricted access here, as it is a relatively popular tourist area. It is one of the most impressive landscapes of Europe, running as a deep chasm through the shoulder of Astraka Mountain (see p. 39) for a distance of about 20 km. A sign-post at one point claims that it is the deepest gorge in the world. Whether that is true or not, it is still incredibly impressive, with vast sheer cliffs of limestone, and tumbling screes and forests reaching down to the Voidomatis River at the bottom.

In places, especially around Monodendri, there are some fine forests with most of the species you could expect in montane Balkan woodland: several maples, native horse-chestnuts, downy lime, hazel, hornbeam, hop-hornbeam, elms, cherry, and many others. There is a path down into the gorge from Monodendri which passes through the forest, and also gives access to the grassier and rocky ledges. Here, and in clearings in the forest, there are mixtures of flowers such as Madonna lily (often in abundance), the endemic *Ramonda serbica*, related to African violets and growing in masses on shaded boulders, the white-flowered *Salvia candidissima*, a St. John's-wort *Hypericum rumeliacum*, the larkspur *Consolida orientalis*, purple and ivy broomrape, several bellflowers, aubri-

Alpine swift *Apus melba*

The spectacular Vikos gorge seen from below Micro Papingo, in autumn

etas, ground-pine, an endemic knapweed *Centaurea pawlowskii*, perennial honesty, a pretty umbellifer *Athamanta macedonica*, the intensely magenta soapwort *Saponaria calabrica*, and many others. It is not especially rich in orchids, though pyramidal and greater butterfly orchids are not uncommon.

The vegetation at the bottom of the gorge is more limited, with alders, willows, planes, and cornelian cherry, but it does give a better chance of seeing Greek stream frogs, yellow-bellied toads, grey wagtails, and a reasonable range of dragonflies, mayflies, stoneflies, and caddisflies. In hot weather, towards midsummer, butterflies gather in large numbers in the damper areas – Camberwell beauties, a selection of fritillaries including cardinals and Niobe, swallowtails, southern white admirals, ilex hairstreak, and many more. Cicadas call from almost every tree, and bush-crickets, grasshoppers and praying mantids occur in remarkable abundance.

Above Monodendri, a dirt road leads on upwards to Oxia, from where there is a short walk to the most extraordinary viewpoint, perched at the top of some of the highest, sheerest cliffs in the middle section of the gorge. The road to Oxia passes through some fascinating jumbled limestone rock pinnacles, washed around with open forest. There are good flowers in the shadier sections, such as the leopard's-bane *Doronicum columnae*, the pretty reddish *Geranium macrorrhizum*, purple broomrape, several saxifrages, *Fritillaria graeca*, garlics, fleabanes (*Inula*) and many others. It is an exceptional area for butterflies, and the grassy bank just before the viewpoint has to be one of the world's great picnic spots, with extraordinary views, eagles overhead, peregrines calling nearby, flowers in abundance, and a marvellous variety of butterflies including Camberwell beauties, scarce swallowtail, Cleopatra, Balkan marbled whites, blue-spot hairstreak, large tortoiseshells, many fritillaries, skippers, and clouded Apollos,

North-west Greece

Digitalis lanata

to name but a few! There is also an abundance of ascalaphids – active predatory relatives of ant-lions, looking like dragonflies, but with long, clubbed antennae; there are two species here, *Libelloides coccajus* and *L. macaronius*. In the stonier areas, the beautiful little ladybird spider occurs in small numbers.

Birds to be seen here and elsewhere in the gorge include alpine choughs (in very large numbers), alpine swifts, kestrels, peregrines, crag martins, red-rumped swallows, occasional lammergeiers, griffon vultures, booted and short-toed eagles, alpine accentors, and many more. Wallcreepers move downwards into the gorge during the cooler months.

There is a good access point – especially suitable for less keen walkers – to the bottom of the gorge where the road up to the Papingo villages (see p. 39) crosses the river, with paths for a short

way up or down the river. There is fine Oriental plane forest here, an old monastery perched on a cliff, exceptional butterflies and other insects, and some good flowers including some of the special foxgloves *Digitalis lanatus* and *D. ferruginea*, spotted orchids, early spider orchids, a rather thin delphinium *Delphinium fissum*, the lovely clary sage, and a selection of bear's breeches including the rarer *Acanthus balcanicus*. Balkan green lizards scurry between rocks, demoiselle agrion damselflies perch in sunny clearings by the river, and dippers and grey wagtails ply back and forth. You can sometimes see dice snakes swimming in the river. Tortoises, especially marginated tortoises, are frequent, and can often be seen crossing the road. It is even a good area for lichens, with demanding species such as tree lungwort quite luxuriant on some of the planes.

The other good way to see the gorge, if you are prepared for a stiff walk, is by following the path from Vikos village to Micro Papingo, or vice versa. This crosses some marvellous screes, passes through good forest, goes below some fine cliffs, and has good views throughout. Additional species here include the impressive marsh-orchid *Dactylorhiza saccifera* in damp places, some fine stands of the Balkan form of lizard orchid, now known as *Himantoglossum caprinum*, with a stronger colour than the western and central European species, lots of stands of the shrubby pink *Drypis spinosa*, bastard balm, red helleborine, *Alyssum* species, the swollen-fruited *Alyssoides utriculata*, and many more, together with the usual abundance of butterflies and other insects.

The gorge is worth a visit at any time between April and early December; during the rest of the year there may be snow, and the weather is often cold and wet.

^{SITE}5 **Mt. Timfi**

Spectacular mountain scenery, rich in plants and animals.
Grid reference: 40°N 20°50'E; part of the Vikos-Aoós National Park.

The peaks of Mt. Timfi, including Astraka (2436 m) and Gamila (2497 m) tower above the two gorges of Vikos and Aoós, forming an extensive area of superb mountain scenery, with high cliffs, peaks, screes, small snowfields, glacial lakes, and alpine pastures. There is no vehicular access to the area, but access on foot is not too difficult from the west. The beautiful old stone Zagorian village of Micro Papingo lies on the western slopes of the mountain, below the buttresses of Astraka, and from here there is a good mule track which climbs steadily for about 1000 m to the first main ridge of Astraka. There is good accommodation in Micro and Macro Papingo, and the ascent, with reasonable time for a look around at the top, can easily be made in a day. There is a refuge on the ridge, which serves food and drinks through the summer, and simple accommodation can be arranged for a longer stay at high altitude.

The walk up passes through pastures and open woods, gradually turning to an impressive forest of trees of *Juniperus foetidissima*, which gives way to screes and pastures, heavily grazed by sheep. Different flowers begin to appear, such as a mountain tea *Sideritis scardica* with yellow flowers, widely collected by the locals; two attractive crane's-bills *Geranium cinereum* subspecies *subcaulescens* and *G. macrorrhizum*, masses of *Drypis spinosa* covered with burnet moths and other insects, a creamy-flowered daphne *Daphne oleoides*, and the first saxifrages and aubrietas, amongst others. Ring ouzels, blue rock thrushes, northern and black-eared wheatears, woodlarks, and black redstarts nest amongst the rocks, and both species of chough circle overhead.

Daphne oleoides

At the refuge, perched high on a spur, a completely new vista opens up, and from that point onwards you are in high mountain country. The list of flowers to be found here is enormous. The north-east facing slope below the refuge is particularly good in late June, with two species of *Aubrieta*, pretty mats of *Globularia cordifolia*, alpine basil thyme, and the rather similar *Thymus teucrioides*, the beautiful *Salvia candidissima*, Gargano dead-nettle, clusters of the bellflower relative *Edraianthus graminifolius*, a small creamy-flowered pink *Dianthus minutiflorus*, together with a variety of saxifrages, St. John's-worts, thrifts, knapweeds, speedwells, and many more. Out of the wind, there are a good variety of butterflies, including a strong population of Greek clouded yellow, heath fritillaries, and brown argus, with visitors from lower areas such as Camberwell beauty and painted lady. Scorpions can be found under stones here and there. At the bottom of the slope, there are lakes and marshy areas, and beyond, on the slopes

of Gamila, lies Drakolimni, or dragon lake, perched on the edge of the Aoós Gorge. Even in high summer there can be snow here, with *Crocus veluchensis*, alpine squill, spring gentians, and other high mountain plants brightening up the pastures. On the higher cliffs of Gamila, there are many choice high alpines such as *Saxifraga marginata*, *S. taygetea*, *S. sempervivum*, and purple saxifrage (at its only Greek locality); aubrietas including *Aubrieta gracilis*, *Achillea* species, a snowbell *Soldanella hungarica*, several louseworts, and many more.

The cliffs in these high areas are home to wallcreepers in summer, together with snowfinches, choughs, ravens, golden eagles, both crag and house martins, and other high altitude birds. Alpine newts occur in some of the lakes.

There are alternative ways up into the mountains, including a spectacular walk from the village of Skamneli, to the east, and a long climb from the Aoós Gorge (see p. 36).

SITE 6 Mt. Smolikas

A large, isolated mountain in the north Pindos Mountains.
Grid reference: 40°10'N 21°E, with a rich flora.

Smolikas is a large rather rounded mountain, consisting mainly of serpentine rock, with some limestone. Its highest point of 2637 m makes it the second highest mountain in Greece, though it is little-known and rarely-visited. It is of particular interest to botanists, because the large outcrop of serpentine rock supports a number of special endemic plants, as well as a wide range of Balkan and central European mountain flowers.

There are extensive forests of black pine and Bosnian pine, with beech or mixed beech–fir forest in places.

North-west Greece

Mixed deciduous woodlands on the unstable lower slopes of Mount Smolikas

Typically, there is much more flowing water than on a limestone mountain, and there are many streams, pools and boggy areas, and a small lake – Drakolimni (not the same lake as mentioned under Mt. Timfi – p. 40). Above about 2000 m, there are extensive grazed alpine pastures and screes, and it is here that many of the special flowers occur. These include the beautiful pink violet *Viola magellensis*, *Silene pindicola*, the snowbell *Soldanella pindicola*, two butterworts *Pinguicula crystallina* subspecies *hirtiflora* and *P. balcanica*, saxifrages such as *Saxifraga exarata*, *S. taygetea* and *S. luteoviridis*, a crucifer *Bornmuellera baldaccii*, a rare west Balkan endemic bog asphodel *Narthecium scardicum*, the almost hairless *Aubrieta gracilis* subspecies *glabrescens* and *Alyssum heldreichii*, amongst many others. More widespread mountain species, many of which only just extend into Greece at this point, include grass-of-Parnassus, wild tulip, the pretty yellow bartsia relative *Tozzia alpina*, coralroot orchid and others. Lower down, there are plants such as the heath *Erica herbacea*, yellow gentian, whorled Solomon's seal, a

Saxifraga exarata

bellflower *Campanula hawkinsiana*, and the small fritillary *Fritillaria epirotica*.

The bird life is poorly known, but seems to be broadly similar to that of the forests of Aoós and Vikos. Red-breasted flycatchers have recently been recorded here as a breeding species, at 1840 m in mixed forest, and there are high-altitude specialists such as choughs and alpine accentors.

Access onto the mountain is not very easy. There are paths up from near Pades on the south side, from Aghia Paraskevi in the north, or from Samarina (the highest inhabited village in Greece) on the east side. All routes involve a long walk.

7 Pindos National Park

SITE

A remote mountain National Park, also known as Valia Kalda, covering 6930 ha. Grid reference: 39°54'N 21°06'E.

The Pindos National Park lies in the north-eastern part of the Pindos Mountains, and it must be one of the least-visited and least-known of any European National Park. It is not sign-posted from nearby main roads, and there are no facilities within the park.

Geum coccineum

However, it is well worth a visit, especially if you are prepared to walk.

It consists mainly of a large wooded valley, ringed with peaks reaching over 2000 m, such as Mt. Mavrovouni (2159 m) in the south part. There are extensive forests dominated by black pine, with Balkan pine higher up, and stretches of beech on north-facing slopes. There are a few Scots pines, which are very rare in Greece, and many other trees in smaller quantities, such as the Greek whitebeam, and various maples.

The underlying rock is mainly serpentine, which – apart from giving a different topography compared to limestone – supports a specialized range of plants. The valley is well-known for its botanical specialities, many of which are confined to the north Pindos and adjacent areas. These include the crucifers *Bornmuellera baldacci*, *B. tymphaea*, and *Thlaspi epirotum*; the garlic *Allium brevirradium*, the catchfly *Silene pindicola*, a golden drop *Onosma pygmaeum*, a pink *Dianthus haematocalyx* subspecies *ventricosus*, and subspecies *pindicola*, two violets *Viola albanica* and *V. dukadjinica* and a snowbell *Soldanella pindicola*, amongst many others. Flowers are generally quite abundant, and other interesting species

Erhard's wall lizard *Podarcis erhardii* (Peter Wilson)

include an attractive avens *Geum coccineum* in damp woodland clearings, *Campanula hawkinsiana*, a pretty annual bellflower often found on serpentine, bird's-nest orchid, coralroot orchid, and a rare cousin of small-white orchid *Pseudorchis frivaldii*, now classified as *Gymnadenia frivaldii* putting it closer to the fragrant orchids.

It is a rewarding area for birds, with just under 80 species known to breed. Many of these are of particular interest, including Imperial eagle (though their breeding status is uncertain), golden eagle, lanner falcon, goshawk, Levant sparrowhawk, short-toed eagle, and Egyptian vulture; there are probably eight species of woodpeckers breeding, including black, Syrian, white-backed, and middle-spotted. Shore larks nest here in the very highest parts of the park, and wallcreepers may occasionally be seen, though they seem to prefer the limestone mountains.

Brown bears are considered still to live here in the extensive forests, together with a few wolves, wild cat, beech martens, roe deer, red squirrel, and wild boar amongst other mammals, though you are only likely to see deer and squirrels in a short stay. Otters are not infrequent along the streams.

Middle-spotted woodpecker *Dendrocopos medius*

There is also a good list of reptiles and amphibians. Greek stream frogs, common frogs, yellow-bellied and green toads, and alpine newts occur in wetter areas, while fire salamanders are common in the humid forests, especially of beech. Both green lizard and Balkan green lizard occur in sunny clearings, with Erhard's wall lizard, smooth snake, dice snake, Dahl's whip snake, nose-horned viper, and Hermann's tortoise. Butterflies are moderately abundant – though not quite as varied as in some of the limestone areas –

and include good populations of Camberwell beauty and large tortoiseshell. Other insects of interest include abundant longhorn beetles.

The best road in comes from the north, via the village of Perivoli (where there is a hotel), though unfortunately it does not connect easily with any well-used main road. There is a track in from the west side of the Katara Pass (see below), branching off a minor road near Milia, though it is not sign-posted, and can be difficult after rain.

SITE 8 Katara Pass and Metsovo

The main E92 road gives access to some marvellous mountain country where it crosses the Pindos between Ioannina and Kalambaka, with abundant flowers and other wildlife.

Good roads in the Pindos are few and far between, and it is fortunate that the E92 crosses over at a particularly interesting place. The highest point lies at about 1600 m, at the Katara Pass, and all the way from here westwards, down to the town of Metsovo and beyond is of great interest. Although almost anywhere within this stretch is worth looking at, the main areas of interest fall into three zones: the beech woods and grassy clearings around Metsovo; damp pastures and scrub higher up the pass, at about 1400 m; and grassy and rocky clearings in the mixed deciduous and coniferous woodland around the highest parts of the pass. The underlying rock is serpentine, which becomes particularly apparent in the higher parts, where soil depth is least.

Metsovo is an attractive old town which has suffered from being the main

focus for tourism and ski development, though it still provides a useful base for exploring the area, with ample hotels. Around the town, and especially along the road up to the pass, there are some fine beech woods. These have a good flora including red helleborine, a green-flowered form of greater butterfly orchid, bird's-nest orchid, coralroot bittercress, herb-Paris, serrated wintergreen, two

Gladiolus imbricatus

sweet-pea relatives *Lathyrus laxiflorus* and *L. vernus*, and an intriguing pinkish-red bladder campion that is virtually confined to serpentine areas: *Silene fabarioides*. There are sparrowhawks and several woodpeckers breeding in the woods. In grassy clearings, there are beautiful clumps of the broom relative *Chamaecytisus hirsutus*, with *Putoria calabrica*, a woodruff relative that grows in flower-covered mats. Clary sage grows here and there along the roadsides – a striking tall spike of flowers.

Higher up, there are more meadows, interspersed with scrub. They are wet or dry, and most are cut for hay at some time, then grazed. They have a good mixture of flowers, in great swathes of colour. Early in the year, there are thousands of crocuses, followed shortly afterwards by masses of poet's eye narcissus. By June, the damper areas have quantities of a marsh-gladiolus *Gladiolus imbricatus*, an oxeye daisy *Leucanthemum praecox* (which differs in minor details from the widespread central European oxeye daisy), white false helleborine, the pretty

bittercress *Cardamine raphanifolia*, marsh-marigolds, common valerian, and the marsh-orchids *Dactylorhiza saccifera* and elder-flowered orchid, in red and yellow forms. Masses of bug orchids occur around the edges of damp places.

In drier areas, there are clustered bellflowers, *Stachys scardica*, *Inula oculus-solis*, *Geranium asphodelioides*, a thrift *Armeria canescens*, wild clary, cut-leaved selfheal, downy woundwort, the spurge *Euphorbia myrsinites*, and many more.

Not surprisingly, these meadows and bushy areas are good for butterflies; a list made recently in late June included bavius, common and baton blues, Cleopatra, brimstone, scarce and common swallowtails, black-veined white, Queen of Spain and spotted fritillaries, Camberwell beauty, white-banded grayling, greenish black-tips, common clouded yellow, purple-shot copper, large tortoiseshell, and quite a few more. There are also bee-flies, transparent burnet moths, small elephant and humming-bird hawk-moths, violet carpenter bees, a very attractive longhorn called *Leptura cordigera*, the largest hymenopteran in Europe: *Scolia flavifrons*, a large shield bug *Carpocoris fuscipinus*, crab spiders, and much else to see. Black-headed buntings sing from the wires, and red-backed shrikes call from the hawthorn bushes.

Higher up, the soil becomes thinner, and there are open woods of beech and Bosnian pine. Along the roadsides, there are special serpentine flowers such as the pretty bell-

Camberwell beauty *Nymphalis antiopa*

North-west Greece

Cotoneaster nebrodensis

flower *Campanula hawkinsiana*, the thyme *Thymus teucrioides*, a bushy white crucifer *Bornmuellera tymphaea* and the catchfly *Silene pindicola*. Among bushes, there are hellebores especially *Helleborus cyclophyllus*, the yellow-flowered *Lilium albanicum*, two species of daphne *Daphne oleoides* and *D. blagayana*, the snowbell *Soldanella pindicola*, and wild tulips, amongst others.

The best time to visit is probably June, but any time between late April and July is worthwhile.

SITE 9 Kalamas Estuary

Large coastal wetlands, north of Igoumenitsa, running almost to the Albanian border.

The delta of the Kalamas River is the most northerly of the wetlands on the west coast of Greece, tucked up almost against the Albanian border. It is a complex site, as the river has been channelled and parts have been drained, so the main bulk of interesting habitat lies well south of the river mouth. Maps of the area are rather poor, both as regards roads and the topography, so you need to explore, looking particularly for saltmarsh, lagoons, and reedbeds.

Unfortunately, the delta is a shadow of what it must have been once, thanks to uncontrolled drainage, arable cultivation, shooting, fishing, tourism, and other activities, though a good deal of interest remains. Breeding birds include black-winged stilts, collared pratincoles, little and common terns, stone curlews, short-toed larks, marsh harriers, and olive tree warblers, though numbers are generally declining. There are hilly areas within the delta, where birds of prey such as lesser spotted eagle may still breed. In winter, there are waders and wildfowl,

usually several spotted eagles, great white egrets, and moderate numbers of Dalmatian pelicans.

It is primarily an ornithological site, though there are flowers on the low dunes, native hollyhocks along the tracks, and plenty of reptiles and amphibians.

Not far inland, the Kalamas River passes through a gorge (grid reference: 39°35'N 20°14'E), where there is a colony of griffon vultures, with other birds of prey such as lesser kestrels.

Lake Limnopouli lies 18 km from Igoumenitsa, east and slightly south. It is a substantial freshwater lake, covering 600 ha, full in winter but drying down to marshes in summer. There are white storks, marsh harriers, short-toed eagles, booted eagles, and ferruginous ducks in the breeding season.

The Acheron Delta on the coast south of Parga, once considered to be a good wetland, is now almost entirely destroyed by drainage, dumping, and development, though there are a few good wetlands inland up the river.

Saltmarsh and scrub around a lagoon in the Kalamas estuary

10 Aoós Gorge

A beautiful, largely wooded gorge on the northern side of the Timfi massif.

Although close to the Vikos Gorge, and often linked with it, the Aoós Gorge is quite different in character, and much less well known or visited. It is more V-shaped, with fewer spectacular cliffs, but this has allowed more forest to develop and survive, and there is a vast area of wild and virtually unvisited wooded country within its confines.

Botanically, it is rich. The rock-dwelling scabious *Pterocephalus perennis* is abundant here, and usually covered with masses of flowers, and there are other scabiouses such as the pretty little *Scabiosa triniifolia* and the robust *Cephalaria leucanthema*. There are at least two species of lilies, *Lilium carniolicum*, and the pure white Madonna

Madonna lily *Lilium candidum*

lily, together with orchids such as narrow-leaved, broad-leaved, and dark-red helleborines, and the endemic *Ramonda serbica* on shaded rocks. A fine large thistle *Ptilostemon afer* is abundant in sunnier areas and a magnet for butterflies. There are rare endemics here,

North-west Greece

An ascalaphid, *Libelloides macaronius*

too, such as the golden drop *Onosma epiroticum*, a borage relative *Lithodora goulandriorum*, a catchfly *Silene intonsa*, and the diminutive *Minuartia pseudosaxifraga*. The forests are mixed and varied, with common beech, Bosnian pine, and a wealth of other species including limes, elms, smoke-bush, several maples, hornbeams and hop-hornbeams, and eastern strawberry-tree, to mention just a few.

It is a fine site for insects, with its mixture of old woodland, sunny flowery clearings, and a permanent river. Stag beetles are common, several species of cicadas sing almost continuously from the trees (and they are easier to see here than

in many places, as the steep slopes often bring you to their level), and there are ascalaphids in the clearings. On the sandy river beaches, there are colonies of a pretty tiger beetle *Cicindela hybrida* subspecies *riparia*. Dragonflies and damselflies are quite abundant, such as golden-ringed dragonfly, broad-bodied chaser, one of the club-tailed group *Onychogomphus serpentinus*, which frequently settles on riverside rocks, and a lovely powder-blue skimmer *Orthetrum brunneum*, as well as two different demoiselle species.

The butterflies are marvellous here, and often in great abundance, especially in the hot dry weather of July and August, when there is little water elsewhere. There are Camberwell beauties and cardinal fritillaries in abundance, great banded graylings, eastern wood white, nettle tree, Cleopatra and brimstone, niobe and silver-washed fritillaries, Lulworth skippers, several blues, and many more.

Yellow-bellied toads are common in pools and quieter patches of the river, while Greek stream frogs are widespread, and dice snakes swim in the water looking for tadpoles. The Dalmatian algyroides (a

Aoós Gorge

Ramonda serbica

lizard) is frequent, and various other reptiles are recorded. The Aoós Gorge is

probably also the best place for mammals in the region, as its extensive forests and steep trackless slopes give ample cover and protection. Wild boars, roe deer, wild cats, and red squirrels are relatively frequent, with otters along the river. Brown bears may still occur, though recent records are few. The bird life is roughly similar to that of the Vikos Gorge, with griffon vultures, common buzzard, dipper, grey wagtail, black, middle-spotted, and white-backed woodpeckers, and many more.

Access is easy. Just south of Konitsa on the main E90 road, there is a lay-by leading to the old bridge over the river Aoós at the mouth of the gorge. You can park here, or drive a further kilometre up the gorge on a rough track. From here on there is a good path along the river, which then climbs through the woods to a monastery. A smaller path carries on beyond the monastery, and paths also climb up the steep slopes to Mt. Timfi.

SITE 11 Ioannina

A variety of interesting habitats around the town of Ioannina.

Clematis viticella

Ioannina is an attractive and bustling town that serves as a focal point for a large area

of north-west Greece, and it makes an excellent base for looking around the region. It is of particular interest to the naturalist, as it lies on the shores of a large natural lake – Lake Pamvotida or Lake Ioannina, with surrounding marshy areas. Much of the western side of the lake, where the town lies, has been built up, though it is still accessible, providing rea-

North-west Greece

sonable views of open water and any birds. The eastern and southern sides, though, are largely undeveloped.

The lake itself is large and quite shallow, fed by springs, and fringed with a wide belt of reeds in the more undisturbed areas. These support vast numbers of great reed warblers – which can be heard from a kilometre away up the nearby mountain – and common reed warblers, together with purple and grey herons, little bittern, little, great-crested, and black-necked grebes, marsh harrier, and Cetti's warblers, ferruginous duck plus other aquatic and waterside birds. White storks breed quite commonly in nearby towns and villages, and they can frequently be seen feeding around the lake or on the marshes. Lesser kestrels are fairly abundant in the surrounding area, nesting on cliffs and old buildings. In winter, there are pygmy cormorants and masses of wildfowl on the lake.

Marsh frogs are abundant, and they probably form the main food of the herons and storks. European pond terrapins are quite often seen, though hard to get close to, and there are more dice snakes here than anywhere else I have seen. If you stand on a knoll overlooking open water near the reeds, you can often see several at once. Tortoises occur nearby, usually Hermann's tortoise, and tree frogs can sometimes be heard calling from the reeds, where there are often large colonies.

It is not really a botanical site, though it is surprising what does occur around the lake. The pink flowers of flowering-rush, yellow irises, amphibious bistort, together with fringed and white water-lilies on the lake, make an attractive combination. In drier areas there is an impressive thistle *Onopordon illyricum*, usually awash with insects, the joint-pine *Ephedra fragilis*, spiny bear's breeches, Jerusalem sage, love-in-a-mist, red star thistle, and more. Along the lake shore one finds the erect white and dark red spikes of an unusual loosestrife *Lysimachia atropurpurea*, and the little *Biarum tenuifolium* hidden away under bushes.

Dragonflies are abundant, though hard to survey in detail, as they tend to fly over the water and perch on emergent plants well away from the shore. The list certainly includes emperor, lesser emperor, black-tailed skimmer, and the striking nail-varnish pink *Crocothemis erythraea*. It is a generally good area for insects, with abundant ant-lions, hymenopterans (including the impressive *Scolia flavifrons*, looking like a

Part of the vast reed-beds that fringe Lake Ioannina

huge hornet but quite harmless), praying mantises, bush-crickets, mayflies, and a good range of butterflies.

From Ioannina, it is possible to arrange boat trips on the lake, or to the island of Nissa (Ali Pasha's Island), which gives

Great reed warbler *Acrocephalus arundinaceus*

good views of the lake and some of its inhabitants. There is a minor road on the east side, which runs south-eastwards from the Katara Pass road, and this gives fine views of the reedbeds, with occasional clear views out into open water. It is particularly good around the monastery of Dourachanis, though all the roadsides are unpleasantly rubbishy.

South-west of Ioannina lies the classical site of Dodona, near the village of Dodoni (well sign-posted from the main road south of Ioannina). It is an impressive, yet little-visited site, with a huge amphitheatre and other ruins, in a dramatic setting. From late April through May, it is marvellously flowery, with orchids such as early spider, pyramidal and lizard; Madonna lilies, and a host of annuals, depending on the current management of the site. Subalpine warblers breed on the nearby scrubby slopes, and there are snakes and lizards everywhere.

SITE 12 Athamanon Mountains (Central Pindos)

High mountains, including Peristeri, running along the border between the states of Trikala and Ioannina.
Grid reference: 39°25'N 21°10'E.

The general title of Athamanon Mountains includes a large region of high remote country, running south-wards from Mt. Peristeri (2295 m) and Mt. Lakmos (south-west of Metsovo) to Mt. Athamanon itself (2393 m) and Mt. Pachtouri (2092 m). It is an inaccessible, little-known, and rarely visited area, largely forested by beech, fir, and pine,

with alpine pastures and cliffs above the tree-line.

Peristeri is probably the best-known mountain botanically. It is mainly limestone, with high cliffs and screes, and snow patches persisting well into the summer. *Crocus veluchensis* is common in the high pastures, together with alpine squills and gentians. On cliffs or amongst scree, there

North-west Greece

Baneberry Actaea spicata

are leopard's-banes *Doronicum orientale*, saxifrages such as *Saxifraga sempervivum* and *S. scardica*, aubrietas, crane's-bills, and many others. Lower down, there are orchids such as tongue and woodcock orchids, with elder-flowered orchid growing in damper pastures, and other gems like *Daphne oleoides* and baneberry. The pretty, autumn-flowering sowbread grows abundantly in the woods.

At the southernmost point of this group lies Kakarditsa (2393 m) – the highest point in the area, with Mt. Pachtourion to the west. These are inaccessible and rarely visited peaks, but known to be botanically rich. On Kakarditsa, for instance, there are: *Alkanna nonneiformis* (otherwise only found in Macedonia), the extremely rare *Solenanthus pindicus*, a member of the borage family known only from this area, growing at heights over 2000 m; the bellflower *Campanula pindica*, *Allium guicciardii*, and many others. Pachtourion is a striking mountain, with high cliffs and several distinct peaks. Above the beech forest, in the largely acidic pastures, there are many unusual flowers such as the groundsel *Senecio viscosus*, the bellflower relative *Asyneuma canescens* and a recently discovered knapweed *Centaurea triamularia* (there are quite a few new plants still being discovered in these mountains). The cushions of *Acantholimon androsaceum*, covered with pink flowers, are abundant in places, and aromatic herbs such as *Satureja parnassica*, *Nepeta spruneri*, and *Artemisia absinthium* all occur frequently.

Overall, the area is known to be good for mountain birds, though there is very little accurate information. It is an important area for vultures, with griffon and Egyptian breeding regularly, and lammergeier still possibly occurring. Amongst the woodpecker species, middle-spotted is of special interest.

There is no simple access route into this massif, but it is generally best approached from the network of forest tracks on the west side; Peristeri can be approached via minor roads from the E92 west of Metsovo, through Mega Peristeri village.

$\overset{\text{SITE}}{13}$ Mt. Kerketio

Mountainous, forested country west of Trikala, rich in all forms of wildlife. Grid reference: 39°35'N 21°32'E.

Westwards from Kalambaka and Trikala there is a vast region of beautiful, wooded, mountainous country, with few roads and virtually no visitors. Although there are many peaks over 2000 m in the area, very few of them are named on general maps. Mt. Kerketio (also known as Mt. Koziakas) is by no means the highest, though it pro-

Stream frog *Rana graeca*

vides a useful reference point as it is named on most maps. There is a good, partly new road (hardly used at all) which does a circuit of the area, branching off the main E92/N6 north-west of Kalambaka, passing through Kastanea, and crossing a high pass before dropping down to 'three rivers' and continuing southwards then eastwards to arrive at Pili, from where it is a short drive to Trikala.

The area includes the protected forest area of Pertouli, around the village of the same name to the west of Kerketio, where there are extensive stands of Greek fir and the hybrid *Abies borisii-regis*, while elsewhere there are beeches and oaks, with Oriental planes along the valleys. The parasitic mistletoe relative *Loranthus europaeus* is abundant on deciduous trees such as sweet chestnut, readily visible as large green clumps in the trees, and the much smaller parasite *Arceuthobium oxycedri* occurs on juniper, though hard to spot as its leaves look rather similar to those of the tree. There are grassy clearings, especially in the valleys, full of flowers and butterflies: cowslips, primroses, butterburs, marsh-

marigolds, violets, bugle, various marsh-orchids, crocuses, and squills, giving way later in the summer to roses, golden-rod, great meadow-rue, mallows, martagon lily, and many others. Typical butterflies here, often in abundance, include Duke of Burgundy, fritillaries such as Queen of Spain and cardinal, scarce and common swallowtails, orange tip, large tortoise-shell, and Camberwell beauty. In wet places, alpine newts, and common and stream frogs breed, while smooth snakes and other reptiles are common.

Most of the northern part of this area is underlain by acidic rocks, with rounded hills, plentiful streams, and thick forests. As you move southwards around the circuit described above, you reach a limestone area. As you enter it, there is a high

Alpine newt *Triturus alpestris*

limestone cliff with a shrine, and a short gorge; this is a good site for the insectivorous butterwort *Pinguicula crystallina* subspecies *hirtiflora*, together with other plants such as sad stock and the sage *Salvia argentea*. Crag martins and lesser kestrels breed nearby.

Mt. Koziakas itself is best approached from the village of Elati to its south, and the track upwards passes through extensive hybrid fir forest. It is a limestone mountain, very rich in flowers, with a mixture of Greek and alpine or central European species. In the woods, there are baneberry, martagon lilies, Solomon's seal, great meadow-rue, a crane's-bill *Geranium macrorrhizum*, and saxifrages such as *Saxifraga paniculata* and *S. sempervivum*, as well as many more widespread woodland species such as sanicle, greater butterfly orchids and violets. Higher, above the highest trees of *Abies borisii-regis* at about 1700 m, there is an alpine zone, rich in flowers, and with three particular rarities: the garlic *Allium heldreichii* confined to the Pindos and Olympus, a crane's-bill *Geranium aristatum*, and the gromwell *Lithospermum (Lithodora) goulandriorum* in one of its subspecies.

Although the birds have not been fully studied here, the area is known to be good for birds of prey and many woodland species. There are breeding populations of griffon and Egyptian vultures, peregrine, and booted and golden eagles. Woodpeckers, tits, firecrests, woodlark, rock bunting, red-backed shrikes, and many more breed in the lower areas.

Continuing the circuit on as far as Pili, there is a scenic limestone gorge, with an ancient church at its mouth, and a lovely old pack-horse bridge. There is a reasonable range of limestone gorge and slope plants here, though it tends to be overgrazed.

SITE 14 Meteora

Wooded hills, famous for the rock pinnacle monasteries of Meteora, but also notable for birds and flowers.

Just north of Kalambaka is Meteora, one of the most extraordinary locations in Greece. There is a series of conglomerate rock pinnacles and cliffs, with a dozen or more monasteries built into sheer rock faces or on the top of the pinnacles. Not surprisingly, it is a famous tourist site, well-visited in summer (though surprisingly quiet out of season). However, it is much more than just a tourist site – the scenery, even without the monasteries, is quite spectacular, and it lies on the edge of a varied area of fine unspoilt countryside, rich in plants and animals.

It is worth spending a few days in the Meteora area itself. White storks nest in the villages and can be seen flying to and from the nearby valley, while a few of the more secretive black storks nest in the woods. Crag martins, house martins, alpine swifts, and red-rumped swallows are everywhere, and you can often get very close views from the pinnacles. Egyptian vultures, rock doves, kestrels, and jackdaws breed on the cliffs, and can be constantly seen or heard; it is probably the best site in Greece for Egyptian vultures, with around 50 pairs breeding.

Around the base of the pinnacles, above the little village of Kastraki (incidentally, a much more pleasant place to stay in than noisy Kalambaka), there are

The extraordinary cliffs and pinnacles of Meteora, topped by monasteries

unimproved grasslands, oak and plane woodlands, and bare areas of sloping rock, which collectively have a surprisingly good flora. The list includes a basil thyme *Acinos suaveolens* that smells of lemon, several fritillary species including *Fritillaria mutabilis*, an alkanet *Alkanna pindicola*, the leopard's-bane *Doronicum orientale*, gargano deadnettle, wild clary, the striking dragon arum (with an incredibly strong smell of rotting meat!), masses of peacock anemones in different colours, and a reasonable selection of orchids, such as green-winged orchid and spider orchid relatives, particularly *Ophrys mammosa*. In shadier parts there are violets, primroses, two sweet pea relatives, the pretty bluish-purple *Lathyrus laxiflorus*, and the yellow and blue *Vicia barbazitae*. A little later, lilies come into flower, including the striking *Lilium chalchedonicum*. In drier areas, there are abundant sun-roses, especially the pink *Cistus creticus*, native hollyhocks *Althaea pallida*, bladder senna, and the striking

spikes of clary sage. Mulleins are also abundant, though with so many Greek species, these are hard to identify.

There are also two knapweed species that are almost endemic to the area: the yellow-flowered *Centaurea chrysocephala*, and the extremely rare *C. kalambakiensis* which appears to be confined to the village of Theopetra.

Not surprisingly, the whole area is good for butterflies and other insects, particularly grasshoppers and crickets. The mixture of scrub, sunny grassland, woodland, and hot rock slopes makes a perfect insect habitat. Butterflies include scarce and common swallowtails, large tortoiseshell, nettle-tree butterfly, southern festoon, green-underside blue, brown argus, small and lesser fiery coppers, green hairstreak, Camberwell beauty, and many more. The striking red-and-black fire bugs are abundant, especially when they emerge from hibernation and sunbathe together in masses. Other insects of interest include rose chafers, ascalaphids

North-west Greece

Lathyrus laxiflorus

(see p. 48), mantids, bush-crickets, green tiger beetles, longhorn beetles, and humming bird hawkmoths.

Balkan green lizards are common in sunny areas with scrub or rocks, tortoises can often be seen feeding in the woods or grasslands, and tree frogs call from more vegetated areas, especially around springs.

Northwards and eastwards from Meteora lie the Antihassia Hills, a quiet, relatively unspoilt area, with extensive wooded hills and peaks up to 1400 m in the east, and steep conglomerate cliffs here and there. It is noted for its bird life, especially birds of prey, including lesser spotted and booted eagles, Levant sparrowhawks, honey buzzards, eagle owls, and black kites. The beautifully coloured rollers can be seen along roadsides, perched on wires (though they seem to be declining in numbers here, as elsewhere), and sombre tits, red-backed shrikes, and several woodpeckers complete the picture. In spring, there are masses of

sand-crocuses, peacock anemones, and stars-of-Bethlehem.

Access to Meteora is easy by road from Kalambaka, passing through Kastraki on the way. To reach the quieter parts of the Antihassia Hills, follow minor roads from south of Kalambaka eastwards through Kallithea, or from Meteora northwards to Vlahava and Skepari. The whole area is interesting.

Red-rumped swallow *Hirundo daurica*

North Greece

North Greece

North Greece

Introduction

North Greece, as defined here, covers a large area of central northern Greece, stretching northwards from Larissa and Trikala through the mountainous areas that run along all of Greece's northern areas to the Macedonian (FYROM) border. It is less spectacular than north-west Greece, but remarkably varied and interesting. In the south it includes most of the vast area of the plains of Thessaly, former lake beds that have been gradually drained, cultivated, and settled, and are now used for the intensive cultivation of cotton, grain, and tobacco. East of here lies the hook-shaped Pilion Peninsula, which is a world apart, with ancient stone villages set in mountain forests and slopes tumbling down to the sea – despite increasing tourism here, this is still an unspoilt and little-known area.

Northwards from Larissa, the ground rises sharply, and the whole of this part of Greece is dominated by Greece's highest and most famous mountain, Mt. Olympus, which rises to almost 3000 m, far higher than anything else in the area. Olympus is a quite remarkable place, with a wonderful range of plants and animals, though it is also the high point of a marvellously unspoilt area which stretches away westwards. As with so much of Greece, you do not need to visit just the highlights to find

Fritillaries and copper butterflies on thistles

Previous page: **Mt. Olympus**

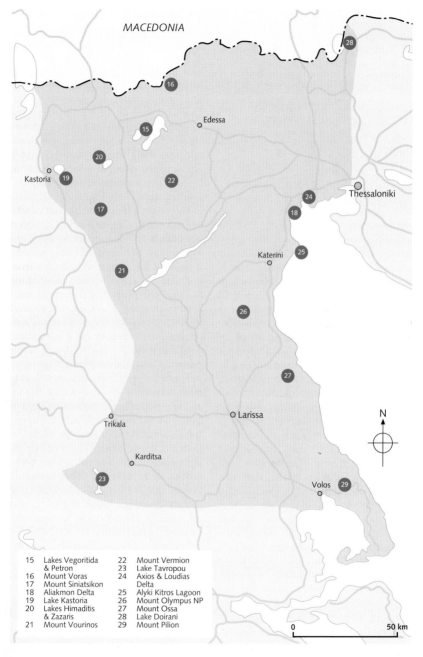

15	Lakes Vegoritida & Petron	22	Mount Vermion
16	Mount Voras	23	Lake Tavropou
17	Mount Siniatsikon	24	Axios & Loudias Delta
18	Aliakmon Delta	25	Alyki Kitros Lagoon
19	Lake Kastoria	26	Mount Olympus NP
20	Lakes Himaditis & Zazaris	27	Mount Ossa
21	Mount Vourinos	28	Lake Doirani
		29	Mount Pilion

attractive species-rich countryside; west from Olympus, there are marvellous areas of forests and hills that hardly anyone from outside the region ever visits.

This part of Greece also has an extensive Aegean coast along the west shore of the Thessalonikan or Thermaikos Gulf. This is not the most beautiful of Greek

Aquilegia amaliae

coasts, often rather flat, and without marked bays or offshore islands. Once it was an area of huge marshy deltas where a series of rivers met the sea on land barely above sea level, forming vast areas of lagoons, saltmarshes, and freshwater marshes among a shifting matrix of silt brought down by the rivers. Such areas must have been extraordinarily rich in wildlife, even into quite recent historic times, but they have been drained, cultivated, built on, dumped on, shot over, and generally abused. There are a few good areas still, such as the combined deltas of the Axios, Loudias, and Aliakmon rivers, south-west of Thessaloniki, where 11 800 ha have been declared as a Ramsar Site (an internationally important wetland), and there is hope that what is left can be retrieved and improved. Elsewhere, though, the shadows of the former interest are only visible in the lines of giant reeds lining slow-moving polluted ditches, or in pools half-filled with rubbish.

The north-western part of this region, running up to the Albanian border at Prespa, is something of a lake district, which always comes as a bit of a surprise. Those who know Greece as a country of hot, dry summers and relatively mild winters naturally assume that all these lakes are of artificial origin. In fact, the combination of much higher rainfall in

the north, lower temperatures generally, especially in winter, and a high output of year-round springs has produced a series of natural lakes. The shallowest ones have filled in with peat and been claimed for agriculture, but the deeper larger ones remain and are generally quite clean and unspoilt. They receive no management to speak of, and some – such as Himaditis – are steadily filling up with silt and peat, while there are signs of increasing agricultural and industrial pollution, but they remain gems of scenic and natural beauty.

The whole of the international border of Greece in this region is with the state of Macedonia (FYROM), reaching almost to Albania at the western end, and to Bulgaria at the eastern end. This is a wild, mountainous region on both sides of the frontier, with peaks reaching to well over 2000 m all along. It is a harsh area anywhere, with cold, snowy winters and hot, relatively dry summers, but it has a lower population than it might have, a result partly of long-running border disputes and military restrictions. Nowadays it is more accessible – an area of great beauty and interest, with new discoveries at every turn. This northern border area has a central European feel to it, reflected in the flora and fauna: extensive beech forests, alpine flowers such as white false helleborine and spring gentian, breeding crested tits, and butterflies such as white admirals, common glider, and others that are rare within Greece outside the extreme north.

There is no single good time to visit this region. In general, spring comes a little later than in the south, and much later in the mountains. Late April and May are good for the lowlands, whilst any time up to late July is good for the highest areas. In autumn, the wetlands are exciting places for birds, and the autumn colours are outstanding. Winters are harsh, but the coastal wetlands usually remain open for birds and can be exceptional if the weather to the north is especially cold.

SITE 15 Lakes Vegoritida and Petron

*Two large natural freshwater lakes around Amindeo, south-east of
Florina, particularly noted for birds.
Grid reference (Vegoritida): 40°45'N 21°40'E.*

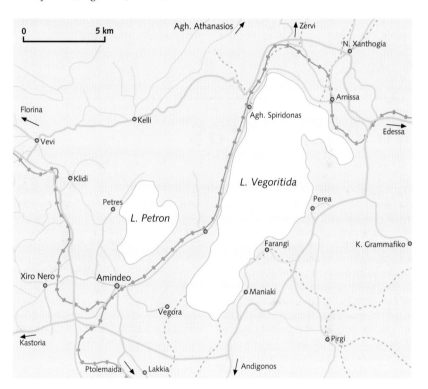

This site consists of sizeable lakes with interesting areas of surrounding countryside
west of Edessa, conveniently close to the
road from Thessaloniki to the Prespa Lakes
National Park (see p. 30). This is primarily a
bird site, though there are other features of
interest, such as dragonflies, frogs, terrapins,
dice snakes, and waterside flowers.

The lakes lie about 500 m above sea
level, in a basin surrounded by hills, or
higher mountains to the east and north.
An area of about 17 000 ha is regarded as

an important bird area here, and the best
parts are being considered as a Special
Area for Conservation. Vegoritida is much
the largest and deepest of the lakes,
becoming shallower towards its narrower
southern end. It is not an easy lake to
watch, although at various times there can
be pelicans, grebes, red-crested pochard,
coot, duck, and pygmy cormorants on the
water. The hills around the lake are probably more interesting, with good sites for
lesser kestrels, Egyptian vultures, rollers,

long-legged buzzards, and barred warblers, amongst others.

Lake Petron, to the west, is smaller and more secluded, and less subject to pollution at present. There is a small mixed heronry here, though it is not doing well. Collared pratincoles and black-winged stilts still breed in small numbers in damp areas. It is unfortunate that these sites .have not warranted Ramsar Site status, and are completely unprotected, so their value is steadily declining.

In winter, depending on the state of the water (in some years they become frozen), the lakes are visited by good numbers of wildfowl, including ferruginous duck (which breeds at the nearby site of Lake Himaditis (see p. 68) and others. Birds of prey pass through or winter here, including white-tailed eagle, spotted eagle, and harriers.

There is a minor road that skirts lake Vegoritida along the south-east corner near Farangi, and a good road follows much of the west side en route from Amindeo to Arnissa. Lake Petron is less accessible, but can be reached on the west side northwards from Petres.

SITE 16 Mt. Voras

An extensive remote mountain range along the Macedonian border, reaching 2524 m at its highest point, with a rich flora. Grid reference: 40°55′N 21°56′E.

Viola gracilis

The name 'Mt. Voras' applies to a large area of high mountains running along the Macedonian border from roughly north of Edessa south-westwards to a point north of Lake Petron, though similar mountains carry on westwards from here along the border. It includes the peak known as Kajmakcalan, at 2524 m the highest point in the massif. Access to this mountain has become easier in recent years, as border controls have been relaxed, though it is still little known and barely visited.

On the slopes, there are extensive beech woods, with a tree-line at about 1700 m. The rock is mainly of acid schists, so there is abundant water on the mountain compared to the limestone peaks. The flora is rich, more Balkan than Greek, with a fascinating mixture of species. In damp, grassy, forest clearings, there are masses of marsh-orchids *Dactylorhiza majalis*, meadowsweet, lady's-mantle, great meadow-rue, the avens *Geum coccineum*, a

leopard's-bane *Doronicum orphanidea*, buttercups such as *Ranunculus serbica* and *R. polyanthemos*, the yellow anemone *Anemone ranunculoides*, clumps of the curious spike-heath with bright red, heather-like flowers, and white false helleborine, among others. Higher up, above the tree-line, the flora in damp places includes the insectivorous butterwort *Pinguicula balcanica*, the rare orchid *Pseudorchis (Gymnadenia) frivaldii*, alpine dock, a subspecies of marsh-marigold, louseworts such as *Pedicularis olympica* (formerly *P. limnogena*) and *P. orthantha*, the bittercress *Cardamine raphanifolia*, and several saxifrages. In drier places, there are violets and pansies such as *Viola gracilis* and the rare yellow-flowered *V.*

Wild boar *Sus scrofa*

eximia, saxifrages, cinquefoils, *Silene roemeri*, and the catchfly *Lychnis viscaria* subspecies *atropurpureal.*

On the highest ridges and peaks, especially where some limestone appears, there is a further range of flowers, including the little *Minuartia recurva*, spring gentian, a felwort *Gentianella albanica*, *Gentiana punctata*, a newly discovered white buttercup *Ranunculus cacuminis*, apparently confined to the top of this peak, saxifrages such as *Saxifraga pedemontana* subspecies *cymosa*, forget-me-nots, cinquefoils, and many more. Earlier in the year, with a peak flowering in early May, there is a marvellous display of crocuses, especially the rare and impressive purplish-flowered *Crocus pelistericus* which is found in great abundance, and the more widespread *C. veluchensis*. *Crocus sieberi* and *C. chrysanthus* have also been recorded.

This area was the scene of heavy fighting during the First World War, when the Serbian army suffered huge casualties storming the summit ridge, and some of the fortifications are still visible around the summit.

The bird life has not been as well studied as the flowers, but it is noted as an important area for birds, with a number

Tengmalm's owl *Aegolius funereus*

of special species. Imperial eagles occur (but probably do not breed), while lammergeiers may still breed here. Other birds of prey include golden, booted, and short-toed eagles in reasonable numbers, long-legged buzzards, and Egyptian vultures. In the woods, there are black, white-backed, and middle-spotted woodpeckers amongst other more common species, and Tengmalm's owl probably breeds. Roe deer and wild boar are frequent, and wolves may still be here.

The virgin forest of Pefkoto Arideas – an ancient beech forest – has 33 ha under

special protection, and is noted for its undisturbed primeval character.

Access is relatively easy, once you have reached the area, from a network of minor roads running northwards from Aridea (north of Edessa), or up the ski station road off the main road west of Edessa, turning off just north of lake Vegoritida, heading towards Zeryi and Aghia Athanasios.

Between Edessa and Aridea, the road passes through the Apsalos Gorge, where there are breeding Egyptian vultures, peregrines, lesser grey shrike, and olive-tree warblers.

SITE 17 Mt. Siniatsikon

A remote and uninhabited mountain area south-west of Ptolemaida, with a rich flora. Grid reference: 40°30'N 21°36'E.

Mt. Siniatsikon is actually the northernmost and highest peak (2111 m) of a medium-height mountain range stretching from the E90 Kozani to Siatista road, northwards, and often known as Mt. Askio. It is composed of hard limestones and schists, and is generally rather bare, with little forest and an open scrub of hawthorns, Christ's thorn, junipers, and other bushes, reflecting the poor soil and long history of grazing.

It is a good place for bulbs, with two species of crocus, *Crocus sieberi* subspecies *sublimis* and *C. veluchensis*, wild tulips *Tulipa australis*, the pretty little pale yellow *Sternbergia colchiciflora* that flowers in autumn, with several *Colchicum* species. Other notable plants include a leopard's-bane *Doronicum orientale*, the shrubby *Prunus tenella*, various saxifrages, cinquefoils and violets, fritillaries, *Genista carinalis*, the little *Minuartia viscosa*, the rare mouse-ear *Cerastium rectum* subspecies *petricola*, alpine woundwort, a thyme *Thymus parnassicus*, white asphodel, and many more. On low cliffs and scree near the

summit is found the milk-vetch *Oxytropis purpurea*, rare in Greece, and *Astragalus mayeri*, only recently discovered in Greece, together with the rare spleenwort (fern) *Asplenium lepidum*.

Prunus tenella

Striking red cliffs and wooded slopes on the western fringe of Mt. Siniatsikon

The bird life is not known to be exceptional, probably due to the absence of extensive woods and high cliffs, but there are reasonably good numbers of the more widespread butterfly species.

Access is difficult from any direction. There are three possible routes, though none is well-used. The easiest is probably from Ardassa on the north-east side of the massif, passing through the hamlet of Bekreveniki. A good alternative is to head for Anarahi then Vlasti on the north side of the mountain, taking the path by the church just before Vlasti. It is also possible to ascend from above Eratira, on the south-west side.

18 Aliakmon Delta
SITE

The southernmost part of the great Axios–Loudias–Aliakmon deltas complex. Grid reference: 40°27'N 22°40'E.

The northernmost part of this important coastal wetland is covered separately on pp. 73–75. In general, the Aliakmon Delta is broadly similar, with large areas of salt-marsh, lagoons, and other coastal wetland habitats, with rather less agricul-

North Greece

Black-winged stilt *Himantopus himantopus*

ture than the northern parts. The bird fauna is also rather similar.

There are two particularly good places within the delta. There is a large lagoon just west of the Loudias mouth, with track access in a circuit, either following the course of the Loudias to its mouth, or from the village of Klidi, just off the main Athens–Thessaloniki highway. The better-known and more watchable site is a lagoon just north-east of Nea Agathoupoli, at the south-west end of the delta habitats. This supports a good range of birds at most times of year. In the breeding season, there are black-winged stilts, whiskered terns, and many feeding Mediterranean gulls from the nearby breeding colonies. Later in the summer one may see glossy ibis, spoonbills, egrets,

black-tailed godwits, marsh sandpipers, slender-billed gulls, sand martins, and many other species, while in winter there can be pygmy cormorants, occasional pelicans, numerous gulls, and waterfowl, with birds of prey such as marsh harriers, spotted eagle, and white-tailed eagle.

In drier areas near the lagoons, there are lesser grey shrikes, Cetti's and olivaceous warblers, nightingales, golden orioles, and Syrian woodpeckers, amongst others.

There is a track running northwards from Nea Agathoupoli near the shore, from which a path branches off towards the lagoon, just by a rubbish tip.

In the whole Ramsar Site (i.e. including Axios and Loudos), 30 species of freshwater fish have been recorded.

SITE
19 Lake Kastoria

A large natural lake almost encircling the old town of Kastoria, with interesting birds and other wildlife.

Lake Kastoria is a kidney-shaped natural freshwater lake, lying at an altitude of

620 m, with the old fur-trading town of Kastoria built on a peninsula extending

Lake Kastoria

into the lake. There are areas of marsh, reedbeds, wet meadows, and wetland forest in places around the margins, though many areas are now intensively used for agriculture, and drainage continues to take place. Despite disturbance and pollution, and a lack of protection (except for restricted shooting), the lake has retained a good bird population, and is certainly worth a look for anyone in the general area.

The range of breeding wetland birds here includes, amongst others, purple heron, little bittern, night heron and squacco heron, ferruginous duck, kingfisher, great-crested grebe, terns, and several species of waterside warblers. Pelicans come here from their breeding areas at Lake Prespa to feed in spring,

when the waters of Prespa are still too cold. Both white and Dalmatian pelicans can turn up here, in variable numbers. In autumn, and at some other times, pygmy cormorants can be abundant, sitting in the trees by the water, and white-tailed eagles are regular winter visitors. Goosanders have been recorded wintering in recent years, in small numbers.

Access is easy, with some good views from Kastoria or quieter access points just north of the town, in the north-west corner of the lake where a minor road reaches the shore, and around the village of Mavrochori on the east side.

The hills round about are mainly well-wooded, harbouring birds of prey such as lesser spotted and short-toed eagles, and occasional rollers.

SITE 20 Lakes Himaditis and Zazaris

Two neighbouring, though very different lakes, set in remote and sparsely populated countryside. Both are important bird sites.

These are two remarkably unspoilt lakes. They lie in the 'lake district' of north Greece, between Lake Kastoria and Lake Vegoritsida, though isolated from both of these.

Lake Zazaris is the smaller of the two, and arguably the more beautiful. Although it has more populated margins, and much less reedbed, it is hemmed in by mountains and extremely picturesque. Ornithologically, it is the least important of the two, though well worth a visit. White storks breed in Limnochori and other nearby villages, feeding in the marshes and lake margins. Both pelicans (white and Dalmatian) can occur here at any time, feeding, roosting, or moving from the lakes further north if they become ice-bound, and pygmy cor-

morants visit occasionally. Great-crested grebes breed in good numbers, and typical waterside birds include Cetti's warbler, great reed warbler, water rail, and little bittern.

It is a reasonable site for amphibians, with marsh frogs, grass snakes, and dice snakes in abundance. Dragonflies are numerous, mainly widespread species such as emperor, various darters, and broad-bodied chaser.

Lake Himaditis (also written as Kheimaditis sometimes) is much larger and less sheltered, with a remarkably unpopulated catchment area (though still subject to overgrazing and deforestation, unfortunately). There are extensive reedbeds and *Typha* beds, and large areas of open water, especially on the north-west side. Most maps show no roads running close to the shore, though there is a reasonable track running southwards from Limnochori along the west shore which gives good access and a few viewpoints. Himaditis is an important bird site, though subject to no protection at all.

Montagu's harriers breed in small numbers in the fields and marshes at the northern end of the lake, and marsh harriers are common. Both whiskered and black terns breed here (neither are at all common as breeding birds in Greece) in shallow, well-vegetated areas of water, though the survival of both here is precarious. There is a substantial breeding population of little bitterns, large numbers of *Acrocephalus* warblers, especially

Reedbeds around the beautiful Lake Zazaris

great reed, and numerous ducks. This was one of the most important sites in Greece for the rare ferruginous duck, though numbers have declined in the last few decades, and small numbers of pochard breed here. Kingfishers are common, and good numbers of white storks breed and feed in the area.

The hills round about are still of interest despite the steady loss of forest, supporting extensive tracts of scrub oak with cornelian cherry, and a few areas of more mature forest, especially higher up. There are breeding populations of Levant sparrowhawks, lesser spotted eagles and possibly still golden eagles and long-legged buzzards, though both are rare.

In winter, the lake is used by both Dalmatian and white pelicans, large numbers of coot and great-crested grebes, and various other waterfowl. Red-crested pochard often winter here in reasonable numbers (though apparently they do not breed), and white-tailed eagles or spotted eagles may pass through, together with the much more common marsh harriers, common buzzards, and other birds of prey.

Himaditis is not noted as an important site for amphibians, invertebrates, or flowers. However, dragonflies and amphibians are both abundant – though difficult to study closely here – and it is such a poorly known area that almost anything could turn up.

Access is largely unrestricted, though by no means easy. There is a newly improved road near the south-east side and a reasonable (except in wet weather) track along the west side from Limnochori to Variko. The best time for a visit is probably between late April and mid-June, though almost any time is of interest.

Ferruginous duck *Aythya nyroca*

SITE 21 Mt. Vourinos

A serpentine mountain, reaching 1866 m, south-west of Kozani,
with a rich flora. Grid reference: 40°12'N 21°40'E.

Although relatively low, Mt. Vourinos is a noted botanical locality, particularly rich in the special flowers of serpentine rock, with at least one species that is only known from here. On the middle slopes of the mountain, up to about 1600 m, there are extensive areas of grazed scrub with bare patches. The flora here includes a subspecies of kidney vetch *Anthyllis vulneraria* subspecies *bulgarica*, a thrift *Armeria canescens*, yellow woundwort, *Dorycnium pentaphyllum* subspecies *germanicum*, an endemic rock-rose *Fumana bonapartei*, bloody crane's-bill, the pretty *Lychnis coronaria*, a beautiful golden drop *Onosma elegantissima* that is known nowhere else in the world, and the perennial cushion-forming bindweed *Convolvulus boissieri* subspecies *compactus*, amongst many others.

Higher up, on the exposed summit ridges, there is juniper scrub, with open black pine woodland *Pinus nigra* subspecies *nigra*. Among the many species of particular interest here are the white crucifer *Bornmuellera*

tymphaea, and its special broomrape parasite *Orobanche rechingeri*, both uncommon plants of serpentine rock; fragrant orchid, *Inula ensifolia*, at least two lilies including *Lilium chalcedonicum*, cowslips, rock-roses, *Polygonum alpinum*, a rare lousewort *Pedicularis graeca*, the bittercress *Cardamine plumieri* in rock crevices, and spring sandwort.

The flora is a marvellous mixture of plants, similar in many ways to that of north Pindos, but at lower altitude and with its own special features. This is also a useful bird site, with breeding long-legged buzzard, golden eagle, lesser grey shrike, lanner falcon, griffon vultures, and a good range of other forest and mountain birds, though lacking the real high altitude specialities such as shore lark or wallcreeper. Jackals can still be seen in the area.

Access is not easy, though there is a reasonable track on the south-west side from between Varis and Exarchos.

SITE 22 Mt. Vermion

A large mountain block, reaching over 2000 m, particularly rich
in plants.

Mt. Vermion is a long, high ridge running roughly north-westwards, to the west of Naoussa and Veria. It is isolated and poorly known, and generally little visited, except for during the short skiing season. There is now a good ski road to a small ski station,

favoured particularly by Thessalonikans, which has made access much easier.

There are vast areas of beech woodland on the lower slopes, with sweet chestnut coppice here and there, and hop-hornbeam, amongst other species.

North Greece

Lilium chalcedonicum

Widespread species such as bird's-nest orchid, yellow bird's-nest, wintergreens, and sanicle are joined by more unusual plants such as the beautiful purple *Iris sintenisii*, cross gentian, *Lilium chalchedonicum*, and the scabious *Knautia drymia*. In higher woodlands, such as near the ski station, there is one of the specialities of the mountain – Mt. Vermion woad – found nowhere else in the world, and an attractive crane's-bill *Geranium reflexum*.

The mountain consists mainly of limestone, with more acid rock in places, such as around the peak of Mavri Petra (2026 m), where there are damp meadows and boggy areas (see below). Most of the high parts are heavily grazed and plants have to be searched for, though there are protected hollows and crevices in the rocks where more interesting species can be found. In mid-May, the high pastures are a mass of the orange-yellow crocus *Crocus cvijicii*, a rare species generally but this is one of its best localities, where it is easier to find than to pronounce. Another crocus *C. sieberi sublimis* occurs here, too, as on many Greek mountains. Other noteworthy bulbs in these high pastures, flowering at various times, include *Colchicum hungaricum* and the grape-hyacinth *Muscari neglectum*. In more humid rocky hollows one can find baneberry, herb-Paris, yellow archangel, sweet woodruff, and whorled Solomon's seal – suggesting that woodland was present not long ago. Other plants of the high rocky pastures include pink butterfly orchids, an endemic yellow woundwort *Stachys iva*, a globularia *G. bisnagarica*, burnt candytuft, *Aubrieta deltoidea*, a St. John's-wort *Hypericum barbatum*, the bell-flower relative (that looks more like a small lily at first) *Asyneuma limonifolium*, maiden pink, cowslips, the less common yellow asphodel *Asphodeline liburnica*, *Inula hirta*, and a house-leek *Jovibarba heuffelii*. In rock crevices, there is a splendid bell-flower *Campanula formanekiana*, together with other crevice plants.

On the northern slopes of the massif, in the north-western corner of the range, there is a high acidic peak called Mavri Petra (2026 m), marked on some maps (such as the Efstathiadis 1:300 000 atlas map), but not many. Because the rock that forms Mavri Petra is not porous, there are masses of streams, rivulets, boggy areas, and marshy meadows, with a particularly good flora. Plants recorded here include the scarlet avens *Geum coccineum*, several marsh-orchids, a bittercress *Cardamine raphanifolia* subspecies *acris*, a butterwort *Pinguicula balcanica* subspecies *balcanica*, alpine knotgrass, and many others.

There are few records for other groups of species on Vermion, though more information will undoubtedly become available with the easier access from the ski roads. There are tortoises and Balkan green lizards in sunny clearings, several woodpeckers in the woods, and shore larks breeding on the high tops.

Access is best from the east side, with Naoussa as a useful base. Roads lead up to Pende Pigadia ski station, or the Seli ski station further south. The crocuses are at their best in mid-May, and the season continues through the summer for other plants.

SITE 23 Lake Tavropou

A large reservoir set in wild, hilly, wooded country.

Lake Tavropou is a very large reservoir to the west of Karditsa, formed by damming a series of valleys. It has become something of a tourist attraction in an otherwise quiet area, and there are now quite good facilities, information boards, and green initiatives in the surrounding villages.

The lake itself has not developed its full potential, though there are good

Lake Tavropou from the west, showing the extensive fir forests on the surrounding hills

numbers of grebes (mainly little and great-crested), coot, and cormorants at present, and ospreys may stop over briefly on passage. It is likely that its value to birds and aquatic life will gradually improve as the vegetation and food sources develop, especially as it is large enough to retain undisturbed areas. The surrounding forests, though, are already outstandingly beautiful, dominated by Greek and hybrid firs, several oaks, and sweet chestnuts, with flowers below such as *Crocus veluchensis*, *C. sieberi* and the orange *C. chrysanthus*, Greek hellebores, various foxgloves such as *Digitalis lanata*, alpine squill, yellow archangel, peacock anemone, and *Anemone blanda*, widow iris including a daffodil-yellow form, and many others. The distinctive mistletoe *Loranthus europaeus* is common on deciduous trees. There is a rich and varied bird life in the forests, including woodpeckers such as middle spotted and white-backed, Levant sparrowhawk, short-toed eagle, sombre tit, mistle thrush, and several owls. It should be a good area for butterflies, with its combination of flowery glades and forest, though more survey is required. Interestingly, though, there is a roadside information point at Neohori that includes a computer terminal from which one can access a list of insects recorded from the area!

Just north of Neohori, on the lake shore, a botanic garden is being developed. It is still very immature, and would not merit a mention in any North European country, but since botanic gardens are virtually absent from Greece, it is worth visiting if only to give encouragement. A wide range of Greek species should eventually be grown.

There is a good road across from Karditsa, and a road all around the lake, with many side branches into temptingly wild country.

SITE 24 Axios and Loudias Delta

An important coastal wetland, designated as a Ramsar Site, with birds at all times of year.

The Axios Delta lies about 20 km southwest of Thessaloniki, and the area covered here runs as far west as the Loudias River. The equally interesting region south and west of the Loudias is covered as a separate site – the Aliakmon Delta – because there is no access within the site across the Loudias. They both lie within the same protected Ramsar Site.

The Axios Delta is almost exclusively a bird site, though there are some other features of interest. Once, the Axios reached the Gulf of Thessaloniki in a dynamic shifting delta, full of wetland habitats. In recent years, though, the river has been canalized and reduced in flow, and the bulk of the delta has been converted to agricultural use, especially rice and cotton. The greater part of the interesting habitats are confined to the coastal fringes, though there are pools, ditches, reed fringes, and other minor habitats throughout the delta, albeit usually rather polluted. The key remaining habitats include large areas of saltmarsh, lagoons, and reedbeds, with rice paddies provid-

North Greece

Great white egret *Egretta alba* (Mike Lane)

ing additional feeding areas when they are flooded. Shooting is now partially under control, and there are plans to construct a Ramsar visitor centre, as scheduled for all of Greece's Ramsar Sites.

Spring is a great time to visit. The spring passage period brings vast numbers of waders, including a few rarer species. Slender-billed curlew can occur in small

Penduline tit *Remiz pendulinus*

numbers – it is said to be the third most important site in Greece for this species – and broad-billed sandpipers. Terns, raptors such as red-footed falcon (frequently in large numbers), and many other species pass through. Breeding birds of interest include collared pratincoles in the salt-marshes, little bittern, little terns, black-winged stilts, avocets, redshank, stone curlew, water rail, little egret, great white egret (in very small numbers), night heron, purple heron, penduline tit and many other wetland birds. A few rufous bush robins nest in scrub along the riversides.

Winter is a very good time to visit the delta, as there can be a quite different range of species, often in large numbers. Spotted and white-tailed eagles hunt over the marshes, though nowadays in very small numbers. By contrast, there may be enormous numbers of marsh harriers; a couple of us recently counted over a hundred birds going to roost in the reedbeds before the light became too poor to count with certainty. The sight of so many harriers floating in against the sunset, with the snows of Mt. Olympus beyond, was one

The Axios delta at sunset, looking towards Mount Olympus

that will be hard to forget! Other birds seen at the same time included greater flamingos, a few Dalmatian pelicans, pygmy cormorant in reasonable numbers, redshank, greenshank, little stint, kingfishers, water rail, several heron and egret species, large flocks of corn buntings, snipe, and various duck. Bitterns are often recorded, though in declining numbers. Mediterranean, slender-billed, and black-headed gulls are frequent, especially near the river mouth and around the lagoons.

You would probably not visit the delta just for groups other than birds, but it does have abundant tree frogs and other amphibians, a reasonable range of dragonflies such as red-veined darter and the striking *Crocothemis erythraea*, and an abundance of saltmarsh plants such as sea aster.

There is no direct access from the main Athens–Thessaloniki highway, so you need to head for Halastra to get to the east side, or Nea Malgara for the west side, taking good tracks that go under the motorway in either case. Motorable tracks permeate the area, though they can be difficult after heavy rain.

^{SITE}
25 Alyki Kitros Lagoon

A coastal lagoon and saltpans, with important gull colonies.
Grid reference: 40°22'N 22°40'E.

The coastal lagoon and saltpans of Alyki Kitros lie on the coast just north-east of Katerini, not far from the village of Kitros, and the old port of Pidna.

The salt works are the most interesting part. They became well known in the 1980s, when a vast Mediterranean gull colony gradually established, peaking at

7300 pairs in 1988 though since then it has dispersed, and breeding areas are less clear-cut. However, it is still a good place to see Mediterranean gulls, and it is also the only breeding site in Greece for slen-der-billed gulls, though numbers have fluctuated substantially, and it is hard to be sure what will be present in any one year. There are also breeding gull-billed and little terns, collared pratincoles, black-winged stilts, avocets, and stone curlews, amongst others. Penduline tits breed on the edge of the salt works, with more common species such as Cetti's warbler. Cattle egrets also occur here, in one of their very few Greek sites.

From August onwards through the autumn and winter, there is a constant stream of birds. Greater flamingos are becoming more frequent, kingfishers are always present, and Caspian terns, spoonbills, and a wide variety of waders and wildfowl occur. About 170 species of bird have been recorded. Not surprisingly, this attracts birds of prey, and peregrines, marsh harriers, kestrels, and short-toed eagles are all regular visitors. White-tailed and spotted eagles, saker and red-footed falcons and hobbies all occur, but are less predictable.

Access is easy. You need to leave the main Athens–Thessaloniki highway at Methonia if coming from the north, or Katerini from the south, taking the old main road, then following sign-posts for 'Port of Pidna' and 'salt works'.

SITE 26 Mt. Olympus National Park

The highest and most famous mountain in Greece, partly protected by a National Park, with an exceptionally rich flora and fauna. Grid reference: 40°05'N 22°20'E.

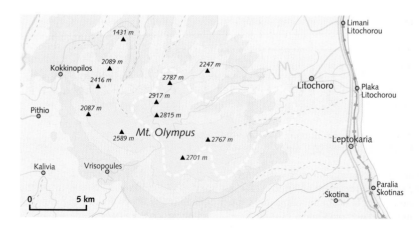

Mt. Olympus, 2917 m at its highest point, covers a vast area, perhaps 40 000 ha in all, with 4450 ha on the north-east side of the mountain protected as a National Park. It is wonderfully varied, mainly on limestone, comprising hot scrub on the lower slopes, deciduous and coniferous woodland at various altitudes, shady ravines, exposed cliffs, high screes and pastures, streams, and snow-fields, in a landscape of great beauty. The flora is exceptional, with about 1800 species, of which about 25 (depending on whose taxonomy you follow) are restricted to Olympus, and many are rare or local.

It is impossible to do justice to Olympus in full, but we can get a good look at the variety by following the most usual route up the mountain, passing through various vegetation zones. The easiest and most popular route is from the east, starting at the town of Litochoro, where there are several hotels. From here, you can walk all the way, via Prionia, or – as most people do – drive to Prionia. Around Litochoro there is extensive scrub, and an impressive gorge. The scrub is made up of the usual species such as kermes and ilex oak, prickly juniper, strawberry-tree and eastern strawberry-tree, Christ's thorn, hop-hornbeam, terebinth, and Judas tree, with an abundance of the pink-flowered shrubby thyme *Coridothymus capitatus*. It is a good place for orchids, such as four-spotted, pyramidal, green-winged, monkey, the yellow few-flowered orchid, and various others including *Ophrys mammosa* and similar species. There are many other herbaceous flowers including tulips, *Fritillaria messanensis, Iris reichenbachii*, dragon arum, and peacock anemone. In the gorge to the west of the town there are a few chasmophytes, such as the blue bellflower relative *Trachelium jacquinii, Campanula versicolor* (flowering in late summer), the pretty, yellow-flowered *Inula verbascifolia* with snow-white downy leaves, and a common golden drop *Onosma echioides*.

The minor road from Litochoro upwards passes through the scrub, then enters black pine forest, with occasional firs *Abies borisii-regis* and beeches, and attractive plants like the tall blue sage *Salvia ringens*, peach-leaved bellflower, and various thistles and mulleins. The end of the road is at Prionia, where there is a car-park and café, and a stream emerges from the rocks. Despite having become busy in recent years, it is a very interesting spot, with a rich flora. Plants of note here include the butterwort *Pinguicula balcanica*, a columbine *Aquilegia ottonis* subspecies *amaliae*, the large crane's-bill *Geranium macrorrhizum*, gargano dead-nettle, marsh-orchids *Dactylorhiza saccifera* and many more. It is well worth exploring this area. From here, you have to walk (or hire a mule), and the path climbs

Saxifraga scardica

North Greece

Viola delphinantha

steadily through rocky forest of beech and other species. In May, this is one of the best areas for the most famous Olympus speciality, *Jankaea heldreichii*, which is locally common on shadier rocks in places. In the beech woods, there are bird's-nest orchids, yellow bird's-nest in abundance, red, white, and narrow-leaved helleborines (and, in some years, ghost orchids, as unpredictable in their appearance here as anywhere else), several wintergreens, spurge laurel and mezereon, coral root bitter-cress, and more.

Above about 1500 m, the montane elements of the flora become more pronounced, and there are more open areas. Characteristic flowers include masses of the yellow toadflax *Linaria peloponnesiaca*, a dwarf broom *Genista radiata*, the tall, dull-red flowered spikes of *Phlomis samia*, more *Salvia ringens*, a pink *Dianthus haematocalyx*, lily-of-the-valley, mountain germander, and St. Bernard's lily (rare in Greece). In pinewoods, there is an abundance of a shrubby composite *Staehelina uniflosculosa*, and the saprophytic orchid, violet limodore. Bosnian pine gradually becomes a more significant part of the woodland as you climb higher, eventually becoming dominant.

Between about 1700 and 2100 m, where the first main refuge stands, there is a mar-

vellous array of flowers, especially in sunny clearings or on cliffs. These include pinks such as *Dianthus minutiflorus*, a yellow rattle *Rhinanthus pubescens*, *Saxifraga scardica* – these last three all being endemic to the Balkans – sad stock, a yellowish soapwort *Saponaria bellidifolia*, candytufts such as *Iberis sempervirens*, and an endemic woodruff with small white flowers *Asperula muscosa*. In ravines, there are additional species such as the columbine *Aquilegia ottonis* subspecies *amaliae*, with blue and white flowers.

The refuge stands in a dramatic position, with cliffs and rocks amongst old Bosnian pine forest, and fine views. It serves food and drinks, and you can stay here (though this will need to be booked in advance in July and August or at weekends). Because the pattern of summer weather on Olympus tends to be one of clear mornings, gradually clouding up to produce thunderstorms in the afternoon, it is really essential to stay on the mountain to have any time in the upper areas. Olympus thunderstorms are definitely best avoided, and the mist can be thick and treacherous.

The path carries on above the refuge through increasingly open pine woodland, home to numerous interesting plants. Some rock faces are covered with cushions of a rare violet *Viola delphinantha*, together with the Olympus endemic *Campanula oreadum*, the blue-flowered *Omphalodes luciliae*, and several saxifrages including *Saxifraga scardica* and *S. sempervivum*. Above this height, there are some marvellously contorted ancient pines, broken by snow and hit by lightning, but still growing and probably extremely old. At about 2500 m the path reaches a saddle, and the real high-alpine zone of Olympus begins. Here, many of the endemics and rarities occur, though they are often very small in stature. They include a mouse-ear *Cerastium theophrasti*, an alison *Alyssum handelii*, a cabbage relative *Brassica nivalis*, a violet *Viola striis-notata* – all endemic –

together with yarrows, cinquefoils, saxifrages, thymes, spurges, and many
others. There is a tiny relative of the sea
beet *Beta nana* that grows in stony turf
near snow patches, on a few Greek mountains and nowhere else. From here, it is a
relatively easy walk to the summit of Skala
(2866 m), and the flora is still rich and
varied: well over 50 species have been
recorded over 2800 m. The bellflower
Campanula oreadum is here again,
together with *Saxifraga spruneri, S.
exarata*, and the bellflower relative
Edraianthus graminifolius.

At this height, there are many other
possibilities, depending on time and
energy, though the habitats remain
broadly the same. The highest point,
Mitikas, can be climbed, or the high pastures of Profitas Ilias are worth a visit.

For birdwatchers, these high areas are a
paradise. It is one of the best places
in Greece to see wallcreepers, which
are not uncommon on the high cliffs, especially on the west side of the Skala–Mitikas
ridge. Alpine swifts and alpine accentors
are common in the high areas, and alpine
choughs can frequently be heard calling.
Shore larks breed in the high stony areas,
while lammergeiers are still to be found,
apparently often visiting the rubbish
dumps near refuges. Griffon vultures and
eagles, including golden and booted, soar
overhead, while peregrines and lanner falcons are not infrequent.

A little lower down in the higher parts of
the forests, there are rock buntings, Levant
sparrowhawks, firecrests, crossbills, crested
tits, and several woodpecker species. The
rare three-toed woodpecker, which is only
known from one other area in Greece,
breeds in a small area of Scots pine at about
1200 m, and black, middle-spotted, white-
backed, and grey-headed wookpeckers
occur elsewhere in the woods. Black vultures used to breed on Olympus until
recently, but now they appear to have disappeared, at least as a breeding species.

It is not a great site for mammals,
though chamois are present in reason-

High cliffs and snow patches on Mt. Olympus

able numbers, officially protected but
unofficially hunted. Roe deer, wild boar,
wild cat, red squirrel, beech marten, and
badgers all occur. Fire-bellied toads and
stream frogs live in the streams, and
there are Balkan green lizards among
others. Butterflies are abundant, including the impressive Apollo, though not
noticeably better than many another
Greek mountain – it is definitely the
flowers, and to some extent the birds,
that are most special on Olympus.

There are other approaches and other
sites on and around Olympus. A reasonable road can be followed from Katerini,
through Petra and across the north-west
shoulder of the mountain. A path leads
off from here, climbing, via an interesting
ravine (with abundant *Jankaea*) to the top
of Mitikas. From the south-west, there is a
road via Olimbiada that climbs up to a
refuge at about 1850 m. The whole area,
even the lower slopes, is generally
unspoilt and barely populated. It is an
exceptional site, in which it is well worth
spending several days.

North Greece

27 Mt. Ossa

An attractive conical mountain, south-east of Olympus.
Grid reference: 39°43'N 22°43'E.

Mt. Ossa is a distinctive, medium-height mountain, reaching 1978 m, with the top 400 m or so above the tree-line. On the lower slopes, there are extensive forests of sweet chestnut, mainly managed, with a reasonable flora that includes bear's breeches, the shrubby *Anthyllis barba-jovis*, and other interesting but widespread species. Higher up, there is beech forest, with a flora similar to that described for Olympus and elsewhere, including red and narrow-leaved helleborines, bird's-nest orchid, martagon lily, greater butterfly orchid (in a curious greenish form), wintergreens, and the marsh-orchid *Dactylorhiza saccifera*. There is an outlying population of native horse-chestnut here, too.

Higher up, the mountain becomes bare and grazed, and here there are masses of crocuses in spring (mainly *Crocus veluchensis*), with *Corydalis solida*, *Berberis cretica*, wild tulip, *Saxifraga scardica* and other saxifrages, squills, yellow stars-of-bethlehem, and many more. In high summer, you can see blue *Eryngium amethystinum*, a horehound *Marrubium thessalum*, *Astragalus angustifolius*, a toadflax *Linaria halepensis*, yellow asphodel, Jerusalem sage, whorled clary, and the yellow composite *Inula oculus-christi*. There is a pretty storksbill *Erodium absinthoides* in rocky places, a house-leek *Jovibarba heuffelii*, and various pinks and other flowers. Towards autumn, *Colchicum bivonae* with lovely, chequered pink flowers starts to appear. Along the roadsides, the distinctive mullein *Verbascum macrurus* is frequent, normally a lowland species, but reaching to about 1600 m here.

Ossa is part of a Special Protection Area for birds, covering almost 17 000 ha of wild uplands, noted for birds of prey including lanner falcon and Levant sparrowhawk, eagle owl, and semi-collared flycatchers.

Ossa can be reached by road from the west via Sikourio and Spilia; or from the north-east by a reasonable road that climbs up from just north of Karitsa.

28 Lake Doirani

A remote lake on the Macedonian border, with good bird populations.

Lake Doirani lies on the Macedonian border to the north-west of Thessaloniki. It is shared with Macedonia, and only about one third of the lake is in Greece. The lake and its surrounding habitats cover about 2000 ha within Greece. It is a shallow eutrophic lake, sheltered by hills on three sides, and partly fringed with reed and carr woodland. Although used for summer water sports and as a beach area to some extent, it remains generally undeveloped, and is undisturbed for most of the year.

It is particularly important for wintering waterbirds, though much depends on the

headed duck have been recorded here in winter, though they are rare, as in Greece in general. The lake as a whole was a good breeding site for egrets, white pelicans, purple heron, and others but its value seems to have declined, perhaps due to over-fishing and disturbance. More records are needed from this little-visited site. Cetti's warblers, reed warblers, and great reed warblers are still common in the surrounding reedbeds and other tall vegetation.

There are few records for other groups, though it certainly supports breeding green toads, marsh frogs, and European terrapins, and dragonflies include southern hawker, emperor, broad-bodied chaser, black-tailed skimmer, and various darters. Freshwater mussels, of several species, are common in the lake – a good indication of clean water.

Access is easy off the main road north of Kilkis to the small border village of Doirani, from where there is a road along much of the eastern shore. Note that there are sometimes border limitations in this politically rather unstable area.

weather to the north, and also whether the lake freezes. In good years, it can hold large numbers of pygmy cormorants and a few common cormorants, reasonable numbers of Dalmatian pelicans, occasional white pelicans, hundreds of great-crested and a few black-necked grebes, black-throated divers, pochard, occasional red-crested pochard, mallard, coot, and other waterfowl. White-

29 Mt. Pilion

Forested mountains on an attractive peninsula, reaching 1610 m.
Grid reference: 39°26'N 23°03'E

The Volos Peninsula, with Volos at its armpit, curves down like a hook from the east coast of Greece. Mt. Pilion occupies the northern part of the peninsula, forming a wooded spine reaching just over 1600 m at the highest point. While not a spectacular area, it is very impressive, with wooded convoluted hills falling eastwards to the sea, and fine forests of beech, sweet chestnut, and fir. It is high enough to have heavy snow in winter, and there is a small ski station at Hania.

Eleonora's falcon *Falco eleonorae*

North Greece

Hypericum olympicum

Despite its relatively low elevation, there is a good flora here, including some endemics. Near the top, there are clumps of a bellflower *Campanula incurva*, described by Polunin as the finest of all Balkan campanulas: 'domes of glorious pale blue-violet flowers, sometimes a metre across, with several hundred large bells opening to the sun at the same time'. It is one of Greece's especially rare Red Data Book plants. In the same area, there are other choice plants, including two foxgloves *Digitalis laevigata* and *D. grandiflora*, a catchfly *Silene compacta*, and three special rarities of the area: an unusual figwort relative *Siphonostegia syriaca* (at its only European locality here), a sage *Salvia eichlerana*, and a mullein *Verbascum pelium*, whose specific name indicates its connection with the area. In spring, there are masses of crocuses *Crocus veluchensis* in the high areas.

Lower down, such as around Makrinitsa on the west side, there is a good, general, unspoilt 'Mediterranean' hill flora, similar to many Peloponnese hills, with snake's head irises, scarlet peacock anemones and the St. John's-wort *Hypericum olympicum*,

amongst others. Pilion is also the only site in the east Mediterranean (apart from one locality on Crete) for Cornish moneywort, found in damp places on the lower slopes.

The whole Pilion area is considered to be particularly good for birds of prey, including short-toed eagle, honey buzzard,

Hypericum olympicum

booted eagle, golden eagle, long-legged buzzard, and Eleonora's falcon. The forest clearings and higher parts are particularly good for butterflies.

Access into the area is easy, though slow. There is a good road from southeast of Volos up to the ski station at (C)Hania, which goes on over to the coastal hill villages. Tracks lead upwards into the hills from most of the east coast villages, and there are now reasonable tourist facilities. The villages are considered to be amongst the most attractive in Greece.

North-east Greece

Introduction

North-east Greece, as defined here, is bordered on the west by a line roughly from the city of Thessaloniki, due north to the Bulgarian border. From here, it extends eastwards to include all the north-eastern mainland, sandwiched between Bulgaria and the Aegean Sea, as far as the Turkish border, and including a few islands just offshore. It is a very varied area, noted particularly for its bird-rich wetlands, including 5 of Greece's 10 Ramsar Sites (internationally important wetlands).

Along the extensive coastline there is a series of wetlands, mainly associated with river mouths. All have declined in value over the past few decades, with some of them, such as the Strymon Delta, to the point of being excluded from our list. However, it is a sign of the enormous importance of this region that the remaining wetlands are still outstandingly important, as well as being very extensive, despite the losses they have sustained. The area lies on an important migratory route, with a distinct bottleneck in places such as Evros, and vast numbers of birds pass through at passage periods. Although winters are nothing like as mild as southern Greece, and can be quite harsh at times, the coastal wet-

Wolf *Canis lupus*

Opposite page: **Agios Mamantos Marsh**

North-east Greece

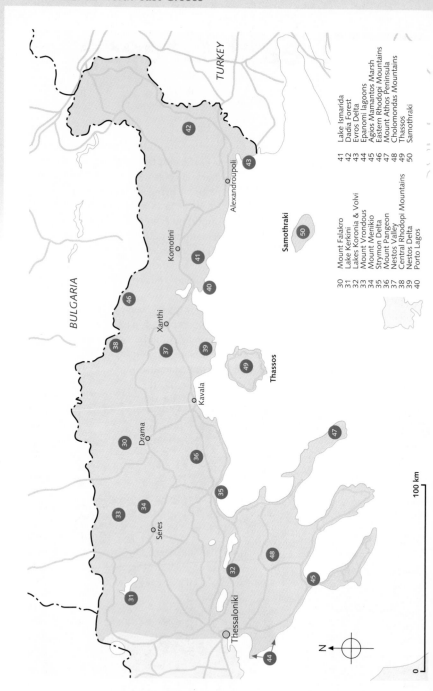

TURKEY

BULGARIA

Samothraki

Thassos

Alexandroupoli

Komotini

Xanthi

Kavala

Drama

Seres

Thessaloniki

N

0 ——— 100 km

30 Mount Falakro
31 Lake Kerkini
32 Lakes Koronia & Volvi
33 Mount Vrondous
34 Mount Menikio
35 Strymon Delta
36 Mount Pangeon
37 Nestos Valley
38 Central Rhodopi Mountains
39 Nestos Delta
40 Porto Lagos

41 Lake Ismarida
42 Dadia Forest
43 Evros Delta
44 Epanomi lagoons
45 Agios Mamantos Marsh
46 Eastern Rhodopi Mountains
47 Mount Athos Peninsula
48 Cholomondas Mountains
49 Thassos
50 Samothraki

lands do remain virtually ice-free, so they provide an important wintering area for very large numbers of birds. The Aegean is largely unpolluted and rich in marine life, while to the north of the coast lie vast areas of unspoilt, partly wooded hilly country, providing an unrivalled combination of habitats for visiting birds.

Inland, there are a few natural lakes that have retained some value as natural sites, although distinctly degraded, but the most remarkable inland wetland is Lake Kerkini, which is actually a 60-year-old reservoir. By a fortunate combination of location and topography it has become a species-rich wetland, recognized by designation as a Ramsar Site, which gives an idea of how good other wetlands could be in this fascinating part of Europe, given more protection and management.

Virtually the whole northern border of our area is formed by Bulgaria, running from its junction with Macedonia (FYROM) in the west, to the Turkish border near Edirne in the east. This is a largely unspoilt area, always hilly and frequently mountainous, rising to around 2000 m in places, and extensively wooded. Wildlife does not recognize political boundaries, and since the southern parts of Bulgaria are very unspoilt and natural, there is a symbiotic relationship between the two countries that makes each more important, and the whole greater than the sum of its parts. For example, wolves, brown bears, and other species have a greater reservoir of populations over the border to the north, which allows them to recolonize the less-favoured Greek parts in times of strong population numbers. This area, on both sides of the border, is known generally as the Rhodopi Mountains. We have picked out some areas of high interest, but it is unlikely that anywhere along this zone will disappoint the visitor, though access is still poor, with few good roads. At the extreme eastern end, just out of the Rhodopi, lies the Dadia Forest, which is the most important known area in Europe for birds of prey, but also good for many other things. It is quite exceptional, and easier to visit than most, too, with good facilities. However, you can't help noticing, when you travel around this forgotten and little-known part of Greece, that there are many other areas which look very similar to Dadia and may well turn out to be as fine. Many of these birds of prey need vast areas of habitat to do well in, and probably the surroundings contribute to Dadia's importance, and vice versa.

Finally, there is the lovely Chalkidiki area, which has such a distinctive shape – the palm of a hand with just three fingers, or perhaps the leaf of a plane tree. Despite its proximity to Thessaloniki (Greece's second city), and popularity with holidaymakers, it remains very unspoilt away from the key beach resorts. There are fine coastal wetlands, vast areas of rocky *garrigue*, and some surprisingly high mountains, reaching over 2000 m at Mt. Athos. The Athos Peninsula is one of the most extraordinary areas in Europe for many reasons, and it remains as if in a medieval time-warp, set aside from the rest of Europe and covered with fine natural habitats. Spread across the north of the three 'fingers', the Cholomondas or Holomondas Mountains are unspoilt and partly wooded, and they link northwards via high areas such as Mt. Pangeon and the Lekanos Mountains to the Rhodopi and Bulgaria.

Overall, it is a fascinating and varied region. For the general naturalist, May and June are probably the best months to be here, with October and November good for autumn colour, late butterflies, and a few bulbs. For the birdwatcher, almost any time between August and June is worthwhile, with peaks in September, midwinter, and April–May, when there is the perfect combination of breeding birds, passage species, and generally pleasant weather.

North-east Greece

30 Mt. Falakro

An impressive high mountain north of Drama, with a rich flora and fauna. Grid reference: 41°21'N 24°6'E.

Mt. Falakro, also known as Boz Dagh of Drama, is an impressive limestone mountain rising to 2232 m, with high cliffs and screes. It lies about 10 km north of the town of Drama, and there is now an easy road giving access almost to the top, thanks to a small ski station that has been recently built. It has a rich flora, which includes a number of arctic-alpine species at or near their southern limit, amongst a total of over 800 species for the mountain as a whole.

The lower slopes have typical north Greek *maquis*, dominated by kermes oak, Christ's thorn, smoke bush, Oriental hornbeam, prickly juniper (with its parasite *Arceuthobium oxycedri*), and terebinth, with herbaceous plants such as ground-pine, blue bugle, basil thyme, the foxglove *Digitalis ferruginea*, pinks such as *Dianthus gracilis*, the catchfly *Lychnis coronaria*, and a few orchids such as lady, pyramidal, and early purple.

Higher up, there are extensive beech woods with a characteristic flora which includes bird's-nest orchid, yellow bird's-nest, swallow-wort, red helleborine, birthwort, baneberry, common columbine,

round-leaved saxifrage, wild strawberry, wood crane's-bill, *Haberlea rhodopensis*, and many others. Both crested cow-wheat and field cow-wheat occur here, though they are very rare generally in Greece. At about 1500–1700 m there is some attractive beech wood pasture, with ancient pollards and flowery grassland in the more open areas – grazed, but not usually overgrazed. The more sheltered areas are particularly good for butterflies and other insects, and the first flowers of crocuses such as *Crocus veluchensis* and *C. chrysanthus* can be found here in spring, with alpine squill and dog's-tooth violet. Above here, there is coniferous forest, mainly of the fir *Abies borisii-regis* and pines. Higher still, there are extensive open pastures, and some high cliffs and screes in the summit area, which has an astonishing amphitheatre of cliffs and a deep, snow-filled pit.

The higher areas have a particularly rich and varied flora, which includes mountain avens in quantity near the summit – this is normally an arctic-alpine, at the extreme south of its range here, and the same applies to the little eyebright

Haberlea rhodopensis

Euphrasia hirtella. Cross gentian *Gentiana cruciata* in its subspecies *phlogifolia*, an autumn gentian *Gentianella austriaca*, and spring gentian all occur in high pastures, together with two lady's-mantles *Alchemilla monticola* and *A. filicaulis*, the harebell *Campanula velebitica* (a Balkan endemic, only just reaching into Greece), the crane's-bill *Geranium reflexum* at the eastern edge of its range, a scabious *Scabiosa rhodopensis* at its only known Greek locality, pinks such as *Dianthus stefanoffii*, and many more. Other plants of interest on the mountain include autumn-crocus relative *Merendera rhodopea* flowering in autumn, a true crocus *Crocus pulchellus* that also flowers in autumn, martagon lily, St. Bernard's lily, vanilla orchid, a rare endemic fritillary *Fritillaria drenovskii*, several species of stars-of-Bethlehem, elder-flowered orchid, the hellebore *Helleborus cyclophyllus*, the rare and endemic violet *Viola delphinantha* (see also Mt. Olympus and Mt. Pangeon), and *Haberlea rhodopensis* (believed to be a survivor through the ice ages from the Tertiary geological period) with its reddish-purple flowers, growing on shady rocks and in rock crevices.

Birds have not been recorded in detail, though it has a good variety of birds of prey, with near-perfect habitat for them. It was here that I had my best ever view of a wall-creeper, as one flew alongside the car, then perched and fed on a roadside cliff a few metres from us; this was in autumn, but they probably breed here as there is suitable habitat. There are breeding nightjars and golden oriole on the lower slopes. It is also an excellent locality for butterflies, with an appealing mixture of northern, southern, eastern, and upland species. Apart from the abundant common species such as cardinals, brimstones, blues, and coppers, there are special species such as large and black ringlets, Dils' grayling, safflower skipper, eastern large skipper, Weaver's fritillary, Higgins' anomalous blue, and the Phalakron blue. The Phalakron blue is named after Mt. Falakro, and only

Black pine forest on the high slopes of Mt. Falakro

North-east Greece

found in a tiny area of mountains around here. It is closely related to the common blue, but differs in being larger and shinier, and in microscopic anatomical differences. It is common here in sunny, grassy clearings in the woods.

The ski station is not unduly intrusive at present, and most of the mountain habitats are in good condition.

Access is easy by road from Drama, to Prosotsani then almost to Volatas, from where a surfaced road climbs through pastures and forest to the ski station, not far from the summits.

The whole area is of interest and well worth exploring, with extensive oak forests and scrub lower down, and beech and pine/fir forests higher up.

SITE 31 Lake Kerkini

A long-established reservoir that has become an outstandingly good bird site.

There are high hills to the north, along the Bulgarian border, and west, making a very impressive setting. The whole area of interest covers over 10000 ha.

It is primarily a bird site, and one of Greece's network of Ramsar Sites, which may give it some added protection and the possibility of conservation management in the near future. For the visitor, one of its great advantages, apart from the large numbers of birds, is that it is so

Lake Kerkini must be one of the most attractive and atmospheric reservoirs anywhere in Europe. This is partly because it has been established for over 60 years, but it is also unusual in that it lies in a broad shallow valley (the bed of a former lake and latterly a river oxbow) and has no high dam. When the water draws down (as it does for much of the year), it reveals a vast area of wet grassland and marshes, with scattered pollard willows, mud, and pools – a paradise for feeding birds. Most of this exposed area is grazed as available, but it all has a pleasantly low-key and unexploited feel to it.

Pygmy cormorant Phalacrocorax pygmeus

Kerkini at sunset

easy to observe, with an embanked road or track for most of the way round.

Breeding birds include a substantial mixed heronry that has night herons, grey and purple herons, squacco, little egrets, glossy ibis (at times), and spoonbills. Both cormorants and pygmy cormorants breed in large and increasing numbers. Some sheltered bays, especially on the west side, have more floating vegetation such as white water-lilies, which is where black and whiskered terns nest, and there are scattered common terns in places. Little bittern, water rail, bearded tit, Cetti's and great reed warblers, amongst others, nest in the reeds, while penduline tits breed in willows nearby. The vast expanse of wooded hills and mountains in the area supports numerous breeding birds of prey such as short-toed, golden, booted, and lesser spotted eagles, black kite, and Levant sparrowhawk, many of which hunt over the lake and surroundings. Incidentally, common sparrowhawks also occur here com-

monly, giving a good opportunity to compare the two in summer. Don't forget to check whether the eyes are yellow or reddish-brown as they flash past you! Both black and white stork also occur in good numbers, breeding nearby.

Winter bird-watching here can be marvellous, though the weather is unpredictable and can be poor for days on end. There are huge numbers of pygmy cormorants (we estimated that one 'raft' had about 5000 birds, on one occasion recently), as well as common cormorant in its *sinensis* race. Dalmatian pelicans visit in large numbers, with the added bonus that they have learnt to follow the local fishermen as they pull in their nets, which means they can be very closely approached. The extreme south of the lake is probably the best area to see them, with large flocks of juveniles and a few adults waiting expectantly. It is hoped that Kerkini may eventually become an important breeding site for Dalmatian pelicans, as birds are staying all year.

North-east Greece

Dalmatian pelicans awaiting food from the local fishermen

There are so few other sites for this endangered species, with its tiny world population, that any new breeding colonies are to be welcomed. White pelicans occur in smaller numbers, especially on passage. Kingfishers are abundant, and there are masses of great-crested, black-necked, and little grebes. As you might expect, there are numerous north European ducks, and both little and great white egrets hunt in the shallows. A few white-headed ducks have spent part of the winter here in recent years, and there are small numbers of red-crested pochard. At passage periods, there can be good numbers of waders, depending on the state of the water, though nothing exceptional. They include grey plover, redshank, wood, green, and marsh sand-pipers, dunlin, little stint and curlew, to name but a few.

The main interest here is undoubtedly birds, though there are reasonable numbers of amphibians including tree frogs, green frogs, and terrapins. The best areas tend to be along some of the reed-fringed ditches close to the site, where the poplars, incidentally, are often home to breeding penduline tits.

Access is very easy on the good new road to the Bulgarian border from Serres. There are motorable tracks most of the way around the lake. Any points where

Pelicans

Dalmatian and white pelicans occur at Kerkini, as on several other north Greek wetlands. Dalmatian pelicans are commoner here. White pelicans, though very slightly smaller, are the more striking birds, with a clearer white plumage and boldly defined black wing tips and trailing edges in flight. Their throat sac and face mask are yellowish or pale orange. Dalmatian pelicans are generally duller in colour, more greyish, with less clearly defined dark patches on the wings; their throat sacs and face masks are more reddish-orange. The legs are grey at all stages, whereas those of white pelican are pinkish, even in young birds. Juvenile white pelicans are much darker on the back than Dalmatians.

rivers enter or leave are also likely to be of interest. Siderikastri has hotels that are open all year.

To the north lies the high and rather forbidding range of Mt. Kerkini, which forms the border with Bulgaria at this point. It is little-known and not very accessible, but home to the breeding birds of prey mentioned above, together with black storks, Egyptian vulture, and other woodland or cliff species. It also has a rich montane flora. Westwards and south-westwards there is a huge area of oak-clad hills and low mountains that would undoubtedly repay exploration in spring and early summer.

SITE
32 Lakes Koronia and Volvi

Two large shallow lakes, with good birds and other wildlife.
Grid reference: 40°41'N 23°20'E.

These two large, shallow lakes lie in a broad valley to the north of the Chalkidiki Peninsula. Lake Volvi is the larger, easternmost lake – one of the largest natural lakes in Greece – while Lake Koronia (also known as Lake Langada) is smaller and further west. Old accounts of these lakes make depressing reading: descriptions of an unspoilt, marshy paradise, full of birds. Sadly, the situation has changed very rapidly, as most of the former marshy areas are under arable cultivation, and the lakes have become much more polluted. However, they are still of value, and are declared as Ramsar Sites of international importance; fortunately, Greece is now taking its responsibilities towards these sites quite seriously, and the decline should be halted or reversed.

Around parts of the shorelines, there are areas of high-quality aquatic habitats such as reedbeds and marshland – though much reduced in size – particularly in the south-west corner of Volvi, or the north-west corner of Koroni. The fine habitat that linked the two lakes ecologically is now all but gone, but nevertheless there is much to see. Breeding birds include night, squacco, and purple herons, little bittern, little egrets, ruddy shelduck, Levant sparrowhawk, penduline tits, water rails, and warblers such as reed, great reed, and

North-east Greece

Cetti's. White storks nest here and there, and there are often Spanish sparrows breeding in their nests.

Pelicans are regular visitors outside the breeding season, with considerable numbers of white and a few Dalmatians. Nowadays, there are often groups of greater flamingos, as they are generally on the increase in this part of Greece. Large numbers of waterfowl, including grebes – mainly great-crested, little, and black-necked – can occur in winter (with up to 20 000 birds recorded, mainly of coot), though Koronia often freezes over for several weeks in midwinter. Pygmy cormorants (another species that seems to be on the increase at present) appear in reasonable numbers, together with pochard, great white egret, common cormorants, kingfishers, coot, and gulls.

There is a reasonable aquatic and marginal flora, though this has declined in recent years as the nutrient and pollutant levels in the lakes have gone up. Water chestnut is present, together with white water-lilies, water milfoil, duckweeds, and pondweeds. The amphibians and fishes were of special interest, though numbers and diversity have declined. There are still green toads, European pond terrapins, agile frogs, and common tree frogs, whilst in the area around there are spur-thighed and Hermann's tortoises, Balkan green lizards, Balkan wall lizards, four-lined snake, leopard snake, large whip snake, and nose-horned viper. Otters probably still occur, and there are substantial numbers of bats which hunt over the lakes. Dragonflies of interest here include *Lindenia tetraphylla*, the emperor, the bright magenta-pink *Crocothemis erythraea*, and several darters.

The surrounding hills are rugged and well-wooded (such as the fine, evergreen oak forest near Asvestochori), and there are a few remaining areas of gallery forest not far from the lake. These are important areas for birds, and breeding species

The striking nail-varnish red male dragonfly *Crocothemis erythraea*

include Levant sparrowhawks, long-legged buzzards, lesser spotted eagles, white storks, eagle owls, and olive-tree warblers. Between Lake Volvi and the sea lies the Rentinas Gorge, through which the lake empties. It is not a spectacular gorge, but still supports small numbers of breeding eagles and vultures, together with nightjars, olive-tree warblers, and possibly black storks and eagle owls.

The lakes are easily viewed from the busy E90 (E5) road which runs along the southern edge. There are tracks running down to the shores in various places (though not always passable after rain), such as from

Water Chestnut *Trapa natans*

Peristeronas, or south-east of Langadas. The main road runs through the Rentinas Gorge, and there are several parking places.

SITE 33 Mt. Vrondous

A botanically rich mountain at the edge of the Rhodopi range. Grid reference: 41°20'N 23°36'E.

Mt. Vrondous (1849 m) lies on the edge of a huge area of unspoilt and interesting countryside, extending away northwards into Bulgaria (see also sites 38 and 46). It is worth considering separately, as it is composed of more acid rock than most of the surrounding mountains, and has a different flora and fauna. It also has good road access from nearby Serres.

Most of the slopes are clothed with forests of either Scots pine (which is relatively unusual in Greece) or beech, especially on the north-facing slopes, with small amounts of the rare maple *Acer heldreichii*. The flora here has more in common with central European mountains than with most of Greece; for example, bilberry, goldenrod, common juniper, alpine knotweed, deadly nightshade, large meadow-rue, wall lettuce, and purple lettuce are common. Plants with more Balkan affinities include red lungwort, a bell-

flower *Campanula moesiaca*, leguminous shrubs such as *Genista carinalis* and *Chamaecytisus eriocarpus*, and the figwort *Scrophularia scopolii*.

There is very little in the way of open alpine pasture, but there are clearings (often wet) in the forest, which again have a rich flora, and good butterflies. Familiar northern species such as bistort, water avens, wood club-rush, and tufted hair grass rub shoulders with a local species of avens *Geum rhodopeum*, with yellow nodding flowers, thistles such as *Cirsium appendiculatum*, a leopard's-bane *Doronicum austriacum*, and a mass of sedges and rushes such as star sedge, beaked sedge, broad-leaved cotton-grass, and the black-flowered *Juncus thomasii*.

Other flowers of interest here include the red-flowered spike-heath (very closely related to the *Erica* heaths, but differing in having the sepals fused into

North-east Greece

Capercaillie *Tetrao urogallus* (Mike Lane)

a tube for about half their length), St. John's-worts such as *Hypericum barbatum* and *H. cerastioides*, fireweed, various mulleins, and the foxglove *Digitalis viridiflora*, with a long spike of dull yellowish-green flowers.

The butterflies have not been studied in detail, but are abundant and diverse, thanks to the mixture of flowery grassland, scrub, wet places, and forest. Species recorded include Apollo, clouded Apollo, lesser spotted fritillary, lattice brown, scarce swallowtail, Balkan marbled white, black-veined white, and large skipper, plus an abundance of blues.

This is a superb area for mountain and forest birds, though undoubtedly much remains to be discovered and recorded. Imperial eagles have been recorded nearby, and golden and booted eagles are relatively common. Griffon and Egyptian vultures have breeding colonies not far away, and they can often be seen overhead. Capercaillie are known to occur in forest clearings in the pines, and hazel grouse may be here – both birds are decidedly rare in Greece. Black, middle-spotted, and white-backed woodpeckers all breed, and Tengmalm's owls are proba-

bly present. It is on the southern edge of an area where brown bear are still present in reasonable numbers, so a chance encounter is always a possibility, though not very likely.

Access is easy, northwards from Serres. There is a good asphalt road as far as the modest ski centre, and a small mountain refuge, open by arrangement only.

Booted eagle *Hieraaetus pennatus*

SITE 34 Mt. Menikio

A beautiful forested mountain area north-west of Serres.
Grid reference: 41°12'N 23°39'E.

Mt. Menikio (also known as Boz Dagh of Serres) is the highest point (1963 m) of a broad, spreading mountain mass lying just north-west of Serres, not far from Mt. Vrondous (p. 95). The vast lower slopes are covered with splendid oak forests (mainly

Oak forests on Mt. Menikio, ablaze with colour in late autumn

North-east Greece

Turkey and Hungarian oaks though other species probably occur in this notoriously difficult area for oaks!). Within the oak forest area, there are grazed flowery grasslands, with scattered prickly and common juniper, maples, smoke bush, terebinth tree, wild pear, sloe, old man's beard and other shrubs. In autumn, the colours are quite stunning, like so much of the forested areas of northern Greece; in my opinion, it is the finest area for autumn colour in Europe. On the higher slopes, there are extensive areas of black pine forest, with some firs.

The western end of Mt. Menikio, sometimes known as Mt. Kouskouras (1623 m) is an important area for breeding birds. There is a strong griffon vulture colony on cliffs, together with smaller numbers of Egyptian vultures, golden eagles, and booted eagles. Peregrines and Levant sparrowhawks both breed in the area, together with eagle owls, wryneck, middle-spotted woodpecker, woodlark, tree pipit, nightingale, and many others. The underlying rock is limestone through most of the region, which supports a rich flora. Spring brings forth crocuses such as *Crocus veluchensis*, while in autumn there are blue *Crocus cancellatus*, cyclamens *Cyclamen neapolitanum*, and meadow saffrons *Colchicum* species. The orchid flora is moderately rich (though not by south Greece standards): lady, military (extremely rare in Greece, with only a few known sites on northern mountains), green-winged, early purple, naked man, early spider, and others, though rarely in great abundance. In the high rocky pastures, there are interesting plants such as alpine aster, at one of its few Greek localities.

Access to the area is either by the very beautiful road that goes around the massif to the north, from Serres north-east to Kato Vrondou, then on to Panorama, passing through some very accessible rich habitat; or up a smaller road from just east of Serres via Hionochori, and on to the southern high slopes.

35 Strymon Delta

A small delta at the mouth of the river Strymon. Grid reference: 40°47'N 23°09'E.

The river Strymon meets the Thracian Sea in a relatively small delta. The flow rate and silt load of the river has declined in recent decades, thanks to reservoirs and irrigation schemes, and it is not a major river now when it reaches the coast. Parts of the delta have been drained, and the whole area has a rather sad and rubbish-ridden air about it. It is not worth a long detour, but it is worth a look whilst passing by, perhaps on the way to Dadia or Evros further east.

There are small lagoons on either side of the river, and limited amounts of wetland, saltmarsh, and low sand dunes. It can become busy with mainly Greek holiday-makers in summer. Breeding birds include collared pratincoles, black-winged stilts, little terns, and stone curlews, with white storks not far away. Orphean warbler and rufous bush robin breed in the scrubby hills just to the west.

At passage periods, there are reasonable numbers of waders, and winter brings grebes, a few flamingos, ducks, great white egret, kingfishers, and occasional birds of prey and scavengers such as black kite. Black-headed and yellow-legged gulls are always around.

The dunes have a modest, though rather trampled, flora, including sea-holly, stinking inula, stranglewort, branched catchfly, sea daffodil, the viper's-bugloss *Echium angustifolium*, and naturalized pampas grass as the main components. In the hills nearby, there are some fine displays of the autumn-flowering heather *Erica manipuliflora*, and masses of autumn squill.

Access to the site is easy, via Nea Kerdilia on the west side of the river, or by crossing the river on the main Kavala road and heading down the east side of the river.

SITE
36 # Mt. Pangeon

*A small, rather isolated mountain, with a remarkably rich
flora and interesting butterflies.
Grid reference: approx. 45°N 25°E.*

Mt. Pangeon (or Pangaion) is a little-known and not especially high mountain, reaching only 1956 m, yet it has a remarkably rich flora, and is an important bird site. The name is said to come from pan (whole) + Aegea (Aegean), meaning that you can see the whole Aegean from the highest point, reflecting its position close to the coast. Despite its isolation from the main mountain mass to the north, it supports a very wide range of Balkan endemics (including some shared only with Mts Olympus and Athos) as well as more widespread species, and a few that occur nowhere else in Greece. In all, about 700 species of higher plants have been recorded. Because there is a broadcasting station on the highest point, there

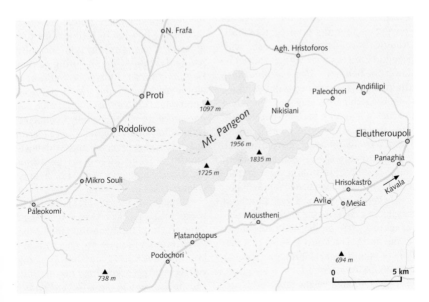

Erica manipuliflora

rated wintergreen, hard shield fern, round-leaved saxifrage, alpine woundwort, and the avens-like *Aremonia agrimonioides*. The pretty snowdrop *Galanthus elwesii* subspecies *minor* occurs in clearings in spring together with two *Romulea* species, and the lovely yellow *Sternbergia lutea* can be found in autumn, together with *Crocus pulchellus* and *C. cancellatus*. Wherever limestone rocks outcrop, especially higher up, there is a whole new range of flowers including bloody crane's-bill and *Geranium macrorrhizum*, ploughman's-spikenard, some regional endemics such as a house-leek *Sempervivum marmoreum*, an iris *Iris reichenbachii*, and the clover *Trifolium heldreichianum*, plus a few local endemics such as the knapweed *Centaurea pangaea* and the woundwort *Stachys pangaea*, whose names clearly show their distribution.

Above the tree-line, there are extensive alpine meadows with snow-filled hollows and rocky areas, all particularly rich in flowers. *Crocus veluchensis* flowers as soon as the snow melts, mainly in late April and May, followed by a selection of small snow-field plants such as the rupturewort *Herniaria nigrimontium*, cross gentian, a plantain *Plantago gentianoides*, and a buttercup *Ranunculus sartorianus*. In drier, rockier places, there are many interesting flowers, including a feather-grass *Stipa epilosa*, cushions of spiny *Astragalus angustifolius*, spring gentian *Gentiana verna* subspecies *balcanica*, alpine rock-rose, and two bellflowers *Campanula orphanidea* and *Edraianthus graminifolius*. The widely collected, yellow-flowered, mountain tea *Sideritis scardica* occurs here, together with cushions of a white mouse-ear *Cerastium decalvans*, and the pink or creamy-coloured *Daphne oleoides*.

Some of the rarer or more special plants occur in rock crevices at this height. These include the beautiful violet *Viola delphinantha* (also on Mt. Olympus and Mt. Chelmos, but generally rare), two yellow saxifrages *Saxifraga juniperifolia* subspecies *sancta* and *S. ferdinandi-*

is an easily-motorable road right to the top, which makes exploration and enjoyment of the mountain rather easier.

The mountain consists mainly of marbles, hard limestones, and schists, with a few areas of gneiss. The slopes up to about 700 m are covered with fairly typical maquis, dominated by kermes oak, with prickly juniper (often with its intriguing little parasite *Arceuthobium oxycedri*, looking like a tuft of cypress growing on a juniper branch), terebinth, Oriental hornbeam, manna ash, wild pear and Christ's thorn, with the autumn-flowering heather *Erica manipuliflora* often common. Amongst the maquis, there is a rich herbaceous flora including peacock anemones, stars-of-bethlehem, blue bugle, the little semi-parasite *Parentucellia latifolia*, blue gromwell, the hound's tongue *Cynoglossum creticum*, and a few orchids such as bee orchid, though this is not a rich area for orchids.

Above about 700 m a vast swathe of beech forest encircles the mountain, reaching up to 1700 m on the south side, lower on the north. The forest is home to a rich flora of mainly central European species, including willow gentian, sweet woodruff, bird's-nest orchid, yellow bird's-nest, ser-

Eastern greenish black-tip *Elphinstonia penia*

coburgii, as well as *S. sempervivum* and *S. paniculata*; the rare and local gesneriad (African violet family) *Haberlea rhodopensis*, which also occurs lower down, and is believed – like the other European members of this family – to be a survivor through the ice ages from the Tertiary period of geological history. There are clumps of a rare, blue-flowered borage relative *Omphalodes luciliae*, with *Draba athoa* (named after Mt. Athos), the endemic knapweed *Centaurea pangaea*, and a yarrow *Achillea ageratifolia*.

The whole mountain is recognized to be important for birds, though unfortunately it has no specific protection, and exploitation for marble and timber are proving detrimental. Breeding species of interest include black stork, eagle owl, Bonelli's warbler, and several woodpeckers such as grey-headed, black, and middle-spotted amongst others in the forested areas. Golden, booted, and short-toed eagles all breed and hunt here,

mainly in the higher areas, and peregrines can often be seen. In more open country olive-tree warbler, rock partridge, rufous bush robin, and lesser grey shrike can be seen, occasionally with rollers.

It is an excellent area for butterflies, with a nice blend of southern, northern, and montane species. Common species include scarce, common, and southern swallowtails, brimstone, wood white, mountain small white, eastern Bath white, pearl-bordered, Glanville, knapweed, dark green, and lesser spotted fritillaries. Some rarer species recorded here include the blue argus (the males of which resemble chalkhill blues), eastern greenish black-tip, Higgins' anomalous blue (which is brown), the Macedonian chalkhill blue, and many more. Apollos occur in small numbers at the highest levels.

The easiest access, especially to the high areas, is via the TV station road that leads from Eleutheroupoli at the eastern end of the mountain, although any of the roads up from the villages that encircle the mountain will take you into interesting country. There is a nunnery on the north slopes, and two refuges.

Aremonia agrimonioides

SITE 37 Nestos Valley

The valley of the Nestos River, especially where it passes through a gorge, with fine bird populations.
Grid reference: 41°10'N 24°45'E.

From the village of Paranesti down to the point where the river Nestos reaches the coastal plain at Toxotes, it passes through a steep-sided valley or gorge, fringed by largely unspoilt wooded hills. There are areas of riverine forest, and pristine maquis on the drier hills. On either side, the hills rise to considerable heights,

North-east Greece

Riverine forest on the lower reaches of the Nestos river

blending into the Rhodopi hills sites northwards, and the heights of Mt. Lekani southwards. The gorge sections of the valley have particularly good breeding bird populations, including black storks, Egyptian vultures and golden, booted, short-toed, and Bonelli's eagles. Rock thrushes and rock nuthatches are common and widespread, and Levant sparrowhawk and lesser spotted eagle can be seen occasionally. Eagle owls breed in the forests, and can be heard calling at night early in the year. Nightingales are common in the scrub on the hillsides, and subalpine and Orphean warblers both occur (together with the ubiquitous Sardinian warblers). Kingfishers are resident throughout the year, and pygmy cormorants pass through and sometimes stay in winter.

Access is best from the southern end of the gorge at Galani near Toxoti on the main Kavala to Xanthi road, roughly following the railway line that passes through the gorge. There is also access at the northern end, from Stavropouli.

Nose-horned viper *Vipera ammodytes*

Sardinian and Orphean warblers

These rather similar *Sylvia* warblers frequently occur in the same habitat, though Orphean is a summer visitor and Sardinian is resident. Sardinian warbler males have a bold black cap extending downwards below the red-ringed eye, whereas Orphean males have a greyer cap covering a slightly smaller area, and the eye is pale yellow. Orphean warblers, both sexes, are distinctly larger than Sardinians, by about 2 cm. In this part of the world, Orphean warblers have a much more melodic song than Sardinians, almost like a nightingale or thrush.

SITE 38 Central Rhodopi Mountains

Forested mountains, right against the Bulgarian border,
north of Stavropouli.
Grid reference: 41°32'N 24°40'E, approximately.

To the north of Paranesti and Stavropouli, tight against the Bulgarian border, there is an area of largely forested mountains, reaching almost to 2000 m, though with no major peaks, which includes two areas of protected forests: the virgin forest of Zagradenia, at the north-westernmost point, and the Tsihla forest of Mt. Haindou to the south-east. The main mountains in the area include Mt. Haindou (Drimos), Mt. Giftokastro, and Mt. Koula, though they are rarely marked on maps. The whole area is wild and little-visited, with huge areas of forest stretching away northwards into Bulgaria, and – as with the eastern Rhodopi Mountains – there are no clear boundaries; the whole area is of interest.

The Zagradenia Forest is representative of much of the area, though it covers only 550 ha. There are forests of beech, Norway spruce (at its most south-easterly locality) and the fir *Abies borisii-regis*, with many ancient trees in the protected areas. Within the forests, there are flowery clearings,

streams, and waterfalls. Botanically it is interesting, with many rare or uncommon

Brown bear *Ursus arctos*

North-east Greece

Yellow gentian *Gentiana lutea*

species such as the speedwell *Veronica barrelierii*, related to spiked speedwell, but this is a Balkan endemic, as is the knapweed *Centaurea stenolepis* subspecies *razgradensis*. There are flowers here that are rare generally in Greece, such as redberried elder, yellow gentian, common twayblade orchid, the large white-flowered buttercup *Ranunculus platanifolius*, and *Aconitum nervosum*.

To the south-west, around Mt. Haindou and the Tsihla protected forest, other species occur, including the beautiful Rhodopi lily, differing from other lilies in the area by its lemon-yellow flowers, and found nowhere else in the world apart from this small area of the Rhodopi Mountains; pinks such as *Dianthus superbus* and *D. drenowskianus*, a harebell *Campanula velebitica*, and the closely related *Symphyandra wanneri*, only relatively recently discovered in Greece, just in this locality, in rock crevices at about

Hungarian oak forest in autumn, in the central Rhodopi Mountains

1500 m. It is not an inconspicuous plant, with rosettes bearing pretty blue-violet bellflowers – it is just that this area is still so little known. Other notable flowers found here and there through this area include the snowbell *Soldanella rhodopaea*, the marsh-orchid *Dactylorhiza cordigera*, and three crocuses: *Crocus pulchellus*, flowering in the autumn, and *C. veluchensis* and *C. chrysanthus*, both flowering in the spring.

Brown bears live in the area; there are currently thought to be about 100–120 brown bears in Greece, and this is one of the better areas, with constant interchange with the larger Bulgarian population. Other mammals include roe deer, perhaps a few wolves, wild boar, and red squirrel. As far as birds go, capercaillie and hazelhen are both known to occur in the higher forests, together with black, middle-spotted, and white-backed woodpeckers. Birds of prey are usually visible somewhere in the sky, including golden and short-toed eagles,

buzzard, long-legged buzzard, Levant sparrowhawk, and vultures. Pygmy owls have been recorded here, in their only site in Greece, and are presumed to breed, and red-breasted flycatchers nest in this general area. Butterflies are abundant throughout most of the area, with a wonderful mixture including poplar admiral, white admiral, common glider, Hungarian glider, Balkan copper and other coppers, both Grecian and Higgins' anomalous blues (and many other blues), Nicholl's ringlet, bright-eyed ringlet, Scotch argus and others from this difficult group, and many skippers such as the tufted marbled skipper.

Although not an easy place to get to, it is worth the effort. Any unusual records should be sent to the Hellenic Society for the Protection of Nature, or the Hellenic Ornithological Society (see p. 310 for addresses). Access is via minor roads northwards from Paranesti through Thermia, or from Neochori (just west of Stavroupoli). Allow plenty of time.

SITE 39 Nestos Delta

A large delta on the Aegean coast with rich bird life all year.
Grid reference: 40°56'N 24°30'E.

Sadly, this huge delta has suffered the same fate as most of the other great Greek wetlands – it has been progressively drained, reduced in size, polluted, and built on. Despite this there is a good deal of interest left, and there is some hope for its future now that its status as an internationally important Ramsar Site is at last being taken seriously. Most of the interesting non-coastal delta habitats have gone, though there is some gallery forest left (probably the largest remaining area in Greece), and patches of freshwater and reeds, but the main remaining habitats of interest are the lagoons, dunes, and salt-

North-east Greece

Sea shells, including a cowrie, and eelgrass along the Nestos shoreline

marshes around the fringes, especially west of the river mouth.

The Nestos Delta is primarily a bird site, though there is also much else of interest (see below), and over 300 species have been recorded. In the breeding season, there are about 30 pairs of avocets and 40 pairs of collared pratincoles, together with little, Sandwich, and common terns, black-winged stilts, Kentish plovers, greater flamingos,

Ruddy Shelduck *Tadorna ferruginea*

stone curlews, little bitterns, and Mediterranean gulls, amongst others. It is probably the best remaining site in Greece for breeding spur-winged plover, on sandy coastal stretches where there is not too much disturbance from people or grazing animals; and the rare ferruginous duck breeds here in small numbers in areas of dense wetland vegetation. There are still lesser spotted eagles and Levant sparrowhawks in the remaining forest, though they lead a precarious existence. Along reed-fringed dykes there are bearded tits, and reed, great reed, and Cetti's warblers, amongst others. White storks breed around the area and feed in the marshes.

In spring and autumn, there are masses of waders and other birds, of which some stay on. Around the lagoons and along the shore one may see dunlin, grey plover, redshank, wood sandpiper, marsh sandpiper, Temminck's and little stint, with occasional broad-billed sandpipers, glossy ibis, and others. Winter sees large numbers of wildfowl, with up to 50 000 recorded, including teal, garganey, wigeon, mallard, and other common species, often joined by ruddy shelduck (peaking at 150 birds, though numbers have been lower recently), and red-breasted and lesser white-fronted geese. Common and pygmy cormorants are both common, with good numbers of Dalmatian pelicans and greater flamingos. Great white egrets are readily visible stalking through the shallows, and kingfishers are everywhere in the wetter areas. Birds of prey that are likely to be seen in winter include marsh harrier, common buzzard, and white-tailed and spotted eagles.

Amphibians and reptiles are very evident at Nestos, especially the loud colonies of tree frogs in reeds and giant reeds, dice snakes hunting in the shallows, and stripe-necked and common terrapins around the edges of the lagoons. A number of other snakes are recorded, including four-lined snake and nose-horned viper.

The low dunes that edge the shore in places are quite rich in flowers, though often rather damaged and rubbish-strewn. Common flowers include sea bindweed, sea-holly, the little prostrate purple spurge, sea spurge, several sea-lavenders, stinking inula (good for butterflies in late summer), cottonweed (now extinct in Britain), joint-pine, stranglewort, a sheep's-bit *Jasione heldreichii*, and sea daffodil. Prickly saltwort is common along the edges of dunes,

Spur-winged plover *Vanellus spinosus*

together with oraches, and there are several species of glasswort and annual sea-blite in the saltmarshes. Eelgrasses *Zostera* species are common in suitable habitats, providing good grazing for waterfowl. Here and there along the strand line, there are masses of washed-up shells, including fine examples of cowries, *Murex*, and many others.

Access into the delta is easy off the main Karvala–Xanthi road by following sign-posts to the airport or to Chrisoupoli. The best areas are down the western side, reached by following roads west from Agiasma; around Keramoti, and near the mouth of the river. There are also some remnants of forest readily visible at the top of the delta, where the main road crosses the Nestos near Toxotes.

40 Porto Lagos

SITE

A lovely coastal area, with a mosaic of wetland habitats, rich in birds, amphibians, fishes, and other forms of wildlife.

Around the little port of Porto Lagos lies one of the great wetlands of Greece. It is one of six Ramsar Sites in north-east Greece, and part of a proposed National Park of Macedonia and East Thrace. We have separated the component parts of this proposed National Park into three distinct sites – this one, the Nestos Delta,

North-east Greece

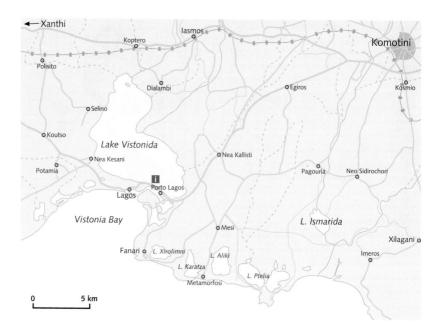

```
←— Xanthi
            Koptero        Iasmos
   Polisito                                              Komotini
            Dialambi              o Egiros        Kosmio
        o Selino
 o Koutso
        Lake Vistonida
        o Nea Kesani       o Nea Kallisti
 Potamia                              Pagouria   Neo Sidirochori
              Porto Lagos
         Lagos
    Vistonia Bay                              L. Ismarida
                        o Mesi                        Xilagani o
         Fanari o  L. Xirolimni                Imeros
                           L. Aliki
              L. Karatza
                              L. Ptelia
                 Metamorfosi
 0        5 km
```

and Lake Ismarida – as the park could not be said to be a cohesive whole at present, and the sites are quite separate geographically and ecologically. Collectively, the combined Ramsar Site covers 24 400 ha – a vast area of top-quality habitats.

Night heron *Nycticorax nycticorax* **(Peter Wilson)**

Porto Lagos village lies roughly at the centre of a huge region of fine, coastal wetland habitats. To the north lies the vast Lake Vistonida, which covers 4200 ha but is nowhere more than 3 m deep; it has a marked salinity gradient from salty at the south to fresh at the north. The port lies on a sandbar that separates Vistonida from the sea; to the south-east of this bar, there is a series of lagoons of varying character, running along the coast for about 20 km, whilst westwards there are a few smaller lagoons and patches of other coastal habitats. For the visiting naturalist, around the port is probably the best place to see birds, with lagoons, reedbeds, sandbars, beach, woodland, and scrub all close by. There is even the 'Flamingo taverna', with good views of open water and reeds!

The area is best known for its birds, which are marvellous. Over 300 species have been recorded, many in large numbers. There is a woodland heronry near the port with grey herons, little egret, night heron, and squacco heron. Other breeding birds include pygmy cormorant, ferruginous duck, the rare and

Greater flamingos and other waterfowl at Porto Lagos in winter

elusive spur-winged plover, avocets, black-winged stilts, collared pratincoles, short-eared owls, hoopoes, Isabelline wheatear, masked shrike, and Calandra lark. Greater flamingos are resident in substantial numbers, and it is expected to become a regular breeding colony in due course. At passage times, vast numbers of birds pass through, and the lagoon edges and shallows are especially good for waders. It is the second best site in Greece (after Evros) for slender-billed curlew, and many other rare species may turn up. It is also excellent during winter, though one should not imagine that the climate is always mild here – it can be extremely cold, and frosts are not infrequent. Large numbers of Dalmatian pelicans spend all or part of the winter here, together with a few white pelicans, and it is a joy to watch them as they fly between lagoons. There can be vast numbers of pygmy cormorants, enormous numbers of the usual North European ducks such as teal, wigeon, pintail, and shoveler. Lake Vistonida may support a thousand or more black-necked grebes, together with little and great-crested grebes in smaller numbers. The area is considered to be the best wintering site in Greece for geese, including lesser white-fronts and red-breasted, though both are in small numbers. There

is usually a reasonable number of birds of prey around, such as harriers and small eagles, though numbers here seem to be lower than at comparable wetlands nearby. Recent counts have recorded up to four white-tailed eagles and five wintering spotted eagles. Interestingly, there are now hundreds of Sandwich terns beginning to winter here, and they can be watched at close range sitting on the sandbars in company with slender-billed, black-headed, and other gulls. The rich pink colour of the slender-billed gulls stands out from a distance. In winter, kingfishers are abundant here, as on many parts of the Greek coast.

Although visitors are most likely to come here to see birds, it has much else to offer, especially in spring and summer. The wetlands and reedbeds are alive with the harsh bird-like calls of common tree frogs, and the gentler croaking of marsh frogs. In early spring green toads, common toads, and yellow-bellied toads all call from the shallow water areas, and they are fairly easy to locate at this period. Both species of terrapin (stripe-necked and common) can be seen in the lagoons, but tend to be nervous of close approaches. While watching the water margins, you will quite often see one of the more aquatic snakes swimming by, perhaps in search of tadpoles. The com-

North-east Greece

Black-necked grebe *Podiceps nigricollis*

monest two here are grass snake and dice snake. There is also the usual assortment of tortoises, lizards including Kotschy's gecko, glass lizard, Balkan wall lizard, and Erhard's lizard, and more terrestrial snakes, such as four-lined snake, leopard snake, and nose-horned viper.

Although the list of mammals recorded is quite long, numbers are generally low in this open habitat, and there are not many you are likely to see. Foxes are frequent, and brown hares can often be glimpsed at a distance, while eastern hedgehogs may be seen at night or on the roads. There is also a small population of jackals, listed as vulnerable in the red data book of mammals of Greece.

They are mainly nocturnal and most likely to be seen crossing a road at night, though bear in mind that some stray dogs (of which there are many here) can look rather similar – a jackal resembles a small wolf, in a uniform sandy coat with a reddish tinge. Otters are present but hard to see, and there are small numbers of roe deer, wild cat, and occasional wolves. Common dolphins are fairly frequent offshore.

This is not a great site for plants, though there are some interesting localities. There are low dunes on many of the coastal frontages, and these have sea-holly, cottonweed, sea daffodil, sea medick, sea rocket, stocks, purple and sea spurges, stranglewort, yellow star thistle, and many others, and can be very attractive at times between March and July. In wooded areas, especially along water courses, there are manna ashes with beautiful frothy white flowers in May, Oriental planes, elms, white willow, and other trees. The saltmarsh areas look superb in late summer when the sea-lavenders and sea asters are in flower, and the glassworts are beginning to turn red.

Part of the huge saltmarsh area at Porto Lagos

Cynanchum acutum

There are extensive beds of Neptune-grass offshore, which provide food and shelter for many marine species, and are a good indication of clean water.

Dragonflies and damselflies are abundant, and a surprising number breed even where the water is brackish. These include ruddy, red-veined and other darters, Norfolk hawker, and lesser emperor, as well as abundant damselflies.

The fishes should also be mentioned, as there is a rich and diverse fauna, including a few specialities. To date 34 species have been recorded, often in abundance, including a shad *Alosa caspia vistonica*, endemic to this area, *Chalchaburnus chalchoides*, a loach *Cobitis strumicae*, as well as the more common species like eel, carp, and mullet.

Black-headed and Mediterranean gulls

Both of these species occur in abundance here, and at a number of coastal sites. Although superficially similar and easily confused, there are enough differences to make identification straightforward. The quickest way is to look at the undersides of the wings: those of Mediterranean are almost white, while those of black-headed are black-tipped and otherwise greyish (though not as black of those of little gull). In summer plumage, the chocolate-brown head of black-headed does not extend down the nape of the neck, while the black head of Mediterranean (and little gull) does. Mediterranean gull is also rather larger, with a distinctly heavier bill.

Access is generally very easy, as the main coastal road passes through the area and gives good direct views. Numerous tracks lead off both southwards and northwards, and the road to Fanari and beyond gives further possibilities. There is an excellent visitor centre just west of Porto Lagos on the north side of the main road, with leaflets and knowledgeable staff.

_{SITE}
41 Lake Ismarida

A freshwater lake with important breeding bird populations.

Lake Ismarida (or Lake Mitrikou) lies within the Porto Lagos area (about 15 km east of Porto Lagos village). It is part of the proposed National Park, but differs from the other sites in being a wholly freshwater ecosystem, set well back from the coast. The lake itself covers 340 ha, with a maximum depth of 1.5 m, though the area is extended by some peripheral wetland habitats including parts of the valleys of the Filiouris and Himaros rivers.

In summer, much of the lake is covered with yellow and white water-lilies, water chestnut, and other floating plants, and edged with yellow irises, rushes, and reeds. These provide excellent habitat for black and whiskered terns, squacco herons, moorhens, water rails, and other birds. Most of the heron species nest in the area, and can frequently be seen fishing or stalking their prey. At times, there are great white egrets, spoonbills, glossy ibis, ferruginous ducks, and various grebes, including red-necked. In winter, Dalmatian pelicans, white-headed ducks, lesser white-fronted geese, and other uncommon species may occur, though numbers and times are unpredictable. In spring and summer, rollers, bee-eaters, hoopoes, and other birds of open country occur around the lake, and collared pratincoles nest in the marshes. White storks

from nearby nest-sites, mainly in villages, feed in the marshes, and marsh harriers hunt over the reeds.

It is a good site for dragonflies, though numbers seem to have declined in recent years as the salinity has increased and the water levels have been lower, due to groundwater abstraction and drainage schemes. There are hopes that the recent upsurge of interest in protecting Ramsar Sites in Greece may halt or reverse this trend. Species include damselflies such as the emeralds *Lestes virens* and *L. barbarus*, both species of emperor dragonflies, and a wealth of darters.

Access is easy via small roads from Pagouria or Neo Sidirochori, with signposts pointing to Ismarida.

SITE
42 Dadia Forest

The Dadia Forest, or Dadia-Soufli Forest, is one of the most exciting sites for the naturalist in Greece, with a superb range of birds and other wildlife.

North-east of Alexandroupoli there is a vast area of virtually uninhabited wooded hills known generally as the Evros Hills. It gradually became clear during the 1970s that this was a really major site for birds of prey, and since 1980 a large section has been protected, with the Dadia Forest at its core. At present, there is a central protected area, in two parts, covering 7290 ha, and an outer buffer zone of a further 28 000 ha that includes some fine habitat but has very little protection. It is a hilly region, with summits and crags reaching up to 800 m (or rather higher on the western edge of the area) overlying a mixture of mainly igneous rocks that are both basic and acidic. The whole area is heavily forested with oaks and pines, though there are patches of agricultural land and some parts that are more heavily grazed, with

open scrub and grassland. Large sections of the forest are cut over, but other parts include many old trees.

An extraordinary total of 36 diurnal birds of prey have been recorded here (out of 38 in Europe) together with 7 species of owls. Of these, up to 23 nest in the general area, plus 6 species of owls. There is simply nowhere better in Europe for birds of prey! It is the only forest in Europe where all four vultures occur: black, griffon, Egyptian, and bearded or

Fritillaria pontica

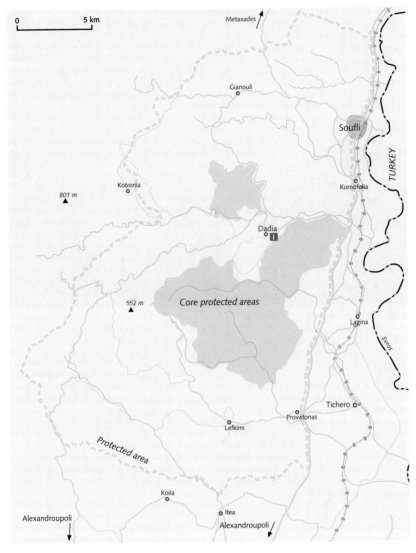

lammergeier. The very rare black vulture had been declining steadily, but seems to have responded well to the policy of putting out carcasses (see below), and numbers are now reaching towards 100 individuals. Griffon vultures are abundant residents, Egyptian vultures visit to breed, and at the time of writing there is a single lammergeier. There are eagles galore: there was a pair of breeding Imperial eagles, but they have moved southwards towards the Evros Delta, though several immatures remain and may well breed in due course. There are four pairs of golden eagles in the protected area, and more round about, together with spotted, lesser spotted, white-tailed (in very small numbers), short-toed, Bonelli's, and booted. Lanner falcons are quite frequent and there are 10 or more pairs of Levant sparrowhawks. Half a dozen or more pairs of eagle owls nest in the general area and their calls can be heard from a number of quiet roads and tracks early in the year. In some years,

Black vultures gathered at the feeding area in Dadia Forest

they nest in a readily visible situation on one of the cliffs in the reserve.

Other birds of interest here include both black and white storks, masked shrike, olive-tree, Orphean, and eastern Bonelli's warblers, rollers, and semi-collared flycatchers, to name but a few.

Naturally enough, it is also a good place to see many other things. Some 36 species of mammal have been recorded, including the normal range of foxes, badgers, red squirrels, and roe deer, but also including edible dormouse, the marmot-like souslik, Günther's vole (virtually confined to this part of Greece), the bicoloured white-toothed shrew, and even occasional wolves.

Altogether, there are 40 species of reptiles and amphibians. The attractive little yellow-bellied toads can be found near most areas of water, green toads call incessantly from wet areas in spring, and newts such as smooth newts can be seen in most ponds or tanks. On dull, wet days, or in the evening, look out for fire salamanders on the woodland roads – they are especially common in the higher oak woods. There are green lizards (a common prey item for some eagles), European glass lizard, Dahl's whip snake, large whip snake, nose-horned viper, two species of tortoise (a main prey item for golden eagles here), and many more.

Neither the invertebrates nor the flowers have been fully recorded yet, though the range and quality of the habitats indicates that a wide range of insects will be present. Butterflies recorded so far include swallowtail, scarce swallowtail, Camberwell beauty, large tortoiseshell, Queen of Spain, cardinal and Glanville fritillaries, wood white, and many

Levant sparrow hawk *Accipiter brevipes*

common species, together with the impressive moon moth. Stag beetles and longhorn beetles are frequent.

The lack of significant areas of limestone rather limits the range of flowers, though there are base-rich igneous rocks here. Cornelian cherry, at least three species of oak, black pine and *Pinus brutia*, smoke bush, wild service tree, eastern hornbeam, hop-hornbeam, and turpentine tree are amongst the woody plants. There are peonies *Paeonia offinalis* in some of the glades, orchids such as *Ophrys mammosa*, loose-flowered orchid, narrow-leaved helleborine, and several tongue orchids. Two lovely dwarf irises occur: *Iris pumila* subspecies *attica* and *I. reichenbachii*, together with wild tulips, *Fritillaria pontica*, and many others. In autumn, there are meadow saffrons *Colchicum* species and true crocuses such as the pretty blue *Crocus pulchellus*. Autumn is also superb for autumn colours (best in November), and there can be good fungi, though it depends a lot when the autumn rains come. It can be a good time to see the vultures, too, as they have to feed more actively in the shorter days: there were 28 black vultures, 23 griffon, and a spotted eagle all together on a recent visit, in late autumn.

The best way to visit the reserve is from the WWF hostel just next to Dadia village (well-sign-posted from the main road and village). It is a comfortable place to stay, and also the starting point for minibus trips to the raptor observation post (the minibus round trip costs three euros, or you can walk – about 3 km each way – free). The current management policy includes the feeding of vultures and other birds on carcasses, placed in front of an observation hide at a distance of about 600 m; this serves the twin purposes of helping the birds to survive and increase their numbers, and of providing a key attraction for visitors. It is well worth visiting, but take a telescope if you have one, and you will need a long telephoto lens if you plan any

Pinus brutia forest

photography. The driver takes a telescope up to the hide, but it may be hard to use for long in busy periods. Otherwise, there are good walks through the forest, and it is worth driving the forest roads such as those to Lefkimi and the radio masts to see all sorts of things.

Whilst in the area, since it is so far from almost anywhere else in Greece, you might find it worthwhile exploring northwards towards the Bulgarian border. The Erithropotamus Valley, especially near Metaxades and Polia, has interesting forested hilly areas near the border; the Ardas River valley near Komara is generally good for birds; and even further north, right on the Bulgarian border, the Evros Valley around Dikea has some unspoilt riverine forest and reed beds, with good heron colonies which include night heron, egrets, and grey herons in large numbers. About 30 000 ha of this area, in two separate blocks, are considered to be particularly important for birds. The whole area is little known, and will probably repay further exploration.

SITE
43 Evros Delta

An extensive and internationally important wetland on the border
with Turkey.

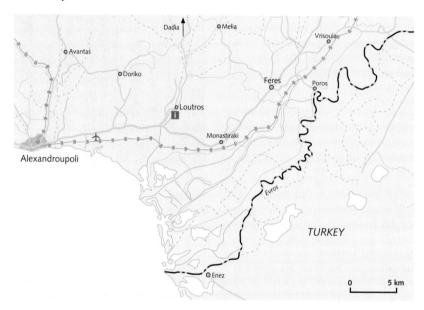

The Evros Delta is, without any doubt, one of the most important wetlands of Greece. Although anyone who knew it 20 or 30 years ago would lament how much it has declined, it is still a remarkable place with a fantastic range of species, and – unlike many Greek wetlands – starting to recover and improve.

The river Evros forms the boundary between Greece and Turkey, and part of the boundary between Greece and Bulgaria. It is the largest river of the Balkans and the second largest in south-east Europe, and it forms a huge delta at its mouth covering 188 square kilometres, of which 110 are in Greece. Although much of the upper part of the delta has been reclaimed for agriculture, there are still vast expanses of semi-natural habitats, mostly lying within a protected area of just under 10 000 ha, with numerous international designations, though the important

area is reckoned to extend to about 19 000 ha – that is, almost half of it is unprotected. These habitats include sand dunes and other sandy areas, saltpans and saltmarshes, freshwater wetlands with reedbeds and other vegetation, non-saline wet meadows, lagoons, tamarisk beds and riverine forests with willows, white and black poplars, narrow-leaved ash, and Oriental plane trees.

The delta is best-known as a bird site and it is a superb one, quite on a par with the other great coastal wetlands of Europe. Over 300 bird species have been recorded, of which 77 are known to breed. Because it lies on a major migration flyway, large numbers of birds pass through at passage periods, and many winter here in a relatively frost-free environment. It is of interest at all times of year, with least to see in late summer and early autumn. It is impossible to do full justice to the birds, but the following gives a flavour of the site.

At passage periods, there are large numbers of white pelicans, both black and white storks, glossy ibis, spoonbill, white-fronted geese, lesser white-fronted geese, and numerous waders, passerines, and birds of prey such as red-footed falcons, lesser kestrels, and pallid harriers. Regular rarities, in smaller numbers, include slender-billed curlews (more likely to be seen here than anywhere else in Europe, with a maximum of 250 birds recorded in spring passage), broad-billed and terek sandpipers, Caspian and sociable plovers, great black-headed gull, and many others, with a distinct eastern bias to the list, as you might expect. The spring passage period is particularly exciting: the site is a major migratory bottleneck, and huge numbers of birds can pass through at critical periods; for example, more than 5000 white storks are regularly recorded here.

The range and number of breeding birds in early summer is excellent, and it includes a number of species otherwise rare in Europe. Isabelline wheatears are quite frequent here close to the western edge of their range, and masked shrike and olive-tree warbler both breed around the site. It is a good place for breeding terns, with gull-billed, common, little, black, and Sandwich in good numbers. Around the lagoons and saltmarshes, there are plenty of Kentish plovers, avocets, black-winged stilts, and gulls, including a good-sized population of Mediterranean gulls (250 birds in 1997). Collared pratincoles breed in the drier parts of the saltmarshes (estimated to be well over 100 pairs throughout the site), and there are a few pairs of the rare spur-winged plovers, especially in the north-west corner. In addition, there are significant numbers of little bitterns, purple herons, little and great white egrets, and many others. Small numbers of ferruginous duck breed here in more secluded vegetated wetland areas. Bee-eaters can be commonly seen, or heard, hawking overhead in search of dragonflies or other insects, and short-toed larks nest here and there.

Winter can be an exciting time here. There is something to see right through, though much depends on the severity of the winter in more northerly sites. January to March is generally considered to be the best time for both quantity and diversity of

Hermann's tortoise *Testudo hermanni*

Giant orchid *Barlia robertiana*

and European – which are both abundant along the dykes and in the lakes. There are two species of tortoises here, Hermann's and spur-thighed, together with the curious little glass lizard, the nose-horned viper, four-lined snake, and *Coluber caspius*. Tree frogs call frequently from the taller patches of vegetation, and marsh frogs leap into the ditches as you approach. Amongst the fishes, the mullet and carp are probably most often noticed as they turn sharply in the lagoons, stirring up the silt, though eels are common, too. There used to be sturgeons, but they have now virtually disappeared.

It is unlikely that anyone would travel as far as the delta just for the flowers, though they are an added bonus if you do, especially in early summer. Most of the 350 or so recorded species are relatively common elsewhere in Greece, though there are some good displays of sand-dune flowers such as sea rocket, sea spurge, sea-holly, and the beautiful sea daffodil, which flowers in midsummer. The pink flowering-rush can be found in freshwater and brackish areas, and there are a few orchids such as giant orchid and marsh-orchid here and there.

As you might expect, there is a wide diversity of insects, of which dragonflies are the most noticeable (apart from mosquitoes!). The exact number of species is not yet known, though it includes red-veined darter, broad-bodied chaser, *Aeshna affinis*, Norfolk hawker, lesser emperor, *Orthetrum brunneum*, and the vivid red *Crocothemis erythraea*.

species, though a recent visit in mid-November provided plenty of interest. There can be vast numbers of ducks such as wigeon, teal, mallard, pintail, and gadwall; a good range of waders such as dunlin, redshank, and greenshank; and variable numbers of Dalmatian pelicans, more or less resident greater flamingos, pygmy cormorants, red-breasted geese, spotted and white-tailed sea eagles, and a good variety of other raptors. A feature of my last visit was a considerable number of slender-billed gulls, still looking very pink in mid-November.

Apart from birds, there is much else of interest. In summary, this amounts to 40 species of mammals, 21 reptiles, 7 amphibians, 46 species of fish, and about 350 species of flowers. The strikingly marked marbled polecat is found here, and its main prey is the souslik – a marmot-like burrowing herbivore. Other mammals include otters in the rivers, wild boar, very occasional wolves, edible dormice, eastern hedgehogs, red squirrels, red fox, and a few wildcats.

Probably the commonest reptiles are the two species of terrapin – stripe-necked

White pelican *Pelecanus onocrotalus*

Saltmarsh and mud-creeks in the Evros delta

Today, most of the estuary is quite accessible. It is best to start with a visit to the excellent EU-funded information centre, well sign-posted off the main E5, just up the Loutros road. The staff provide ample information, and you may be able to find a guide at less busy times. There is a good circular track leading into the area from the river Loutros bridge on the E5, which covers most habitats, and there are side tracks to the west that are well worth following. The track can be navigated by car or bike, except in very wet periods. The more easterly part of the delta is a military area, which you need a permit to enter; this must be obtained in advance, and a good way is through the offices of Charioteer Ltd, an agency in Thessaloniki. Leave plenty of time for this process.

The extraordinary Dadia Forest and neighbouring area (see p. 112) is inextricably linked with the delta ecologically, and is worth visiting at almost any time.

(see p. 112)

SITE
44 Epanomi Lagoons

Small lagoons and salt works, rich in birds, just south of Thessaloniki.
Grid reference: 40°29'N 22°49'E.

On a peninsula south of Thessaloniki, forming the southern arm of the little Gulf of Thessalonika, are several small coastal wetlands, none worth a major trip individually, but collectively worth a detour. They are so close to Thessaloniki airport that they can easily be visited in a short time.

North-east Greece

The saltworks at Angelohori

Angelohori saltpans and lagoon lie just south-west of Angelohori. In early summer, there are small numbers of black-winged stilts and little terns here, and the numbers and diversity of waders and other water-birds goes up considerably in autumn. One can see common species such as dunlin, avocet, and redshank, and less common ones such as spoonbill, glossy ibis, Temminck's stint, Terek sandpiper, and red-necked phalarope, and it is one of the few places in Europe where slender-billed curlew turn up occasionally. In winter the range of species is generally rather low: Mediterranean, slender-billed, and other gulls, little egrets, herons, and a few birds of prey, but rarely more.

The coastal strip has the remains of sand dunes, but they are rather disturbed and rubbish-ridden. Flowers include yellow horned-poppy, sea-holly, sea medick, and others, though frankly there are better places to see them!

Further south, there are two lagoons near Epanomi. The northernmost one is by the roadside, partly reed-fringed though char-acteristically messy. There are great reed and reed warblers, a few dragonflies, and tree frogs, but not a great deal else as a rule. At the tip of a small peninsula west of Epanomis beach there is a better lagoon, though nowadays it is too disturbed to be of enormous value. There are similar birds to Angelohori, with little terns, Mediterranean gulls, avocets, and black-winged stilts amongst others. In the drier surrounding areas are rufous bush robins, stone curlews, and several shrikes in early summer. A large blue summer-flowering thistle *Cardopatium corymbosum* grows in the scrub around here, with *Eryngium creticum*.

Access to the Angelohori salt works is easy by following the road that runs west-wards just south of Angelohori – the salt works are at the end. For the main Epanomi lagoon, head for the EOT camp-site near Nea Michonia, and it is just a few hundred metres away.

Cardopatium corymbosum

SITE 45 Agios Mamantos Marsh

A surprisingly unspoilt coastal marsh at the neck of the Kassandra Peninsula.
Grid reference: 40°14'N 23°20'E.

Just north of the narrowest point on the Kassandra Peninsula, a kilometre or so north of where the road crosses the canal across the isthmus, there is a relatively unspoilt area of coastal marsh, seasonal lagoon, and sand dunes. On a fine day, with the Cholomondas Mountains beyond, the views are impressive, though closer inspection reveals all-too-much rubbish and bulldozing.

In early summer, the area is noted for its large populations of collared pratincoles, breeding on the saltmarsh around the receding lagoon. Avocets, black-winged stilts, redshank, little terns, Kentish plovers, and stone curlews are all common, too. Marsh harriers, Cetti's warblers, and other birds breed in the reeds, and common tree frogs and marsh frogs can be heard calling. In autumn, there are reasonable numbers of waders, and moderate numbers of waterfowl, grebes, coot, and gulls in winter. Peregrines and marsh harriers hunt over the area, as no doubt do other species from time to time. Dragonflies are moderately abundant (though probably limited in population size and diversity by the fact that the lagoon dries out every year) and include emperors, several darters, and the powder-blue skimmer *Orthetrum brunneum*.

On the coastal side, there is a broad strip of low sand dunes. These are quite flowery, but unfortunately incredibly messy. Amongst the rubbish are sea

Collared pratincole *Glareola pratincola* (Peter Wilson)

daffodils, cottonweed, yellow horned-poppies, sea-holly, sea medick, and purple spurge amongst others, and there are glassworts and sea asters on the edge of the saltmarsh.

There is access by a number of small tracks leading eastwards down to the marsh from the main road just north of the isthmus.

The whole Kassandra Peninsula is of interest, with wooded hills rising to just over 300 m, and some rocky ravines. Golden and short-toed eagles breed, with eagle owls, scops owl, nightjars, and many others. Olive-tree warblers occur in … olive trees, and shearwaters can be seen all around the coasts. A good road encircles the high land, and small roads run up over it.

SITE 46 Eastern Rhodopi Mountains

The eastern part of the wooded Rhodopi Mountains near the Bulgarian border.
Grid reference: 41°10'N 25°07'E, approximately.

The Rhodopi Mountains stretch all the way along the border between Greece and Bulgaria, extending widely on either side. They are one of the great wildernesses of Europe, with remarkably low population density and huge areas of forest. Although difficult to get to, in the sense that they are far from airports and population centres, and the roads into them are poor and few and far between, at least there are few political restrictions at present. This site concerns the area from roughly due north of Xanthi, as far as the Kompsatos River valley, west of Komotini, but in an area like this precise boundaries are irrelevant – the whole area is worth exploring.

It is best known as an important locality for birds, particularly forest birds and birds of prey, though there is little doubt that much more remains to be discovered. There are huge tracts of oak scrub and woodland, with smaller patches of conifers, usually at higher altitudes. Some fine riverine forest remains, such as that along the Kompsatos valley. Black storks breed in the forests, though they are hard to spot, as always, and Levant sparrowhawks are fairly common in spring and summer, though finding them is a matter of luck. Birds of prey are a special feature of the area – golden, short-toed, and lesser spotted eagles are all regular in the higher areas, such as around Mt. Papikio.

Just east of Iasmos, where the Kompsatos crosses the main road, there is a fine gorge

Lesser spotted eagle *Aquila pomarina*

running northwards upstream from here. It is a well-known bird-watching site, which offers the possibility of good views of Egyptian and griffon vultures and peregrines. Rock nuthatches are common, and blue rockthrush, ortolan bunting, and red-backed shrikes are all easily found on the hills around.

Access is via minor roads northwards from the Xanthi to Komotini main road, such as to Echinos, in the heart of the area, or up the Kompsatos from Iasmos.

SITE 47 Mt. Athos Peninsula

An extraordinary, anomalous area, owned by its monasteries and open only to males over 18.
Grid reference: 40°10'N 24°34'E.

This is one of the strangest places in Greece, indeed in Europe. Apart from being beautiful and unspoilt, it is owned and controlled by its 20 ruling monasteries, with very restricted access. It is a self-governing monastic enclave within the Hellenic Republic. We have covered it here for completeness, but access is not easy, being mainly restricted to males over 18 years, with special permission.

Unlike most areas of Greek mountains (and much of the Mediterranean area), a large part of Athos has remained ungrazed for most of the thousand years or so of monastic control. Consequently, the vegetation is much more natural, and there are vast areas of near-natural Mediterranean and sub-Mediterranean forest, with sweet chestnut, hop-hornbeam, strawberry-tree, eastern strawberry-tree, bay, wild olive, Hungarian, downy, kermes, and holm oaks, Montpellier maple and other species, often growing very luxuriantly. At the southern end, Mt. Athos itself rises to a remarkable 2033 m, dominating the peninsula and the surroundings. Thanks partly to its height and isolation, there are several species here that occur nowhere else, or only in a few other places: for example the knapweeds *Centaurea chalcidicaea* and *C. rupestris* subspecies *athoa*, *Aubrieta erubescens*, a woad *Isatis tinctoria* subspecies *athoa*, the rare violet *Viola delphinantha*, shared with Mt. Olympus and a few other peaks, a mayweed

Eastern strawberry-tree *Arbutus andrachne*

Anthemis sibthorpii (endemic to Athos alone) and an everlasting *Helichrysum sibthorpii*, amongst others. Some of the endemic species, such as *Armeria sancta*, are coastal. The general mountain flora of the peak of Athos above the tree-line is rich and colourful. A few plants of alpine affinity, such as the fern *Cystopteris alpina*, a forget-me-not *Myosotis alpestris*, *Arabis bryoides*, *Acinos alpinus*, and *Saxifraga sancta*, occur in sheltered spots near the summit, where snow lingers late.

The birds are of interest, too, with breeding golden and short-toed eagles, eagle owl, black stork, and even capercaillie. Eleonora's falcons breed, and Audouin's gulls can be seen around the southern coasts, together with shearwaters.

The mammals of Athos include golden jackal (at one of its most northerly locations), red fox, badger, wild cat, wild boar, roe deer, red squirrel, beech and (possibly) pine martens, weasel, and (appropriately) the rare and threatened monk seal.

SITE 48 Cholomondas Mountains

Unspoilt wooded hills, rising to 1163 m, with good birds and flowers.
Grid reference: 40°23'N 23°30'E.

The Cholomondas (or Holomontas) Mountains run in a broad band across the 'palm' of the Chalkidiki 'hand', forming a barrier against the north winds. Although of no great height, with only one peak above 1000 m, they cover a large area

Beech and mixed forest in late autumn on the Cholomondas mountains

North-east Greece

(about 13 000 ha) and are unspoilt and generally uninhabited. Around the lower slopes, there are vast areas of scrub dominated by kermes oak, turpentine tree (which often has the striking horn-shaped galls, reddening in autumn, that are caused by an aphid *Baizongia pistaciae*), lentisc (or mastic tree), box, juniper, sumac, and others. There are herbs of interest under the scrub, including blue bugle, the little semi-parasite *Parentucellia latifolia*, ground-pine, several crane's-bills, and a few orchids including bee and pyramidal. This is good country for subalpine warblers (the males are quite distinctive, with a reddish-brown throat, and thin, white 'moustache'), Sardinian warblers, Cretzschmar's bunting, rock partridges, and red-backed shrikes. A little higher, the vegetation becomes more temperate in appearance, with a few small fields, grasslands, hedges, and woodlands, with north European birds such as blackbird, robin, wren, and buzzard. In autumn, there are crocuses, autumn crocuses, and cyclamen flowering here.

The highest parts are almost uniformly clothed with dense forest, mainly of beech but with some oaks, rowan, wild cherry, and other trees. There are rocky outcrops and ravines, and a few clearings and fields. The flora here is quite rich, especially in the older, denser parts of the woodland, with yellow bird's-nest, red helleborine, bird's-nest orchid, and others. These higher areas are particularly good for birds

Subalphine warbler *Sylvia cantillans*

of prey such as griffon vulture, short-toed eagle, golden eagle, and peregrine. Eagle owls almost certainly breed, and Eleonora's falcons can be seen regularly in midsummer before they head for their breeding areas on the coast. Black storks are thought to breed here, but this is not proven. Semi-collared flycatchers breed in the higher-altitude beech woods where there are mature trees with old woodpecker holes. Butterflies are abundant, including large species such as the two-tailed pasha, usually seen near strawberry-trees, and the cardinal fritillary.

Access is easy, with several minor roads running through the hills. The best road runs from Palaeokastro westwards past Taxiarchis and on to Arnea, through some of the best forest and close by the highest point. The village of Skagira is the birthplace of the great naturalist and philosopher Aristotle.

SITE
49 Thassos

An unspoilt island off the Nestos Delta, dominated by Ipsali Mountain.
Grid reference: 40°40'N 24°38'E.

Thassos (or Thasos) is an attractive, small, mountainous, and wooded island lying just off the coast of north-east Greece, south of the Nestos Delta. It rises to 1203 m on Mt. Ipsali (or Ipsari), but much of the island is hilly. It has remained well-wooded, especially on the east side, with *Pinus brutia* woodland generally, becoming diluted with fir *Abies borisii-regis*, yew, prickly juniper, hop-hornbeam, and

cilis, the distinctive sage *Salvia triloba* (currently described as part of the *Salvia fruticosa* complex), the yellow-flowered mountain tea *Sideritis scardica*, maidenhair fern, and many more. Above about 900 m the woodland opens out into rocky grassland, with a rich flora including alisons, milkworts, thymes, marjorams, and woundworts – a nectarcollecting insect's paradise (and in fact Thassos is noted for its honey). On tongues of scree that descend through the forest from the higher slopes, one of Thassos's rare plants usually grows: a small St. John's-wort *Hypericum athoum*. A lovely purplish-pink bird's-foot trefoil *Lotus aduncus* occurs here and there in the lowlands.

manna ash higher up. A subspecies of mistletoe is common on the pines, and the little parasite *Arceuthobium oxycedri* is common on the junipers. There is a rich flora in the woods, and especially in rocky clearings or on cliffs, including the bellflower *Campanula trachelium* subspecies *athoum*, the silvery-white rosettes of *Inula verbascifolia*, a scabious *Scabiosa webbiana*, a pink *Dianthus gra-*

Thassos is a generally pleasant place, with olive groves and scrub, and rich with birdsong. The rather scratchy call of Cretzschmar's bunting vies with the more melodious black-headed bunting, and the mournful descending trill of woodlarks. At night, nightjars can be head churring and wing-clapping.

Access is by ferry from Kavala, just to the north-west.

50 Samothraki

A small mountainous island in the north Aegean, south-west of Alexandroupoli.
Grid reference: 40°18'N 25°34'E.

Samothraki is a small oval island off the Aegean coast, effectively a detached portion of the Rhodopi Mountains, though with ecological affinities to Thassos and Athos to the west. It is dominated by a crescent-shaped peak, Mt. Fengari, which rises to an impressive 1611 m, and almost the whole island is hilly apart from the extreme western end. The resident population is small, and the island is relatively unspoilt. There is extensive maquis on

the lower hill slopes, and deciduous oak woodland (dominated by downy oak) higher up, with Oriental planes along the valleys, as in most Greek mountain areas.

Despite its small size, there are some interesting plants, including some rarities. For example the distinctive knotgrass *Polygonum icaricum* grows as a chasmophyte (i.e. on cliffs in gorges) on Mt. Fengari, and is endemic to here and Ikaria. Mountain cinquefoil *Potentilla montana* subspecies *halacsyana* grows near the summit of Fengari, and the attractive bellflower relative *Symphyandra cretica* subspecies *samothracica* with blue flowers grows commonly as a chasmophyte in shadier cliffs on Samothraki. The St. John's-wort *Hypericum athoum* (see also Thassos) occurs occasionally in damp gullies. It is a surprisingly good place for ferns and their relatives, with interesting recent records including forked spleenwort, oak fern, Jersey fern, maidenhair spleenwort, *Cheilanthes persica*, and two species of adder's tongue fern, together with a quillwort *Isoetes durieui* (which is normally a west Mediterranean species) in temporary pools.

The bird life is broadly similar to that of Thassos or nearby mainland hilly areas. Black-headed buntings and lesser grey shrikes are found in lower areas, with sparrowhawk, buzzard, peregrine, and common kestrel, and there are scops owls in the villages.

Scops owl *Otus scops* (Peter Wilson)

Access to Samothraki is by ferry from Kavala or Alexandroupoli.

Central Greece

Introduction

Central Greece, as defined here, comprises the southern portion of what is often thought of as mainland Greece, together with the large island or peninsula of Evvia. It extends across from the western wetlands on the Ionian coast, through the southernmost Pindos Mountains and Mt. Parnassos to Athens and the Attican Mountains, and finally the Aegean coast, so it is an extremely varied area.

The western coast of Greece, especially towards the north, is distinctly wetter and correspondingly greener than the east, and the westernmost mountains receive a good deal more rain. Although the coastal areas are generally as dry as anywhere by midsummer, the mountains tend to carry on receiving rainfall in patches right through the summer, with powerful thunderstorms building up regularly. This continues to supply the rivers through the summer which, to some extent, contributes to the year-round value of two major wetlands on the west coast within this region: the Amvrakia Gulf and Messolongi. Both are the deltas of one or more rivers and, like other Greek deltas, they have a distinctive character (quite unlike an Atlantic estuary, for example) due to the very small tidal range and the relatively calm seas.

The mountains that dominate this region cover a vast area, and between the sites that we have selected there are many areas of fine wild country, with abundant species. We have tried to pick out the best localities though there are many places, especially in the foothills and lower mountains, which are rarely visited and little known, with more undoubtedly waiting to be discovered. In the western part of the mountains lies the town of Karpenisi. Surrounded by mountains and with a relatively high rainfall, it has a more alpine character than most Greek towns. Karpenisi makes a good base from which to explore the vast expanses of mountainous and wooded country that stretch away in all directions.

Eastwards from here the mountains become drier, extremely rugged, and generally very high – Mt. Parnassos is best known, but Giona is actually higher, at 2507 m, and Vardousia is arguably more spectacular. Together with Mt. Iti and various slightly lower peaks, this comprises a remarkable region of wild high mountains, with very varied geology and a marvellous range of scenery and wildlife that could occupy anyone for years. These mountains are particularly known for their flowers, with more

Crocuses on Mt. Parnassus

Opposite page: **The ruins of ancient Delphi, awash with flowers in spring**

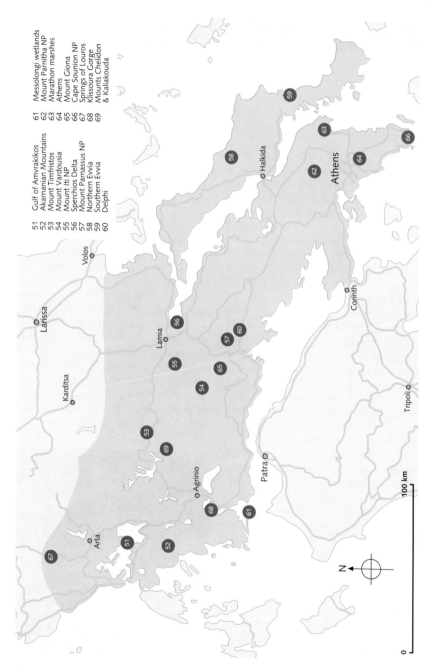

51 Gulf of Amvrakikos
52 Akarnanian Mountains
53 Mount Timfristos
54 Mount Vardousia
55 Mount Iti NP
56 Sperchios Delta
57 Mount Parnassus NP
58 Northern Evvia
59 Southern Evvia
60 Delphi
61 Messolongi wetlands
62 Mount Parnitha NP
63 Marathon marshes
64 Athens
65 Mount Giona
66 Cape Sounion NP
67 Springs of Louros
68 Klissoura Gorge
69 Mounts Chelidon
   & Kaliakouda

than 3000 species recorded, including many endemics or rarities.

Athens, easily the largest city in Greece, is situated on a peninsula at the south-east end of the region. It has a dry, warm climate, and lies in what must once have been a particularly interesting area. Unfortunately, the size of Athens itself, plus its port, suburbs, and the many enlarged coastal towns around the peninsula, have contributed to the demise or decline of many sites and species. Most of the remaining special interest is confined to the higher, more rugged hills that are not suitable for development, or which have special historical significance. There are sites within Athens, too (see p. 161), but you have to search for them.

The easternmost part of the region is formed by the island of Evvia, which comes within a few hundred metres of the mainland (across which there is a bridge). Despite its relative proximity to Athens, it has something of the character of a slightly backward island, with ancient olive groves, small fields, and traditional agriculture, albeit often next to busy coastal resorts or industrial areas. It is actually a very rewarding place to visit (especially if you go by ferry, which gives much more of the feel of going to a remote island, as well as providing the opportunity to see marine birds and wildlife), with great tracts of unspoilt and often mountainous scenery and a

number of special Euboean endemics (that is, confined to Evvia).

For many, this region will be the starting point of a trip to Greece, on days out from Athens, or short trips of a few days, or simply as the first port of call on a longer visit. As the following pages show, there is a tremendous variety of wildlife to be seen here, and it is worth planning a longer trip. Access is easy around most of the area, with good roads except in a few more remote mountain regions.

It is a warm and mild part of Greece, especially in the south-east and on the protected shores of the Gulf of Corinth. April is particularly good for flowers in the lowland sites and up as high as Delphi, or for displays of crocuses in the mountains. May is perfect for mid-altitude and the coastal wetlands, while the higher areas can still be visited through until late July with advantage. The western coastal wetlands are good for birds virtually throughout the year, and the Attican region, in particular, is mild enough in autumn and winter to allow quite a few flowers, especially crocuses, to be in flower.

Gulf of Amvrakikos
SITE 51

A huge harbour, internationally important for its birds.
Grid reference: 39°21'N 21°00'E.

The Gulf of Amvrakikos (sometimes known as the Gulf of Arta) covers 405 square kilometres, and is the biggest natural harbour in Europe (much bigger than Poole, in the UK, which often claims the title). This great expanse of water, with depths of up to 60 m, ebbs and flows into the Ionian Sea through a channel only 600 m wide at the port of Preveza. The southern side is largely mountainous, with only small amounts of littoral and intertidal habitat; on the northern side, however, there are vast areas of

Dalmatian pelican *Pelecanus crispus*

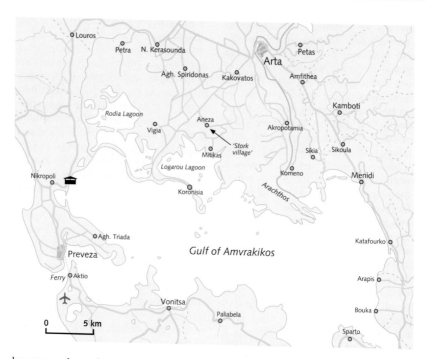

lagoons, saltmarshes, reeds, and other coastal wetlands, in the deltas of two rivers protected from the open sea's erosion. The climate is broadly Mediterranean, though slightly cooler and damper than most of southern Greece. Overall, it is one of Greece's most important wetlands, recognized as being of international importance as a Ramsar Site (internationally important wetland). It has a wide range of interesting features but, like all Greek wetlands, has declined sadly in value in recent years.

Botanically it is not exceptional, though the extensive areas of more or less unspoilt habitat support a reasonable range of species. The saltmarshes are dominated by glasswort, annual seablite, sharp rush, sea spurreys, and others. In drier areas, there is the pretty eryngo *Eryngium creticum* and sometimes *E. amethystinum*, both particularly good for insects, together with Spanish oyster plant, cardoon, the viper's-bugloss *Echium italicum*, and the bluish-flowered chaste tree. In and around brackish or fresh water, you can see reedmace, yellow iris, flowering-rush, white water-lily, sea club-rush, pondweeds, tassel weeds, duckweeds, and water starworts. There are small areas of riparian forest left,

Spoonbill *Platalea leucorodia*

though these have shrunk dramatically over recent decades. They contain Oriental planes, narrow-leaved ash, alder, elm, poplars, and willows, with old man's beard, silk vine, and other climbers. Some of the hills around and within the gulf have extensive typical Greek *maquis*, dominated by kermes oak, junipers, eastern strawberry-tree, tree heather, and holm oak, though some areas are open.

The gulf is best known as a bird site, with good reason. In the breeding season, there are dozens of different species. Dalmatian pelicans breed here, arriving on their nest sites in February and laying by March, at one of their few breeding areas anywhere. The population size was estimated at 37 pairs in 1991, down to about 25 pairs in 1996, a good deal smaller than the Prespa population (see p. 31), but significant nevertheless. Four species of tern breed: gull-billed, common (up to 600 pairs a few years ago), little, and Sandwich, with a few black terns hanging on in the Louros Delta area. There are hundreds of black-winged stilts and collared pratincoles, and reasonable numbers of stone curlews. Kentish plover nest along the shores, with an estimated total population of about 200 pairs. Breeding wetland birds here include squacco heron, night heron, purple heron, little bittern, little egret, and ferruginous duck, for which it is now the best remaining site in Greece, and spoonbills, in small and declining numbers. White storks are abundant here – several nearby towns and villages have striking numbers of nests (often with accompanying Spanish sparrows), such as Aneza and Filipiada, and the storks can be seen in the marshes through the spring and summer. Warblers such as fan-tailed, great reed, Cetti's, and even olive-tree warbler breed around the site, together with a few semi-collared fly-catchers, and kingfishers can be seen at all times of year. In the hills within and around the site, there are several breeding birds of prey, including short-toed and lesser spotted eagles, marsh harrier,

Eryngium creticum

and buzzard, and vultures can often be seen overhead. Rollers used to nest here, but no longer do, in keeping with their general decline. On a lighter note, the ferry across the mouth of the Gulf at Preveza is worth catching just to see the house martins that nest on some of the boats; their nests move to and fro across the channel many times a day! There are also some good colonies of sand martins around the harbour.

At passage periods, in both spring and autumn, there can be vast numbers of birds of great variety and interest. Glossy ibis (which used to breed but no longer do) are regular in variable numbers, sometimes up to a thousand or so, with large numbers of waders (including, very occasionally, the rare slender-billed curlew), all the European flycatchers, an enormous array of warblers, most European birds of prey including osprey, and many others.

In winter, numbers of wildfowl and other birds can build up considerably, depending on the weather elsewhere. This site holds the largest regular concentration of wintering waterfowl in Greece, with an average January maximum (with coot) of 145 000. This includes wigeon, teal, gadwall, pintail, shoveler, red-crested pochard, merganser, and grebes. In addition, there are white pelicans, great white egrets, Mediterranean and slender-billed gulls, and pygmy cormorants. Birds of prey gather – marsh harriers are abundant, and pallid harriers turn up occasionally, together with spotted eagles, peregrines, small numbers of merlin, and occasional white-tailed eagles.

Not surprisingly in such a vast and varied wetland area, there is a great variety of amphibians and reptiles. Common tree frogs call loudly from reedbeds and other tall vegetation, and marsh frogs can be heard along the ditches and lagoons. The curious call of green toads (like distant pumping) can be heard in spring, and there are also smaller populations of common toad, agile frog, and smooth newts. Both European and stripe-necked terrapins are common along canals and lagoons, and loggerhead turtles used to nest on the sandy beaches, though nowa-

days they breed no further north than Zakynthos (see p. 267), which is also the most northerly breeding point in Europe. Hermann's and marginated tortoises are both common, and there are several species of snake, including grass snakes and dice snakes (which can both be seen hunting by swimming in ditches and lagoons, looking for tadpoles, small fishes and frogs), leopard snake, nose-horned viper, Montpellier snake, and Dahl's whip snake. Eleven species of lizard have been recorded, including green and Balkan green, Turkish gecko, Dalmatian algyroides, and Erhard's wall lizard.

Golden jackal still occur here, and other mammals that one might see include eastern hedgehog, pine marten, stoat, and red squirrel. However, it is not really a great area for mammals.

It is a good place for seeing insects, though not exceptional for any one group. There are good numbers of dragonflies, though the salinity of the lagoons excludes many species. Emperor, lesser emperor, several darters including the

The Gulf of Amvrakikos from the north, with saltmarsh and lagoons in the foreground

Leopard snake *Elaphe situla*

striking *Crocothemis erythraea*, and scarce chasers are all frequent. The beautiful lacewing, genus *Nemoptera*, with hind wings like long streamers, can be seen in warm dry areas, violet carpenter bees are everywhere, and bush-crickets such as long-winged conehead and Roesel's bush-cricket are abundant. It is not exceptional for butterflies, though there are plenty about. Two impressive spiders are common in undisturbed tall grassy vegetation: the wasp spider, and its close relative *Argiope lobatus*, with a wavy edge to its very solid-looking body.

Access to the north side is generally easy along the main road from Arta to Preveza (from which there are good views and even hides – though they are not well-sited); the road southwards to Koronissia passes through a good range of habitats, and most other minor roads southwards are worth exploring.

SITE 52 Akarnanian Mountains

Rugged limestone mountains running southwards from the Gulf of Amvrakikos, with a particularly good range of hill birds.
Grid reference: 38°45'N 21°00'E.

Southwards from Vonitsa, on the south shore of the Gulf of Amvrakikos as far as Astakos, there is a rugged range of wild and little-visited limestone mountains, reaching 1589 m at the highest point. On the seaward side, they are bare and rocky – reminiscent of the Mani Peninsula (see pp. 221–229) – thanks to centuries of grazing and burning, though in the central valley it is more humid, and here there is extensive woodland. Maquis, with kermes oak, junipers, smoke bush, strawberry-tree, and maples, is found lower down, with more distinct oak forest higher up. Above this, there are areas of

Greek fir, with open pastures at the highest levels. They are snow-capped in winter and into early spring.

It is a good bird site, though unprotected by any designation. One of the largest colonies of griffon vultures on mainland Greece is still found here – griffons have declined throughout Greece, and there are probably no more than 300 pairs in the country (of which half are on Crete). The colony here used to be 30–40 pairs, though it has diminished further recently to a dozen or so birds. Lammergeiers did breed here, though they no longer do, but there are still Bonelli's

Central Greece

The coastal road from Paleros in the north to Astakos in the south gives a good feel of the area, and some fine views of cliffs and sea, and a detour to the monastery of Aghias Dimitron is worth taking to gain some altitude. The central area is harder to reach, but there is a poor road going south from Monastiraki, and another poor road southwards from Petra on the east side of the massif.

and short-toed eagles, peregrines, and honey buzzards, and eagle owls in the forests and higher areas. In scrub and cultivated areas lower down, there are lesser grey shrikes, olive-tree warblers, rock partridges, and ortolan buntings. In rocky areas the ringing calls of rock nuthatches can usually be heard, and in wooded areas there are middle-spotted woodpeckers.

Bonelli's eagle *Hieraaetus fasciatus*

The bare limestone mountains of Akarnania

SITE 53 Mt. Timfristos

A high, botanically rich mountain.
Grid reference: 38°53'N 21°47'E.

Mt. Timfristos towers above the town of Karpenissi in the central southern Pindos. It reaches 2315 m at the highest point (though few maps actually mark this summit). Its slopes are mostly bare, with just a few areas of sparse Greek fir forest, thanks to heavy and continuous grazing pressure.

On the lower slopes, there are extensive areas of maquis, with prickly juniper, the hawthorn *Crataegus heldreichii*, Spanish broom, and a whitebeam *Sorbus umbellata*, with *Daphne oleoides*, a striking red soapwort *Saponaria calabrica*, ground-pine, the skullcap *Scutellaria orientalis* subspecies *alpina*, the bellflower relative *Asyneuma limonifolium*, and some lovely thistles (often covered with butterflies) such as *Carduus candicans* and *C. macro-cephalus*. Higher up, there is a bare landscape, dotted with hummock 'hedge-hog' plants. The sub-shrub *Acantholimon* *androsaceum*, consisting of hummocks covered with masses of pretty pink flowers, is common; they are a Middle-Eastern group of flowers, related to sea-lavenders and thrift, at the western edge of their range here. The pretty 'snow-in-summer' look-alike *Cerastium candidissimum* is common, together with a house-leek *Jovibarba heuffelii*, and aromatic plants like *Marrubium velutinum* and *Nepeta nuda*.

At the highest levels, *Crocus veluchen-sis* flowers on into the summer, with a snow-patch buttercup *Ranunculus sartorianus*, *Viola aetolica*, alpine squill, the pretty little crane's-bill *Geranium cinereum* subspecies *subcaulescens*, a valerian *Valeriana tuberosa*, and many others.

It is not a great bird site, but there are reasonable numbers of blue rock thrushes, northern wheatears, kestrels, and other widespread birds. Golden eagles occasionally drift by, and shore

A beautiful ancient hummock of *Acantholimon androsaceum* on Mt. Timfristos

larks may nest on the high tops. Butterflies include Damon blue, Greek clouded yellow, fiery copper, weaver's fritillary, and Grecian anomalous blue.

Access is relatively easy now, as a road winds its way up to a newish ski station, from just west of Karpenissi, passing through most of the habitats, and other minor roads climb part way up. There is a huge area of fine, partly wooded country eastwards from here as far as Aghios Georgios.

54 Mt. Vardousia

Extensive, high rugged mountains, rich in flowers and birds.
Grid reference: 38°42'N 22°07'E.

Mt. Vardousia is the general name for an extensive mountain with numerous high rocky peaks, reaching 2495 m at its highest point, but with many peaks over 2000 m. Amongst the high peaks, there are some of the finest cliffs in Greece, huge vertical faces, rarely climbed or visited. It has one of the most varied and interesting floras of any Greek mountain.

On the lower slopes, there are extensive forests of Greek fir, with clearings for villages here and there. Within the forests, there are interesting plants such as *Cyclamen*

repandum, the saprophytic orchid violet limodore, yellow bird's-nest, wintergreens, and *Corydalis solida*. Above the forest one finds extensive grassy pastures, with Greek hellebore, the foxglove *Digitalis lanata*, a mountain variant of swallow-wort, the fritillary *Fritillaria graeca*, cowslips, St. John's-worts, and at least two lilies: martagon lily and *Lilium chalchedonicum*.

The most specialized plants occur on the highest cliffs and screes. These include dwarf shrubs of a maple *Acer heldreichii* and Greek whitebeam.

Edraianthus graminifolius

Herbaceous plants include the bellflower *Campanula rupicola* and its relative *Edraianthus graminifolius*; the sage *Salvia argentea*; and the densely tufted form of *Trifolium hybridum* subspecies *anatolicum*; several saxifrages such as *Saxifraga adscendens*, *S. chrysosplenifolia*, and *S. sempervivum*; a catchfly *Silene barbeyana* that is endemic to just a few mountains around here, and grows only in high-altitude shady limestone cliffs; yellow gentian *Delphinium fissum*; and an avens *Geum heterocarpum* found nowhere else in Greece. High up, there are pockets of arctic-alpine plants such as alpine aster and mountain sorrel.

It is an important bird site, though unprotected and undesignated. Golden and short-toed eagles are frequently seen; lammergeiers have been recorded and may still breed, but Egyptian vultures probably no longer occur; black and white-backed woodpeckers breed in the woods, in addition to more common species. Rock partridges are common residents, and sombre tits are often seen, in a variety of habitats.

Access onto the mountain is usually up the Mornos Valley to the village of Mousounitsa, from where there are paths up the mountain. Several organizations maintain mountain huts here.

SITE 55 Mt. Iti National Park

A beautiful, forested mountain area, with a rich and varied flora and fauna.
Grid reference: 38°48'N 22°15'E.

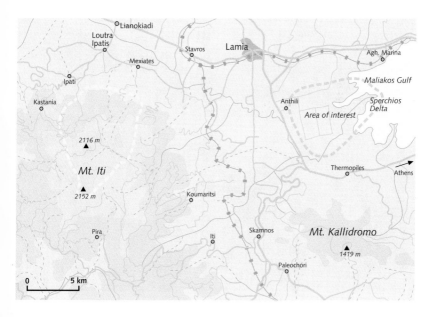

Clouded Apollo *Parnassius mnemosyne*

The Mt. Iti (or Oiti) National Park was established in 1966, and now has a core zone of 3010 ha within an overall territory of 7210 ha. It is famous for its beauty, with good reason; it has a mixture of old fir forest, with flowery grassy glades, topped with alpine pastures. Because the underlying slightly acidic rock is not porous, there is much more surface water than on the nearby limestone mountains such as Parnassus, and there are streams everywhere, tumbling down through the forests, with a few lakes higher up, and some meltwater pools. Despite the cliffs on the north slopes, it is a gentler mountain than many, though it rises to 2152 m, and the weather can be as unpredictable here as anywhere.

The lower slopes have typical maquis with kermes oak, turpentine trees, smoke bush, and *Phillyrea latifolia*, while above about 800 m there are extensive forests of Greek firs, covered in lichens at higher elevations.

Botanically it is very rich and at the moment the grazing pressure seems to be about right – enough to maintain the grassy flowery areas, but not so much as to graze everything to near-extinction. In lower areas, there are masses of flowers: the red lily *Lilium chalchedonicum* occurs along the track-sides and in clearings, together with the prominent spires of *Morina persica*, several mulleins, lots of thistles such as *Onopordon illyricum*, the pretty willowherb *Chamaenerion dodonaei*, downy woundwort, and many others, almost all of which are visited by a steady stream of butterflies. In the more open areas of woodland, there are

Rhinocorys elephas

Iti National Park

vetches such as *Vicia villosa*, large-flowered calamint, foxgloves such as *Digitalis
ferruginea*, several species of *Dianthus*,
pheasant's eye narcissus, yellow gentians, the pretty sweet-pea relative
Lathyrus grandiflorus, and clary sage,
together with many others.

In wetter areas – and there are plenty of
them – grow marsh-orchids such as
Dactylorhiza saccifera and *D. baumanniana*, globeflower (which is extremely rare
in Greece), the curious lousewort relative
Rhinchocorys elephas that has attractive
yellow flowers with a profile that faintly
resembles an elephant, and the crane's-
bill *Geranium asphodelioides*.

Higher up, in pastures and rocky areas
of schist, there are more specialized
plants such as the flax *Linum punctatum*
subspecies *pycnophyllum*, rather too
many species of milk-vetch *Astragalus*,
including *A. parnassi*, *A. creticus*, *A.
mayeri*, and *A. baldaccii*; the violets *Viola
aetolica*, *V. poetica*, and *V. graeca*, and the
autumn-flowering *Colchicum graecum*.

There is an interesting flora around snow
meltwater pools, including species that
are rare elsewhere in Greece, and at least
one endemic to Iti. The list includes
shoreweed, mousetail, a little loosestrife
Lythrum thymifolia, a yellow Stars-of-
Bethlehem *Gagea amblyopetala*, and the
endemic speedwell *Veronica oetaea*.

Chamois still occur here but, despite
the protection of being in a National
Park, are illegally hunted. In fact – like
most Greek National Parks – there is very
little to distinguish the park from the surrounding countryside, though at least
logging seems to be controlled here.
Other mammals include wild boar, red
squirrel, roe deer, and beech marten.
Alpine newts breed in the lake on the
Livadies Plateau, and stream frogs and
yellow-bellied toads occur around the
streams. Birds are abundant here: short-
toed eagles breed in the park, and are
frequently seen hunting over the area,
while griffon vultures and golden eagles
may drift in now and again from else-

A clearing in old fir forest on Iti, rich in flowers and butterflies

where. Peregrines breed on the crags, it is a good area for eagle owls, and honey buzzards breed secretively in the forests. Rock partridges still occur fairly frequently, and can often be heard calling, and the woods are full of woodpeckers: great and middle-spotted, black, white-backed, and possibly others. Red-backed shrikes are common in open areas.

It is an excellent area for butterflies, which are both abundant and diverse.

Eagle owl *Bubo bubo*

The range of species includes Apollo, clouded Apollo, swallowtail, scarce swallowtail, clouded yellow, large copper, zephyr blue, brown argus, great sooty satyr, black-veined white, lattice brown, Balkan marbled white, several fritillaries including lesser spotted, and many more. Thistles such as the pretty *Ptilostemon afer* are particularly good for butterflies and other insects. Jersey tigers are common, and a species of golden-ringed dragonfly *Cordulegaster picta* occurs on the mountain streams. Grasshoppers are extremely abundant on the grassy plateau at high altitude.

Access to Iti is quite easy, though there are few facilities and no significant information. The village of Ipati (on the north side) is the best starting point, and there is a path or a driveable track from here. There is a refuge at about 1800 m, although only usable by groups, but the distances involved are short enough to make it possible to be based at Ipati and still see the full range of habitats.

SITE 56 Sperchios Delta

*One of the few wetlands of any significance outside northern
Greece.*
Grid reference: 38°53'N 22°31'E.

The Sperchios Delta lies at the western
end of the Maliakos Gulf, just south-east of
Lamia. The Sperchios River drains a wide
area of hilly country (including Mt. Iti
National Park – see map p. 139) and has
deposited a substantial delta where it
reaches the sea. The interesting area once
extended well inland, to the main Athens
road and beyond, but it has steadily been
drained, developed, and cultivated, and
only a small proportion is left. This still
constitutes, however, a reasonable amount
of habitat, and it is worth a visit if in the
area – though a number of sites north and
east of here are similar and better.

There are extensive areas of saltmarsh,
with sandbars and mudflats, together with
reed-fringed ditches and small amounts of
freshwater. Much of the delta area is under
rice fields, which can be good for birds at
times, especially in spring.

Breeding birds include black-winged
stilts, collared pratincoles, stone curlew,
Cetti's and fan-tailed warblers, little bittern, white stork, and terns, especially
little and common terns on the sandbars.
Penduline tits, and possibly bearded tits,
breed in the delta. At passage periods
there can be masses of waders, including
distinctive birds such as spoonbills and
glossy ibis, quite large numbers of little
bitterns, terns, and gulls, and wildfowl
including ferruginous duck. Winter
brings avocets (up to 3000 have been
recorded), great white egret, slender-
billed gulls and reasonable numbers of
wildfowl. Spotted eagle, hen harrier, and
the ubiquitous marsh harrier all hunt
over the marshes at times.

Access onto the delta is via dirt tracks
running east from Anthili, on the main
highway south of Lamia. There are
numerous tracks, some of which may
become impassable at times, and others
go nowhere useful, but it is worth
persisting!

SITE 57 Mt. Parnassus National Park

*One of the finest and most accessible mountain areas in Greece,
with an exceptionally rich flora and fauna.*
Grid reference: 38°30'N 22°37'E.

Mt. Parnassus is one of the most impressive, and certainly one of the most
accessible, of the high mountain areas of
Greece, just a couple of hours from
Athens, with good roads almost to the
top. About a third of its area has been a
National Park, covering 3513 ha, since
1938 – the earliest in Greece. However, for
the purpose of this description we will
largely ignore the park boundary, since it

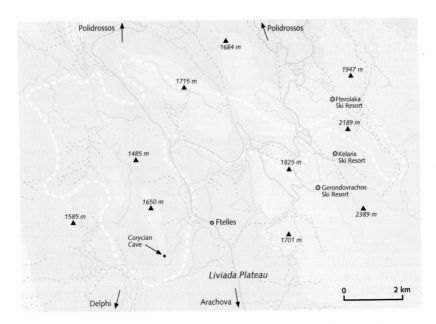

excludes many areas of interest (including most of the highest peaks) and it is impossible to tell by any detectable change in management where the park begins or ends. There is no information on site, no special management of the park's vegetation, and – worst of all – there appears to be no restriction on either house-building or commercial development such as ski centres.

However, it is a marvellous area despite the problems, and protected from some changes by its high altitude and rugged terrain.

The lower slopes are clothed with typical limestone maquis, dominated by tree

Southern swallowtail Papilio alexanor

spurge, terebinth and lentisk, the spiny little broom *Genista acanthoclada*, spiny spurge, and the ubiquitous kermes oak. The flora under the maquis, and the birds associated with it, are broadly as described for Delphi (p. 152), which lies on the lower slopes of Parnassus. From about 800 m upwards, Greek fir forest dominates, at least on the western and northern sides, while the other slopes are largely bare. Within this forest zone there is a rich flora, especially in some of the grassy clearings that become increasingly common towards the upper level of the forest. In early spring (from early April onwards, depending on the amount of snow that fell in the winter), there are some of the finest displays of crocuses anywhere, with vast swathes of blue with a little yellow – *Crocus veluchensis* and *C. sieberi* subspecies *sublimis*, and an apparent hybrid swarm between the two, making identification rather more difficult, and patches of orange-yellow *C. chrysanthus* here and there. The band of crocuses moves up the mountain as the snow melts, so they can be seen in flower until June at least. With them, there are alpine squills, *Corydalis solida*, Greek

Geranium macrorrhizum

hellebore, masses of the pretty *Anemone blanda* in various colour forms, the spurge *Euphorbia myrsinites*, a Stars-of-bethlehem *Ornithogalum montanum*, yellow stars-of-bethlehem *Gagea* species, and the first flowers of *Iris pumila* sub-species *attica* and snake's head iris. Other plants in flower at this height in spring

An ancient tree of *Juniperus foetidissimus* on Mt. Parnassus

Central Greece

Slopes above Delphi

include *Aubrieta deltoides*, the dead-nettle *Lamium garganicum*, pheasant's eye, a pretty speedwell *Veronica glauca*, and grape-hyacinth *Muscari neglectum*. A little later, *Lilium chalchedonicum* and the yellow orchid *Orchis pallens* come into flower. Unfortunately, these lower slopes are all so heavily grazed that it is hard to find plants in flower (and it also reduces the populations of butterflies and other insects); flocks follow the snow up in spring, and I have even seen flocks still on the mountain in December trying to graze through heavy frost and light snow!

Higher up, around the ski station and the end of the road, there are some interesting habitats towards the upper limits of the forest, with cliffs and numerous swallow-holes or *dolines*, which are often deep enough to have their own microclimate, quite humid towards the bottom. May and June are the best times at this altitude (it is all heavily grazed later), and here you can find the large crane's-bill *Geranium macrorrhizum*, the pretty bellflower *Campanula rupicola* in crevices on the cliffs, the white-

flowered cinquefoil *Potentilla speciosa*, with the ragwort *Senecio thapsoides* at the base. There are saxifrages here, such as *Saxifraga sempervivum* and *S. sibthorpii*, leopard's-banes, the aromatic *Nepeta nuda* and *Marrubium velutinum*, a relative of snow-in-summer *Cerastium candidissimum*, a creamy-white flowered daphne *Daphne oleoides*, and mats of *Prunus prostrata*, which has little plum-pink flowers in great masses. The foxglove *Digitalis laevigata* grows along roadsides.

Higher still, amongst the high tops and cliffs, there is another range of flowers, mostly flowering a little later, including more of the special plants of Parnassus. Overall, there are at least 25 Greek endemics and 10 plants endemic to just Parnassus or the immediate area. There are too many to name individually, but here are some of the more interesting

Tulipa orphanidea

Rock partridge *Alectoris graeca*

ones. Three milk-vetches *Astragalus parnassi* (an endemic), *A. baldaccii*, and *A. angustifolius* occur together on ridges, with burnt candytuft, the cat-mint *Nepeta parnassica*, eastern bugle, the St. John's-wort *Hypericum rumeliacum*, *Asperula boissieri*, the bellflowers *Campanula aizoon* and *Edraianthus graminifolius*, *Achillea umbellata* and *A. holosericea*, the familiar rock garden plant *Pterocephalus perennis*, like a mat-forming scabious, and many more. In the late snowfields and on the highest cliffs, there is a pretty dwarf buttercup *Ranunculus brevifolius*; cushions of the pink *Dianthus haematocalyx* and its more familiar spiky relative *Drypis spinosa*; *Draba parnassica*; several more saxifrages including *Saxifraga spruneri*, *S. scardica*, and *S. marginata*; a violet *Viola poetica*; the bellflower relative *Edraianthus parnassicus*, alpine erigeron, and many more, depending on the season.

Lower down, it is worth making a detour along the track to the Corycian Cave, to see some fine trees of *Juniperus foetidissima*, a lot more irises, the endemic mullein *Verbascum delphicum*, and some tulips *Tulipa orphanidea*, amongst others.

Parnassus is also a superb place to watch mountain birds. Apart from the range of birds mentioned in connection with Delphi (p. 154), which can all be seen around the lower slopes of Parnassus, there are many birds with more specific high-altitude connections. Shore larks breed here in reasonable numbers, mainly on the high rocky slopes above about 2000 m. They are resident vertical migrants, only descending as low as necessary to escape the snow, so they can be seen in the Liviada Plateau area and elsewhere during the winter. Alpine accentors and snow finches occur at similar altitudes, though often associated more closely with scrubby or rocky areas, where black redstarts can often be seen, too. Rock partridges can be heard calling from rocky outcrops, and both common and alpine choughs wheel overhead. In the forests, there are at least four species of breeding woodpecker, including black, white-backed, and middle- spotted, as on many other Greek mountains. Tengmalm's owls have been recorded as breeding here, using old black woodpecker nest holes in the fir forest. Like eagle owls (which also occur here) they can be heard calling at night in late winter and very early spring, and occasionally at other times, which is probably the best way to confirm their presence. Birds of prey to be seen here include golden, booted, and short-toed eagles, the occasional lammergeier, griffon vulture, lanner falcon, goshawk, and honey buzzard.

Mammals, reptiles, and amphibians are not significant features of the Parnassus ecosystem, thanks to the lack of surface water, and to hunting and grazing pressures. Wild boar occur in small numbers, with red squirrel and beech marten in the forests. Balkan green lizards are not uncommon. Butterflies are frequent, but not abundant, limited by the heavy grazing pressure. Species preferring rocky sites with sparse vegetation, such as the Grecian grayling, do well here.

Iris pumila
Subspecies *attica*

Other butterflies of interest here include Apollo, Greek clouded yellow and black ringlet at high altitudes, southern swallowtail, eastern orange tip, the Levantine skipper on the southern slopes, and the tiny little grass jewel – almost like a tiny brown argus, feeding here on the spurge relative *Andrachne telephioides*.

Access by road is easy. A good road runs up from Arachova (which makes a useful base) on the south side of the mountain, and from it a road ascends to the ski station not too far from the summit. The road continues down the more forested north side towards Polidrossos. There are reasonable tracks running westwards across the Livadia Plateau. There are marvellous, though demanding, footpaths up from Delphi, or from Ano Tithorea on the north-east side.

SITE 58 Northern Evvia

The northern part of one of the largest Greek islands: wild, remote, and mountainous, with many sites of interest.

The island of Evvia, also known as Euboea, is the largest Greek island after Crete, although as it comes within 100 m of the mainland at its closest point, and there is a main road bridge here, it is not always described as an island. Despite this, and its relative proximity to Athens and the main E75 motorway, it is still a remarkably quiet and unspoilt area. For the purpose of this book, northern Evvia lies northwards from Halkida and the bridge to the mainland.

The dominant mountain here, and the highest on the island, is Mt. Dyrfis, which

Campanula spathulata

Coastal reed-beds and marshes near Nea Artaki

reaches 1743 m. It is a superb area of mountainous scenery, topped by a beautiful conical peak that is snow-capped through the winter, extending over a wide area of countryside southwards to the Mavrovouni Massif (just inland from Kimi) and northwards towards Pilio, with vast tracts of unspoilt forests (mainly of Greek fir, with some sweet chestnut and pine), grassy clearings, limestone screes, and cliffs. It is a well-known and important botanical site, with a number of rarities as well as an abundance of more common montane and forest species, though it is neither high enough nor far enough north to attract many true alpine species. Some of the many specialities to be seen here include: a species of the 'mountain tea' group *Sideritis euboea* which is endemic to Evvia; *Rindera graeca*, a beautiful member of the borage family with clumps of narrow silvery-grey leaves and clusters of reddish-purple tubular flowers, endemic to Greece; a marjoram relative with pinkish-purple flowers *Origanum scabrum* (rare in Greece, though also found on Mt. Taigetos: see p. 232); the endemic violet *Viola euboica*, and

the endemic fritillary *Fritillaria euboeica*, which has pretty clear unchequered yellow flowers and grows on limestone screes or in open woods. Other flowers of interest to be found on Dyrfis include the golden drop *Onosma erectum* subspecies *erectum*; a St. John's-wort *Hypericum delphicum*; wall germander, and mountain germander in its white-hairy subspecies *Teucrium montanum* subspecies *helianthemoides*; a pretty, purplish-flowered skull-cap *Scutellaria rupestris* subspecies *parnassica*; a white-flowered subspecies of common marjoram; Gargano deadnettle in its subspecies *striatum*; the mat-forming scabious *Pterocephalus perennis* subspecies *perennis*; *Campanula spathulata*, an attractive bellflower with very open flowers, and its close relative *Asyneuma limonifolium*, which has spikes of pale blue narrow-petalled flowers. In spring, following the melting snow upwards, the pretty crocus *Crocus sieberi* subspecies *sublimis* flowers in reasonable quantity.

There is now a good road over the shoulder of Dyrfis, giving relatively easy access to the higher areas, and there are forest tracks throughout. Other peaks within the massif include Mt. Pixarias (1343 m) to the north, noted for its extensive box scrub (at its southernmost Greek mountain locality), and Mt. Xerovouni (1417m) to the south-west. Xerovouni is a bare, dry mountain (Xerovouni means 'dry mountain'), but still has a rich flora hidden amongst the rocks, including endemics such as the violets *Viola dirphya* and *V. chelmea*, and the large-flowered dwarf crane's-bill *Geranium subcaulescens*.

It is an important area for birds of prey, with breeding griffon vulture, short-toed and golden eagles, and possibly still Bonelli's eagles, together with peregrine and Eleonora's falcons, plus a few lesser kestrel colonies. Eagle owls occur here and there (though as usual they are underrecorded), and more common species include woodlark, blue rock thrush, and rock, Cretzschmar's, and cirl buntings. Beech martens are common in the more wooded areas.

Northwards from Halkida, there is an area of low, forested mountains known as Mt. Kandilio (or Kantili), reaching 1246 m. North of Nerotrivia, there is a large roadless and little-known area, with extensive coniferous forests (mainly of *Pinus brutia* and Greek fir, with some black pine at higher levels). Within this area, there are small gorges, open limestone grassland areas, and cliffs, with an extensive bare area above the tree-line in the highest parts, and it is known as a good area for birds of prey: Bonelli's eagles and golden

eagles still hang on in small numbers, with honey buzzards, Eleonora's falcons, and lesser kestrels. The higher areas are good for plants, too, with many of the species that occur on Dyrfis, including both *Origanum* species, *Onosma euboicum* – an endemic golden drop that usually occurs in association with serpentine rock – and *Sideritis euboea*. Other flowers recorded here include the endemic and very local ragwort *Senecio eubaeus*, which only occurs here and on the Dyrfi group of mountains, an endemic Daphne *Daphne euboica*, and a rock-rose relative *Fumana pinatzii*, amongst many others.

Just to the south of the Kandilio range, near Nea Artaki, there is a small coastal wetland with reedbeds and saltmarshes, of no great importance but worth looking at for amphibians, terrapins, dragonflies, and passage birds in spring and late summer.

On the north coast, north-north-east of Isteia, there is a coastal wetland covering about 600 ha, made up of a lagoon (marked on some maps as Megalo Livari lagoon) fed by freshwater springs and streams, together with areas of reedbed, woodland, sandy beach, and scrub. While not a major site, it does have breeding little terns and white storks, and a good range of waders, and other birds turn up on passage, including glossy ibis, ferruginous duck, and spoonbill; good numbers of wildfowl may pass the winter here, including quite large flocks of mute swans. It is not a well-studied area, and there is scope for a good deal more to be discovered.

Southern Evvia

A hilly and generally unspoilt region, with mountains rising to 1399 m.

This site covers the part of Evvia southwards from Halkida and the bridge to the mainland.

Lake Distos lies in a large depression amongst the hills south of the village of

Distos. Although it can have open water, it is normally visible only as a sea of reeds and other fen vegetation, and it seems to be steadily drying out. Although nominally covering an area of 2600 ha (a sizeable

Flowery garrigue, with the vast reed-beds of Lake Distos beyond

lake), it is contracting as a result of water abstraction (and possibly climate change), and suffers from shooting, draining, burning, and agricultural pollution. Despite all this it still holds some interest, and is worth a detour from the main road south to Karistos, close to which it lies. Breeding species recorded in recent years include little bitterns, little egrets, night herons, purple herons, Cetti's warbler, great reed warbler, and other common wetland birds. In higher water years, there may be good numbers of passage migrants, particularly in spring, though in spring 2000, despite good winter rain and snow, there was very little water, so its future looks uncertain. Glossy ibis and various other waders have been recorded here in the recent past.

The hills around are mainly unspoilt, and have good flowers in spring including masses of peacock and crown anemones, a few orchids such as yellow bee and lesser yellow bee, the pretty little semi-parasite *Parentucellia latifolia*, two species of Stars-of-Bethlehem, and the attractive sand crocus *Romulea bul-*

bocodium. Breeding birds include Rüppell's and subalpine warblers, lesser grey shrike, rock partridge, rock nuthatch, and a few birds of prey including short-toed eagle. Marsh harriers can be seen quartering the marshes.

South of here, the main road passes through an area of serpentine rock (of which there are several on Evvia) that has an unusual flora, though at present parts of it are being destroyed by the construction of a new road. The iris *Iris unguicularis* is common around here. There is an old quarry by the road that has become flooded, and which has masses of terrapins, together with some dragonflies and marsh frogs.

It is probably worth mentioning that the ferry crossings around here from Evvia to the mainland can be very rewarding, with superb views, and frequent glimpses of seabirds and cetaceans. Agia Marina to Nea Stira is particularly good.

At the southern end of the island lies Mt. Ochi, reaching 1400 m and high enough to hold snow well into the spring. It covers a substantial area of wild and little-known country, worth a visit between April and early July. Flowers of interest here include the endemic yellow fritillary *Fritillaria euboeica*, the endemic 'mountain tea' *Sideritis euboea*, the rare marjoram *Origanum scabrum*, and *O. vulgare* subspecies *hirtum* – a white-flowered form of marjoram, with glandular-hairy leaves and stems, and the endemic violet *Viola euboea*, a form of wild peony, *Hypericum delphicum* along streams, and the variety of primrose known as *Primula vulgaris* variety *sibthorpii*. It is also a good area for birds of prey, though the details are not well-known: short-toed eagles and Bonelli's eagles certainly occur, together with peregrine, Eleonora's falcon (on its way to breeding sites on more remote islands),

and long-legged buzzard. Unfortunately, much of the original forest has been cleared or reduced to scrub, limiting the range of species somewhat.

The little town of Karistos makes a good base for exploring Ochi and other parts of southern Evvia; just to the west of it, there are saltpans, marshy areas, and a river mouth that can be good for migrants in spring, which hold a small range of wetland amphibians, reptiles, and dragonflies.

Access to most sites is straightforward, with a good (and improving) main road and a network of smaller roads. Forest tracks go high on Ochi on the west side from Karistos, or on the east side from Metochi. There is a limited-opening refuge south of the summit, close to almost the only bit of forest here.

SITE 60 Delphi

One of the finest classical sites in Greece, also particularly good for flowers and birds.
Grid reference: 38°30'N 22°25'E.

Delphi is an exceptional place. Its ruins are amongst the finest and most evocative anywhere, but it has the added bonuses of being in a beautiful and spectacular site,

and of having a rich flora and fauna. The ancient site lies tucked under a high cliff on the south-west side of Mt. Parnassus (see p. 143), with the Kastalia Spring emerging from a chasm just to the east, and wide views across a sea of olive trees in the vale of Itea to the Gulf of Corinth and the Peloponnese beyond. I first visited Delphi on a warm December day – entry was free, and there was no one else about, and I was delighted to find the place full of butterflies even at that time of year, with rock nuthatches calling from every rock, and occasional eagles overhead. I have been back at different seasons since, and there is almost always something else to see, though it is best to avoid the hot summer months when it is very busy, dusty, and largely flowerless.

Alkanna orientalis

Within and immediately adjacent to the site itself there is an impressive variety of flowers, and the masses of common flowers in the ungrazed part of the town can look quite stunning in spring. Masses of yellow melilot, with the similar but slightly smaller *Trigonella graeca*, and red poppies flow around the ruins, with vetches such as fodder vetch and *Vicia villosa*. The striking yellow-flowered alkanet *Alkanna orientalis* forms large clumps, and in some years the honeywort *Cerinthe retorta* (currently popular in gardens) does well. In amongst these masses of flowers, there are smaller quantities of a catchfly *Silene behen*, the umbellifers *Bonannia graeca* and *Smyrnium perfoliatum*, with yellow asphodels, slender asphodel, perennial honesty, medicks, and the pretty two-toned wild pea. On old walls (of which there are plenty!), one sees clumps of a golden drop *Onosma frutescens* and the striking bellflower *Campanula topoliana* subspecies *delphica* (the taxonomy of this group is confusing, and there are records of the same plant under several names). Near the stadium, there are clumps of an endemic woundwort *Stachys swainsonii*, a figwort *Scrophularia heterophylla*, and two sainfoins.

On the cliffs by the Kastalia Spring (now unfortunately closed due to falling rocks, though you can still see the cliffs quite well), there are many of the above, with the autumn-flowering bellflower *Campanula versicolor*, catchflies *Silene gigantea* (like *S. italica*, only bigger), another alkanet *Alkanna graeca*, red valerian, and the common shrubby composite *Ptilostemon chamaepeuce*, with long narrow leaves and heads of pinkish-red flowers.

The ancient site used to be mentioned as a good place to see orchids, though this no longer seems to be the case. However, if you walk from new Delphi up the edge of the site to arrive above the stadium, there are marvellous displays of flowers, including orchids. Low cliffs have the same bellflowers, and a little annual bellflower *Campanula drabifolia*, and the terraces under almonds and olives are a mass of colour in spring. Amongst the mayweeds, poppies, and medicks, there are tassel hyacinths and a similar bulb *Bellevalia dubia*, the spider-orchids *Ophrys spruneri* and *O.*

Sternbergia colchiciflora

Colchicum cupanii

mammosa, masses of yellow bee orchids, mirror orchids, early spider orchid, giant orchid, and a few others. There are clumps of the mullein *Verbascum undulatum* and many other flowers. Higher up, towards the top corner of the ancient site, the terraces end and a more natural scrub and grassland habitat commences. Here, there are dwarf oaks, tree spurge, a few clumps of the dwarf *Iris pumila* subspecies *attica*, and fritillaries *Fritillaria graeca*. Tulips used to occur up here, but seem to have gone. On the cliffs, there are clumps of an attractive daphne with pink-flushed flowers *Daphne jasminea*, the shrubby yellow

flax *Linum flavum* and a pretty St. John's-wort *Hypericum rumeliacum*. On the grassy places below, in autumn, there are autumn crocuses *Colchicum cupanii* and the yellow bulbs *Sternbergia lutea* with its smaller relative *S. colchiciflora*.

It is also worth carrying on up the path towards Parnassus if you have time and energy, or exploring below the site.

Besides all the flowers, Delphi is an excellent place to see birds, especially in spring. Rock nuthatches are common, and quite tame, and you can easily come across one of their impressive nests in the old site. There is a marvellous range of buntings in and around the site, with six species occurring regularly: corn, cirl, black-headed, rock, ortolan and Cretzschmar's, and it is a good place to try to sort out the different calls. Woodlarks call mournfully from the slopes, and apart from the ubiquitous Sardinian warbler, there are Rüppell's, Orphean, and occasional olive-tree warblers here. Sombre tits can be found in lower scrubby areas, firecrests are common in the trees, and goldfinches are everywhere. Blue rock thrushes sing from prominent rock outcrops, black-eared wheatears flit amongst the stones, and hoopoes call from the terraces. At passage periods, other birds can turn up – for exam-

Rock nuthatch *Sitta neumayer*

Old terraces above Delphi in early spring

ple red-breasted flycatchers in spring and Levant sparrowhawks in autumn.

It is also a good place to see birds of prey, though few of them actually nest here, and you need to consciously spend time scanning the skies. Golden eagles and peregrines are quite common, griffon vultures (and very occasionally lammergeier) less so, and honey buzzards breed not far away. Many pass over on migration, too.

It is not a great site for butterflies, but they tend to occur in quite large numbers and are easily seen. For example, three swallowtails – scarce, common, and southern – are all regular, with clouded yellows, painted ladies, various skippers, and a few blues. Green lizards and wall lizards are common around the ruins, and the Greek legless skink occurs nearby.

SITE 61 Messolongi wetlands

A vast coastal wetland, particularly rich in birds.
Grid reference: 38°20'N 21°15'E.

The huge complex of lagoons, salt-marshes, and other coastal habitats at Messolongi is essentially the combined deltas of two rivers: the Acheloos and the Evinos. Altogether, there are about 50 000

ha of interesting habitat, of which about 25 000 ha are delta. Part of the site is designated as a Ramsar Site (internationally important wetland) and Special Protection Area, which gives hope that

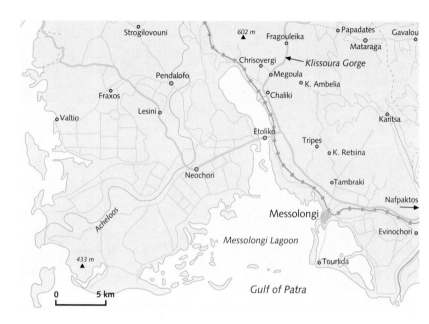

some of the decline of recent years may be halted or reversed at last. It is an area of great beauty, with large shallow lagoons edged with saltmarsh and backed by rugged mountains such as Arakinthos.

The main habitats are shallow lagoons, saltpans, reedbeds, mudflats, salt-marshes, ditches, sandbars, sand dunes, and some forested areas. The saltmarshes are dominated by characteristic plants such as glassworts, annual sea-blite and sharp rush, with sea club-rush in places. Where the water is less saline, there are

Kingfisher *Alcedo atthis* (Peter Wilson)

yellow iris, flowering-rush, pondweeds, common duckweed, white water-lily, and greater and lesser reed-mace. There are some good dunes on the north-west shore of the gulf – good dunes are rare in Greece, and they are often heavily trampled and over-used. These are more extensive and higher than average, and have a good flora, which includes sea medick, the white-flowered sea daffodil, sea bindweed, cottonweed, purple spurge, catchflies, and others, while further inland the communities are more stable, dominated by a scrub of mastic trees, myrtle, and tree heath. There is still some riparian forest left, notably the monument of nature near Lessini, where about 60 ha are protected. This consists of Oriental plane, narrow-leaved ash, white willows, elm, and poplars.

The hills and mountains around the wetland are an important part of the ecosystem, with interchange between the two habitats. There are mountains to the north-east, and a few limestone hills within the delta. Here, there is typical maquis lower down, dominated by kermes oak, mastic tree, turpentine tree, spiny broom, myrtle, and Judas tree, with sun-

Central Greece

roses *Cistus* species and Jerusalem sage below. There are colonies of one of the rarer spider orchids *Ophrys argolica*, here at the northern edge of its distribution (it is much more common in the Peloponnese, see e.g. p. 214). In places, there are more extensive areas of Valonia oak, with its huge acorns and scaly acorn cups.

The region as a whole has some unusual plants; for example, there are at least four noteworthy knapweed species: *Centaurea sonchifolia*, which is rare in Greece generally, and grows on dunes, while *C. heldreichii*, *C. niederi*, and *C. aetolica* all occur in the area. The pink catchfly *Silene ungeri* is fairly frequent in the delta area, flowering in April and May, but it only occurs up the west coast of Greece and just into Albania.

However, Messolongi is best-known amongst naturalists for its birds. As is usual with Greek wetlands, it is nothing like as good as it once was, due to salt-works, drainage, land reclamation, over-use of rivers, population expansion, and the threat of more works higher up the rivers.

Breeding birds include collared pratincoles, gull-billed, little, and Caspian terns, avocets, stone curlews, Kentish plover, and white storks around the lagoons. Penduline tits, Cetti's and reed warblers, Calandra lark, lesser grey shrike, kingfishers, and sand martins breed here and there in the site. On the surrounding hills, and especially on Mt. Arakinthos to the north-west, birds of prey are quite numerous as breeding species, including griffon vultures, lesser spotted, golden, and short-toed eagles, peregrine, and eagle owl. Many of these can be seen soaring over the wetlands.

At passage periods, especially spring, there can be good numbers of waders such as dunlins and common sandpiper, and rarer species such as terek and broad-billed sandpipers. It is one of the few sites where slender-billed curlew – one of the world's rarest waders – may turn up.

In winter there can be large numbers of birds, though it depends on conditions further north and is rarely as good as

Centaurea sonchifolia

Amvrakikos (see pp. 131–135). Maximum counts in most years exceed 20 000 birds. In a good year there can be vast numbers of coot, black-necked grebes, cormorants, pochard, and wigeon, with smaller numbers of great white egret, Mediterranean gulls, slender-billed gulls, and kingfishers. Visiting birds of prey at this time of year include marsh harriers, spotted eagle, Imperial eagle, merlin (a rarity in Greece), and short-eared owls. Both red and black kites can occur here – an exceptional occurrence in Greece, as neither is common, and red are decidedly rare.

It is a good area for reptiles and amphibians, especially around the lagoons and along the ditches and channels. Common tree frogs are abundant, often 'chacking' loudly from the reeds, and marsh frogs and agile frogs line the banks, leaping in as you approach. Both pond and stripe-necked terrapins are common here, often basking in the sun by the lakes. Grass and dice snakes hunt in the shallows, while cat snakes, Balkan whip snakes, Montpellier snakes, four-lined snakes, and others are found in drier areas. Amongst the many

Saltmarsh around the edge of the Messolongi wetlands, with limestone mountains beyond

species of lizard, there are European glass lizards, Balkan wall lizard, Dalmatian algyroides, snake-eyed skink, and Balkan green lizard. Two species of tortoise are frequent in well-vegetated areas: marginated and Hermann's tortoises.

Dragonflies and other insects are broadly similar to those of the Gulf of Amvrakikos.

Access into most of the area is easy. The road through Messolongi town and on southwards to Tourlida gives access to some of the better eastern lagoons, though they are rather over-exploited. The western part is more intact and less-exploited, though more difficult to get to. Tracks leading west or south-west from Neochori take you eventually into good areas.

SITE
62 Mt. Parnitha National Park

A small National Park immediately north of Athens, centred on Mt. Parnitha (1413 m), with a surprisingly rich flora and fauna. Grid reference: 38°10'N 23°43'E.

Mt. Parnitha (also known as Mt. Parnon or Parnes) lies immediately north of the Athens conurbation, with burgeoning developments flowing around its south-

ern flanks. It is probably fair to say that it would not warrant National Park status if it were not so close to Athens, but nevertheless it has plenty of interest, and is

Sardinian warbler *Sylvia melanocephala* (Mike Lane)

well worth a visit if in Athens anyway. It gives a break from the noise and pollution, if nothing else. The National Park covers 3812 ha (and is contiguous with an EU Special Protection Area for birds), with no buffer zone.

Typical limestone maquis clothes the lower slopes, with pink-flowering bushes of *Cistus creticus*, rosemary, terebinth, kermes oak, and sage amongst others. In bare areas, or under bushes, there are masses of herbaceous plants in spring, including some good orchids. These include mirror, horseshoe, four-spotted, pyramidal, sawfly, pink butterfly, bumble bee, and the rare *Ophrys attica* (formerly known as *O. carmeli* subspecies *attica*) amongst others. Other flowers found in this site include burnt candytuft *Aethionema saxatile* subspecies *graeca*, *Anemone blanda* in several shades, and tassel hyacinths.

Higher up, there is a fair amount of Greek fir forest, open in places, but enough to give a woodland atmosphere. It is the only Attican mountain to keep any worthwhile fir forest, thanks to heavy exploitation elsewhere over the years. In clearings, there are pretty few-flowered orchids, reminiscent of cowslips or miniature daffodils from a distance, and four-spotted orchids, with a leopard's-bane *Doronicum caucasicum*, snake's head iris, *Aubrieta deltoides* (common in gardens), *Corydalis solida*, the dwarf iris *Iris pumila* subspecies *attica*, and a yellow star-of-Bethlehem *Gagea reticulata*.

Tulips *Tulipa orphanidea* still occasionally occur, but are increasingly rare. In spring, as the snow melts, the crocus *Crocus sieberi* subspecies *attica* (confined to a relatively small area of mountains), flowers profusely, together with alpine squill. In autumn, there are cyclamens *Cyclamen graecum* and *C. hederifolium*, with autumnal squill and at least three meadow saffrons *Colchicum cupanii*, *C. bivonae*, and *C. lingulatum*. Here and there (mainly just outside the park boundary!), there are patches of the wild peony *Paeonia mascula* subspecies *hellenica*, and the beautiful red lily *Lilium chalcedonicum*.

It is also a good place to see birds. Short-toed eagles, goshawks, and peregrines all breed here, and can be seen or heard moderately frequently – there are several cliffs and ravines around the mountain, though most areas are too disturbed by walkers and climbers to make good bird refuges. Golden eagles often float over, but do not breed here. Eagle owls may still occur, and amongst the scrub there are Rüppell's and Sardinian warblers, black-eared wheatears, Cretzschmar's buntings, and others.

Few-flowered orchid *Orchis pauciflora*

It is quite a good place to see reptiles; two species of tortoise are quite frequent here – Hermann's and spur-thighed – together with a number of snakes and lizards.

Access is straightforward; there is a road that goes all the way up, via Thrakomedones (though it can be surprisingly hard to find!) or you can walk from here, and a bus runs from central Athens. In fact, there is quite an extensive network of footpaths over the mountain, and once you get away from the roads, it can seem quite remote. Spring is best, summer is busy, and winter can be snowy.

SITE

63 Marathon marshes

A small coastal marshland on the eastern side of the Athens peninsula.
Grid reference: 38°10'N 24°02'E.

Just south-east of the town of Marathon, there is an area of coastal marsh that once covered about 1000 ha, but which has been steadily reduced through drainage and coastal development. Nevertheless, there is still a fair range of birds to see, though it all has a slightly unsavoury, messy feel to it. There are marshy areas, lagoons, small reedbeds, and some dunes.

Breeding birds here include little egrets, purple herons, crakes, little bitterns, night herons, and black-winged stilts. Cetti's, reed, great reed, and fantail warblers all nest within the marshland area, and Orphean warblers breed in the scrub not far away. Other birds to be seen in the breeding season in the surrounding scrubby hills include black-eared wheatear, rufous bush robins, black-headed and Cretzschmar's buntings, and rock nuthatches. In damp fields, there are tawny pipits, yellow wagtails, and short-toed larks.

At passage periods there can be lots to see. Glossy ibises (with up to 100 at once

Marathon marshes in winter

recorded), ruffs, little stint, sandpipers (including green), spoonbills, squacco herons, great snipe, and red-throated pipits are all regulars in spring, and many waterfowl stay for the winter. A total of 175 species of birds have been recorded, though this probably inflates its importance as it is particularly well-studied, and several of them may no longer occur.

Apart from the birds, there are tree frogs, marsh frogs, dice snakes, a few ter-rapins, emperor and lesser emperor drag-onflies, and masses of darters.

Access is by a minor road eastwards off the N54 just south of Marathon, to Kato Souli, followed by a right turn after 3 km towards the sea.

The nearby Marathon Lake is a reservoir with relatively little of interest, except for a few gulls, grebes, and duck, though the surrounding limestone hills are pleasant, with extensive maquis, including lots of strawberry-trees.

64 Athens

SITE

A selection of sites within, or close to, Athens.

Athens today is a huge, busy, and rather polluted city, in which development is proceeding apace. However, largely thanks to its geography, there are a few places of interest left either within or very close to the city; these are mainly on steep rocky limestone hills. The finest of these, Parnitha, is protected as a National Park (see p. 158). Other sites include Mt. Hymettos (or Ymittos), Mt. Likavitos, the Acropolis, the Botanic Garden, and Nymphos Hill.

Mt. Hymettos is a major feature, domi-nating the skyline to the east of Athens as a long hog's back rising to over 1000 m. There is some woodland on the lower slopes, but

Athens, from the slopes of Mount Hymettos

Central Greece

it is mainly a vast, bare, natural limestone rock garden, rising above a sea of development and pollution. Lower down, there is a cemetery and chapel at Kaisariani, which is noted for its orchids; these include some particularly attractive ones, such as an uncommon relative of early spider orchid *Ophrys aesculapii*, sawfly orchid, horseshoe orchid, and *O. attica*, with a few plants of mirror orchid. Higher up, in open rocky areas, there are tongue orchids, naked man orchids, few-flowered orchid, four-spotted, and a version of sombre bee orchid *O. iricolor*, with *Clematis cirrhosa* flowering in winter. Here and there are clumps of *Iris pumila* subspecies *attica* in various colours, snake's head (or widow) iris, grape-hyacinths, mainly *Muscari commutatum*, golden drop *Onosma*, and clumps of *Aubrieta deltoides* tumbling down the rocks. The views from the top are superb, especially out of the summer period. In autumn, there are some good bulbs up here: pretty pinkish *Colchicum cupanii*, autumn squill, several crocuses flowering through the early part of winter, including the creamy *Crocus boryi*, *C. laevigatus*, and the Greek saffron crocus *C. cartwrightianus*, thought to be the origin of the cultivated saffron crocus; the stigmas are divided into long reddish branches, and it is these that form the saffron.

It is quite a good place to see birds, though there are no real concentrations. Scrub and open woodland birds such as serin, subalpine, Rüppell's and Sardinian warblers, black-headed and Cretzschmar's buntings, and black-eared wheatears are common lower down, and rock nuthatches breed here and there. Falls of birds can occur in spring and autumn, and it is quite a good place to watch for passing raptors, cranes, and storks. Parties of alpine swifts often pass overhead, and they breed nearby.

Mt. Likavitos is right in the city; it can be walked up easily, or there is a cable car. Flowers of interest here include quite a few rock plants such as the composite *Phagnalon rupestre*, pitch trefoil, the common pink catchfly *Silene colorata*, tassel hyacinth, a notable dark purplish

vetch *Vicia villosa* variety *varia*, large Mediterranean spurge, and an undistinguished pale yellow crucifer that produces distinctive 'two-shield' fruits, giving rise to its name *Biscutella didyma*. There are also patches of the pretty cliff-dwelling bellflower, generally placed under *Campanula rupestris*. There are good views of migrant birds from here, and alpine swifts are always overhead in spring.

Nymphos Hill (with the Filapappou Monument at the top) lies just south of the Acropolis, and there are fine views across from it. In spring, there are masses of attractive flowers here; bushes of shrubby medick with its intriguing spiral fruits, white mignonette, a white deadnettle with white-edged leaves *Lamium moschatum*, a pretty, dark-blotched red poppy *Papaver apulum*, rocket, salsify, a white garlic *Allium neapolitanum*, and a white umbellifer *Tordylium apulum*, which produces rather attractive oval fruits, edged with a thickened crimped border. There are scattered trees of pines, carob, olives, and others. Overhead, there are always some or all of common swift, alpine swift, house martins, and swallows; serins and goldfinches sing from the trees, and Sardinian warblers call from the scrub. In early April 2000, we watched a male scarlet rosefinch singing here – a very rare occurrence in Greece, but it was presumably just passing through, though we saw it again in 2001. Butterflies include swallowtail, scarce swallowtail, painted lady, and wall brown.

The Acropolis hill has broadly similar flowers, plus giant fennel, the figwort *Scrophularia canina*, and the pretty blue stork's-bill *Erodium gruinum*. Alpine swifts are especially conspicuous here.

The Botanic Garden in central Athens is a pleasant place to walk, get away from the traffic, and see a few birds, though as a means of viewing some labelled Greek flowers, it is a serious disappointment.

Ophrys aesculapii

<small>SITE</small> 65 Mt. Giona

One of the major mountains of Greece, with a rich flora and fauna.
Grid reference: 38°37'N 22°15'E.

Mt. Giona is actually higher, at 2510 m, than its much more famous neighbour Mt. Parnassus (see p. 143), yet it is virtually unknown except locally, and amongst Greek climbers and walkers. It towers above the Mornos Valley to the west, where there is one of the highest and finest cliffs in Greece: the Plaka Cliff rises a sheer 1200–1300 m above the village of Sikia, on the west side of the mountain.

On the mountain, there are extensive forests of Greek fir, with patches of broad-leaved beech – eastern hornbeam forest, with maple. It is heavily grazed and there are large areas of pasture, as well as excessive scarring from the bauxite mining that is going on there. It is a beautiful mountain in parts, though sadly changed by the mining.

Lower down, there are noticeably more orchids than on Parnassus, including lady orchid, early purple, and naked man orchid.

Higher up, in the rocky limestone pastures and clearings, there is a rich flora including masses of crocuses early on: mainly *Crocus veluchensis* and *C. sieberi*, as on Parnassus, *Corydalis solida*, bellflowers such as *Campanula radicosa* and *C. tymphaea*, the crane's-bill *Geranium cinereum* subspecies *subcaulescens*, pinks, the curious catchfly *Silene roemeri* with its dense clusters of little creamy flowers, a very pretty perennial cushion bindweed *Convolvulus boissieri* subspecies *compactus*, *Alkanna graeca*, and many others. The large crane's-bill *Geranium macrorrhizum* grows amongst the limestone screes, and on high-altitude cliffs there are clumps of the pretty daphne *Daphne jasminea*, bellflowers including *Campanula aizoon* and *C. rupicola*, *Viola poetica*, and several saxifrages including *Saxifraga spruneri*, *S. graeca*, and *S. adscendens* subspecies *parnassica*. The cinquefoil

Geranium cinereum subspecies *subcaulescens*

Potentilla kionaea occurs here above 2000 m, and is endemic to Giona. Dwarf birch is locally common at high altitudes. Altogether, it is an impressive mixture of endemics, Balkan specialities, and more widespread flowers.

As you might expect, the forest clearings and high pastures are rich in butterflies, and the whole mountain is a noted bird site. One visitor records seeing seven golden eagles in the air together – an encouraging record (though becoming less and less likely now), and there are also short-toed eagles and peregrines. The high Plaka Cliff is a breeding site for griffon vultures and possibly lammergeiers still. In the woods, there are several species of woodpeckers, including black, middle-spotted, and white-backed, and eagle owls can be heard calling early in spring. The distinctive shore lark breeds in the high pastures, with a few snowfinches in similar habitats.

Access nowadays is quite easy, following the mining tracks from Kaloskopi to a considerable height. For keen walkers, there is also a good route from Sikia, on the west side.

Woodpeckers

Middle-spotted, great-spotted, and white-backed woodpeckers all occur here, and are rather similar. Great-spotted (adult) has just a small area of red at the back of the head, and two vertical white patches on its otherwise black back; white-backed (adult) is slightly larger, with a wholly red crown and transverse white barring on the back. Middle-spotted is the smallest of these three, with (adult) a red crown, and less black around the face and chest, giving a paler appearance. White-backed is most likely to be seen in old woodland with ancient trees.

66 Cape Sounion National Park

A small National Park south of Athens, on a limestone headland, with good flowers.
Grid reference: 37°35'N 24°00'E.

Cape Sounion lies at the extreme south of the peninsula on which Athens stands, lying about 45 km from the old airport. The core of the park is tiny – only 525 ha, though it has an outer buffer zone of 4250 ha. It is hard to think of it as a National Park in the European sense, as there is no information, no apparent conservation management, and little development control in the peripheral zone; it seems to exist mainly as an area of open land around the ruins of the fifth-century temple to Poseidon, which are both impressive and impressively sited.

Nonetheless, the area has a good flora and a few other features of interest, and is certainly worth a visit, especially in spring, or even late winter. The *phrygana* is dominated by spiny broom, spiny burnet, the thyme *Coridothymus capitatus*, spiny spurge, the pink sun-rose *Cistus creticus*, Jerusalem sage, and

The ancient temple at the core of the Cape Sounion National Park

mastic tree, amongst others. In open patches there is a rich flora, with masses of colourful flowers – crown anemones, tassel hyacinth, the dwarf iris *Iris pumila* subspecies *attica*, the yellow fenugreek *Trigonella balansae*, and the blue *T. coerulescens*, in addition to poppies, pink catchflies *Silene colorata*, and yellow cresses. It is quite a good area for orchids, including horseshoe, sawfly, both forms of yellow bee (*Ophrys lutea* subspecies *murbeckii* = *O. sicula*, and the darker *O. melena*), bumble bee, sombre, and the uncommon *O. attica*. The ruins themselves are clad with red valerian and stocks (though this varies according to the current herbicide policy).

In summer, there are other fine flowers such as *Convolvulus oleifolius*, the hollyhock relative *Althaea cannabina*, and the pretty shrubby St. John's-wort *Hypericum empetrifolium*. By autumn, there are cyclamens *Cyclamen hederifolium* and *C. graeca*, the delicate little white *Narcissus serotinus*, the lovely yellow *Sternbergia lutea*, and autumn

Yellow bee orchids

There are four members of the yellow bee orchid group in Greece. These used all to be forms or subspecies of *Ophrys lutea*, though now they are described as four separate species. *O. lutea* is the largest, with a lip 14–18 mm long, a broad yellow edge to the lip, and just a very short inverted brown 'V' at the tip of the lip. *O. phryganae* is the least well known of the group; the lip of each flower is held at an angle and the tip is turned up – an easy character to spot; it is also smaller than *lutea*. *O. melena* is easily recognized as the lip is virtually all brown, with just a faint yellow margin. Finally, *O. sicula* has the broad yellow edge of *lutea*, but smaller flowers (with the lip 13 mm long at most), and usually a more marked inverted brown 'V', reaching almost to the edge of the lip.

squill, together with a few crocuses such as *Crocus cartwrightianus*.

Other flowers recorded here include the knapweeds *Centaurea laureotica* and *C. attica* subspecies *asperula*, both endemic to the area, and the sainfoin *Onobrychis ebenoides*, the pink *Dianthus serratifolius*, and *Centaurea raphanina* subspecies *mixta* – all endemic to Greece.

It is not a key bird-watching site, with only a limited range of resident and breeding species. Sardinian warblers are common, with blue rock thrushes, common kestrels, a few Cretzschmar's buntings, and stonechats. At passage periods, there are often fine views of passing or settling birds of prey, including honey buzzards and Eleonora's falcons,

and it is a good place from which to watch the sea for dolphins and porpoises. There are Hermann's tortoises in small numbers, with green and wall lizards.

Cyclamen hederifolium

SITE 67 Springs of Louros

A spring-fed lake, with interesting butterflies and dragonflies.
Grid reference: 39°30'N 20°52'E.

The Louros River, which flows down into the Gulf of Amvrakikos (see p. 131) and contributes considerably to its delta habitats, is partly fed by the springs that issue at the 'Springs of Louros'. This is actually a little lake surrounded by trees, very deep and clear, fed by an abundant supply of clean spring water that overflows at a considerable rate to form part of the Louros. It is a popular 'beauty spot', with an EOT café just nearby. It is not a major wildlife site, and not worth making a large detour for, but it does form an oasis of green in an otherwise dry area, and has a few features of interest.

Kingfishers are resident and quite tame, and can often be watched sitting on a tree branch not too far away. The slopes fall away too steeply for the aquatic flora to be rich, but there are limited shallows around parts of the margin, with a few flowers of

Cardinal fritillary *Argynnis pandora*

interest. These form the emergence points for dragonflies, damselflies, and other insects such as emperor dragonfly, the attractive blue and black-banded hawker *Aeshna affinis*, brilliant emerald in its form *Somatochlora metallica meridionalis*, various darters and chasers, and a selection of damselflies such as beautiful demoiselle in its form *Calopteryx virgo* subspecies *festiva*, and *Lestes* species.

In high summer, when other habitats are becoming dry, the butterflies on the flowers around the margins can be marvellous, with cardinals and other fritillaries, masses of blues, skippers, and coppers, Cleopatra, brimstone, whites, and others on the mints and anything else with nectar. They tend to be quite approachable here, too, which makes photography easier. Bush-crickets and praying mantis are both frequent.

The site is sign-posted from the main Arta to Ioannina road, and lies only a kilometre from the main road, up a narrow lane.

SITE 68 Klissoura Gorge

An impressive limestone gorge, with good birds of prey.
Grid reference: 38°30'N 21°15'E.

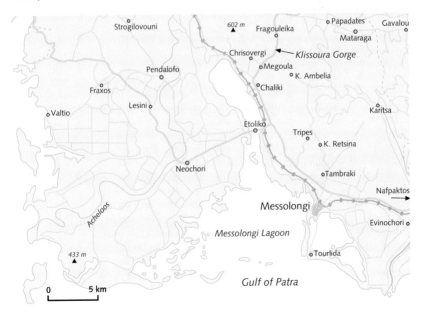

The Klissoura (or Klisura) Gorge lies just north of the Messolongi wetlands, and there is considerable ecological interchange between the two – birds of prey, in particular, from the gorge breeding sites feed over the marshes and lagoons, and the cliffs of the gorge provide safe roosting and breeding sites.

It is a spectacular gorge through limestone, with high steep cliffs; its tranquillity and interest is marred somewhat by the fact that the busy main road from Messolongi to Arta and Ioannina passes through the gorge, though this does make access easier.

The main breeding bird species here include a good colony of griffon vultures, which can be easily seen from the road or soaring overhead. Lesser spotted and short-toed eagles nest here or further into the Arakinthos Hills (which run south-east from here), and long-legged buzzards are frequent here, with more common species such as blue rock thrush, rock bunting, subalpine warbler, kestrel, and peregrine. Wallcreepers have been seen here in winter, and may breed, though the cliffs are generally rather dry.

The main E55/N5 gives direct access into the site, and tracks and paths can take you up the sides. The Arakinthos Hills rise to almost 1000 m and are of great interest, with some good cliffs and imposing rock features. There are minor roads into the hills from Kefalovrissi, or from further south near Messolongi, leading to Kato Retsina and beyond.

SITE 69 Mts Chelidon and Kaliakouda

Remote, well-wooded mountains, rich in flowers and butterflies.
Grid reference: 30°27'N 21°40'E.

South-west from Karpenissi, there is a long valley which climbs gradually into a mountainous area, with Mt. Chelidon (1975 m) to the west, Mt. Kaliakouda (2101 m) to the east, and the Panetoliko ridge (1757 m) at the head of the valley. The whole area is unspoilt and generally unvisited, with precipitous, unstable slopes, gorges, extensive forests – especially of Greek fir – and high, bare mountain-tops and screes. It is an area that would benefit from further exploration, and there is undoubtedly much more to be discovered.

Chelidon is an impressive, though not especially high, limestone mountain, with extensive forests and grassy, flowery clearings, topped with an alpine zone. Grazing pressure is relatively low here. In the forests, there is also juniper, hawthorn, a plum *Prunus cocomilia*, danewort, and other shrubs, and in higher clearings cowslips, early purple and lady orchids, downy woundwort, scabiouses, and other attractive flowers grow. However, the abiding memory from a late June visit (apart from the dramatic thunderstorms!) is the incredible quantity and diversity of butterflies. The combination of flowery limestone grassland, scrub, forest, warmth, and even some surface water, clearly suits a very wide range of species, including scarce and common swallowtails, grizzled skippers of various types, Cleopatra and

Arabis recta

brimstone, heaths, Balkan marbled whites, Apollo, lattice brown, several coppers including fiery, fritillaries such as lesser spotted and silver-washed, Grecian grayling, and several blues including zephyr, to name only a fraction. On the same flowers (especially thistles and danewort), there were clearwing moths and two species of burnet moth.

In the highest areas, there are unusual plants such as the umbellifer *Peucedanum longifolium*, a hawkbit *Leontodon hellenicus* growing in crevices in the hard limestone at up to 1900 m and endemic to here and Kaliakouda, a rare ragwort *Senecio scopolii*, the tall spindly *Delphinium fissum*, spring speedwell, and many others. In autumn, the little bulbous *Sternbergia colchiciflora* is quite frequent, together with a few autumn crocuses.

Mt. Kaliakouda is broadly similar, and shares many of the same flowers and butterflies. There is a rare vetch – *Vicia canescens* subspecies *serinica* – thought to be endemic to a small area in Italy, but recently discovered here, a little yellow Stars-of-Bethlehem *Gagea minima*, the cress *Arabis recta*, and another more widespread vetch *Vicia onobrychioides*, amongst many others. The clouded Apollo butterfly is quite frequently seen.

Birds have been relatively little recorded. Griffon vultures drift over periodically, but probably do not breed here. Short-toed eagles are not infrequent, and golden eagles can be seen occasionally, with the odd booted eagle and common buzzard. Eagle and tawny owls breed in the forests or on the cliffs, and both black and white-backed woodpeckers occur. Firecrests and coal tits are common in the forests, and blue rock thrushes call in rockier areas.

The southern part of the road that passes between Chelidon and Kaliakouda passes along and next to a fine gorge, where crag martins are abundant, alpine swifts chitter overhead, and rock nuthatches call from outcrops. It looks to be a good place for cliff-dwelling plants, too, but they are hard to get at.

Access into the area is easy via the minor road running south-west from Karpenissi to the monastery at Proussos. A poor road goes on beyond this, over Panetoliko, towards Thermos. A reasonable track goes most of the way up Chelidon from the village of Mikro Chorio, passing through stands of native horse-chestnut, and Kaliakouda can be reached by a track from Megalo Chorio. Mt. Oxia (1926 m) (which has good beech forests close to their southern limit) lies about 20 km to the east of Kaliakouda and can be reached via minor roads running south from near Karpenissi, heading for Stavli and climbing from there.

Aegean islands

Introduction

The Aegean epitomizes Greece: a huge
area of warm sea liberally scattered with
hundreds of islands of all sizes; perfect for
relaxing, swimming, sunbathing, and sail-
ing – an idyllic area. The Aegean can lay
claim to being almost wholly Greek in a
way that few other seas can be assigned to
any one country. The islands of Greece
spread eastwards right across the Aegean,
to within 2 km of Turkey at the closest, and
southwards until they meet the Libyan
Sea. This region covers a much greater
area than any other in the book, though of
course the land surfaces are much smaller.

The Aegean islands are grouped
roughly into named clusters: the Cyclades
(or Kiklades), which include Naxos,
Andros, and Mikonos, lying in the sea
south-east of the Athens peninsula; the
Dodecanese, which include all the far
south-east islands such as Kos, Samos,
and Rhodes; and the Sporades, which
form a small group north of Evvia. Other
islands such as Lesvos and Limnos do not
fall readily into any group.

The ecological associations of the islands
of the Aegean are complex. Clearly, the
intervening sea presents a considerable
barrier to the movement of most flowers,
insects, reptiles and amphibians, mammals, and even some birds. This naturally
means that some species, which may be
common elsewhere in Greece, do not occur
on some of the islands. On occasion this
gives other species the opportunity to fill
the gap and become more abundant than
in comparable situations on the mainland.
As the Aegean lies almost at the meeting
point of three continents – Europe, Asia,
and Africa – it is hardly surprising that the
species which have colonized the islands

Old forest on Rhodes

are of many kinds; the western islands have
mainly Greek and south European coloniz-
ing influences, while the islands along the
Turkish coast, such as Rhodes, Kos, and
Samos have quite distinct affinities with
Turkey, such as the presence of Comper's
orchid, Krüper's nuthatch, cinereous
bunting, and Persian squirrel on some or all
of these islands. The southernmost islands,
such as Rhodes, have clear influences from
Africa, too, as indicated by the eastern marbled skipper, which is essentially an African
butterfly, though the distance to Africa is
perhaps too great to allow many species to
have colonized directly.

The Aegean also served as a mild
refuge through the last glaciations, so that
many species have direct links with earlier eras. In most other parts of Europe
the majority of species are post ice-age
recolonizers.

Opposite page: **A Lesvos olive grove in spring, with peacock anemones and other flowers**

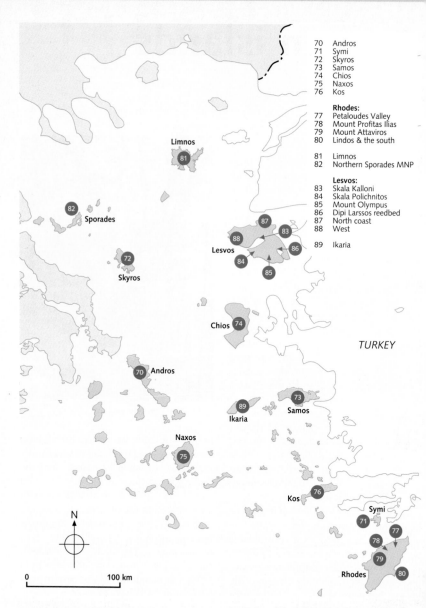

70   Andros
71   Symi
72   Skyros
73   Samos
74   Chios
75   Naxos
76   Kos

Rhodes:
77   Petaloudes Valley
78   Mount Profitas Ilias
79   Mount Attaviros
80   Lindos & the south

81   Limnos
82   Northern Sporades MNP

Lesvos:
83   Skala Kalloni
84   Skala Polichnitos
85   Mount Olympus
86   Dipi Larssos reedbed
87   North coast
88   West

89   Ikaria

On many of the Aegean islands, there are substantial mountains, often rising above 1000 m, such as Mt. Attaviros on Rhodes, Mt. Olympus on Lesvos, and – highest of them all – Mt. Kerkis on Samos, which reaches 1433 m. These have acted as especially isolated areas where species have continued to evolve undisturbed, often from long before the last ice age, gradually separating from their close relatives to become completely new species. There are endemic species, often with tiny populations, on many of the larger islands, and especially on the more mountainous ones. On the Aegean islands as a whole, 80 Greek endemic species of flowers occur, of which 36 are exclusive to the islands. The same process

Loggerhead turtle *Caretta caretta*

has happened with reptiles, especially lizards, and butterflies. No doubt it occurs in other invertebrate groups, too, though not enough work has been done to establish the full range.

Nowadays, the Aegean acts as something of a sanctuary in other ways, too, thanks to its low human population, and relatively low pollution and disturbance. The endangered monk seal finds its main European stronghold here, and other conspicuous vertebrates include loggerhead and green turtles (though, surprisingly, neither breeds here), and various cetaceans such as dolphins, porpoises, and pilot whales.

The climate is generally hot and dry through the long summers, and mild in the winters, especially in the more southerly parts. For most groups of species, a visit at some time between late March and early May is best, though the higher mountains can be visited a little later. Autumn is good for passage birds and some flowers, and winters are good for birds in the wetlands and a surprising number of flowers, such as snowdrops and crocuses.

^{SITE}70 Andros and adjacent islands

A group of islands in the northern Cyclades, with special breeding birds, endemic flowers, and good marine wildlife.

The islands of Andros, Tinos, Mikonos, and Siros form the northern Cyclades, close to the southernmost tip of Evvia. They are generally unspoilt, though well populated, and popular particularly amongst Greeks for holidays. Some parts, especially the more remote and mountainous areas, are good for birds and other wildlife.

North Siros (or Syros) is an important area for birds. It is largely unpopulated, with a rocky coastline that includes cliffs. Here there are breeding shags (an uncommon and shy bird in Greece, with probably no more than 400 resident pairs in the country), Bonelli's eagle, Eleonora's falcon (in good numbers), peregrine, Audouin's gull, and choughs. Cory's shearwaters breed on offshore islands, and small numbers of storm petrels are thought to occur. Inland, there are Rüppell's warblers, Cretzschmar's buntings, and other more widespread birds. Rollers used to breed, but seem to have disappeared, in keeping with their general decline in Greece.

It is a well-known area for passage migrants (as one might expect from the presence of large numbers of breeding Eleonora's falcons), with most of the smaller birds that one might expect, though the lack of good wetlands limits the range. Dalmatian pelicans and white-tailed eagles turn up, and Audouin's gulls winter here in small numbers.

Parts of the other islands have broadly similar habitats and many of the same birds, especially the north-east parts of Andros, Tinos, and Mikonos. The whole area still supports small numbers of monk seals, though they lack the protection of the Sporades.

There is an interesting pale blue bell-flower *Campanula sartorii* which is found only on Andros and Tinos, in rocky shady places on schists or limestone. It has no obvious close relatives, and is considered to be a pre-glacial survivor. Another endemic species, a yellow alison *Alyssum tenium*, is restricted to a few schist slopes around Tsimenas Oros in south-east Tinos. The St. John's-wort *Hypericum delphicum* occurs in a few mountain valleys on Andros.

SITE 71 Symi

A little island north-west of Rhodes, virtually unpopulated, with a rich flora.

Symi is a smallish, little-known island, with an area of about 57 square kilometres. It lies north-west of Rhodes, and within a few kilometres of the Turkish coast. It consists mainly of limestone, with hills reaching to 616 m at Mt. Vigla. The current population is about 3000, mainly living in the town of Symi (or Yialos-Horio), and there are large uncultivated areas with *garrigue* and woodland.

Symi, and its adjacent uninhabited islands, are important for coastal birds. There are good numbers of Eleonora's falcons here, breeding in autumn, with lesser kestrels, ravens, a few breeding Audouin's gulls, and both shearwaters (see p. 194), plus an abundance of common scrub species. As it is one of the less well-known islands, there are undoubtedly many more records to be made, especially at passage periods.

Spur-thighed tortoises are common, and Rhodes dragons occur in warm places. There are few snake species – cat snake, leopard snake and Ottoman viper – and very little in the way of ordinary lizards. Green toads breed here and there.

Botanically it is quite rich, though not exceptional. There are a few rarities, endemics, or eastern specialities here.

For example, the pretty little autumn-flowering *Biarum davisii* (a curious, yellowish-pink, flask-shaped relative of the arums) grows in some quantity (its only other area is in Crete, though the plants on Symi are sometimes treated as a separate Turkish subspecies), and the robust *Cyclamen persicum* can be found in spring in semi-shaded sites. There is only one plant endemic to Symi alone: the pink-flowered, shrubby marjoram relative *Origanum symes*, which occurs around Disalona Bay on the east side, just on one north-facing limestone cliff by the sea. There is also a white or pale purple cushion germander *Teucrium montbretii* subspecies *heliotropiifolium* which is found only in Symi, Karpathos, and a few places in Turkey.

Other plants of interest on Symi include the autumn-flowering *Narcissus serotinus*, an Aegean endemic crocus *Crocus tournefortii*, and several meadow saffrons *Colchicum* species, including the Rhodes-Symi endemics *C. balansae* and *C. macrophyllum*.

There is no airport at the time of writing, and access is by ferry from Rhodes town or Kos. There are places to stay on the island.

SITE
72 Skyros

*An isolated, medium-sized island in the Sporades, important for
seabirds, raptors, and rare flowers.*

Skyros is a largely unspoilt island,
shaped roughly like a dumbbell. The
northern section, around Mt. Olympus
(367 m), is rugged and unspoilt, while
the southern section is mountainous
and virtually unpopulated, rising to
772 m at Mt. Kochilas.

Eleonora's falcons breed in large numbers
around the cliffs and offshore islands, especially in the south, with at least 30 pairs
recorded, and – as usual – this reflects the
density of small and medium-sized birds
coming through on autumn passage.
Audouin's gulls have a strong breeding
colony in the north of the island (estimated
at about 55 birds in 1996), though the
colony is subject to disturbance from tourist
developments. Shearwaters can be regularly
seen just offshore, and probably breed, and
storm petrels may also occur. Cretzschmar's
buntings, Rüppell's and Orphean warblers,
and other small birds breed in the rocky *garrigue*. Monk seals may occur in small
numbers – Skyros is not far from their core
area in the North Sporades Marine Park.

On limestone cliffs on Skyros, especially
around Mt. Kochilas, there are several rare
or endemic flowers. *Aethionema retsina* is
a pinkish-white flowered, shrubby relative
of the more familiar burnt candytuft,

which only grows on cliffs near the sea
here and on Skiropoula, just to the west.
An aubrieta *Aubrieta scyria* with pale pink-
ish-violet flowers grows nearby, and is
endemic to here and one place on nearby
Evvia, and other plants found on or near
the same cliff system include the bellflower *Campanula merxmuelleri*, a yellow
viper's-grass *Scorzonera scyria*, and the
knapweed *Centaurea rechingeri*. The flora
of Mt. Kochilas is generally rich in addition to these endemics, making it an
important botanical locality.

Butterflies of interest recorded on
Skyros, mainly in the south, include the
orbed red-underwing skipper, Oriental
marbled skipper, and the lovely Cleopatra.

Access is by boat from Kimi on Evvia,
or from nearby islands.

Cleopatra *Gonepteryx cleopatra* (Peter Wilson)

SITE
73 Samos

A medium-sized mountainous island, noted for its flora and fauna.

Samos is a medium-sized island (covering just over 450 square kilometres)
which seems larger, thanks to its mountainous nature. It is extremely close to

Turkey (less than 2 km at the closest
point) and shares much with the mainland ecologically. Its extreme proximity to
Turkey does mean that military installa-

tions are prominent here. There are two main mountain ranges: in the west, Kerkis rises to 1433 m, the highest point on any Aegean island, and around the centre Ambelos rises to 1153 m, surmounting a large area of wooded hilly ground. Unfortunately, it was severely affected by fires in summer 2000, and it remains to be seen how it will recover.

Botanically, the island is rich and varied, with a diverse flora that includes several local endemics and a number of rarities in addition to a fine range of common species.

On Mt. Kerkis, at the western end of the island, there is an endemic, very spiny perennial knapweed *Centaurea xylobasis*, which is found on limestone rocks above 1200 m but nowhere else. It grows with cushions of the thrift relative *Acantholimon ulicinum* subspecies *ulicinum* covered in pink flowers, the yellow-flowered greenweed *Genista parnassica*, and other interesting plants. In limestone scree a little lower down the mountain there is an endemic annual, bluish-flowered larkspur *Consolida samia*, which again occurs nowhere else, and only about 100 plants are

Crocus olivieri

known from here. Another endemic on Kerkis is the little annual mayweed *Anthemis rosea* subspecies *rosea*, with reddish flowers, growing with *Aubrieta deltoidea*, a candytuft *Iberis spruneri*, and many other flowers. There is also an endemic reddish-blue grape-hyacinth *Muscari kerkis*, known only from pinewoods on Mt. Kerkis, where it is rare and threatened by recent fires.

Mt. Ambelos has its own special plants, too, including two rare orchids, *Comperia comperiana* and the white-flowered *Cephalanthera epipactioides*, both confined to a few Aegean islands within Greece (and eastwards into Turkey). There is also a rather striking leafy perennial, up to 3 m high with pinnate leaves, called *Datisca cannabina*, which grows here under Oriental planes and pines; elsewhere in Greece, it only occurs on Crete and Lesvos. Other plants of interest in the Ambelos locality include the snowdrop *Galanthus elwesii*, alpine squill, two fritillaries *Fritillaria bithynica* and *F. carica* subspecies *carica* (both endemic to the east Aegean), two crocuses: orange *Crocus olivieri* and bluish *C. cancellatus*, and a locally endemic gladiolus *Gladiolus anatolicus*.

Samos is an excellent place for orchids in general, with at least 60 species recorded. In addition to common species such as pyramidal orchid, and the two rarities already mentioned, the list includes red helleborine, Roman marsh orchid, violet limodore, and numerous *Ophrys* species such as *O. bremifera*, *O. candica*, *O. cornuta*, *O. episcopalis*, *O. heldreichii*, *O. icariensis* (a local endemic), *O. minutula* (an east Aegean endemic), King Ferdinand's orchid (or earwig orchid), horseshoe orchid, and mirror orchid. Other orchids include Provence, Anatolian, bug, holy, monkey, and loose-flowered, plus five species of *Serapias* (the tongue orchid genus).

Samos is a good place to see birds, though it is not as well known as other nearby islands, and its relative lack of wetlands makes watching more difficult. As with flowers, Mt. Kerkis is particularly good, with about 7000 ha recognized as being

Worm snake *Typhlops vermicularis*

important for birds, and partly protected as a Special Protection Area. There are breeding peregrine, honey buzzard, long-legged buzzard, short-toed eagles, and eagle owls in and around the forested areas, blue rock thrush and Rüppell's warblers in more open areas lower down, and the strikingly coloured rock thrush (not to be confused with blue rock thrush) and tawny pipit at the highest levels. Rock thrushes are rare as breeding birds on the islands, and have only quite recently been discovered on Samos.

There are limited areas of wetlands, especially in the south-east of the island, near the airport and further east at Alyki. Greater flamingos are here for much of the year, ruddy shelducks are regulars, and rollers still breed. In the nearby scrub and trees, there are masked shrikes, lesser grey shrikes, Cretzschmar's buntings, and a variety of warblers breeding. At passage periods, there is a similar range of birds to Chios or Kos, though they are not well known yet.

Samos has a fascinating range of reptiles and amphibians, lacking a few species because it is an island, but with others that suit its southerly location and proximity to Turkey. These include the striking agama or Rhodes dragon (see p. 204), which is quite common in the lowlands, the Anatolian lizard which is endemic to Samos and adjacent parts of Turkey, Balkan green lizard, the true Mediterranean chameleon (probably different from the Pylos species – see p. 248), Turkish gecko on walls and in houses, snake-eyed lizard (a rather inconspicuous lizard that lacks any obvious eyelids (hence the name); as one identification guide says, 'touch gently to check' whether it has eyelids or not), golden skink, worm snake, sand boa, Dahl's whip snake, Montpellier snake, and several others. The amphibians are more limited,

partly because there are few wetlands – just common and green toads, marsh frogs, and stripe-necked terrapins.

Butterflies are abundant on Samos, especially in flowery clearings in the mountain woods. There is one species that has its only European site on Samos – the orange-banded hairstreak, which occurs only in the open rocky limestone areas around the treeline on Karvouni and other mountains, above about 1000 m. It does not appear in all European butterfly books, partly because some books treat the far eastern islands as being within the Turkish biome; it seems to be characterized by its *absence* of orange, despite its name! Other butterflies here include the pretty eastern festoon, false Apollo, southern, scarce and common swallowtails, Cleopatra, southern white admiral, eastern rock grayling, Freyer's grayling, white-banded grayling, and a close relative of meadow browns, *Maniola telmessia*, which replaces meadow browns on most south-east Aegean islands.

Just to the west of Samos lie the Fourni islands. They are an important area for several species of birds, especially breeding Eleonora's falcons (with about 50 pairs), lesser kestrels, a small colony of Audouin's gulls, and breeding populations of both Cory's and Yelkouan (Mediterranean) shearwaters.

Samos can be reached by air from Athens, or by ferry from Piraeus and Chios. There is a ferry from Samos to Fourni.

Fritillaria bithynica

^{SITE}74 Chios

A mountainous island off the Turkish coast, with a rich flora and bird list.

Chios (or Hios) is an attractive and unspoilt island just off the coast of Turkey. It rises to 1297 m at Mt. Pelineo in the north, with other substantial mountains in the north and centre of the island. There are few marshes, permanent rivers, or forests, apart from a limited amount of pine and Greek fir forest.

Like Lesvos, Samos, and other islands, it shares much ecologically with Turkey, and there are species that are rare elsewhere in Greece, though it is not as well-recorded as Lesvos, particularly with respect to the birds, and there is probably much more to be discovered.

Breeding birds are of interest, especially in and around the northern mountains, where the few small wetland areas also occur, on the nearby coast. Cinereous bunting, which has its European stronghold in Lesvos (see p. 194) breeds in small numbers here (the only other known Greek breeding site is on Skyros), with no more than two or three pairs currently known. Rufous bush robins can be found in scrub and old river beds in small numbers, Orphean warblers breed in the *garrigue*, often giving themselves away by their almost thrush-like song, the masked shrike breeds in old olive groves, and rock spar-

rows can be found in rocky places. Two other uncommon buntings occur – ortolan and Cretzschmar's – though both are reasonably common here. On the island of Venetiko, an uninhabited rocky islet off the south coast, about 15 pairs of Eleonora's falcons breed, feeding off the abundant passage birds in autumn.

At migration periods vast numbers of birds pass through. To date 211 species of birds have been recorded on the island, of which about 100 are regular passage species. The number of species is pushed up, unfortunately, by records from the active trapping that goes on there. Red-backed shrikes are common (and a frequent target for trappers), with other shrikes, thrush nightingale, bee-eaters, collared flycatchers, rose-coloured starlings, rollers, short-toed larks and many warblers, hirundines, and other species. Rarities have included White's thrush, scarlet rosefinch, and rustic buntings on passage, and white-breasted kingfisher, probably straying in from Turkey. The small coastal wetlands, such as at Kontari (near the airport) and Volissos, attract waders and wildfowl on passage, and keep a few birds through the winter. The southern headlands are the best areas for seeing migrants, and there are often shearwaters offshore.

Botanically it is quite rich. Most of the rock is limestone, giving it a rather different character from Lesvos, and making it somewhat better for orchids. There are also a few complete endemics, and a number of flowers have their main population here.

Orchids are common. In open limestone *garrigue*, there is *Ophrys cornuta* and *O. heldreichii* (both related to woodcock orchids), sombre bee, yellow bee and the browner lesser yellow bee, sawfly, the striking *O. spruneri*, pyramidal, pink butterfly,

Crocus biflorus

and bug orchid, amongst others. There may be a few loose-flowered orchids hanging on in wet places, and in the uplands there are *Orchis anatolica*, the pale yellow spikes of Provence orchid under pines, sometimes growing close to violet limodores, giant orchid, tongue orchids, and others. The helleborine *Cephalanthera epipactioides*, with white-flowers, occurs here and there in open pine woods. It is one of the rarest of Greek orchids, with just a few east Aegean localities. Other plants of interest include the yellow-flowered, spring-flowering *Crocus olivieri* (with its distinctive six-branched style), a form of the bluish-white *C. biflorus*, sand-crocuses including *Romulea bulbocodium*, *R. ramiflora*, and *R. linaresii*, the pretty dwarf blue or yellow *Iris pumila* subspecies *attica*, snake's head or mourning iris, white-flowered *Gagea graeca*, the little bunch-flowered *Narcissus tazetta*, alpine squill near the summit of Pelineo, and many more. The greenish-yellow fritillary *Fritillaria pelinaea* grows on the western and north-eastern slopes of Mt. Pelineon above 500 m, under pines or maples around the villages of Spartounda and Vikio. It is rare here, especially after some recent fires, but grows nowhere else in the world. Other endemics or special rarities on Chios include Persian cyclamen; the slender, small-flowered bellflower *Campanula cymbalaria*, which has its only known Greek locality close to the top of Mt. Pelineon, where it was found in 1991

(it also occurs in Turkey); and a distinctive spiny red thistle *Cirsium steirolepis*, which is probably confined to north-central Chios.

It is also quite a good place for an autumn visit, with the beautiful *Sternbergia lutea*, the more sober *S. colchiciflora*, meadow saffron species such as *Colchicum variegatum*, and others.

Chios has an outstanding range of butterflies which includes the widespread species such as painted lady, clouded yellows, southern white admiral, two-tailed pasha, and small skipper; various eastern species such as eastern festoon, false Apollo, Kreuper's small white (with partly shaded under-wings, and occurring in wilder areas than small white, such as flowery limestone slopes), the attractively named grass jewel, eastern rock grayling, Oriental meadow brown, Balkan marbled white, inky skipper, Levantine skipper, and others; and one endemic, *Maniola chia*, so far known only from Chios and the adjacent island of Inousses. This actually looks and behaves remarkably like the common meadow brown *M. jurtina*, but is apparently distinct on minor morphological and chemical differences, and is easily distinguished in the field because common meadow brown is absent from Chios!

Access to Chios is by air from Athens or direct charter flights from north Europe; or by boat from nearby islands such as Lesvos or Samos.

75 Naxos

A smallish Aegean island, notable for its strong populations of several birds of prey.

Naxos lies at the eastern edge of the Cyclades group of islands. It is a smallish, oval-shaped island, with a backbone of mountains reaching to just over 1000 m at Mt. Zas (or Dias), with steep narrow gorges running down towards the sea. It is mainly

scrub-covered, though there are a few sections of pine forest and some holm oaks. It has remarkably strong populations of several large raptors, including some that are steadily becoming rare elsewhere. There is a colony of about a dozen pairs of griffon vultures, which range widely over the island. Long-legged buzzards (see p. 186) are resident here, with three or four pairs in the hills. Peregrines breed in the mountains, and there are several pairs of Eleonora's falcons breeding on the cliffs and on offshore islands. Bonelli's eagles still breed here (out of a total estimated Greek population of only about 50 pairs). On more open and scrub-covered hillsides,

Galanthus ikariae

there are Rüppell's warblers, Cretzschmar's buntings – both pleasantly common – and more widespread species, such as Sardinian warbler, little owl, and woodlark. Yelkouan and probably Cory's shearwaters both breed around the island, and can be seen offshore or from boats.

Naxos is also a well-known site for spectacular migration of birds, particularly in spring but also in autumn. There is a long list of recorded species, includ-

ing flycatchers such as collared, Isabelline wheatears, red-footed falcons, shrikes, and red-throated pipits.

Although it is not a classic botanical locality, there is plenty of interest, including a good range of orchids – such as man, dense-flowered, early spider, and *Orchis saccata* – and several rare species: the hare's ear *Bupleurum aira* grows here in its only two world localities in open scrub; the shrubby, yellow-flowered treacle mustard *Erysimum naxense* is endemic to Naxos, occurring on cliffs and scree in a number of small populations on Mts Zas, Koronos, and Faanari. A special snowdrop, *Galanthus ikariae*, is confined to Naxos and just a few other Aegean islands. It flowers in March in shady places in the mountains over about 500 m.

The butterflies are nothing special, though southern grayling and Lulworth skipper stand out from among the more widespread species here.

Access is by air or sea from Athens, and there are reasonable roads around the island.

76 **Kos**

An attractive, medium-sized island, with good birds, flowers, and other wildlife.

Kos is the second largest of the islands in the Dodecanese, about 40 km long but nowhere more than 10 km wide. It is not particularly mountainous, with extensive coastal plains and rolling fertile hills, though Mt. Dikios (846 m) in the southeast is a substantial landscape feature, and the highest mountain on the island. At the western end, Mt. Latra reaches 427 m, in an area of moderately wild country. It is only about 4 km from Turkey

at its closest point, so, like Rhodes and Lesvos, it has much in common with Turkey ecologically. Kos is a popular tourist destination, with several extensive coastal developments.

Mt. Dikios covers a substantial area of countryside, with extensive pine and cypress forests and large areas of scrub. By Kos standards it is relatively undisturbed, and is a particularly valuable refuge for birds of prey and other birds.

Breeding species include Bonelli's eagles, long-legged buzzard, peregrine, and both common and lesser kestrels, as well as more widespread scrub and cliff species such as black-eared wheatear, blue rock thrush, and a few Cretzschmar's buntings. Eleonora's falcons feed here in summer, then move to breed on smaller islands nearby. Black woodpeckers have recently been recorded in Kos's forests.

On the central north coast, west of Tingaki, there are several wetlands of interest including Lakes Psalidi and Alyki, which have reedbeds, saltmarsh, brackish lagoons, and *garrigue*. They are an important breeding area for ruddy shelduck and a few other wetland birds such as black-winged stilt and little bittern, with breeding wetland-edge species such as fan-tailed warbler, stone curlew, and tawny pipit. The wetlands are especially good for passage migrants such as waders. The very rare slender-billed curlew and broad-billed sandpiper can both turn up at times in very small numbers, and red-breasted geese are occasional visitors. Greater flamingos pass the winter on the main lagoon at Alyki, sometimes in gatherings of several hundred. Birds of prey include red-footed falcons on passage (in abundance some years), osprey, lesser spotted eagle, and pallid harrier.

At passage periods virtually the whole island can be of interest, especially the coastal wetlands and scrub. Almost anything can turn up, and likely visitors include several species of flycatcher, warblers, buntings, wagtails, terns, all the hirundines, several shrikes, and many more. The very rare bimaculated lark was spotted recently – an indication of the possibilities.

Botanically, Kos is interesting but not exceptional. There are very few plants that are confined solely to Kos, but quite a number of Aegean or east Greek endemics occur here, and a good range of orchids. Some of the special flowers include a species of dutchman's pipe

Aristolochia hirta, the multi-coloured, shrubby *Lithodora hispidula* subspecies *hispidula*, a bellflower *Campanula lyrata*, the distinctive stonecrop relative *Rosularia serrata* on cliffs, and *Quercus aucheri*, a very local species of oak (confined to the east Aegean and adjacent Turkey). Orchids of interest include the rare *Cephalanthera epipactioides*, the east Aegean endemic *Ophrys calypsus* (a slightly contentious version of late spider orchid), and various other *Ophrys* species including *O. candica*, *O. cornuta*, *O. mammosa*, and *O. heldreichii*, with about 35 species in all.

The agama or Rhodes dragon (see p. 204) is quite common at the western end of the island, and other reptiles of interest include Kotschy's gecko, spur-thighed tortoise, golden skink, snake-eyed lizard, European glass lizard, sand boa (see p. 254), and the venomous, though generally unaggressive, Ottoman viper.

Rhodes

Rhodes is one of the larger Greek islands (after Crete, Evvia, and Lesvos), roughly 80 km long and up to 30 km wide. Although it has a higher peak than Lesvos (Mt. Attaviros, 1215 m), it is generally much less rugged and hilly, though there are still substantial areas of wild habitat, especially pine woods and *garrigue*. It is the most south-easterly part of Greece, lying much closer to Turkey than mainland Greece, and has a warm, mild climate where spring comes early. To some extent its wildlife reflects its geographical position, and there are a number of essentially eastern or Turkish species that occur here, plus a few endemics found nowhere else. Geologically, it consists mainly of limestone, especially in the mountain regions, and softer sedimentary rocks. Although it is a popular holiday destination, the areas away from the tourist centres, especially in spring, are remarkably quiet and there are large, unspoilt areas.

Aegean Islands

Petaloudes Valley

*A small valley in the hills south-west of Rhodes town, known as
'butterfly valley', but interesting for other forms of wildlife, too.*

Jersey tiger moth *Euplagia quadripunctaria*

Petaloudes, or 'Butterfly Valley' as it is
more often known, has become a popular tourist attraction on Rhodes. In high
summer, literally millions of Jersey tiger
moths (not butterflies at all, but they are
brightly coloured and day-flying, so the
name is not surprising) gather in the
valley to aestivate (that is, pass the
hottest period of summer in a state of
rest). The valley is steep-sided and shady,
and there are permanent springs, providing a constant humid environment at a

time when the rest of the area is parched.
It is thought that the moths come from
all over Rhodes, and probably from adjacent parts of Turkey, to this one suitable
place. It is a remarkable sight, but it
unfortunately happens in summer when
the other wildlife features of Rhodes are
at their dullest, and the valley does
become very busy. It seems likely that the
excessive use of the site, and the not
infrequent disturbance of the moths to
make them fly up in clouds to create a
more impressive spectacle, is causing the
site to deteriorate.

It is quite an interesting locality for
other reasons. The woodlands are partly
composed of *Liquidambar orientalis* – a
Turkish tree that just reaches into Greece
here; like other liquidambars, it has
superb autumn colours. Other trees
include eastern and common strawberry-
trees, storax, covered in masses of
beautiful white flowers in spring, an
endemic bladder senna *Colutea insularis*,

Storax *Styrax officinalis*

A 'cornfield' near Petaloudes, full of *Gladiolus italicus* and crown daisies

Oriental plane, azarole, bay, Valonia oaks, and other interesting species. Violet limodores grow under Aleppo pines, and there are endemic, pale-coloured cyclamens *Cyclamen repandum* subspecies *rhodense*, and the more robust, deeper-coloured *C. persicum* is also found occasionally. The latter species does not occur in Iran, despite its name, but is an eastern Mediterranean species that just reaches into Greece on a few Aegean islands. Other flowers of interest in and around butterfly valley include Mediterranean orchid, woodcock orchid, giant orchid, small-flowered tongue orchid and the little pinkish *Orchis anatolica* (another primarily Turkish species), the endemic bellflower *Campanula rhodense*, ground-pine as its eastern subspecies, the pretty toadflax *Linaria pelisseriana*, and the curious little corn salad with bladder-like fruits *Valerianella vesicaria*. It is actually quite a good (though not exceptional) area for butterflies, including brimstone, Cleopatra, clouded yellow, Berger's clouded yellow,

eastern wood white, and scarce and common swallowtails.

Access is easy, with good roads signposted from the main northern or southern roads, and ample parking with cafés.

Bongardia chrysogonum

Aegean Islands

78 Mt. Profitas Ilias

The second highest mountain on Rhodes, with an extremely rich flora including several Rhodes specialities.

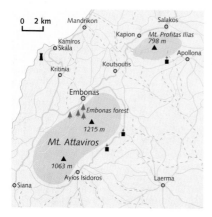

Ophrys heldreichii

Although not very high (798 m), the mountain of Profitas Ilias, lying just north-west of the town of Apollona, has a very rich flora in an unspoilt environment. It is largely wooded with Calabrian pines and cypresses *Cupressus sempervirens*, forming an attractive, old open woodland with masses of flowers below. Cyclamens are abundant, mainly *Cyclamen repandum* subspecies *rhodia* in drifts, but with a few *C. persica*. The rare and beautiful endemic white peony is quite common in the woods, flowering from late April through May. It is a subspecies of *Paeonia clusii* – the species that also grows on Crete as a different subspecies. The pretty blue or

white flowers of *Anemone blanda* are common, and there are masses of orchids: pale yellow spikes of Provence orchids, clumps of white Mediterranean orchid, pink butterfly, man, pyramidal, milky, green-winged, and woodcock orchids (in the strikingly coloured *Ophrys heldreichii* form); the greenish-pink spikes of *O. saccata*, and the various species of spider and bee orchids: *O. reinholdii* with two white diamonds on the lip, *O. candica*, a form of late spider orchid with a rather swollen lip, horseshoe orchid with its distinctive horseshoe (on some specimens), sombre bee orchid, and forms of yellow bee orchid. In places, usually on the lower slopes, violet limodores are extremely abundant, sometimes growing in hundreds under pines, and the pretty *Orchis anatolica* is common

Paeonia clusii **subspecies** *rhodia*

Masses of endemic cyclamen in mixed pine and cypress forest on Profitas Ilias

here and there. Other flowers occurring on and around the mountain include mandrake, Greek Star-of-Bethlehem, fine forms of lesser celandine, friar's cowl, a sand-crocus *Romulea linaresii*, crown anemones, and just occasionally the rather inconspicuous yellowish-green endemic fritillary *Fritillaria rhodia*. In early autumn *Colchicum macrophyllum* flowers, followed by *Muscari parviflorum* and *Crocus boryi*.

On a few north-facing limestone cliffs, there are some very rare plants: the spikes of a bellflower relative *Asyneuma giganteum*, reaching over a metre tall in places,

clumps of an endemic, pale-yellow flowered knapweed *Centaurea lactucifolia*, a bellflower *Campanula hagielia*, and the shrubby cress *Erysimum rhodium*. The rare Comper's orchid and the helleborine *Cephalanthera epipactioides* have both been recorded not far away. Both are essentially Turkish species.

Although it is probably best as a botanical site, there are many other notable features on and around Profitas Ilias, and almost anyone who visits it describes finding the need to go back several times! The flowery clearings and sunny slopes are quite good for butterflies – eastern festoons are easy to find in spring, with orange tips and over-wintered species such as brimstones and red admirals, followed by a series of blues, hairstreaks, swallowtails, fritillaries, and others, though rarely in great abundance. False Apollos can be found occasionally (though they look far more like festoons than Apollos!).

Romulea linaresii

Agama lizards (see p. 204) are common on the lower, warmer slopes and snakes, such as Balkan whip snake and grass snake, are not infrequent.

Birds of interest here include abundant singing and displaying woodlarks, cuckoos, common buzzards, and long-legged buzzards (which are probably more common on Rhodes as breeding birds than anywhere else in Greece), kestrels, and possibly lanner falcons.

Honey buzzards are summer visitors to Rhodes. They are more slender than either of the other buzzards, with a thinner tail, very small head, and thin neck. The wings are narrower, with a definite pinched appearance, and there are well-marked, thick dark bars at either end of the tail. Rough-legged buzzards, which breed in Russia and Scandinavia, pass through at passage periods. They most resemble common buzzards, but have a

Buzzards

Both common and long-legged buzzards are frequent in Rhodes, resident throughout the year. They are rather similar birds, and both are very variable, though there are a few consistent differences. Long-legged buzzards are distinctly more reddish, especially noticeable in flight, and they have an unbarred, rusty-coloured tail in contrast to common buzzard's black-and-white barred tail. Immature long-legged buzzards are rather darker, with a slightly barred rufous tail. Long-legged are a little larger than common buzzards.

pale breast and dark belly (usually the other way round in common buzzard), and a heavy, dark, terminal tail band. They often hover in search of food.

Long-legged buzzard *Buteo rufinus*

---

79 Mt. Attaviros

The highest mountain on Rhodes, mainly bare on the south side, with fine cypress forests on the north side. The whole site is good for flowers.

Mt. Attaviros is an impressive limestone mountain, reaching to 1215 m. The south side rises up sharply from the surroundings, and looks almost entirely bare from a distance. On the north side there is an extensive area of natural forest, 135 ha of which is preserved as a 'protected monument of nature'. These forests are

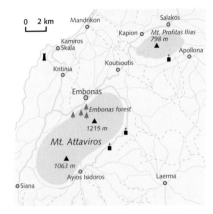

perhaps because they are denser, with fewer flowery clearings. There are small amounts of Provence orchid, Mediterranean orchid, Rhodes cyclamen, and *Anemone blanda*, with the unusual relative of wall pennywort, *Rosularia serrata*, on shady rocks and cliffs. This resembles a wall pennywort, except that it has a distinctive rosette of leaves and small, reddish-purple flowers; within Greece it is confined to Crete and the east Aegean. The rare orchid *Cephalanthera epipactioides* also occurs here sparsely.

The south side of the mountain, with its abundance of open limestone habitats, is rich in orchids, though access is not very easy. Species recorded here include green-winged orchid (as *Orchis picta*), the pink *O. anatolica*, pyramidal, naked man, pink butterfly, and giant orchids, with the following *Ophrys* species: horseshoe, *O. reinholdii*, *O. strausii*, *O. candica*, yellow bee, lesser yellow bee, and others. The very local *O. rhodia* (recently split off from the more widespread *O. umbilicata*) grows here

remnants of the natural forests which covered much of Rhodes, and elsewhere, after the last ice age; they consist mainly of cypresses *Cupressus sempervirens* variety *horizontalis* (a rare species in Greece, confined to a few southern islands) and *Pinus brutia*. Despite the nominal protection they are still subject to some grazing, though felling appears to have ceased.

For some reason these forests are not as species-rich as those of Profitas Ilias,

The protected coniferous forest of Embonas, on the north slopes of Attaviros

and there on the lower slopes, though its distribution is very patchy. Incidentally, despite its name it is not endemic to Rhodes, and has also been found in Cyprus and Karpathos.

Cretzschmar's buntings breed here, and short-toed eagles and long-legged buzzards can often be seen overhead. Amongst the butterflies, there is an interesting form of the rare white-banded grayling Aegean subspecies, known as *Pseudochazara anthelea* subspecies *anthelea* variety *atavirensis*.

The forest can easily be reached by following the road west from Embonas, and a road roughly encircles the mountain. There is a path to the summit from Embonas.

SITE
80 Lindos and the south

The hottest and driest part of Rhodes, with a North African or Middle Eastern feel to the wildlife.

Lindos itself is a fascinating little town, of Moorish appearance, with a striking acropolis on the hill that towers above it to the seaward. It makes an excellent base for exploring the south and centre of the island, and there is plenty to see around the town. The acropolis is well worth a visit, not only for itself, but for the views it affords: there are agama lizards (see p. 204) everywhere, and a substantial colony of lesser kestrels on the adjacent cliffs, which can be watched at close range from every angle. Alpine swifts race overhead in large groups, blue rock thrushes sing from crags, and the views down to the sea and along the coast are dramatic. Scops owls are common in the town, and they can usually be heard, and occasionally seen at close quarters, when eating out in the town's restaurants. The walls

Earwig orchid *Ophrys regis-fernandii*

of the acropolis have flowers such as the yellow henbane *Hyoscyamus albus*, the lovely bellflower which is a form of *Campanula rupestris* known as *C. hagielia*, the stocks *Malcolmia chia* and *Matthiola tricuspidata*, squirting cucumber, the annual bellflower *Campanula rhodensis* (an endemic relative of the widespread annual *C. drabifolia*, but with larger flowers), the red-flowered, shrubby composite *Ptilostemon chamaepeuce*, *Rosularia serrata*, and a pretty everlasting *Helichrysum orientale*, with yellow flow-

Campanula rhodensis

The striking town of Lindos, with its ancient acropolis

ers. The turban buttercup occurs around Lindos, mainly in yellow and white forms; the striking poppy-red form still turns up occasionally, but it is much rarer.

Southwards from Lindos the island is surprisingly wild and unspoilt, presumably because it is furthest from the airport and port. There are extensive beaches and dunes, and large areas of flowery *garrigue*. Both loggerhead and green turtles can occur all around this coast, though neither is known to breed here – loggerheads breed mainly west of here, while green turtles breed eastwards from Rhodes. The warm southern scrub and sandy areas are good for orchids, including a few that are rare further north. Perhaps the most unusual is King Ferdinand's orchid (or earwig orchid!), which is closely related to the mirror orchid but quite distinctly different with its very slender, almost tubular, lip. It is endemic to a few islands in the eastern Aegean and adjacent Turkey, and south Rhodes is one of its main strongholds. A good place for it is around Plymiri Beach, where one can also find bug orchid, holy orchid, pyramidal orchid, a rare relative of the sombre bee orchid known as *Ophrys funerea* (formerly *O. fusca* subspecies *funerea*), tongue orchids

such as *Serapias cordigera* and *S. parviflora*, and others. In the scrub, there is spiny *Teucrium brevifolium*, a spiny greenweed *Genista acanthoclada*, a little yellow flax *Linum trigynum*, the pink mallow *Malva aegyptiaca*, a grape-hyacinth *Muscari weissii*, various plantains including the silky *Plantago bellardii*, red turban buttercups, sun-roses, including *Cistus creticus* and *C. parviflorus* with their close relative *Fumana arabica*. On the beach itself, there are sea medicks, the pretty little rayless *Anthemis rigida*, sea rocket, stocks, *Hypecoum procumbens*, the pink cress *Erucaria hispanica*, and sea holly. This general pattern is repeated around the southern part of the coast. Inland, such as in the hills to the north of Kattavia, there is some really striking flowery *garrigue*, in wild country dominated by *Cistus* bushes covered in flowers, the shrubby, yellow-flowered *Anthyllis hermanniae*, the spiny, yellow-flowered *Genista acanthoclada*, with endemic bladder senna, various *Astragalus* species and others – a striking mixture in April.

This southern part has an interesting bird fauna. Chukars (the eastern equivalent of rock partridge), little owls, nightjars, short-toed larks, woodlarks,

red-rumped swallows, rufous bush robins, black-eared and possibly Isabelline wheatears, Orphean warblers, woodchat shrikes, and Cretzschmar's and black-headed buntings all breed here. At passage periods small birds can become abundant in shrubby areas, and waders at marshy pools around the coast. It is not a great locality for butterflies, though

Ophrys reinholdii

there are a few interesting species including eastern festoon, powdered brimstone (very similar to brimstone, but generally yellower underneath rather than green (males only), feeding on Christ's thorn), possibly the tiny little grass jewel, Loew's blue, eastern rock grayling, Oriental meadow brown, the eastern marbled skipper (a mainly African species), Levantine skipper, and pygmy skipper, amongst the more common species.

Inland from Lardos to Laerma, and eventually on to Apollonia where it merges with Mt. Attaviros, there is a splendid area of rolling hilly country, with extensive Calabrian pine woods interspersed with olive groves, small fields, *garrigue*, rough grassy areas, seasonal streams, and even a few wetlands (which usually dry up by the end of spring). It covers a very large expanse with a low population density, and has probably never been fully explored. In marshy

areas along the roadside, there are masses of loose-flowered orchids in places, with *Ophrys reinholdii*, bumble bee, late spider in the form known as *O. candida*, the woodcock orchid in a rather confusing mixture of forms that extend into all of *O. scolopax*, *O. heldreichii*, and *O. cornuta*, tongue orchids such as *Serapias bergonii*, crown anemones, the yellow restharrow *Ononis natrix*, and much else. Marsh frogs and green toads both breed here. The arable fields are often rich in special weeds such as Venus' looking-glass, wild gladiolus, shepherd's needle, blue woodruff, and tassel hyacinth. The pine woods have their own flowers such as Provence, sombre, naked man, horseshoe, and other orchids; the less-common gladiolus *Gladiolus illyricus*, sun-roses, and heathers. The birds do not seem to be special here, though there is enough habitat to make the area worth exploring more fully and there is undoubtedly much more to be discovered.

There is easy access into most of the areas mentioned, especially via the coast road from Lindos to Kattavia, and on the road from Lardos to Laerma, which is partly surfaced. The road from Kattavia to Messanagros is passable but rough, giving access to some lovely wild countryside.

Arum dioscoridis

SITE
81 Limnos

A large isolated island in the north Aegean Sea, with some important ornithological areas.

Limnos is one of the larger Aegean islands, little known outside Greece and not yet seriously affected by tourism. Overall, it is much less hilly than islands such as Lesvos and Rhodes, with few hills reaching over 300 m, and the highest point a mere 355 m. It is not noted for its

flowers – though there are the usual good displays of widespread species in spring – but is best-known for a complex of coastal wetlands on the east side.

About 14 000 ha have been noted as an important area for birds, though most of this has no protection. The habitats include extensive saltmarshes, brackish and freshwater marshes, reedbeds, and sand flats. The non-tidal wetlands tend to be wet only in winter and spring, drying out by about June. The main site is the lagoon of Alyki, on the north-east peninsula, and other habitats spread south-west from here to the Moudros Gulf. Noteworthy breeding species here include a few ruddy shelduck (recently estimated at four pairs), avocets, stone curlew, black-winged stilts, and fan-tailed warblers. Up to 5000 greater flamingos have been recorded on Alyki Lagoon in winter, when there are also masses of shelduck and other waterfowl. At passage periods, there are waders such as wood and green sandpiper, terns, and duck including ferruginous. The few fragments of woodland attract other species such as flycatchers on passage.

In general, the island supports good numbers of lesser kestrel, and a recent survey has shown that there are strong populations of Audouin's gull and Eleonora's falcon on cliffs and islets around Limnos.

Access to Limnos is by air from Athens or Lesvos, or by sea from Kavala or adjacent islands.

SITE 82 Northern Sporades Marine National Park

Greece's first Marine National Park, set aside as a pristine area for the protection of monk seals and other specialized wildlife.

The Alonissos–Northern Sporades Marine National Park lies in the northern Aegean Sea; the closest adjacent islands are Skopelos and Skiathos to the west, with the closest mainland – the Mt. Pilion peninsula – just west again. It was set up as a sea park in 1986, and declared a marine National Park in 1992, the first in Greece. The park covers an area of sea and a group of islands, one inhabited (Alonissos), six smaller islands, and a couple of dozen islets. It falls into two areas: the more strictly protected Zone A, which covers 1578 square kilometres, and the 678 square kilometres of Zone B, which includes the inhabited area. Piperi Island, in the east of Zone A, is the nucleus of the park, a former monument of nature and a special place.

The islands are all of limestone and consist mainly of low hills, rising to a maximum of 570 m on Gioura Island, with rocky slopes and inlets, and a series of caves which provide the base for the monk seal population. It is a very beauti-

Kotschy's gecko *Cyrtodactylus kotschyi*

ful and unspoilt area, with a wealth of marine and island wildlife.

On the largest island, Alonissos, there are Aleppo pine forests, and scrub with Phoenician juniper, strawberry-tree, mastic tree, tree heather, kermes and holm oaks, Mediterranean buckthorn, and others. Most of the smaller islands are dominated by scrub or open limestone habitats, though on Piperi there are extensive pine forests covering about 60% of the island.

The park was established mainly to give a protected area for the monk seal. This is an extremely rare mammal, for which the Aegean is its European stronghold, and the park now forms its core area. There are presently thought to be about 30 adults in the park, with a reasonably strong breeding success; outside protected areas, the monk seal is subject to so many pressures – being killed by fishermen, dynamite fishing, pollution, disturbance, and injury by boats – that the population has been steadily declining for years. It is hoped that the better protection of the park, together with the establishment of a network of reserves across the Aegean, will promote its recovery. Monk seals are dark brown, with a white patch below, but since there

are no other seal species normally found in the Aegean it is unlikely to be confused with anything else. It breeds mainly in caves, often those that only have underwater entrances, and has become mainly nocturnal, although it is believed to be essentially a daylight-loving creature more suited to pupping on open sandy beaches; disturbance and hunting have forced it to alter its habitats, though these may change again within better-protected areas.

However, monk seals are by no means the only interesting creatures within the park. Gioura has a population of about 500 wild goats, similar to the kri-kri of Crete but differing in minor details. There are over 300 species of fishes recorded, and a good range of cetaceans: common dolphin, striped dolphin, long-finned pilot whale, sperm whale, and very occasionally the killer whale (which is actually a large dolphin). Reptiles of interest include Erhard's wall lizard (the commonest lizard here, and food for several birds of prey), cat snake, smooth snake, and the intriguing little Kotschy's gecko.

It is also a very important area for birds. About 80 species have been recorded – not a long list by mainland standards, but it includes good populations of a number of rare species. Of these, Eleonora's falcon is perhaps the most conspicuous. They are positively common as a breeding bird around the islands, with at least 200 pairs within the park (one estimate suggests that there are 3000 pairs, including up to 400 on Piperi alone, but this seems unlikely). They arrive in early summer and breed in late summer and through the autumn, feeding on birds migrating southwards. This is an indication of the abundance of suitable migrant birds here, though records are still sparse. Other birds of prey include Bonelli's eagle, peregrine, common buzzard, and lesser kestrels. The rare Audouin's gull breeds on the islands in reasonable numbers, with at least 50 pairs concentrated around the northern islets and Piperi. Cory's shearwaters are summer visitors to breed on the islands, and Mediterranean (yelkouan) shearwaters are resident in large numbers. Other birds of interest include breeding rock nuthatches, crag martins, alpine swifts, olivaceous and olive-tree warblers, together with large numbers of birds at passage periods.

The whole area is of interest botanically. In addition to the usual displays of spring flowers, there are a number of rare or endemic species spread over most of the islands. The rare mespil *Amelanchier chelmea* occurs in small quantity on Gioura from sea level up to the top of the hills; its

occurrence here is rather curious, as in its few other localities (e.g. Mt. Chelmos – see p. 236) it is a mountain tree, growing only above about 1200 m. There are a number of special chasmophytes here (i.e. plants growing on cliffs) including the bellflower *Campanula reiseri*, confined to cliffs on Gioura and Kiri Panagia, *C. rechingeri*, *C. chalcidica*, the flax *Linum gyaricum*, and the little sandwort *Arenaria phitosiana*, whose only known world population, consisting of about 100 plants, occurs on a sea cliff on Gioura. Other plants of interest known from the islands include a scabious *Scabiosa hymetta* (a Greek endemic), a treacle mustard *Erysimum senoneri* (endemic to the Aegean), the yellow composite *Inula limonella*, a knapweed *Centaurea rechingerii* (endemic to the area), a dwarf, dark-purplish fritillary *Fritillaria sporadum*, known only from scattered populations on Gioura and Kyra Panagia, a fine bellflower relative *Symphyandra sporadum* (endemic to the Aegean area), and the thyme relative *Satureja athoa*.

An integrated management plan is being drawn up for the park in conjunction with the local people and non-governmental organizations such as the Monk Seal Protection Society, and the Greek government has made public pledges with regard to its protection, so there is reasonable hope for its future, though plenty of problems and conflicts remain.

Access is not particularly easy, though it is possible to fly from Gatwick to Skiathos (in summer only) then transfer by hydrofoil to Alonissos. There are regular boats to Alonissos from Aghios Konstantinos in the Lamia Gulf, Volos, or Kimi on Evvia. Movement within the less-protected Zone B is generally unrestricted, though access to the islands in the core of the park is more tightly controlled. For example, Piperi Island is viewed as sacrosanct, and no landing or even close approach is permitted. However, close approach to, and limited landing on, Kyra Panagia, Gioura, Psathoura, and Skantzoura is permitted. They are all uninhabited, but there are historic monuments such as restored monasteries and limited

Cory's shearwater *Calonectris diomedea*

Shearwaters

Two species occur in Greek waters, and both are common within the park area. Cory's shearwater is much the larger, with a wingspan of over a metre, and a rather front-heavy appearance. It is brownish-grey above, much paler than the Mediterranean yelkouan, with a dark tail bar, and almost pure white below except for dark wing margins and tips. The yelkouan shearwater has a wingspan of about 80 cm; it is very dark brown above, and dirty grey below rather than pure white. At close quarters, the dark bill of the yelkouan can be distinguished from the yellowish-black tipped Cory's bill. Cory's shearwaters are summer visitors only.

facilities. Arrangements can easily be made in the port at Alonissos.

Lesvos

Lesvos (also often written as Lesbos) is the second or third largest of the Greek islands, after Crete and Evvia (which is not always viewed as an island), and is twice the size of Corfu, which is much better known. It lies in the eastern Aegean, less than 10 km from the Turkish mainland but about 200 km from the closest part of

mainland Greece, so it is little surprise that its natural life is as much Turkish and Asian as Greek, with species such as Comper's orchid, Persian squirrel, and Krüper's nuthatch. It is a rugged island, with mountains reaching almost to 1000 m in both the north and south, and large areas of wild, middle-altitude hills in between. Unlike most Greek islands, the predominant rocks are not limestone but mainly volcanic, with a tendency towards more acid soil. This restricts the flora slightly, and certainly limits the number of orchid species, but it has given rise to a beautiful and varied landscape with many features of interest. Olive growing is the predominant land use, and there are said to be 11 million olive trees on the island, accounting for about 25% of Greece's olive production. From the wildlife point of view, this could be a great disappointment if the olive groves were like the most highly managed of those on Crete or in Spain; but in practice, the olive groves make up a huge wildlife resource, more like the cork oak *dehesa* of western Iberia, rich in flowers, breeding birds, and mammals, in a landscape of great charm.

Although the following pages pick out a number of sites considered to be of particular appeal, especially wetland areas where there are good concentrations of birds, it is fair to say that almost all parts of Lesvos are of interest to the naturalist, and there is plenty more waiting to be discovered.

SITE 83 Skala Kalloni

The northern part of the Kallonis Gulf, which is noticeably rich in birds and other wetland species.

The area around the small coastal village of Skala Kalloni, at the head of the Kallonis Gulf, has become well known in recent years, especially through Richard Brooks' excellent books on bird-watching

on Lesvos (see further reading) as a prime ornithological site where birds can be watched easily, often at close quarters. There is a fine combination of relatively unspoilt coastal and wetland habitats

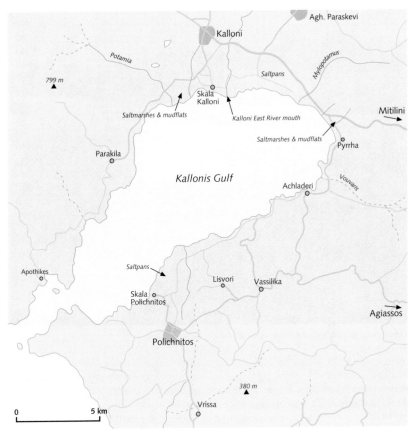

which collectively attract large numbers of birds (though sadly, even in this quiet island, where green tourism is of great importance, there is destruction and loss of habitat taking place continually).

Within the village there is the substantial freshwater Kalloni Pool, which contains water through the winter and spring up until about early July, depending on the season. Although small, it attracts considerable numbers of birds which can easily be watched from the surrounding paths and roads: breeding birds include black-winged stilt, garganey, and avocet, though its main interest is for migrants and wintering birds. In spring, there are usually glossy ibis, most herons including squacco, night, purple, and grey, little bittern, white stork, ferruginous duck, Montagu's

and marsh harriers, little and Temminck's stints, curlew sandpiper, wood sandpiper, occasional spur-winged plovers, various terns, masses of hirundines, and many more. Autumn is generally less good, as the availability of water is more unpredictable at the main passage period, but many similar species can turn up if it is wet. In winter there is usually a good selection of ducks, grey herons, various waders, and a few kingfishers.

Just to the west of Skala Kalloni there is a small river mouth, and a vast area of saltmarshes and mudflats. It is a harder locale in which to get close to birds because of the extensive flat areas, though there is plenty to see. Breeding birds here include Kentish and little ringed plovers, black-winged stilt, stone curlews, fan-tailed warblers, and a few other birds of

Kalloni pool, probably the best-known birdwatching site on Lesvos

open country. In spring there is a good mixture of species, such as great white egrets, greater flamingos, occasional black storks and spoonbills, avocets, and a variety of other waders; marsh harriers hunt over the area, with occasional Montagu's and even pallid harriers, plus common and long-legged buzzards, and numerous passerines such as yellow, citrine, and white wagtails, plus various pipits. Just offshore, there are often great-crested and black-necked grebes, and mergansers. At the mouth of the river there is apparently a large colony of common shrews, which may attract birds of prey.

Inland from here, the Potamia Valley and a small freshwater pool are both excellent areas. The pool attracts similar birds to those of Kalloni Pool (see above), and it is also a good spot to see both stripe-necked and the much rarer (in Lesvos) European pond terrapins, as well as marsh frogs, dice snakes, and common tree frogs. It often remains wet through to autumn, and is then a good place to see autumn passage migrants. The Potamia Valley con-

tains drier habitats, including olive groves and open woodland, good for breeding olive-tree warblers, Orphean warblers, masked shrike, sombre tit, and nightjars.

Just to the east of Skala Kalloni village another river – generally described as Kalloni East River – reaches the sea. This is probably the best place to watch birds on the whole of Lesvos, with very easy access and good watching points along the banks. As with the other sites here, spring is probably the best time, with large numbers of migrants passing through or arriving to nest. Passage birds include tawny and other pipits, rufous bush robin, Cretzschmar's and cinereous bunting (which both breed on the island), bittern and little bittern, most herons, including great white, glossy ibis, both black and white storks, collared and black-winged pratincoles, spur-winged plovers, whiskered, little, black, and white-winged black terns, wrynecks, rose-coloured starling, and too many others to mention. Birds of prey include short-toed and booted eagles, common and long-legged buzzards, goshawk, Levant sparrowhawk, osprey, red-footed falcon, and four harriers – marsh, hen, pallid, and Montagu's. Breeding birds here and inland include bee-eaters, little bitterns, rufous bush robins, hoopoes, western rock nuthatch, and many others.

Eastwards again, between the main Kalloni–Mitilini road and the sea, there is a large area of saltpans which are also very attractive to birds, and these extend eastwards into saltmarshes just beyond the Pyrrha–Achladeri turn-off. Many of the low-lying fields around here are flowery and unimproved, and the whole area has a wealth of interest. Passage migrants include an abundance of waders, mainly common species but with collared and black-winged pratincoles, green and wood sandpipers, spur-winged plovers, and curlew sandpipers, amongst others; gulls, including a few slender-billed, terns including gull-billed, great spotted cuckoos, Calandra larks, rollers, several shrikes, rose-coloured starling, and a host of others. In autumn, there are many similar species, though white and Dalmatian pelicans can turn up, as can black and white storks, Eleonora's falcon, and broad-billed sandpipers. In winter, egrets, flamingos, grebes, various ducks, including the distinctive ruddy shelduck, several bird of prey species, and many others find this frost free and productive environment very congenial.

Other wetlands around the northern part of the gulf can be found at the mouths of the Vouvaris and Mylopotamus rivers, just north of Achladeri, and westwards along the road to Parakila. This area also holds breeding Krüper's nuthatch, masked shrike, and other special birds.

This part of Lesvos is not particularly notable for flowers, though a few of the marshy fields contain loose-flowered orchids, water-dropworts, and yellow iris, and the tongue orchid *Serapias bergonii* is not uncommon. Here and there one sees masses of pink hawksbeard, purple viper's-bugloss, peacock anemones, common poppies, and other annuals – a marvellous sight in spring. Where there are pine woods, there are often yellow Provence orchids and violet limodores. Almost anywhere within the area is good for tree frogs, marsh frogs, stripe-necked terrapins, and green toads. Butterflies found here include swallowtail and scarce swallowtail, eastern festoon, lesser spotted fritillary, and small and Mediterranean skippers.

Skala Kalloni itself makes an excellent base, though it is likely to be full of birdwatchers during April and May, and becomes busy with general holidaymakers later.

SITE 84 Skala Polichnitos

Coastal habitats on the southern side of the Gulf of Kalloni, with abundant birds and flowers.

The area around Skala Polichnitos – the beach for the small town of Polichnitos which lies just south – is still very unspoilt, with extensive undeveloped areas of beach, low dunes and other sandy habitats, saltpans, pools, saltmarsh, and other coastal wetlands. As with other wetlands around the gulf, it is very rich in birds, especially at passage periods, and there is an abundance of spring flowers.

In spring a vast range of birds may turn up, depending on the time and weather. Likely species include great white egret, flamingo, glossy ibis, squacco and purple herons, both black and white storks, and spoonbill; ducks such as garganey and

pintail; birds of prey including marsh, hen, and Montagu's harriers, short-toed eagles, red-footed and Eleonora's falcons; collared pratincoles and a wide variety of waders; rollers, hoopoes, golden oriole, bee-eaters, terns, gulls and many more, though numbers tend to be lower here than at the Kalloni group of sites. It is also a good area for breeding birds, including bee-eaters, Kentish and little ringed plovers, black-winged stilts, stone curlews, fan-tailed warbler, tawny pipit, and Orphean warbler. White storks nest in Polichnitos village.

A good selection of birds may pass through at autumn passage periods, especially around the saltpans to the north-east of the village, which may remain wet though this cannot be guaranteed. Species of interest at this time include egrets, both storks, black-necked grebe, hen and marsh harriers, various waders, gulls, osprey, and Eleonora's falcon, plus a mixture of smaller birds. Greater flamingos often spend the whole autumn and winter here. In winter there is

Trithemis annulata

usually a good mixture of waterfowl, birds of prey, waders such as avocets, Sandwich terns, red-breasted mergansers offshore, and a pleasant array of other birds.

The low, sandy habitats along the gulf shore are still remarkably unspoilt (though there are signs of increasing numbers of tracks and casual building) and are extremely flowery in spring. The main species producing the colour include common poppies, a yellow fenugreek *Trigonella balansae*, stocks, including *Matthiola tricuspidata*, with its distinctive three-horned fruits, the pretty pinkish-red catchfly *Silene colorata*, and barbary nut, the dwarf iris which only comes out after lunch. Beautiful electric blue *Eryngium creticum* flowers and sea-lavenders add to the variety, and in high summer sea daffodils appear. The inland wetlands along the small river are good for tree frogs, marsh frogs, and terrapins.

The beach is worth investigating. Shells are often abundant, including little cowries, the striking spiny *Murex*, and huge examples of fan mussels *Pinna* species, looking rather like discarded pitta bread at first sight.

Not far away to the south, there is a rather similar area at the developing beach resort of Vatera, which lies on the southern open sea coast, and is therefore more exposed to the wind. There is a mixture of habitats, including freshwater wetlands, sandy beach and foreshore, scrub, pine woods, and olive groves. It is not as rich as Skala Polichnitos, but worth a visit; it is definitely best in April–May, before the main tourist season. Breeding birds here include Kentish and little ringed plovers, fan-tailed and Cetti's warblers, rufous bush robins, hoopoes, bee-eaters, black-winged stilts, olivaceous and olive-tree warblers, red-rumped swallows, crag martins, spotted flycatchers, and many more. Cinereous buntings possibly breed on the rocky areas to the west, towards the mouth of the Gulf of Kalloni. The headland just to the west of Vatera, Aghios Fokas, where there is a small chapel, is a good spot for watching birds

The extraordinary displays of spring coastal flowers at Skala Polichnitos

offshore, and possibly cetaceans such as common and bottle-nosed dolphins, which are more likely to be seen from here than anywhere else on Lesvos.

The wetland areas around Vatera have the usual assortment of amphibians and reptiles, including stripe-necked terrapins, and dragonflies such as the darters *Sympetrum meridionale*, yellow-winged, and red-veined; the striking red *Crocothemis erythraea*, and the plum-coloured *Trithemis annulata*.

SITE 85 Mt. Olympus

A beautiful mountain area, reaching 968 m, with a wealth of birds, flowers, and other wildlife, including many rarities.

Strictly speaking, Mt. Olympus is not the highest mountain on Lesvos, as the Lepetimnos range in the north of the island rises to 1 m higher (depending on which map you consult), though in practice it is the most significant mountain terrain on the island.

Around the lower slopes of Olympus, such as along the road from Keramia to Agiassos, there are extensive old olive groves on hilly land, with masses of flowers such as peacock and crown anemones, barbary nut – these last three often in startling and colourful abundance – blue lupins, mayweeds, and various orchids, especially green-winged (in the form *Orchis picta*), tongue orchids such as *Serapias vomeracea*, *S. lingua*, and *S. bergonii*, pink butterfly, naked man, yellow bee, four-spotted, and sombre bee amongst others. Around Agiassos there is an area of limestone (quite

rare on Lesvos) that is worth exploring, and which has a fine rock garden of flowers such as the dwarf iris *Iris pumila* sub-species *attica*, more orchids, such as four-spotted and lesser yellow bee *Ophrys sicula*, and abundant grape-hyacinths and anemones. Balkan green lizards are quite common here, too.

Above Agiassos the more natural mountain habitats commence, as olive groves give way to cherry orchards, then to natural woodlands. There are extensive woods of *Pinus brutia* and sweet chestnut, with flowery clearings, and this is probably the most rewarding zone for the naturalist. These woods are best known as the main site for Krüper's nuthatch in Europe (though it is widespread in Turkey and other sites are now known on Lesvos); they are quite frequent here, and easily located if you can tune in to their call, which partly sounds like common nuthatch but also includes a harsher ticking sound. The first time I visited the woods, I found them within 30 seconds of leaving the car, but have not always been so lucky! Other birds of interest in these woods include short-toed tree-creepers, sombre tits, eastern Bonelli's and subalpine warblers, middle-spotted woodpeckers, redstarts, nightingales, honey buzzards, sparrowhawks, and many others. It is a beautiful place in spring sunshine, alive with bird calls and the first spring flowers and butterflies. Persian

Krüper's nuthatch *Sitta krueperi*

Aegean Islands

squirrels are quite common – similar to red squirrels, but lacking the prominent ear tufts, and with identification made easier by the absence of red squirrels! Lesvos is the only part of Europe where they occur – another indication of how much more Asian Lesvos is than European.

These woodlands, and especially the clearings and roadsides, are good for flowers, though the main flowering period is later than on the coast, due to the altitude – May is usually best here. Flowers within the woods, especially where there is chestnut, include wild peonies, wild tulips (*Tulipa orphanidea* – probably a relict of cultivation here as it occurs along old field borders), green-winged, four-spotted, horseshoe, and toothed orchids, sword-leaved helleborines, peacock anemones, leopard's-bane, the extraordinary dragon arum, and a large arum *Arum elongatum*, cyclamens including *Cyclamen hederifolium* and *C. graecum*, the grey-leaved spurge *Euphorbia rigida*, and many more. Under pines, there are often different species, and it is here that the very rare and striking orchid *Comperia comperiana* grows in small numbers; it is a close relative of the more familiar lizard orchid, and essentially a Turkish and west Asian species that just extends into the Aegean islands such as Lesvos and Rhodes. Other orchids include Provence orchid, violet limodore, and woodcock orchid, with sun-roses and other flowers. In clearings, there are wild pears and wild *Prunus* species, which are magnets for bees and over-wintered butterflies.

Above the woods the land becomes more open, and this is a good place to find the fritillary *Fritillaria pontica* subspecies *substipelata*, a tall plant with green unchequered flowers, often seen in abundance, growing with the broad-leaved snowdrop *Galanthus elwesii* (which flowers earlier), a Star-of-Bethlehem *Ornithogalum montanum*, and alpine squill. In autumn, a meadow saffron *Colchicum variegatum* with pink chequered flowers is fairly frequent, and the yellow *Sternbergia lutea* can be seen here and there. In some areas, there are a few special plants, including a species of

Comper's orchid *Comperia comperiana*

'mountain tea' *Sideritis sipylea* (a mainly Turkish species), the endemic alison *Alyssum lesbiacum* (growing on a serpentine outcrop at about 700 m), the umbellifer *Tordylium hirtocarpum*, the saxifrage *Saxifraga graecum*, a speedwell *Veronica grisebachii*, and the Star-of-Bethlehem *Ornithogalum tenuifolium*.

The higher woods and ridges are also of interest for lichens and bryophytes (mosses and liverworts), though as yet there are few detailed records. Lichens recorded here include *Nephroma laevigatum*, and various *Cladonia* and *Usnea* species; bryophytes include *Ceratodon purpureusi*, *Bartramia pomiformis*, *Camptothecium aureum*, *Scleropodium touretii*, and *Polytrichum juniperinum* – one of the commonest hair-mosses in north Europe, but very rare here.

The highest areas of the main peak are bare, though access is rather difficult. The road to Plomari goes to just over 900 m, giving easy access to some high country, but the strong military presence in the area limits exploration and especially photography. In general, the road from Keramia (just off the main Mitilini–Kalloni road) through Agiassos and on towards Plomari on the south coast gives easy access to most of the good areas. In the lower areas towards the south coast, some of the more sheltered and less heavily grazed valleys hold the lovely yellow azalea *Rhododendron luteum*, at its only native site in Greece, and one of its few European locations.

SITE 86 Dipi Larssos reedbed

A substantial reedbed and associated wetlands, with an excellent range of birds.

The Dipi Larssos reedbed is the only one of any size in Lesvos (and there are very few in the eastern Aegean islands as a whole), thus assuming relatively greater importance. It lies west of the village of Keramia, where a small river reaches the Gulf of Geras, just south of the main Mitilini–Kalloni road. The main habitat here is reedbed, but there is also a series of open water pools, a small river, beach and sandbanks, scrub, and nearby rocky crags, woodland, and olive groves.

Breeding birds of interest include water rail, fan-tailed and Cetti's warblers, nightingales, rufous bush robins, and others, though its main interest is for winter visitors and passage migrants. In spring a great variety of birds pass through, including black-necked grebes, little bittern, squacco, night and purple herons, green and wood sandpiper, olivaceous and barred warblers, terns (with virtually all the possible species being recorded), hirundines, and many others. Birds of prey include long-legged buzzard, osprey, marsh harrier, short-toed eagle, peregrine and Eleonora's falcons, hobby, and others. A number of birds pass most of the winter here (though very few people visit at this time of year), including great white egrets, black-necked and great-crested grebes, goshawk, marsh harrier, Sandwich tern, kingfisher, and masses of Mediterranean gulls, amongst others. In the pools, there are marsh frogs, green toads, stripe-necked terrapins, and occasional dice snakes, with tree frogs calling nearby. Otters probably occur here, as road casualties have been seen nearby.

Squacco heron *Ardeola ralloides* (Mike Powles)

In the surrounding habitats, there are other birds, such as black-headed bunting, sparrowhawk, crag martins, Rüppell's and Sardinian warblers, and hoopoe. Under the pines, there are occasional violet limodores, Provence, sombre bee, yellow bee, and tongue orchids.

Access is best from the coast road to Perama, which crosses the two small rivers then runs roughly along the southern shore of the gulf. Tracks lead in both directions from this into the main area of habitat.

SITE 87 North coast

A wild and rugged area lying along the north coast eastwards from Mithimna, and including the highest point on the island, at Mt. Lepetimnos.

The Mt. Lepetimnos range of mountains runs across the north of Lesvos, but just inland, leaving a steep area of land that runs down to an unspoilt section of coast punctuated by occasional fishing villages.

The mountains themselves rise to 968 m, and are largely bare and unforested. It is a good area for some specialized breeding birds, such as Bonelli's eagles, which probably have a resident pair here, the more common short-toed eagles, long-legged buzzard, peregrine and possibly lanner falcons, chukar, cirl, rock, and Cretzschmar's buntings, alpine swifts, rock nuthatches (with several of their extraordinary nests visible on cliffs along the road), woodlark, crag martins, and possibly white-throated robins, though

Masses of spring flowers on the beach at Petra

Ornithogalum nutans

their current status is uncertain. In general, there is much more uncultivated country here than further south, with fewer olive groves or arable fields, and consequently a different range of birds, though densities are generally lower.

Botanically, it is moderately rich, though lacking in spectacular displays of spring flowers. There are many areas of scrub with spiny broom (which smells wonderful when flowering en masse), French lavender, eastern strawberry-tree, *Phillyrea latifolia*, kermes oak, a small copse of narrow-leaved ash, spiny burnet, and wild pear *Pyrus spinosa* (= *amygdaliformis*). Herbaceous flowers include dragon arum, peacock anemones, asphodels, the striking giant fennel, barbary nut, two species of autumn-flowering cyclamen, the confusingly named one-flowered clover (which only has one flower per head, but produces masses of pink or white flowers in a mat), and a few orchids, though they are not particularly at home on this volcanic soil. Where there are pine woods, such as near Klio, there are Provence orchids, a large saxifrage *Saxifraga chrysosplenifolia*, the greenish-white spikes of a Star-of-Bethlehem *Ornithogalum nutans*, yellow stars-of-

Bethlehem *Gagea* species, woodcock orchid, yellow bee orchid, and tongue orchids, amongst others. On rocks and cliffs within the mountain area, there are interesting flowers, such as the umbellifer *Smyrnium apiifolium*, the alkanet *Anchusa leptophylla* subspecies *incana* in crevices close to the summit (thought until recently to be endemic to Turkey), several figworts, Gargano dead-nettle, and the little saxifrage *Saxifraga hederacea*. It is an interesting area for lichens, too, including *Dermatocarpon miniatum*, *Pertusaria pertusa*, *Parmelia pulla*, and *P. tinctina*, all of which occur on or around the summit rocks.

The lower slopes are good for butterflies and other insects, without being exceptional. Eastern festoons are frequent, with orange tips, common and scarce swallowtails, Bath white and eastern dappled white, brimstone and Cleopatra, fritillaries, including lesser spotted and silver-washed, Balkan marbled white, eastern rock grayling, and various skippers. Humming bird hawk-moths are common, and migrant butterflies such as painted ladies and clouded yellows may appear in large numbers at times. It is also a good area for reptiles, especially in the lower areas. Spur-thighed tortoises are common here, with Balkan wall lizard, Balkan green lizard, Turkish gecko, whip snake, cat snake, Ottoman viper, and Montpellier snake, and agama lizards in the coastal areas. These last-named are an essentially Eastern species, occurring mainly in North Africa and west Asia, with a few outposts in Greece. They have a dragon-like appearance, and may reach 30 cm long – hence the name Rhodes dragon. They are common in places, such as along the coastal strip west of Skala Sikaminia.

The coastal area is very scenic, and the fishing village of Skala Sikaminia is probably the most beautiful village in Lesvos. It is a good spot from which to watch coastal birds that include Cory's and Mediterranean shearwaters, shags, cormorants, Mediterranean gulls, a few

Audouin's gulls in spring and autumn, and more common species.

The area around Mithimna (commonerly known as Molivos) has many fine habitats. Scops owls are common in the village and alpine swifts frequently 'chitter' overhead; Rüppell's, subalpine, and Orphean warblers, blue rock thrushes, black-eared wheatears, and peregrines are all present in scrub or around nearby cliffs. The orchid *Ophrys mammosa* occurs near Petra, and there are masses of beach flowers nearby.

Access into the area is easy via the Mithimna–Klio road, and back to the south of the massif via Stipsi. There are many tracks off these roads, though those into the mountains are quite rough.

88 West Lesvos

A wild and unspoilt area, with many rare birds, some endemic flowers, and one of the finest fossil forests in Europe.

Western Lesvos, defined here as the part of the island to the west of a line from Kalloni to Mithimna (Molivos), is a remarkable region. The scenery is extraordinarily rugged and stony, lacking any high peaks but wild, hilly, and unspoilt almost throughout. There is very little woodland, and most places are covered by rocky *garrigue* or a mass of small, stony stone-walled fields, with olive groves in the more fertile parts such as the valleys near Skoutaros. Valonia oaks are frequent, though mainly as scattered trees, giving the feel of ancient pasture woodland, and most parts are grazed by wandering sheep, goat, or cow herds. There are a few species that are confined to the west end of the island, and a number that are more common here than anywhere else.

The old olive groves and adjacent habitats, especially where there are scattered oaks and a few rock outcrops, are good for breeding birds such as the delightful masked shrike (with a song that sounds almost like a great reed warbler!), olive-tree warbler, Rüppell's, subalpine, and Orphean warblers, hoopoe, sombre tit, blue rock thrush, and possibly hawfinches, amongst others. In the wilder rocky areas, such as around Moni Ipsilon (a not particularly attractive monastery in a striking location), or between Sigri and Eressos, there are different birds. Rock sparrows have colonies around villages or old buildings, black-eared wheatears are

Sea daffodil *Pancratium maritimum*

Campanula sparsa

frequent, rock nuthatches nest on most suitable cliffs, and there are several pairs of long-legged buzzards, most notably around Moni Ipsilon. The rocky parts of the west of the island are the main stronghold of cinereous bunting, one of Europe's rarest birds, and they can be found through most of the wilder areas, together with Cretzschmar's, black-headed, ortolan, and cirl buntings. A few pairs of Isabelline wheatear (and possibly pied wheatear) breed in the region, particularly near Sigri, and lesser kestrels are fairly common. Other breeding birds of interest that may be seen within the region include short-toed eagles, nightjars, chukars, peregrine and lanner falcons, alpine swifts, crag martins, red-rumped swallows, hoopoes, turtle doves, red-backed, lesser grey, and woodchat shrikes, and many more – a remarkable list that reflects the dry rocky nature of the terrain and the eastern position of Lesvos.

Botanically, it is rather patchy; large areas of the west appear to hold little of note, though almost anywhere is worth exploring as it is so little known. Expanses that may look dry and barren (even in spring) can have species of interest, such as *Ornithogalum narbonense*, bellflowers from the *Campanula sparsa* group, the tiny stonecrop *Sedum caespitosum*, or the

Striking volcanic cliffs at Skala Eressos, West Lesvos.

Black-eared wheatear *Oenanthe hispanica*

toadflax *Linaria pelisseriana*. There is an endemic orchid *Ophrys lesbis*, which is in the *O. argolica* group, with reddish-purple sepals and petals, and two 'eyes' or a horseshoe on the furry, brownish-yellow lower lip. It is scattered through the west of the island in scrub, *garrigue*, and open woods, mainly on more alkaline soils such as on the limestone hills near Gavathas (see below). It flowers early, from March until late April, and should be looked for anywhere in west Lesvos. There are some good, flowery, beach–sand dune areas; at Kampas, the flowers on the dunes include the blue fenugreek *Trigonella coerulescens* and the yellow *T. balansae*, with the stocks *Malcolmia flexuosa* and *Matthiola incana*, sea medick, sea holly, sea daffodil, sea spurge, an attractive bellflower in the *Campanula lyrata* group, and others. Just west of Skala Eressos there is a very species-rich area of low dunes, where the following grow: yellow horned-poppy, the very pretty black and red poppy *Papaver nigrotinctum* (amongst other poppies), the curious little yellow poppy relative *Hypecoum imberbe*, dyer's alkanet, sea medick, broomrapes, including purple broomrape, a Venus' looking-glass *Legousia tetragonum*, sea daffodil, three-horned stock, mayweeds such as *Anthemis tomentosa*, hare's-tail plantain, purple bugloss, narrow-leaved clover, and many others. On the cliffs nearby grow clumps of capers, *Inula verbascifolia*, *Phagnalon rupestre*, and various other flowers.

On the north coast there is an area of limestone that is steadily being lost to quarrying. It has a slightly different range of flowers, including *Ophrys lesbis*, other orchids including pyramidal, yellow bee and lesser yellow bee, tongue orchids, one of the Dutchman's pipes *Aristolochia rotunda* (a food plant of eastern festoon butterfly), cyclamens, lice-bane, *Silene dichotoma*, the pretty vetch *Vicia melanops*, foetid bean trefoil, little robin, and other limestone plants.

The olive groves and areas where there are more trees are good for Persian squirrel and beech martens; eastern hedgehogs are abundant, and brown hares can be seen occasionally, though they are rarer than they should be due to shooting. Spur-thighed tortoises can be seen in suitable patchily vegetated sites, and several snakes are frequent, such as leopard snake and cat snake. The curious little sand boa (see p. 254) is found occasionally, though it is probably more common than records suggest. In the lower areas, such as on the coast between Sigri and Skala Eressos, the agama lizard (see p. 204) is common, with occasional Turkish geckoes. In wetlands, such as along the river that emerges on the wild coast between Sigri and Skala Eressos, there are stripe-necked terrapins, marsh frogs, green toads, tree frogs, dice snakes, and wetland birds such as squacco herons and little bittern in spring. Butterflies are not a special feature of the area, though there is a reasonable range

Malope malacoides

of more common species such as clouded yellows, eastern rock grayling, eastern festoon, and the swallowtails.

Between Moni Ipsilon and Sigri there is a very well-marked turn-off for the famous fossil forest. This is worth a visit, and some of the trees are very impressive. You have to pay to go in, and it is open on weekdays from 8 am to 3 pm. There is also an unfenced and unannounced area of forest along the Sigri–Eressos road (a rough track) which is more pleasant to visit.

SITE 89 Ikaria

An isolated and little-known island lying to the west of Samos,
with a rich flora and good breeding bird populations.

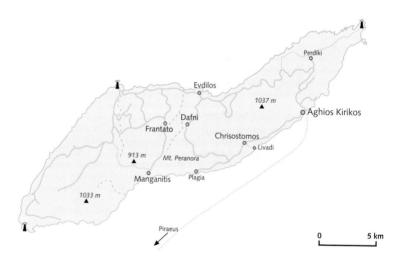

Ikaria is a smallish Aegean island, long and thin, but with mountains reaching to about 1000 m all along its length. Away from the eastern end, where the main town and port of Aghios Kirikos lies, it is wild and sparsely populated. The central parts have *Pinus brutia* and oak woodland in places, and there are a number of fine cliffs.

It is particularly noted for its birds of prey. There are several pairs of long-legged buzzards breeding and resident here, with one or two pairs of Bonelli's eagle still surviving. Around the coasts and on offshore islands, there are large numbers of breeding Eleonora's falcons,

feeding themselves and their young on the substantial numbers of late-summer and autumn passage migrants that pass through on their way south. There are small numbers of lesser kestrels breeding on cliffs, and cinereous bunting may possibly breed. White-tailed eagles move through on passage.

Botanically, it is rather special by virtue of a dozen or so rare flowers, some confined to the island, that occur on the cliffs of central and western Ikaria. The crucifer *Erysimum senoneri* subspecies *icaricum* is a shrubby relative of the wallflower, with bright yellow flowers. It is restricted to just five cliffs, and is a particularly specialized member of this more widespread group. The spring-flowering snowdrop *Galanthus ikariae* subspecies *ikariae* is confined to damp, shady places in the hills of Ikaria (there is another subspecies, which grows on a few other islands, including Naxos, though recent work has indicated that they should all simply be called *Galanthus ikariae*). The unusual, shrubby pink candytuft *Iberis runemarkii* is confined to one cliff on the south side of Mt. Peranora, to the north of Plagia. The plant grows along about 2 km of cliff, but only in very small numbers. Other endemics include the yellow-cress *Rorippa icarica* and the knotweed *Polygonum icaricum*, together with another half dozen special plants, and it is generally believed amongst conservation circles that the mountain areas of central Ikaria should be given special protection for their rare plants. Ikaria is currently listed as a potential Natura 2000 site (with Samos) for its flowers, birds, and invertebrates, and as a monk seal sanctuary.

Access is by sea from Samos or Piraeus.

Peloponnese

Introduction

The Peloponnese forms the southern-most part of mainland Greece. Although it is sometimes described as an island since the construction of the Corinth canal, in practice, from the ecological point of view, it is part of the mainland. It has been attached to the mainland via a narrow isthmus (in fact the original isthmus, after which this geographical feature is named) for a long time, and shares a high proportion of species with the rest of Greece.

It is a quite extraordinarily diverse area, with a marvellous wealth of natural history interest in a region that encompasses some of the driest and most barren parts of Europe, high mountains to 2500 m that are snow-capped well into summer, and one of the most important wetlands in Greece, as well as all points in between. It is a very unspoilt region, with few large towns and relatively little large-scale agricultural development. Patra is much the largest town, and the north-western coastal strip is the main intensive agricultural area, though there are olives and grape vines in many parts, including the famous regions of Kalamata (for olives) and Nemea (for its wine), in addition to Corinth, from which the name currant derives.

The Peloponnese is extremely mountainous. There is a block of roughly

Roadside flowers in spring on the Mani Peninsula

Opposite page: **Koskarakas Gorge**

Peloponnese

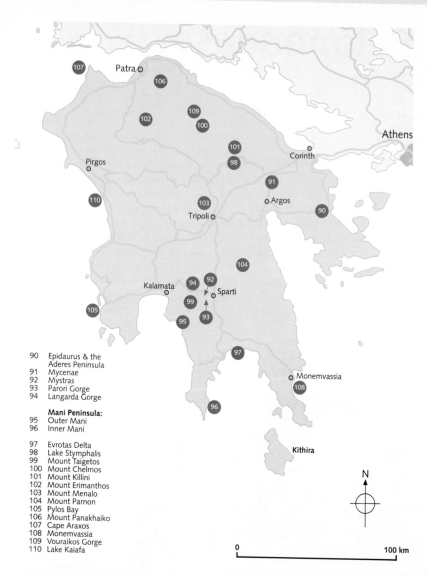

90 Epidaurus & the
    Aderes Peninsula
91 Mycenae
92 Mystras
93 Parori Gorge
94 Langarda Gorge

Mani Peninsula:
95 Outer Mani
96 Inner Mani

97   Evrotas Delta
98   Lake Stymphalis
99   Mount Taigetos
100 Mount Chelmos
101 Mount Killini
102 Mount Erimanthos
103 Mount Menalo
104 Mount Parnon
105 Pylos Bay
106 Mount Panakhaiko
107 Cape Araxos
108 Monemvassia
109 Vouraikos Gorge
110 Lake Kaiafa

0   100 km

T-shaped mountains which fills the centre of the region, with outliers in all directions. Across the north there is a long, broad mountain range which includes Erimanthos, Panahaiko, Chelmos, Killini, and others, reaching 2374 m at its highest point and broad enough from north to south to present a substantial barrier to the movement of species, as well as separating rather different climates. With a few interruptions, a tongue of mountains proj- ects southwards down the middle of the Peloponnese, through Mt. Menalo to the Taigetos range which dominates the south and provides the highest point in the area at 2404 m. The Mani Peninsula (the middle 'finger') of the Peloponnese is a mountainous extension of the Taigetos range, with peaks over 1000 m almost to its tip. The south-eastern part of the region has extensive mountain areas, too, running southwards from Mt. Parnon; though not especially high, these mountains collectively form a wild and rugged area that is little known and rarely visited. As with so many mountain areas, it is not simply the high peaks that are of interest – the vast areas of rocky scrub on the lower slopes, the extensive natural woods, and the high cliffs all contribute to the value of the area. The mountains of the Peloponnese are especially noted for their gorges, such as the Viros, Parori, and Langarda Gorges around Taigetos, or the Vouraikos Gorge in the north; these frequently act as secure homes for cliff-nesting birds of prey such as eagles (and formerly vultures, though these have virtually disappeared from the Peloponnese, probably due largely to hunting pressure), and are the site of special flowers which enjoy the increased humidity and the lack of grazing or browsing by goats.

The northern band of mountains, especially around Chelmos, has higher rainfall and snowfall than the rest of the peninsula, and there are extensive forests in this area which are partly unexploited. Many believe that the area around Chelmos should be given National Park status to protect its remarkable combina-tion of habitats and species, though there is no sign of this happening at present. There are no National Parks in the Peloponnese, and little in the way of protected areas, despite its extraordinary diversity and interest.

The lowlands have a quite different character, and include some of the warmest and driest parts of Greece. The central and eastern peninsulas are especially noted for their climate, mild or warm in winter and very hot in summer, with a very different range of species compared to the mountains – a different world, in many ways. Despite the relative aridity of the lowlands, there are wetlands here (there were once more), thanks to the spring-fed year-round rivers and snow-melt through the spring. The Evrotas Delta was once a fine wetland, attracting large numbers of birds; it is still important enough to be considered as part of Greece's network of European Natura 2000 sites, though it is a shadow of its former self. The finest wetland in the region, and one of the best in Greece, lies around Cape Araxos and to its south, in the north-western point of the Peloponnese. There is a marvellous combination of coastal habi-

Kardamili Bay

tats here, combined with freshwater marshland and undisturbed woodlands, to produce an exceptional matrix of relatively undisturbed, semi-natural habitats which is unique in Greece.

For the lowlands, and especially the southern peninsulas, you need to go early to see them at their best. The best displays of flowers are going over by mid-April (though paradoxically, the area can often experience some of the coldest weather of the winter in this period), though it is best a little later for birds and butterflies. The high areas, especially the northern mountains, are best visited from May to late July or early August. There are flowers through the autumn and right through the winter (such as crocuses and snowdrops), and the frost-free wetlands are good for birds in winter.

90 Epidaurus and the Aderes Peninsula

A classical site on the edge of unspoilt hilly country, with good flowers.

The ancient site of Epidaurus is one of many famous classical sites in the Peloponnese, especially in this north-east corner. To be honest, the site itself does not hold an enormous amount of interest for the naturalist (though well worth visiting for other reasons, of course), but it is certainly worth exploring while you are there, and it is the gateway to an area of interesting country. Southwards and eastwards from here, the landscape is still surprisingly remote and unspoilt.

At Epidaurus itself, there are some interesting flowers, where herbicides have not been used. Orchids are quite common, including tongue orchids (mainly in the *Serapias vomeracea* group, including the more slender *S. bergonii*), yellow bee orchids, horseshoe orchid, and the speciality of the area: *Ophrys argolica* (see p. 220), named after nearby Argos. On rocks and walls, where herbicide has not been applied recently, there are bellflowers *Campanula rupestris* agg. ('agg.' is a botanical convention and stands for 'aggregate', indicating species which closely resemble each other), golden drops *Onosma frutescens*, and the little annual bellflower *C. drabifolia*. In more fertile areas, crown anemones, tassel hyacinths, and the ubiquitous mayweed *Anthemis chia* abound, making a tapestry of colour. Rock nuthatches are common around the ruins, where they nest, and serins, goldfinches, and firecrests sing from the trees. In autumn, there are some interesting bulbs in this area, including the yellow *Sternbergia sicula*, crocuses such as the white *Crocus boryi*, autumn squill, and sometimes a few *Colchicum* species.

It is worth travelling on south-eastwards, in spring at least, to the north coast of the peninsula, along the north side of the Aderes massif. The pretty magenta-coloured soapwort *Saponaria calabrica* clothes the roadsides, and here and there one can find rich patches of *Ophrys heldreichii*, the striking relative of woodcock orchid, man orchid, yellow bee orchid, and sawfly orchid, with four-spotted orchids in drifts amongst scrub. In autumn, there are bulbs such as autumn squill, and even through the winter there is something of interest, such as the Greek saffron crocus *Crocus cartwrightianus*.

Spring flowers near Epidaurus, dominated by *Silene colorata* **and mayweed**

Epidaurus is well sign-posted and easily reached from Nafplio (an attractive old town with plenty of accommodation and good flowery spring walks on the nearby headland).

SITE 91 Mycenae

A famous prehistoric site set amongst hilly country, with good flowers and birds.

Mycenae (or Mykenai) lies just a few kilometres north of the ancient town of Argos, in a spectacular setting with superb views. Although herbicides are used on key parts of the site, there are still large areas of untouched cliffs, walls, and rocky turf, which can be good for flowers at the right season. In spring this is a good area for orchids, especially the local specialities *Ophrys argolica, O. reinholdii,* and *O. spruneri,* sometimes with horseshoe orchid as well (see p. 220 for a guide to the differ-

ences between these similar species). More common and more widespread orchids here include naked man orchid, four-spotted orchid, yellow bee, and sawfly. On walls and cliffs, there are rock alisons *Alyssum saxatile,* the shrubby composite *Phagnalon rupestre,* the pretty bellflower *Campanula rupestris* agg., the golden drop *Onosma frutescens,* and a navelwort *Umbilicus horizontalis,* together with more widespread species such as red valerian. In more fertile areas, there are masses of mayweeds, pop-

The ruins of Mycenae

pies, the yellow fenugreek *Trigonella bal-ansae*, with its pretty little 'Christmas trees' of hanging fruits, white asphodel, and pitch trefoil, with its distinctive tarry smell and electric-blue flowers.

In autumn, there are masses of the yellow crocus-like *Sternbergia sicula* down the southern slopes of the site, and commoner bulbs such as autumn squill.

There are good birds to be seen at Mycenae; rock nuthatches are common and obvious within the site (as they are at many of the classical sites – the topography seems to suit them); in scrub and olive groves nearby, there are Rüppell's warblers, rufous bush robins, sombre tits, and – of course – Sardinian warblers, while blue rock thrushes sing from the crags.

Access is easy and well sign-posted from the new main road into the Peloponnese that runs southwards from Corinth towards Tripoli. The site is open all year.

SITE

92 Mystras

A magnificent ruined Byzantine city, tumbling down the east slopes of Mt. Taigetos. Grid reference: 37°05'N 22°20'E.

Mystras is one of the great sights of the Greek world. It is a beautiful, large, ruined Byzantine city, still with numerous surviving churches and monasteries, in a lovely situation on the lower slopes of Taigetos, with cliffs and snow-clad mountains towering over it.

It is a good place botanically, too. Although most of the flowers also occur elsewhere nearby, the absence of grazing

A clerid beetle *Trichodes alvearius*

allows some of them to do particularly well, and they can be seen and appreciated in superb surroundings. If you are with a group, or have sympathetic transport, it is worth being taken to the top entrance and walking down, perhaps with a detour to the top castle if you feel energetic. The path to the entrance from the top of the road has some lovely flowers, before you even enter the site. It is at its best in April, when there are some beautiful displays. There are three white saxifrages: *Saxifraga chrysosplenifolia* with large flowers, *S. hederacea* with small flowers and rounded leaves (always growing in shady places), and rue-leaved saxifrage, more erect, with small flowers and fingered leaves. The golden drop *Onosma frutescens* is common, with bellflowers of the *Campanula rupestris* group (probably now called *C. andrewsii*), nettle-leaved figwort, perennial honesty, the yellow clumps of rock alison (familiar in rock gardens), masses of peacock anemones, mainly in scarlet, and giant orchids. In autumn the yellow *Sternbergia lutea* grows here, outside the site, and the attractive bellflower *Campanula versicolor* and the garlic *Allium callimischon* are in flower. Inside the site, there are clumps of Mediterranean spurge, looking especially fine here, Judas trees, white irises *Iris florentina*, terebinth tree, a few pretty vetches, including the striking *Vicia melanops*, the blue Bithynian vetch, and the pale yellow *V. hybrida*. There are a few orchids (though it is better to visit the nearby Parori Gorge for these – see p. 218),

including horseshoe, sombre, and yellow bee orchids. A little later giant fennels come into flower, often well over 2 m high. Tassel hyacinths are common, but much rarer is the pretty little toadflax *Cymbalaria microcalyx*, growing only on a few cliffs here (but easier to find in Parori). Other flowers to be seen in and around the site include starry clover, the dark violet alkanet *Anchusa hybrida*, common stars-of-Bethlehem, Nottingham catchfly, Jerusalem sage, Virginia stock, the common white asphodel *Asphodelus aestivus*, slender asphodel, wild pea, and shining crane's-bill.

It is quite a good place to see birds, though there is nothing unusual. Rock nuthatches are common, noisy and tame here, and you often have good close views. Blue rock thrushes sing from the higher crags, alpine swifts circle overhead, and there are Cetti's and Sardinian warblers in abundance. Although no large birds of prey breed on the site, you can occasionally see them passing high overhead; both Bonelli's and booted eagles can occur, and peregrines are not uncommon.

Vicia melanops

It is not a great place for butterflies, but there are reasonable numbers of some more widespread species such as brimstone, Cleopatra, holly blue, wall brown, common orange tip, and the usual migrants such as clouded yellow. Other insects include violet carpenter bee and the pretty red and blue beetle *Trichodes alvearius*. In autumn there can be surprisingly large numbers of butterflies – masses of Cleopatras, occasional two-tailed pashas, swallowtails, southern commas, pearly heath, and lots of blues

and skippers. Additional interest at Mystras is provided by the presence of green lizards and a few tortoises.

Access is easy and well sign-posted from Sparti. The site is open all year. It is worth exploring the little paths and olive groves around, and particularly above, the site, where there is a small gorge with open woods of downy oak. It is a scenic and productive area. The Parori Gorge (below) and the Langarda Gorge (p. 220) are within 10 minutes drive, and both are worth visiting.

SITE 93 Parori Gorge

A small, limestone gorge with easy access, very rich in flowers, butterflies, and birds.
Grid reference: 37°04'N 22°21'E.

Just south-east of Mystras (see map on p. 233), a few kilometres west of Sparti, lies the little village of Parori, tucked in at the bottom of Mt. Taigetos. Starting almost from the village centre, there is a small gorge with a track for about half a kilometre, and a path beyond for about as far again up to a little rock chapel, giving access to a fine mix of Greek nature, especially in spring.

Horseshoe orchid *Ophrys ferrum-equinum*

There is a shady Oriental plane tree and seating area by a spring and some piped water in the village, where there is friar's cowl, maidenhair fern, little-robin, shining crane's-bill, and a few other flowers, before the gorge proper (and there is a café here).

The gorge itself is a marvellous place for flowers; shrubs and trees such as false scorpion vetch, nettle tree (with nettle tree butterflies around it!), turpentine tree, maples such as *Acer sempervirens*, the shrubby St John's-wort *Hypericum empetrifolium* grow on the banks, and the joint-pine *Ephedra fragilis* hangs down from the steep sides. Orchids are good here, and it is an excellent place to compare some of the similar and rather difficult species of this area (see below); horseshoe orchid, *Ophrys spruneri*, *O. argolica*, *O. reinholdii* and *O. mammosa* all occur, with some probable hybrids. There

Gruner's orange-tip on burnt candytuft, its larval food-plant

Ophrys spruneri

little Gruner's orange tip), grass pea, Nottingham catchfly, and other flowers. On some of the cliffs, there are bellflowers such as *Campanula versicolor* (flowering in late summer), and *C. andrewsii* (flowering in spring), the beautiful furry-leaved woundwort *Stachys candida*, an endemic catchfly *Silene goulimyi*, and other choice plants, mostly well out of reach. Higher up, on the grassy slopes, there are four-spotted orchids, lots of spring-flowering cyclamens *Cyclamen repandum*, including plants in the form 'pelops' with beautiful leaves, sometimes now called subspecies *peloponnesiacum*. Along the path side, there are patches of the pretty little rock-dwelling toadflax *Cymbalaria microcalyx*, related to ivy-leaved toadflax but daintier and not as invasive, a bulb *Bellevalia dubia*, small *Malcolmia* species, the white saxifrage *Saxifraga chrysosplenifolia*, white ramping-fumitory, and many others.

is also yellow bee, four-spotted orchid, *O. attica*, and sometimes others. Along the track, there are thistles and other composites – milk thistles, the shrubby cliff-dwelling *Ptilostemon chamaepeuce*, and the valerian *Valeriana dioscoridis*, all alive with butterflies on a good day. At the base of the slopes there is a spreading bellflower *Campanula spathulata*, burnt candytuft (food-plant for the pretty

It is an excellent place for butterflies. On a calm sunny day, they can be seen in some abundance around the flowers in the lower parts of the gorge. Nettle tree butterflies

Parori Gorge

Lesser kestrel *Falco naumanni*

(also known sometimes as the snout, due to its protruding palps) are common, with brimstone, Cleopatra, common clouded yellow, eastern orange tip, Gruner's orange tip, southern comma, speckled wood (in its more orange southern form), green hairstreak, scarce swallowtail, Camberwell beauty, and many others. It is a good place for cliff-dwelling snails, there are scorpions under the stones, and many other invertebrates of interest. Tortoises and green lizards are both common.

Birds are more or less what you would expect in a small gorge here. Blue rock thrushes, crag martins, and jackdaws are common. There is a small colony of lesser kestrels (a rare and declining bird over much of Greece), and other birds of prey such as peregrine and short-toed eagle can be seen occasionally.

Some difficult spider orchids

The Peloponnese is a marvellous region for orchids, with a number of endemics. Parori, and other sites, are good places to compare some of the similar ones as they all occur together. There are five similar spider orchid *Ophrys* species here: *O. reinholdii*, *O. argolica*, horseshoe orchid *O. ferrum-equinum*, *O. spruneri*, and *O. mammosa*.

O. argolica, sometimes called the eyed orchid, has a broad, undivided lower lip, with white-hairy shoulders, and usually two bluish eye spots, sometimes joined. *O. reinholdii* is rather similar in having hairy shoulders to the lip, but the lip is much narrower and nearly always deeply divided, with an 'arm' at each side, and two eye spots that are whitish or grey, sometimes joined.

The remaining three species do not have the white-hairy shoulders. The horseshoe orchid has a roughly round, undivided lip, with silvery-blue speculum markings; these can be just two stripes, or a horseshoe, but they never reach into the centre of the flower and surround it. *O. spruneri* can look very similar, but it nearly always has a three-lobed lip, with distinct 'arms' at the side, and the blue speculum reaches right into the centre of the flower at the 'top' of the lip. *O. mammosa* often looks different straight away as its sepals (the three equal outermost 'petals') are usually green or two-toned green and pink, rather than all pink or purple; and the characteristic which gives it its scientific name *mammosa* is the presence of two large, breast-like swellings on the lip. All these orchids occur in the area, but *O. argolica* (named after Argos) and *O. spruneri* are Greek endemics.

94 Langarda Gorge

SITE

A limestone gorge, cutting deep into the mountains.
Grid reference: 37°07'N 22°18'E.

The main Sparti–Kalamata road, the N82, climbs high over the Taigetos Mountains. Coming west from Sparti, it begins to climb near the village of Tripi, and enters the large and spectacular Langarda (or Tripi) Gorge (see map p. 233). This is a well-known botanical site, and a good place for birds. Despite the fact that the main road runs through it, access is actually more difficult than the Parori Gorge, though there are a few places to stop.

The floor of the gorge is lined with Oriental planes, while higher up there are black pines and Greek firs. Next to the road, there are wet cliffs with maidenhair fern, and elsewhere there are dry, sunny, and shaded cliffs, steep rocky slopes, scrub, and grassland, rich in flowers. In spring Spanish broom, Jerusalem sage, and *Malcolmia* species light up the slopes and roadsides. On the cliffs, there are clumps of the pinkish-flowered, downy-leaved *Stachys candida*, the endemic catchfly *Silene goulimyi*, the saxifrage *Saxifraga chrysosplenifolium*, *Aubrieta deltoides*, so familiar in rock gardens, and at least three species of golden drop *Onosma frutescens*, *O. montana*, and *O. erecta*. The little bluish-purple flowers of a rock-cress *Arabis verna* grow on ledges and crevices, and four-spotted orchid grows amongst scrub. There is a pink flowered, mat-forming scabious *Scabiosa crenata* subspecies *breviscapa*, the curious little *Thalictrum orientale*, with its few, largish white flowers looking more like an *Isopyrum* than a meadow-rue, bellflowers such as *Campanula andrewsii*, and the endemic squill *Scilla messeniaca*, with more leaves than flowers. In the woods, there are anemones *Anemone blanda*, cyclamen *C. repandum*, primroses, the attractive orange-yellow leopard's-bane *Doronicum orientale*, the small white-flowered comfrey *Symphytum ottomanum*, and snake's head iris.

In autumn, there are other flowers here, including a pinkish-lilac unchequered *Colchicum, C. boissieri*, almost unique in having stolons from its corms, the bell-flower *Campanula versicolor*, and in the woods, from late October to Christmas, the pretty white flowers of

Doronicum orientale

the snowdrop *Galanthus reginae-olgae*. This is the only Greek autumn-flowering snowdrop, looking rather like the common snowdrop except that the flowers appear before the leaves; they are beautifully scented. Nearby, there are usually a few creamy-white *Crocus boryi* clumps, flowering in late autumn.

Altogether, it is a very rich area botanically, with many unusual and endemic species, worth visiting in spring and early summer, or in autumn.

Langarda Gorge is also good for birds, though not to the same degree as for flowers. Large raptors breed in the area, including Bonelli's and short-toed eagles, honey buzzard, and eagle owl, and probably others. There is often some bird of prey overhead. In the gorge, there are crag martins, alpine swifts, blue rock thrushes, rock nuthatches, and others. It is not as good for butterflies as the Parori Gorge (p. 218), perhaps because it is more exposed and windy, though certainly worth a look.

Following the main road up, westwards, you reach a pass at about 1300 m, with a useful hotel that claims to be open all year, though this road has become quieter since the alternative main road to Athens from Kalambata was improved, so things may change. At this point, you are in black pine forest, and from here tracks branch off, especially southwards, to give access to some fine wooded country with flowery clearings. In April, it is still quite wintery here, but by May and early June there is a blaze of flowers, including the mayweed *Anthemis cretica*, leopard's-banes, lesser butterfly orchid, the crane's-bill *Geranium asphodelioides*, the vetch *Vicia melanops*, yellow spikes of Provence orchid, pale pink toothed orchid, and marsh-orchids here and there. There are serins and firecrests in the forests, and butterflies such as Cleopatra and Queen of Spain fritillary in the glades.

Mani

The Mani Peninsula is the central finger of the three-pronged southern section of the Peloponnese. Although it does not look large on the map, it is so complex, and so poorly served with main roads (fortunately, since this is one reason that it has remained so unspoilt) that we have split it into several areas. It is of great interest to the naturalist, and warrants detailed treatment. The Outer Mani (Exo Mani in Greek) is the more northerly area running roughly from Areopolis northwards almost to Kalamata, though we are looking here only at the western side, leaving out the great mass of Mt. Taigetos, which is treated as a separate site (p. 232).

The peninsula consists largely of hard limestone. It was well-wooded once, but a combination of fires, over-grazing, and a hot, dry climate have combined to make most of the countryside bare and seem-ingly barren. The coastal plains are culti-vated and settled, while the few hill villages rely on stony terraces with vines and olives for their livelihood. As you go further southwards, and particularly into Inner Mani (see p. 226), the ground becomes stonier and the climate harsher, and there is less and less cultivation. One of the great pleasures of Mani for the visi-tor (though possibly not for the locals) is that the stony ground on the hills has pre-vented ploughing and spraying of the terraces; consequently, these are a quite extraordinary mass of flowers in spring, with a surprising number in autumn and winter, too. It is simply a pleasure to walk or drive through, even without looking closely at anything.

SITE 95 Outer Mani

Spectacular, arid limestone scenery in one of the warmest and driest parts of Greece, with a rich flora, including endemics.

The old town of Kardamili makes an excellent base, with plenty of good accom-modation and some fine old buildings. It lies right next to one of the key features of Outer Mani – the great Viros Gorge (not to be confused with Vikos Gorge in north-west Greece). This stretches right from the coast almost to the heart of Taigetos, and can be walked in its entirety, or 'dipped into' at several points. At the base, it is pos-sible to walk into the gorge and see some of the special flowers; there are clumps of a shrubby gromwell on the cliffs with white or blue flowers *Lithodora zahnii* – endemic to just this area, together with the striking, mauve-flowered, shrubby com-posite *Ptilostemon chamaepeuce*, and wild capers, amongst others. In shadier places, the local endemic meadow-rue *Thalictrum orientale* is quite common (and there is more of it up in old Kardamili), early spider orchids, and woodcock orchids push up through the spiny burnet, and the joint-pine *Ephedra fragilis* hangs down from the cliffs. The pale blue lice-bane grows in hot places, and the interesting evergreen birthwort (the only evergreen European one, with rather strik-ing flowers) sprawls over walls. At nearby Kardamili Harbour, there are many of the same plants, often more accessible, together with horned woodcock orchid, the spider orchid *Ophrys mammosa* (see p. 220), and some yellow *Fumana* species: *F. arabica* (big flowers) and *F. thymifolia* (small flowers). Sometimes the striking red fungus *Clathrus ruber* turns up here; it has no English name, but should be called the red geodesic dome fungus.

Further up, two villages – Exohori and Tseria – face each other across the gorge; it is a long way round by road, but they are linked by a footpath that climbs down into the gorge and up again, via an old settlement. There are superb views, abundant flowers here, and good birds. There are many of the lower altitude flowers, such as *Lithodora zahnii*, but also golden drops, the squill *Scilla messeniaca*, burnt candytuft, two of the yellow bee orchids and other *Ophrys* orchids, an autumn-flowering heather *Erica manipuliflora*, several autumn bulbs such as *Cyclamen graecum* and *C. hederifolium*, the white *Crocus boryi*, and the daffodil *Narcissus serotinus*, amongst others. The pink-purple European plumbago is quite common around here, flowering in autumn.

There is another, rather similar gorge further north, near Orovas, that is also worth exploring.

The terraces below Exohori, and other villages at the same height, such as Kastania, are a mass of flowers in spring. Swathes of scarlet peacock anemones, blue narrow-leaved lupins, the honeywort *Cerinthe retorta* (now widely grown in gardens), and lots of orchids – tongue orchids such as *Serapias orientalis*, giant orchids, two yellow bee orchids, *Ophrys reinholdii*, *O. spruneri*, *O. argolica*, and horseshoe orchid (see p. 220 for distinctions between them), sawfly, naked man,

and others. Wild pear trees are covered with frothy white blossom, and the annual soapwort *Saponaria calabrica* lines the edges.

Birds are rarely abundant here, though there is plenty of interest. Rock nuthatches are common, often nesting in the villages, as are crag and house martins, and blue rock thrushes. Black-eared wheatears breed in drier areas, woodlarks sing from the hillsides, and buzzards and Bonelli's eagles soar overhead. At passage periods, other birds of prey, and numerous smaller passerines, are funnelled up the peninsula. Higher still, above the village of Sidonia, there is an area of 'protected forest' dominated by Greek fir, described in more detail under Mt. Taigetos (p. 232).

Down on the coast, a minor road follows the sea edge southwards from the port of Aghias Dimitrios towards Trachila. There is an extensive, tufa-like, eroded limestone beach, with coastal flowers such as yellow horned-poppy, three-horned stock, sea rocket, sea-lavenders, stinking inula, golden-samphire, the sweet pea *Lathyrus clymenum*, and the yellow fenugreek *Trigonella balansae*. There are often groups of waders, especially at passage

Golden jackal *Canis aureus*

Lithodora zahnii

bellflower *C. drabifolia*, a pretty knap-weed with rosettes and sessile purplish flowers *Centaurea raphanina mixta*, red valerian, *Saponaria calabrica*, tree spurge, *Ptilostemon chamaepeuce*, pitch trefoil, and its broomrape parasite *Orobanche lavandulacea*, a blue stork's-bill *Erodium botrys*, and many others. There are lesser kestrels breeding here,

periods: little egrets, black-winged stilts, sandpipers, and stints, and kingfishers are frequent in autumn and winter. At the time of writing, there are ominous signs of increasing development here, so things may change. The masses of fibrous sea balls washed up are evidence of beds of the flowering plant Neptune-grass off-shore, a good sign of a healthy marine ecosystem. Further on, the road passes along the base of a large west-facing cliff that is a mass of flowers in spring: great mats of the bellflower *Campanula topo-liana* covered in flowers, an annual

Horseshoe orchid *Ophrys ferrum-equinum*

One of the superbly flowery olive groves for which the Mani is famous

The spectacular sweep of Limeni Bay and the mountains of Mani, with tree spurge in the foreground

and we have seen Eleonora's falcon, though they probably do not breed here (there is a colony not far away on Kithira, and they are very mobile birds). Rock nuthatches, black-eared wheatears, and blue rock thrush are common, and noteworthy butterflies include Bath white, dappled white, wall brown, and other common species.

Further south along the main Areopolis road, there are some beautiful flowery olive groves between Aghias Nikon and Itilo. They are separated by stone walls, with masses of limestone boulders in them, and the flowers are quite stunning from late March to mid-April. Amongst the masses of Pyrenean crane's-bill (in its large-flowered Peloponnese form) and *Cerinthe retorta*, there are tongue orchids, hyacinth relatives *Bellevalia dubia*, masses of pink hawksbeard, and yellow asphodels.

Kotschy's geckos live in the walls, often in large numbers, there are little owls in the old olive trees, Bonelli's eagles overhead, and woodchat shrikes in the bushes. A fine spot indeed!

Summers in Mani are rather too hot and dry, but by October it is surprising what is appearing. On a recent trip in October, we recorded over 30 butterflies, some in large numbers. There are meadow saffrons *Colchicum* species, yellow *Sternbergia lutea*, daffodils, masses of *Cyclamen graecum*, crocuses such as *Crocus boryi, C. niveus, C. goulimyi*, and others. Butterflies include coppers, Lang's short-tailed blue, Mediterranean skipper, plain tiger (related to milkweeds), Oriental marbled skipper, eastern rock grayling, Freyer's dappled white, and lots of others, congregating especially on the flowers of stinking inula.

Golden jackals are quite frequent around the Stoupa area (seen mainly at night), and beech martens are common wherever there are villages. Some of the old churches have good colonies of bats roosting or breeding.

Peloponnese

96 Inner Mani

The southernmost part of mainland Greece, notable for its special flowers and migrant birds.

Colchicum bivonae

Also known as Mesa Mani in Greek, this is the southernmost part of the central 'finger' of the Peloponnese, and also the southernmost part of mainland Greece (if you accept the Peloponnese as being part of the mainland – it is often said that since the completion of the Corinth Canal, it is actually a large island). Its scenery is spectacular yet barren, beautiful to some, daunting to others. High limestone hills, virtually treeless, dominate the view, and most of the coastline is rocky and desolate – the overwhelming impression is of bare rock. As with the Outer Mani (see p. 222), this is due to a combination of clearance of forest, grazing, fire, and a harsh arid climate, but the effect is even more marked here.

However, to the botanist it is a fascinating place, rich in flowers, some of which occur nowhere else. Although largely lacking in woodland, this is made up for by the abundance of plants of dry open places, but you do need to go early: March and early April is the peak time, with a reasonable amount to see in late October, then a continuing series of flowers through the mild winter, though rarely in abundance. Birds are best seen in April, when large numbers of migrants on passage join the residents and breeding species.

For the purpose of this book, we are taking the Inner Mani as being that part of the peninsula lying south of the Areopolis–Gythion road. In fact, this road provides a fine starting point, as it passes across the high central spine of the peninsula, giving access to some good localities. Where the road crosses the higher, bare, limestone areas, there are extensive patches of low *garrigue*, heavily grazed and regularly burnt, leaving a low cover of spiny bushes such as spiny burnet. However, paths into the *garrigue* soon reveal a rich flora: orchids galore include four-spotted, bumble bee, yellow, mirror, pink butterfly, horseshoe, sawfly, the pale pink toothed orchid, and others. Pink cyclamens *Cyclamen repandum* are in flower, with

Southern festoon *Zerynthia polyxena*

Spring flowers in an Inner Mani olive grove near Areopolis

Anemone blanda, the curiously named pretty blue iris, Barbary nut (which only comes into flower at lunchtime – you can often see them coming out while you are

Ranunculus millefoliatus

eating a picnic!), a distinctive yellow buttercup with ferny leaves *Ranunculus millefoliatus*, and bulbs such as tassel hyacinth and *Bellevalia dubia*. Here and there, some special plants need to be searched for: bright orange-red tulips (*Tulipa goulimyi* and *T. orphanidea*) in small clumps, and two fritillaries: the more common is the Greek fritillary, with greyish-green leaves and hanging purplish flowers with a green stripe on each petal; rarer (though locally common) is a fritillary that occurs nowhere else in the world but Mani: *Fritillaria davisii*; it is shorter (up to 15 cm rather than up to 25 cm), with shiny green leaves, and darker smaller flowers that lack the stripe. It also tends to flower a bit earlier, and is usually over by early April.

Bonelli's eagles are frequent over these hills, ravens are common, and cirl bunting, woodlark, black-eared wheatear, and woodchat shrikes are all common or abundant. Alpine and common swifts, together with hirundines, are usually overhead.

On the east side, around Passavas, there are a few more fertile areas where there is

Peloponnese

Nettle-tree butterfly *Libythea celtis*

extensive terracing (though often disused), and even some trees, mainly Valonia oak (with the largest acorns and cups of any European species). Here there is a rather different range of flowers, in greater abundance but with fewer rarities: various vetches including Bithynian, *Vicia melanops*, the striking blue-purple of *V. villosa* variety *varia*, deep red asparagus pea, brick red *Lathyrus cicera* and pale yellow *L. aphaca*; pink hawksbeards and salsify are common, and there are orchids galore – pink butterfly, giant, naked man, bumble bee, various *Ophrys* species including the rare *O. attica*, tongue orchids, etc., with the shrubby legume foetid bean trefoil giving some shade. In autumn, there are masses of *Cyclamen graecum*, the thin spikes of autumn ladies tresses, autumn squill in abundance, and occasional *Colchicum* species and bright yellow-orange *Sternbergia lutea*.

Southwards from Areopolis lie the impressive caves of Pyrgos Dirou, well worth a visit in their own right. The roadsides and olive groves nearby are particularly good for flowers with, amongst others, the striking silvery-leaved, white-flowered *Astragalus lusitanicus* subspecies *orientalis*, slightly reminiscent of a silvery broad bean plant, yellow fenugreeks *Trigonella balansae* (with bunches of hanging narrow fruits), and *T. graeca*, with flattened rounded fruit. There are at least three tongue orchids: *Serapias parviflora*, *S. orientalis* (large, with a hairy lip), and *S. lingua* (smaller with a pinker lip), horseshoe orchids, *Ophrys reinholdii*, a Dutchman's pipes *Aristolochia longa*,

scarlet pheasant's-eyes, blue larkspurs, fritillaries, large lord's and ladies, and *Trifolium boissieri*, a clover with large bright orange-yellow heads. In autumn, there are lots of *Sternbergia lutea* here, and masses of crocuses, together with a few meadow saffrons *Colchicum* species.

Other plants of interest worth looking out for on this southernmost part of Mani include the rare *Tulipa goulimyii* (only found here, at one site in Crete, and on the nearby island of Kithira). It flowers in late March and early April on the southernmost point of the peninsula. Crocuses to be found on the Mani, mainly between October and March, include white *Crocus niveus*, *C. hadriaticus*, and *C. boryi*, and the endemic lilac-flowered *C. goulimyi*; and meadow saffron *Colchicum* species include *C. psoridis*, the chequered *C. bivonae*, and *C. parlatoris*.

Some of the breeding birds have already been mentioned. Others include Rüppell's warbler in some of the higher scrub areas, eagle owls here and there on the higher slopes, scops owls around towns and villages, short-toed eagles, and Eleonora's falcons and peregrines, especially along the coast. In April, there is a large and varied influx of passage migrants, often making their first landfall since Africa, though most do not stay long. Masses of warblers, all the pied flycatchers (pied, collared, and semi-collared), rarer, more easterly wheatears such as Isabelline, rollers, and many others pass through, best seen soon after dawn.

From early April through to about the end of May, and then again in autumn,

Mantis *Empusa fasciata*

there are good numbers of butterflies, though it is not an outstanding site. Southern festoons are quite frequent, feeding as larvae on the Dutchman's pipes *Aristolochia* species, together with eastern Bath white, eastern dappled white, eastern baton blue, nettle tree, pygmy skipper, Lang's long-tailed blue, swallowtails, plain tigers, and many others, though not matching the abundance of mountain pastures.

Mammals are not a big feature of the Mani, except for a few: golden jackal are quite common here (see p. 110 for identification features). Although rarely seen during the day, they are often seen at night, especially near Areopolis. Beech

martens are common around villages, and – as with Outer Mani – some of the old churches have colonies of bats. Kotschy's gecko is the most frequent of the geckos, and Balkan green lizard and Peloponnese wall lizard are common throughout.

While in the Mani, it is worth seeking out some of the many old Byzantine churches, sometimes clustered together in villages, sometimes miles from anywhere, and often filled with neglected frescoes. It is also famous for its extraordinary tower houses, many of which still remain in the villages, with the best group at Vathia towards the south of Inner Mani. There is a fascinating story behind these houses, too long to be told here, but worth reading up.

97 Evrotas Delta

An important, though degraded, estuary complex in the southern Peloponnese.

The Evrotas Delta is the largest remaining wetland in the southern Peloponnese, lying between the central and eastern peninsulas. Although it must have covered a considerable area once, now it is largely drained and under intensive agricultural or residential use, leaving the remaining pieces of habitat fragmented and isolated, though some are well worth searching out. It is still a significant passage bird site, the third most important

area in Greece for breeding loggerhead turtles (after Zakynthos and Crete), and home to a good range of coastal and wetland plants and animals. It has recently received greater attention and protection as a European Natura 2000 site, and there are clear signs of a determination to protect and manage the remainder under a co-operative agreement between the government, the Sea Turtle Protection Society, and the Hellenic Ornithological Society, with the aid of EU money. It is estimated that about 3000 ha of habitat remain, as sand dunes, saltmarsh, seasonal and permanent lagoons, reedbeds, ditches, and *garrigue*.

Loggerhead turtles (see p. 268) breed here in moderate numbers, with about 200 nests recorded in 1999. They can be found all round the bay, concentrated in the least accessible areas, and are usually marked and protected straightaway to

Peloponnese

Glossy ibis *Plegadis falcinellus*

prevent trampling or predation by dogs and foxes. There is sometimes a turtle information kiosk on the beach at Leimonas in high season. Green turtles, which do not breed here (or anywhere in Greece), are often seen offshore, as are dolphins and porpoises.

The birds are best in spring and autumn. About 210 species have been recorded, including waders such as wood and green sandpiper, glossy ibis (up to 100 have been recorded at one time, with 500 or more during the season), and spoonbill; birds of prey such as marsh harrier, peregrine, and Eleonora's falcon, and even the occasional Imperial eagle. Both spotted eagles and Imperial eagles may spend part of the winter here, though they are rare. Herons can be particularly abundant at passage times, including good numbers of squacco, purple, and little bitterns (which are often very tame). Breeding birds are not exceptional, though the list includes little terns, Kentish plovers, kingfishers, and egrets, and much larger numbers of kingfishers winter here. The Divari lagoon and estuary, to the east of the delta, is especially good for birds, and other areas vary according to water levels and season. A few pairs of lesser kestrels breed within the delta, on old buildings and cliffs.

The dunes and beaches are excellent for flowers, especially in spring (though the beautiful sea daffodil flowers in July and August). Species to be found here include sea holly, sea medick, wild caper, purple spurge, a blue globe-thistle *Echinops spinosissimus*, spiny restharrow, the spiny umbellifer *Echinophora spinosa*, the ubiquitous but very pretty catchfly *Silene colorata*, and an endemic pale pink flax *Linum phitosianum*, which occurs nowhere else. It grows in just one area, where there are about 200 plants in *garrigue*, near Vlachiotis, in company with an interesting mixture of flowers, including the endemic *Tulipa goulimyi*, the very rare relative of Cretan sainfoin *Ebenus sibthorpii*, and the pretty little pink-flowered primrose relative *Coris monspeliensis*, amongst others. There are extensive beds of Neptune grass offshore, and inconspicuous flowers such as tasselweed and several pondweeds *Potamogeton* species at the river mouths. Good areas for flowers include Leimonas beach dunes and the beach at Trinisia. There is also a good spot a few kilometres west of the main site at an unnamed bay marked by the prominent rusting wreck of the *Dmitri*; in addition to flowers here, there are a few turtle nests and some good seasonally wet habitats.

There are few mammals to be seen, though jackals still occur in small numbers, together with foxes, badgers, and beech martens, amongst others. Both stripe-necked and European terrapins are common in the rivers, with the former being more abundant. Water snakes, especially dice and grass snakes, are common, preying on tadpoles and various small fishes or invertebrates. It is a good ploy to stand on the main road bridge at Trinisa, or the bridge over the Vasilopotamus south of Leimonas, and watch quietly for a

Tree frog *Hyla arborea*

Scarabeus semipunctatus

including the bright blue *Orthetrum brunneum*, darters, including the bright red *Sympetrum fonscolombei*, and the nail-varnish pink *Crocothemis erythraea*. The striking, plum-coloured *Trithemis annulata* is common, especially in late summer, and damselflies include small red-eyed (well outside its normal range) and blue-tailed. Along the strand-line, throughout the bay, there are masses of a pretty little tiger beetle *Cicindela hybrida* feeding on other strand-line insects.

while. You are almost certain to see terrapins, water snakes, and marsh frogs, and you may see or hear tree frogs which are abundant in more vegetated parts, especially those with giant reeds or milk thistles. Kingfishers often pass by. There are also two special freshwater fishes here: *Leuciscus keadicus* is only found here, while *Tropidophoxinellus spartiaticus* is endemic to the rivers of the Peloponnese.

Dragonflies are abundant in places, and can be seen throughout the area. Where the little spring-fed river meets the sea at Trinisa, there are emperors, skimmers,

The *garrigue* around the delta is generally good for flowers in spring (March–April), with abundant orchids, several species of *Cistus*, and many others.

There is a good new information centre just south of Skala on the Leimonas road, with exhibits, leaflets, and helpful staff, open during normal office hours. Access is easy from the main Gythion–Neapoli road, which touches the site in several places, and via roads leading south from Skala or Vlachiotis.

SITE 98 Lake Stymphalis

A spring-fed lake in the mountains of northern Peloponnese, with interesting birds.

Lake (or Limni) Stymphalis is a medium-sized lake lying in a depression that extends to about 2300 ha, though the area of good habitat covers no more than 1300 ha. Although often described as seasonal, it seems always to have some water, and is probably best described as fluctuating. There is a large area of open freshwater, mainly on the southern and eastern edges, and substantial areas of reedbeds. The western parts dry up more readily, and other parts of the basin have been drained for agricultural use.

Its primary interest is as a bird site, with features of value for most of the year.

Lakes such as this are rare in southern Greece, and it consequently acts as a magnet for migrating birds. It is a notable site for migrant herons including purple heron, glossy ibis, gull-billed and black terns, storks and many other birds. In winter, there are night herons, hen and marsh harriers, grey herons, and usually a few eagles and other birds of prey. In the breeding season, there are reasonable numbers of grey herons, marsh harriers, little bitterns (with up to 30 pairs), great-crested grebes, great reed warblers and a few other waterside birds, though it is not a major site. Ferruginous duck breed here in small numbers.

The surrounding hills are pretty unspoilt, with Greek fir, oak, and mixed woodland, as well as bare areas and *phrygana*, and there is a good range of typical scrub and open country birds, including rock partridges.

Botanically it is not rich; apart from a few wetland flowers such as purple-loosestrife and yellow iris, there are flowers of damp grassland such as pennyroyal and small-leaved mint, white horehound, and a little annual hare's ear *Bupleurum trichopodum*. The shrubby thyme *Thymus capitatus* is common along roadsides, and usually attracts butterflies. In spring, as any winter snow clears, there are crocuses in the grass, mainly the pretty lilac-blue *Crocus sieberi*.

The water levels may be too variable for a very rich aquatic fauna to develop, but there are plenty of marsh frogs, a few dice snakes, and reasonable dragonflies, although fewer than one might expect.

There are roads all around the lake, including a newly enlarged one on the south side, and ample parking places, though no observation areas, and no apparent protection for the site.

An interesting archaeological site, ancient Stymphalia, is being excavated on the north side.

SITE 99 Mt. Taigetos

Mt. Taigetos is the highest, most isolated, and barest mountain in the Peloponnese, though it has a surprisingly rich flora.

Mt. Taigetos is a broad name for the highest part of the chain of mountains that dominates the northern part of the Mani,

A fiery copper butterfly on *Drypis spinosa*

running northwards to Sparti and beyond. The highest point – Profitas Ilias – lies about 15 km south of Sparti, and reaches 2404 m, making it the highest mountain in the Peloponnese.

The lower parts of the mountain and its manifold gorges are covered in other site descriptions. The high areas soar above these, snow-covered through the winter and spring, and far more inaccessible.

The western slopes are remarkably bare except in a few places, but on the eastern slopes there are woods of Greek fir and some fine black pines, with Oriental planes in the valleys. The trees peter out at around 1800 m, giving way to bare limestone, though this is proba-

as red helleborine and pyramidal orchid, bastard balm, bellflowers, the lovely *Morina persica* (an anomalous member of the teasel family, whose whorls of creamy flowers turn deep red), and many others are common. In spring, there are primroses, peacock anemones, Gargano dead-nettle, 4-spotted orchids, lesser celandines, the tiny arum relative *Biarum tenuifolium*, and scattered populations of the snowdrop *Galanthus reginae-olgae*. These clearings are excellent places for butterflies and other insects in summer, including white-banded grayling, two-tailed pasha, brimstone and Cleopatra, fritillaries including silver-washed, clouded yellows, blues, coppers including fiery copper, eastern orange tip, hairstreaks, browns, and many others. Dragonflies, from goodness knows where, patrol the clearings and tracks, including the striking *Lindenia tetraphylla* at times.

At about 1600 m, there is an EOS refuge among black pines, and from here on up the forest begins to thin out, and there are

bly lower than the natural tree-line. The forested areas are very attractive, with flowery, grassy clearings amongst old trees, and occasional wet areas. Red lilies *Lilium chalchedonicum*, foxgloves, especially *Digitalis ferruginea*, orchids such

The Taigetos range in spring, seen from the north-east

Biarum tenuifolium

no motorable tracks. The flowers become steadily smaller, thanks partly to heavy grazing but also to the increasing altitude and duration of snow cover. The variety, if anything, increases though, and there are many special plants on these higher areas. From about 1700 to 2000 m, there are vast areas of bare rocky limestone, with some scrub and occasional cliffs. Here, there are widespread species such as the snow-in-summer relative *Cerastium candidissimum*, the pretty large-flowered *Hypericum olympicum*, little pinks such as *Dianthus cruentus*, the familiar lilac-purple clumps of *Aubrieta deltoidea* (frequently grown in gardens), large tussocks of the striking scabious *Pterocephalus perennis*, and small bushes of a spiny barberry *Berberis creticus*. In spring, there are masses of *Anemone blanda*, *Cyclamen repandum*, alpine squill, tight rosettes of the knapweed *Centaurea raphanina*, mats of the beautiful *Prunus prostrata* covered in pinkish flowers, and a form of the purplish *Corydalis solida* sometimes known as *C. densiflora*. There are many rarer species, too: the endemic crocus *Crocus sieberi*

An old olive grove on Taigetos, full of peacock anemones and *Euphorbia rigida*

subspecies *nivalis*, which differs from the other subspecies in having a hairless throat, only occurs on Taigetos, flowering in spring as soon as the snows melt. Later, there are masses of the sprawling marjoram *Origanum scabrum* (endemic to Greek mountains), an unusual cushion bellflower *Campanula papillosa*, the skullcap *Scutellaria rupestris* subspecies *rupestris*, saxifrages such as *Saxifraga marginata*, *S. sibthorpii*, and the larger white-flowered *S. chrysosplenifolia*. There are big tussocks of the pink-flowered *Acantholimon androsaceum*, sprawling plants of grey-leaved *Sideritis clandestina* (one of the components of the popular Greek mountain tea), all too many tussocks of spiny *Astragalus* plants, mainly *A. creticus* subspecies *rumelicus* and *A. angustifolius* with white flowers, clumps of one of the most attractive of mulleins, the dwarf *Verbascum acaule*, and too many other species to mention. None grows large here, though they are individually often very pretty and worth seeking out.

Galanthus reginae-olgae

Taigetos could not be described as a great bird-watching site, though it is of some interest. Golden eagles used to breed here, though it seems unlikely that they still do; they are generally very rare in the Peloponnese now, though a major prey species, the rock partridge, still occurs here. Short-toed eagles are not uncommon still, there are one or two pairs of Bonelli's eagles, and honey buzzards and eagle owls breed, though inconspicuously. The high barren plateaux and valleys of Taigetos are perfect for shore larks, and they breed here in small numbers close to the summit ridge. Both choughs and alpine choughs can be found in the high areas.

On the south-west side, above the village of Saidona, there is an area of 'protected forest' dominated by Greek fir, with a few evergreen maples, sweet chestnut, holm oak, and other deciduous trees. The forest climbs high into the Taigetos massif, to the edge of the treeline, with the trees diminishing in size as you ascend. In sheltered places, there are masses of pale-flowered primroses, blue and white *Anemone blanda*, and red peacock anemone, the white-flowered penny-cress *Thlaspi graeca*, bright blue alpine squills and the endemic *Scilla messeniaca*, the beautiful local form of *Iris unguicularis* in great flowery clumps, and ferns such as *Asplenium onopteris*. As the snow melts, there are masses of blue and white *Crocus sieberi* subspecies *nivalis*. Other flowers here include a snow-in-summer *Cerastium candidissimum*, and shrubs such as the yellow legume *Cytisus villosus*, prickly juniper, and eastern hornbeam. In wet areas, there are stream frogs and palmate newts. The habitat is particularly fine, with flowery, grassy clearings and many old trees. Butterflies are common, including large tortoiseshells, Cleopatras, southern festoon, and fiery copper, and the impressive giant peacock moth. Regular birds include woodchat shrike, Cretzschmar's bunting, several woodpeckers, rock nuthatch, and subalpine warbler. Eagles and other birds of prey regularly pass overhead.

The best access is from the east side. There is now a good road up the mountain from the main Sparti–Gythion road, through Palaeopanagia. At about 1100 m, it becomes a dirt track which can be followed with difficulty as far as the EOS refuge. There is a good track above Saidona up into the protected fir forest, and on over the ridge. The best time for a visit is from May to July. There is a good 1:50 000 'Road Editions' map, *Taygetos*, that covers the whole area.

SITE
100 Mt. Chelmos

Also known as Aroania, this is one of the most beautiful, spectacular, and interesting mountains in Greece.

Mt. Chelmos is a general name for a group of mountains lying roughly in a horseshoe around the valley of the river Styx, or Mavroneri. The highest peak is Psili Korfi, which reaches 2355 m, but the whole region has the feeling of a mountain range, with substantial areas at high altitude and many villages with a mountain character. It is a much damper region than the mountains of the southern Peloponnese, and there are vast tracts of forest, especially on the east side. From the natural history point of view, the region of interest extends far beyond the high mountains, east towards Killini (see p. 239), and north-west to Kalavrita and the Vouraikos Gorge (see p. 255).

As a botanical site, it is superb, with a very large range of species which are mostly growing well in ungrazed or only lightly grazed conditions. The best area is

Colchicum triphyllum

undoubtedly the upper valley of the Styx, though there is no easy way to reach it. Probably the best way is to follow the motorable track southwards from Peristera on the east side of the mountain, then the waymarked trail which climbs steadily up the valley, and becomes gradually more difficult as the high screes are reached. The woodlands of pine and spruce are magnificent (see below), but the plants become more special as the trees open out higher up, from about 1800 m onwards. On steep limestone cliffs and rocks, there is a beautiful

Teucrium aroanium

The summit range of Mt. Chelmos from the Styx valley

little cushion plant tightly covered in blue flowers – *Campanula* (*Trachelium*) *asperuloides* – which occurs from medium altitudes right up to the high tops; incidentally, if you read *Flora Europaea*, and any subsequent book that has copied it, the flowers are described as pink; however, at all its known sites (and it is endemic to quite a small area) it is quite definitely blue. It was probably described originally from herbarium specimens, and the mistake was simply perpetuated. Other cliff flowers include the shrubby composite *Staehelinia uniflosculosa*, the blue *Scilla messeniaca*, the widespread cushion scabious *Pterocephalus perennis*, and a very unusual germander *Teucrium aroanium*, which grows in extensive cushions covered with dull purple flowers, and is almost confined to Chelmos. In fact, it is a good area for germanders, with wall germander, mountain germander, and yellow germander all common. On scree slopes and in crevices, there is a very unusual and distinctive borage relative *Arnebia densiflora*, with clusters

of showy yellow flowers, at its only European site apart from a small population on Mt. Giona (see p. 163). Curiously enough, there is another borage relative *Solenanthus stamineus* which has its only European site here, except for a small population on Giona. There is a third interesting borage here, the endemic *Rindera graeca*, which has greyish leaves and clusters of purple flowers. The beautiful *Viola delphinantha* occurs here on a few cliffs (see p. 78), together with alpine aster (in a variant sometimes considered to be subspecies *cylleneus*), two yarrows, the white cushiony *Achillea umbellata*, and the yellow *A. holosericea*, amongst others. Yellow betony is frequent just above the tree-line, with the beautiful sage *Salvia ringens*.

At about 1900 m, at the foot of a high wet cliff, there is a cave from which a stream (the infant river Styx) issues, and over which a waterfall flows for part of the year. In this particularly damp environment, there are some splendid flowers that continue blooming well into high

Open scrub on limestone near the tree line on Mt. Chelmos

summer: a butterwort *Pinguicula crystal-lina* subspecies *hirtiflora* occurs in masses on wet ledges, while within the cave there is a swathe of a lovely columbine *Aquilegia ottonis* subspecies *ottonis*, which only grows here and in southern Italy. A pretty yellow saxifrage *Saxifraga sibthorpii* is common in the damp shade, amongst a mass of herb Robert. Other species of interest include an endemic flax *Linum aroanium*, an endemic globularia *Globularia stygia* that only occurs here and on Killini (see p. 240), several catchfly species, including *Silene auriculata* and *S. radicosa*, the lousewort *Pedicularis graeca*, the pink woodruff *Asperula boissieri*, and many others. Spring gentian occurs here at its southernmost European locality.

In this same area, there are crag martins and alpine choughs on the cliffs, wallcreepers, ravens, grey wagtails, and a few common kestrels.

The Chelmos range is quite exceptional for butterflies, with a vast range of species recorded that include rarities and some

confined to this area, although curiously butterflies are not as abundant here as on some other mountains with fewer species, such as Menalo (p. 243) or Chelidon (p. 168). Apart from common species such as swallowtails, Cleopatra, brimstone, and Gruner's orange tip, there are special species including southern swallowtail, the striking Apollo, and the less conspicuous clouded Apollo; the pretty eastern greenish black-tip (like a Moroccan orange tip but with black, not orange wing-tips) is frequent, Greek clouded yellow occurs above about 1100 m, and fiery coppers cluster around nectar flowers such as *Drypis spinosa*. There is a remarkable number of species of blue butterfly here, making identification of individual specimens quite difficult. Apart from common species, there are Bavius blue (an uncommon south-eastern species), Zephyr blue (widespread but uncommon), blue argus (south-eastern), the delightfully named Grecian anomalous blue, which occurs on a number of Greek mountains and is, of course, brown; the Pontic blue, which is virtually confined to this area within Europe; and finally, Chelmos blue which, as the name suggests, is confined to Mt. Chelmos at higher altitudes (though it does occur elsewhere outside Europe). Other species of interest here include a strikingly coloured variant of the large grizzled skipper, the tufted marbled skipper, and the Grecian grayling.

An alternative approach to the high parts of Chelmos, which involves less climbing, is via the new road to the Kalavrita ski resort, and on to the EOS refuge at over 2000 m. From here, one can cross the summit ridges and descend into the Styx Valley, though the path is no easier. Other plants of interest around the high areas include the stemless mullein *Verbascum acaule*, the prostrate plum *Prunus prostrata*, the skullcap *Scutellaria orientalis*, a soapwort *Saponaria bellidifolia*, and many more. Shore larks breed up here in small numbers, and alpine accentors can be found here and there.

Flowing around the slopes of Chelmos, and especially on the east side, is a vast area of forest, dominated mainly by Greek fir, pines, and oaks such as Hungarian. The path up the Styx Valley travels through good forest, or there is a superb unmetalled road from Zarouchla to Pheneos which passes through the whole range of mid-altitude forest. It is a good area for orchids, with red, white, sword-leaved, and broad-leaved helleborines, pyramidal and 4-spotted orchids, violet limodore, early spider, greater butterfly, and bird's-nest, amongst others. A large marsh-orchid *Dactylorhiza saccifera* is common in ditches and flushes, and here you can also see a fine thistle *Cirsium creticum*, square-stemmed St John's-wort, spiny restharrow, and more. Other flowers in the woods and clearings include large-flowered calamint, tree heather, a distinctive bellflower *Campanula trachelium* sub-species *athoa* (a subspecies of nettle-leaved bellflower), wintergreens, the blue and white vetchling *Lathyrus laxiflorus*, bastard balm, foxgloves such as *Digitalis laevigata* and *D. ferruginea*, downy woundwort, *Phlomis samia*, and many others.

The clearings are particularly good for butterflies, with Balkan marbled whites, southern white admiral, white-banded graylings, fritillaries including silver-washed, cardinal and lesser spotted, wood whites, hairstreaks, and many others. Eastern greenish black-tip also occurs here.

In spring, the forests are alive with birds – crossbills, four or five woodpeckers, serins, tits, firecrests, Bonelli's warblers, spotted flycatchers, nightingales, and many others. Beech martens are common in the woods, and you frequently come across their droppings. Altogether, it is one of the best areas in Greece for the naturalist, though little known and rarely visited. I spent a day there in mid-July 2000 with a friend, and we saw no one (not even local people) all day.

SITE 101 Mt. Killini

Extensive, high limestone mountains in the north-east Peloponnese, reaching 2374 m, rich in mountain flowers.

Although Killini (Ziria) is slightly higher than nearby Chelmos, it is less varied and spectacular, with fewer high cliffs, humid gorges, or forested areas, and as a result it feels less like a high mountain area. Most of the slopes and higher parts are of bare limestone, though there are patches of old forest high on the northern and eastern slopes, and lower down on the southern slopes, such as around the village of

Above this, the mountain consists mainly of bare limestone with low vegetation, though the flora is actually quite rich. Interesting species growing here include the same form of alpine aster as on Chelmos (see p. 237), the endemic *Globularia stygia*, saxifrages including *Saxifraga scardica*, which forms huge clumps over rocks, the scabious *Pterocephalus perennis*, the same two yarrows as on Chelmos (*Achillea umbellata* and *A. holosericea*), a houseleek *Sempervivum marmoreum*, the hemispherical hummocks of *Acantholimon androsaceum* covered in pink flowers, the large-flowered speedwell *Veronica austriaca*, and masses of *Drypis spinosa*. The last plant is a bushy relative of the stitchworts, covered in pink flowers which are a magnet for any montane butterfly such as coppers, blues, small fritillaries, and hairstreaks, and for burnet moths. The bellflower relative *Asyneuma limonifolium* is quite common – its pale blue starry flowers look almost like a squill, especially as the spikes are usually grazed down to a few centimetres, but they have five petals not six. The mountain plant *Sideritis clandestina* is quite common, with grey leaves and pale yellow flowers striped with reddish-brown, sold in local villages as 'mountain tea'.

Kastania; this has the appearance of a declining resource: burnt, over-grazed, and mistreated. Killini has the advantage of having a good metalled road up high on the north side above Trikala (which makes a useful base), from where a rough track goes all the way round the mountain. Although this can make access easier, it has almost certainly added to the burden of grazing and forest destruction, and removed some of the mountain's essential wildness.

At about 1500–1600 m, there are large areas of juniper, hawthorn (mainly *Crataegus pycnoloba*), spiny *Astragalus* hummocks, clumps of the electric blue *Eryngium amethystinum* (which is especially good for butterflies), and numerous thistles, including the striking *Ptilostemon afer*, the white *Cirsium hypopsilum*, and the large-flowered *C. macrocephalon*, all alive with butterflies on calm, sunny days. This habitat is particularly good for red-backed shrikes, which are abundant, and rock nuthatches are frequent in suitable places.

At the upper edges of the forest, especially where there are cliffs, you can find clumps of the large blue bellflower *Campanula versicolor*, spikes of a pennywort *Umbilicus horizontalis*, pink and white spikes of *Morina persica*, globe thistles such as *Echinops microcephalus*, yellow St Barnaby's thistles, and many more. Butterflies are common (though not as abundant as on some of the more vegetated Greek mountains), as well as other interesting insects such as longhorn beetles, sand-wasps, rose chafers, and a wealth of bumble bees.

An early spring visit towards the snowline on Killini should turn up *Crocus sieberi* subspecies *sublimis*, including the strikingly three-coloured form sometimes known as forma *tricolor*, wild tulips, especially *Tulipa*

Drypis spinosa

Mt. Killini

sylvestris subspecies *australis*, and yellow stars-of-Bethlehem. In autumn, there are good numbers of bulbs including the pinkish-purple *Colchicum pulchellum* and *C. graecum*, and the small yellow flowers of *Sternbergia colchiciflora*.

The whole site could not be described as exceptional for mountain birds, perhaps because of the lack of forest and the excessive grazing pressure. Red-rumped swallows are common around the middle slopes, with common wheatears, stonechats, and other widespread species. Alpine accentors are rare at the highest levels, and peregrines are seen occasionally.

On the north-east slopes of the mountain, there are two natural temporary lakes which dry out by midsummer. They do not appear to have any special interest, but are worth a look when there is water in them.

Access is easy onto the mountain, as described above, or via rough tracks from almost any angle. A new 1:50 000 map, in the 'Road Editions' series, is due to be published soon which should make exploration here easier.

SITE 102 Mt. Erimanthos

A substantial block of mountains in the north-west Peloponnese, rising to 2221 m, with vast expanses of wild, inaccessible country.

Mt. Erimanthos, and its associated peaks of Mt. Skiadovouni, Mt. Lambia, and Mt. Kaliphoni, forms a vast area of high, wild country to the south of Patra, dominating the north-western corner of the Peloponnese where it rises like a wall from the plains. Biologically, these peaks are rather less rich than Killini and Chelmos, though this may partly be because there is more waiting to be found. In general, they are bare of forest, though there are scattered patches of good fir and pine forest.

In the woodland areas (such as above Kaletzi), Greek hellebores are abundant at their only site in the Peloponnese (they are much more common further north on 'mainland' Greece). Other plants of interest in this zone include foxgloves such as *Digitalis ferruginea*, eastern bugle, Gargano and bifid dead-nettles, four-spotted orchids, the yellowish carline thistle *Carlina corymbosa*, and the usual assortment of montane roadside thistles.

Higher up, there are some more special plants, though they are not easy to find. The scattered, dark-foliaged, surprisingly large trees are usually *Juniperus foetidissima*, and other junipers occur. A rare bellflower relative *Edraianthus parnassicus* has its only Peloponnese site here, clumps of purplish *Aubrieta intermedia* occur, as well as *Morina persica*, *Inula verbascifolia* at unusually high altitudes, the scabious *Pterocephalus perennis*, the

endemic bedstraw *Galium taygeteum*, the mountain tea *Sideritis clandestina*, the white-flowered *Daphne oleoides*, one of the yellow stars-of-Bethlehem *Gagea fistulosa*, *Colchicum graecum* (which flowers in early autumn), a fritillary *Fritillaria mutabilis*, the little autumn-flowering yellow *Sternbergia colchiciflora*, and many others, though all are small and often hidden in clumps of something tougher or spinier.

Butterflies include rock grayling, white-banded grayling, southern swallowtail (and the more common swallowtails), mountain small white, Iolas blue, Gruner's orange tip, Cleopatra, lesser spotted fritillary, scarce copper and many more, though it is not a major butterfly site. Apollos have been recorded here. It is always worth checking the thistles and blue *Eryngium amethystinum* that are so common at mid-altitudes, or higher along tracks.

Several tracks climb high onto the mountain, notably from Kaletzi on the west side, or near Vlasia to the north-east.

The view from Mt. Erimanthos encompasses some superb unspoilt limestone scenery

^{SITE}
103 Mt. Menalo

A moderately high limestone mountain, rich in flowers and butterflies.

Clypeola jonthlaspi

Mt. Menalo lies just north-west of Tripoli, rising to 1980 m, bare-topped above its forests of Greek fir. Although not of outstanding importance, it is now very easily accessible, thanks to the combination of the Corinth–Tripoli motorway and a good ski station road almost to the top, and it is certainly worth a detour any time between April and July.

In spring, while the tops are still snow-covered, the lower slopes have a good mixture of flowers and early butterflies. The pink cinquefoil *Potentilla micrantha*, a yellow crocus *Crocus olivieri* (easily recognized, thanks to its six-branched style – the only yellow crocus with this feature), *Crocus chrysanthus* (with three-branched style), purplish *Crocus sieberi*, alpine squill, *Anemone blanda*, a stars-of-Bethlehem *Ornithogalum oligophyllum*, the dwarf iris *Iris pumila* subspecies *attica* in its yellowish form, widow (mourning) iris *Hermodactylus tuberosus*, burnt candytuft, and various others. The last-named is a pretty pink cress, the main food-plant of Gruner's orange tip, which also occurs here. Other flowers at this time include the striking spurge *Euphorbia rigida*, disc cress, two forms of yellow bee orchid, and yellow stars-of-Bethlehem. Lower still, in the lightly cultivated zone, there are fields full of the striking and uncommon cornfield weed *Leontice leontopetalum*, a yellow-flowered herbaceous member of the barberry family that can reach about 70 cm high, with masses of the deep blue speedwell *Veronica glauca*, and a range of forms of early spider orchid.

Mount Menalo, with masses of the rare cornfield weed *Leontice leontopetalum* in the foreground

Early butterflies include over-wintered large tortoiseshells and brimstones, common, eastern, and Gruner's orange tips (see box), painted ladies, etc. Most of the birds are common and widespread, and include such species as buzzard, wren, coal tit, blackbird, and subalpine warbler.

Higher up, later in the summer, there are masses of flowers such as thistles (e.g. *Ptilostemon afer* and *Onopordum illyricum*), *Eryngium amethystinum*, fox-gloves that include *Digitalis ferruginea*, *Campanula versicolor* on cliffs, the pink hawksbeard *Crepis incana*, and violet limodores. Higher still, there are low-grow-ing flowers such as the white-flowered *Astragalus angustifolius*, pinkish-purple *Pterocephalus perennis*, yellow *Sideritis clandestina*, and the white snow-in-summer *Cerastium candidissimum*.

In the upper forest clearings, butterflies and other insects are abundant in midsum-mer. White-banded grayling, great sooty satyr, cardinal, brimstone, Cleopatra, clouded yellows, scarce and common swal-lowtails, zephyr blue, and many more, all busily taking nectar from thistles, *Eryngium amethystinum*, *Campanula versicolor*, and other suitable flowers. Menalo probably has more bee-hives on it than any comparable Greek mountain, perhaps partly due to its proximity to Tripoli and easy road access, but it must also be an indication of the great amount of nectar that is available from flow-ers. Other insects here include vast numbers of red-flashing grasshoppers, and longhorn beetles such as the impressive *Ergates faber*, which is brown and very large.

Red-backed shrikes are common in the scrub zone at middle altitudes, and ravens are frequently seen overhead, though it is not a large or high enough area to attract the real mountain specialists. Wall lizards, in the form *albanica*, occur here too.

Orange tip butterflies

There are places in Greece, such as Menalo and Parori (see p. 218), where three orange tip species may be on the wing together. They are reasonably distinctive when settled, and with practice can be distinguished while in flight. Males of all three species have patches of orange towards the wing-tips, as the names suggest. Common orange tip, familiar to most north European naturalists, has a basically white ground colour above, with green, white, and black marbled hind-wings below. Gruner's orange tip is noticeably smaller, similar in pattern but with a pale yellow ground colour, especially on the fore-wings. The east-ern orange tip is a more striking but-terfly (very similar to the Moroccan orange tip of south-western Europe), with a bolder yellow ground colour, strongly marked orange patches, and yellow and black marbled hind-wing undersides (with no white). Females are harder to identify, and could be confused with other species.

104 Mt. Parnon

A gem of a mountain, hidden away in the wild country north-east of Sparti.

North-east from Sparti, towards Astros on the east coast of the Peloponnese, there is a huge area of unspoilt, sparsely popu-lated countryside on a rolling plateau that lies at 700–1000 m. Mt. Parnon rises steadily above the plateau, covering a wide area and reaching 1934 m at its highest point (though most maps place the name Mt. Parnon a little further south, amongst the lower peaks).

The Tripoli–Sparti road skirts the western edge of this large region of open countryside, passing through at almost 1000 m, and anywhere along here is of interest. In spring, there are great clumps of the beautiful *Iris unguicularis* in its particularly nice Peloponnese form, together with the pretty periwinkle *Vinca herbacea*, widow iris, a few early orchids, peacock anemones, burnt candytuft, and others, with a sparse population of early butterflies such as Gruner's orange tip. All the rolling countryside between here and Mt. Parnon is virtually uninhabited, but such fields as there are often have interesting cornfield weeds, including some good populations of wild tulips *Tulipa orphanidea*. There are quite good populations of the more common steppe-breeding birds here, such as Cretzschmar's bunting, woodlark, woodchat shrike, black-eared and common wheatears, tawny pipits (best located by listening for their distinctive song-perch song, which is a bit like that of a tree-pipit but with fewer notes), and short-toed larks.

Around the monastery of Malevi (east of Aghios Petros and marked on most maps), there is an area of very unusual scenery, extensive rolling steppe country dominated by Syrian juniper, here at its only European locality! It is quite a striking plant, possessing unusually long needles for a juniper and much larger cones, with the seeds united into a single stone, rather like a plum.

Closer to Mt. Parnon itself, there are extensive forests of Greek fir, pines including both *Pinus brutia* and black pine, and scattered trees of stinking juniper, especially higher up. These forests are little known and barely visited by anyone, but are well worth exploring. Neither Mt. Parnon nor the surrounding forest and plateau are listed as an 'important bird area' by ICBP, partly because there are no rare raptors known to be breeding here, but perhaps also because the area is under-studied; it would certainly repay detailed exploration. The flowers are generally widespread species, such as the foxgloves *Digitalis laevigata* and *D. ferruginea*, the shrubby *Anthyllis hermanniae*, tree heather, smoke bush, common strawberry-tree, and a few orchids such as four-spotted, early spider, violet limodore,

Open forest of Syrian juniper at its only European locality

Peloponnese

Large ant-lion *Palpares* species

and broad-leaved helleborine. In the upper forest areas, a very large ant-lion occurs, resembling *Palpares libelluloides* though not yet identified with certainty.

Below the highest peak, to the west, there is an attractive, flat-bottomed, *polje* (internally drained valley), of the type quite common in the limestone mountains of Greece. It is heavily grazed, but not cultivated and certainly worth a visit, being quite rich in birds, butterflies, and flowers. A distinctive and uncommon mullein *Verbascum mallophorum*, with downy white leaves, a branched inflorescence, and violet filament hairs, is common here, together with masses of *Eryngium amethysteum*, lots of thistles, a spurge *Euphorbia rigida*, a little brownish-flowered garlic *Allium callimischon*, the mountain tea *Sideritis clandestina*, cushions of *Astragalus*, a couple of pinks, globe thistles, and the reddish-flowered *Phlomis samia*. In spring, there are crocuses, grape-hyacinths, alpine squill, both white and yellow stars-of-Bethlehem, and various other fine flowers. Cirl buntings, wheatears, and goldfinches are common.

Amongst the butterflies visiting the flowers, you may find the tiny and little-known odd-spot blue, one of Europe's smallest butterflies and extremely rare.

The highest parts of the mountain are best for the special flowers, which grow mainly on the high-altitude bare slopes, especially on the east side down towards the village of Kastanitsa. A woundwort *Stachys chrysantha* with silvery-white leaves and pale yellow flowers grows here (and elsewhere, lower down around the mountain, wherever there are suitable limestone rock faces), with a red-flowered, very spiny knapweed *Centaurea laconica*, the yellow spikes of a toadflax *Linaria peloponnesiaca*, and the bushy, white-flowered *Cerastium candidissimum*. Dwarf species in the higher parts include the creeping mats of *Paronychia kapela*, the rock-cress *Draba lasiocarpa*, two yarrow relatives, the yellow-flowered *Achillea holosericea* and white-flowered *A. umbellata*, prostrate mats of the pink woodruff *Asperula boissieri*, a low-growing, perennial, shrubby plantain *Plantago holosteum*, in a dwarf form sometimes known as variety *alpestris*, tiny stonecrops such as *Sedum rubens* and *S. sartorianum* (a high-altitude version of the more familiar wall-pepper, but with the lower stems covered in dead leaf-bases, and each leaf with a distinct spur at the base), and various others.

There is a reasonable track up to the chapel below the highest point, and various other trails through the area. There is an accurate 1:50 000 map of the whole area in the 'Road Editions' series.

SITE 105 Pylos Bay

A fascinating area, with a rich and varied bird life almost all year, and one of the few European sites for chameleons.

Immediately north of Pylos (site of a famous battle between Athens and Sparti) on the west coast of the Peloponnese lies Pylos Bay, protected by

a small island. The northern part of the existing bay is terminated by a long sandbar which holds back the sizeable Dinari Lagoon and an area of saltmarsh, cover-

Natura 2000 site. Unusually for Greece, there are nature trails and information boards (with useful, well-presented information), as well as a tower hide overlooking the lagoon. The main habitats are brackish open water, saltmarsh, sand dune, and scrub, with rocky *garrigue* on the nearby headland. There is very little in the way of reedbeds. Offshore lie some of the best Neptune-grass beds in southern Greece.

It is probably best known as a bird site, with year-round interest. In spring, the area is alive with birds as breeding species, passage migrants, and the last winter visitors combine. Breeding species include black-winged stilt, marsh harrier (in small numbers, probably because of the lack of reedbeds), collared pratincoles in small numbers on the saltmarsh, Kentish plovers, little terns, kingfishers, little bitterns (apparently in quite large numbers), and fan-tailed warblers. Short-toed eagles are often seen over the area, probably breeding on the nearby headland or island. Reasonable numbers of greater

ing about 2000 ha in all. To the west of the lagoon lies a rocky peninsula, topped by an ancient castle. The whole combination is very scenic, and it is a popular beach in summer. The bay itself is not of special importance, but the lagoon and sandbar are now being managed and partly protected with the aid of EU money as a

Pylos Bay

Rosa sempervirens

flamingos winter here, staying on quite late into spring, though as yet they are not known to breed, and a good range of waders passes through. Unfortunately the site can still be heavily disturbed in winter by shooting, despite its status, which reduces the number of birds using it. Other birds seen on a recent spring visit include hoopoes, cormorants, common tern, rock nuthatch, wheatear, little egrets in abundance, great white egrets, and grey herons.

The sandbar is covered by scrub and low dunes. Although the seaward side is considerably disturbed in summer, the amount of parking and driving on the sand has been greatly reduced by notices recently, and quite large areas away from the beach are relatively undisturbed. The flowers are interesting, and include sea-holly, the spiny umbellifer *Echinophora spinosa*, white asphodel, a pretty little red-flowered restharrow *Ononis diffusa*, honeywort, and various sea-lavenders, including *Limonium oleifolium* and *L. vulgare*. Shrubs include the olive relative *Phillyrea latifolia*, sea buckthorn, and *Pistacia* species.

The most interesting feature of this site, however, is the presence of chameleons. Chameleons are extremely rare in Europe, and the population here seems to be closer to the north African species *Chamaeleo africanus* than the normal European ones, though it may turn out to be a different species altogether. It appears that the adults live mainly away from the coastal strip, returning here in July (females) or August (males) for mating and egg-laying. The females lay about 50 eggs in nests in the sand, where they develop over a period of almost a year, incubated by the heat of the sun. Uncontrolled camping and parking had been damaging large numbers of the nests or killing the young hatchlings, so control of this should help to increase the population. After mating and laying, the adults gradually disperse from the sandbar.

Other features of interest in the area include two species of tortoise (Hermann's and marginated), tree frogs, grass snakes, and green toads, which breed in the lagoon. In early spring (until about the end of March), the curious, persistent call of the green toads, sounding like a distant pump, can be heard as they mate and lay strings of eggs.

There is a good road which crosses the sandbar into the site from near Gialova, and from here tracks lead northwards.

SITE 106 Mt. Panakhaiko

A moderately high limestone mountain, reaching 1926 m, with a good flora.

Mt. Panakhaiko (sometimes called Voida, after its highest peak) seems to tower over Patra and the adjacent coast thanks to its steep northern slopes, though it is not particularly high, and does not rate a mention in books on Greek mountains. However, it is high enough to have a reasonable flora and fauna, rather similar to that of Erimanthos or Chelmos (see p. 236), though lacking in some of the special species of these mountains. There are limited stands of Greek fir, with some pines, reduced by fire and over-grazing. Above the trees, there is a typical 'hedgehog' zone dominated by the white-flowered spiny *Astragalus angustifolius*, with other spiny species such as the sea-holly relative *Eryngium amethystinum* (always worth looking at for butterflies), a carline thistle *Carlina corymbosa*, and thistles such as *Onopordum illyricum*. The snow-in-summer relative *Cerastium candidissimum* is abundant here, as on most limestone mountains in central Greece, together with pinks such as *Dianthus pinifolius*, *Aubrieta intermedia*, and the pretty blue knapweed *Centaurea triumfettii*. Other flowers of interest include the white-flowered *Achillea umbellata*, the little, yellow-flowered daffodil relative *Sternbergia colchiciflora* (flowering in October), crocuses, including the spring-flowering *Crocus sieberi* subspecies *sublimis* and the autumn-flowering *C. cancellatus*, a fritillary *Fritillaria muta-*

bilis with purplish-brown chequered flowers, and the autumn-flowering *Colchicum graecum*.

The eastern area of the Panakhaiko range is considered particularly important for birds, including the impressive gorge of the river Selinoundas, and as far eastwards as Mt. Clokas (or Klokas), which rises to 1367 m. This is a fine region of partly wooded mountainous country, with extensive roadless stretches. There was a strong colony of griffon vultures in the Selinoundas Valley (the only breeding colony in the Peloponnese), but sadly this has continued to decline, due mainly to illegal shooting. Booted eagles, and the much scarcer Bonelli's eagles still occur in the area, together with peregrines, rock partridges, honey buzzards, several woodpecker species, and probably eagle owls.

There are reasonable roads and tracks into the mountain area from all directions, and access is easy.

1̊0̊7̊ Cape Araxos

Extensive and remarkably unspoilt wetlands and other habitats, collectively making up easily the best wetland in the Peloponnese.

Cape Araxos projects north-westwards into the Ionian Sea to the south-west of Patra, making it the north-west corner of the Peloponnese. It is a remarkable location that has escaped development and exploitation, thanks to a combination of circumstances, including church ownership of a large section. The area of interest extends patchily southwards down the coast from Cape Araxos for almost 50 km to Kotichi Lake, and inland almost as far as the main road in places. Within this region, there are good examples of brackish lagoons, sand dunes, saltmarsh, grassland, freshwater marshes, pine and oak woodland, and dry limestone hills. Although it is a Ramsar Site (internation-

ally important wetland), and a Special Protection Area in part, as well as a candidate Special Area for Conservation, it appears to have no practical protection at present, and it is hard to escape the thought that it could be a really major wet-

Male Ladybird spider *Eresus niger*

dunes, and sandy beaches, with vast areas of glasswort, sea purslane, sea club-rush, marram grass, and common reeds. There are limestone hills scattered within the area, reaching no great height but providing a quite different habitat, with new nesting and feeding opportunities. There are good examples west of Araxos. The whole area has a wonderfully unspoilt feel to it, with little of the littered, bulldozed, and overgrazed nature that characterizes so many otherwise attractive Greek sites. The combination of good habitats, intimately mixed and able to contribute to each other ecologically, is particularly important, too.

It is especially well known ornithologically (though this is by no means its only value, as shown below). Breeding birds here include marshland and saltmarsh species such as collared pratincoles, black-winged stilts, a good population of little bitterns, and a few white storks which breed in the forest, at their only Peloponnese site. Kingfishers are common at all times of year, Kentish plovers are frequent along the seaward margins, and little terns, common terns, and calandra larks nest on the sandy dunes. Stone curlews and hoopoes are both quite common, marsh harriers are abundant for much of the year, and both little and great-crested grebes breed. Olive-tree warblers occur relatively frequently, especially in the 'parkland' areas, with a population estimated recently at 70.

At passage periods, there can be large numbers of waders, wildfowl, birds of prey, and passerines. These include glossy ibis, Dalmatian pelicans (a few

land complex with better protection and integrated conservation management. It is well worth a visit at almost any time of year, and there is a great deal to see.

Before looking at the detailed species of interest, it is worth describing something of the habitat, since there are now very few comparable examples of unspoilt, mixed coastal habitats anywhere else in Greece. There are extensive forests of umbrella and Aleppo pines and Valonia oaks, known collectively as the Strofilia Forest (Strofilies is a Greek word for umbrella pines), lying mainly to the south of Kalogria. The forest varies from dense to open, and there are patches of oak woodland that are more like parkland or pasture–woodland than pure woodland. Here and there, extensive marshlands occur, which flood in winter and then gradually dry out in spring, and there are also stretches of more permanent freshwater marsh, with some reedbeds, such as the area to the south of the Kalogria–Araxos road. The large, sheltered bay running inland from Cape Araxos has something of the character of a lagoon, though it is deeper than most, while Kotichi Lake is a fine example of a shallow coastal lagoon. Along most of the coast between Kalogria and Kotichi, there are extensive areas of saltmarsh, sand

Kentish plover *Charadrius alexandrinus* (Mike lane)

Spring-fed lakes and limestone mountains at Kalogria

non-breeding individuals on Kotichi Lake), black-necked grebes, redshanks, sandpipers (including up to 250 marsh sandpipers), various terns, most herons, turtle doves, hirundines, and masses of warblers, flycatchers, and other small birds. A small number of ferruginous duck usually pass through, together with many more common species of wildfowl. The lagoons and marshes remain unfrozen through normal winters, when they are used by egrets, herons, a few pygmy cormorants, marsh and hen harriers, duck such as wigeon, pintail, shoveler, and pochard, and many more. Visiting birds of prey in winter or on passage include peregrine, red-footed falcon, spotted and short-toed eagles, hobby, osprey, lesser kestrel, merlin, and common buzzard.

It is an excellent place to see and hear reptiles and amphibians. At least 5 amphibians and 20 reptiles have been recorded, and many of them are found in large numbers here. For example, the marshland south of the Araxos–Kalogria road pulsates with amphibian calls in spring. Marsh frogs

are extremely abundant (providing food for many of the other inhabitants of the marsh), but this is also a good site for the relatively recently described *Rana epeirotica*, which differs mainly from the more widespread marsh frog in its call, as well as in minor morphological features. Tree frogs are frequent throughout the damper areas wherever there is slightly taller vegetation, green toads breed in the shallow waters, and common toads are widespread. Snakes are quite common, especially grass and dice snakes, which can be seen swimming in the lakes and rivers, but also cat snake, leopard snake, Dahl's and Balkan whip snakes, Aesculapian snake, and nose-horned viper, to name a few. Balkan green lizards and Balkan wall lizards are common, while Turkish geckos and Greek algyroides are not infrequent. Both stripe-necked and European terrapins occur here, though the former is probably the commonest at this site. Hermann's and marginated tortoises are common in *garrigue*, open grassland, and rough grassland.

The beach stretching from Kalogria southwards to Kotichi Lake is one of the

Calandra lark *Melanocorypha calandra*

few mainland breeding sites for logger-head turtles. Up to 85 nests have been recorded here in recent years, but the site is poorly protected and numbers are probably declining.

It is not an important mammal site, and there are few reliable recent records, though otters and golden jackals (see p. 110) may still occur, and beech martens and eastern hedgehogs are both common. Brown hares can occasionally be spotted loping away through the dunes or grassy areas, though they are not common.

It is not a major site botanically, though there is plenty to interest anyone visiting mainly for other reasons. The pine woods and limestone hills are quite good for orchids, such as early spider, yellow bee, and the distinctive *Ophrys mammosa*, with bug orchid, loose-flowered, and toothed orchid here and there. On the sand dunes, there is sea medick, sea holly, the beautiful sea daffodil, the spiny umbellifer *Echinophora spinosa*, the distinctive sedge-like *Cyperus capitatus*, and

sea spurge, amongst others. In scrub and open woodland areas, there are shrubs such as tree heather, Phoenician and prickly juniper, mock privet, myrtle, and masses of pretty herbaceous species such as peacock anemone, barbary nut, and white asphodels. In the marshes, there are yellow irises, purple-loosestrife, flowering-rush, and many others.

It is also an excellent place for insects and other invertebrates, not surprisingly given the range of habitats available. Dragonflies and damselflies are abundant in early summer, including darters such as common, southern, and red-veined, emperor and lesser emperor, the distinctive plum-coloured *Trithemis annulata*, the hawker *Aeshna affinis*, and many others. Butterflies include Camberwell beauties, large tortoiseshells, Cleopatras, brimstones, and fritillaries. It is an excellent place for other groups of insects and other invertebrates; for example, a recent visit in spring turned up velvet ants, various solitary wasps and bees, colonies of the large, blue-black bee *Chalicodoma parietina* which builds multiple homes in the form of a sheet of hole-filled 'mortar' over rocks and buildings, ladybird spiders, jumping spiders, ruby-tailed wasps (striking little parasites on solitary wasps), and many others.

Roads permeate the area westwards from the main Patra–Pirgos road. The best starting point is the Araxos–Kalogria road, then southwards.

108 Monemvassia

Unspoilt hilly country, with the medieval town of Monemvassia as its showpiece and main attraction.

Monemvassia is a remarkable place – the 'Greek Gibraltar', but better! It is an ancient town built on the southern side of a dramatic limestone peninsula jutting eastwards from the Neapoli Peninsula. It

is one of those wonderful ancient Greek sites (like Mystras and Delphi) where you can enjoy spectacular scenery, a marvellous historical site, and abundant features of natural interest, all together.

Unlike Mystras or old Delphi, however, Monemvassia is still inhabited and can be freely entered at any time.

The south-facing cliff and slope where it is built is a superb botanical site with many other features of interest. Wild leeks are common, together with masses of yellow horned-poppy, various colour forms of hoary stock (partly derived from cultivation), *Malcolmia* species, rock alison, pitch trefoil and its blue broomrape parasite *Orobanche lavandulacea*, squirting cucumber, sea squill, joint-pine, several scabiouses, yellow asphodel, tree mallow, and many more. On cliffs and old walls, there are rarer plants such as the borage rel-

Hyoscyamus albus

ative *Procopiana cretica*, a henbane with creamy-yellow flowers *Hyoscamus albus*, a beautiful mat-forming bellflower, often covered with blue-purple flowers *Campanula andrewsii*, the white-leaved and yellow-flowered *Inula verbascifolia*, and at least two rare woundworts: *Stachys candida*, and the extremely rare *S. spreitzenhoferi*, which occurs nowhere else. Both have white flowers marked with pink, but *S. spreitzenhoferi* has very short calyx teeth, and leaves that are green above and white below (rather than white-woolly all over). Tree spurge is abundant on the warmer parts of the cliffs, with its masses of grey-green leaves turning reddish almost as soon as summer starts, and the tall stately spikes of giant fennel are everywhere, often reaching 2 m or more in height. Ferns such as rusty-back and *Cheilanthes fragrans* are common.

Rock nuthatches call loudly from the cliffs, male blue rock thrushes sing from vantage points, and a peregrine can often be seen overhead. Both lesser kestrels and Eleonora's falcons can also often be seen here. Rüppell's warblers and black-eared wheatears breed on top of the peninsula, and short-toed eagles are regular visitors. Peloponnese wall lizards and Greek rock lizards are common.

It is also a surprisingly good place for butterflies and other insects; the beautiful southern swallowtail breeds here, together with common and scarce swallowtails, dappled whites, Mediterranean skippers, southern meadow brown, southern comma, the monarch relative plain tiger (probably only as a migrant), graylings, and many others. The splendid giant peacock moths are common, and can sometimes be found in quantity during the day, settled around somewhere where a light has been on at night.

The nearby beaches can be extremely colourful in spring, with masses of pink-purple stock, especially *Malcolmia flexuosa*, sheets of the yellow fenugreeks *Trigonella graeca* and *T. balansae*, mixed with other attractive plants such as yellow *Lotus cytisoides*, the sea heath *Frankenia hirsuta*, a tiny little campion *Silene sedoides* in holes in the rocks, a rare garlic *Allium circinnatum* with spirally curled leaves, endemic to the Aegean, bladder vetch, pink kidney-vetch, barbary nut, the yellow *Fumana arabica*, and a few orchids such as mirror, bug, and some of the tongue orchids.

The area on the mainland around Monemvassia is especially known for reptiles, perhaps partly because of the particularly warm climate but also because it has been relatively well studied. Widespread species recorded commonly here include marginated tortoise, Hermann's tortoise, terrapins, Greek algyroides, Greek rock lizard, Peloponnese wall lizard, Balkan green lizard, worm snake, the curious little snake-eyed skink (rather like a slow-worm with very short legs), the Greek legless skink (like a small slow-worm, with a more pointed snout), slow-worm itself, European glass lizard, Dahl's whip snake, and Montpellier snake. Rarer species include Kotschy's gecko and sand boa. The latter is the only European representative of this mainly tropical

family, which just creeps into south-east Europe. The sand boa is little known and rarely recorded, partly because it is not common, but also because it spends most of the daylight hours either hidden or hunting in the galleries of small mammals. It is a smallish brown and white mottled snake, with a pointed snout, unlike anything else in Europe.

The hills and low mountains northwards from Monemvassia are wild and rugged, and largely unpopulated. Some 80 000 ha are recognized as an important bird area (IBA), known collectively as the East Lakonia Mountains. The highest peaks reach almost to 1300 m (e.g. Mt. Chionovouni), and many are above 1000 m, where there is a small amount of Greek fir woodland. Breeding birds here include short-toed and Bonelli's eagles, blue rock thrush, black-eared wheatear, rock nuthatch, and woodchat shrike. Three uncommon warblers all breed here in moderate numbers: Rüppell's, Orphean and olive-tree, and Cretzschmar's bunting is present but rare. These eastern coastal

Medieval town of Monemvassia

Snake-eyed skink *Ablepharus kitaibelii*

mountains are an important corridor for migrating passerines and birds of prey, though there is certainly a great deal more to be discovered. Cape Maleas, at the extreme south-east end of the peninsula, is well known as a passage bird-watching site. Regular sightings include all three black and white flycatchers (pied, collared, and semi-collared), rollers, hoopoes,

masses of warblers, various wheatears including Isabelline, all the possible shrikes, and the tiny scops owl, whose distinctive call sounds rather like sonar.

Despite the attraction of Monemvassia town and large tracts of unspoilt country, this is a very poorly known area, with much waiting to be discovered. Besides the obvious times to visit, in April and May, it is also worth coming in late autumn or winter, when the weather can be remarkably good, and there are yellow *Sternbergia lutea* flowers, several meadow saffron *Colchicum* species, and winter-flowering crocuses such as the Greek saffron crocus *Crocus cartwrightianus*.

Peleponnese

SITE 109 Vouraikos Gorge

A dramatic gorge running down to the Gulf of Corinth, noted for its birds and flowers.

The Vouraikos Gorge runs roughly northwards from Kalavrita to the sea. In parts, it has striking cliffs, on one of which there

Mega Spileo monastery and the cliffs of the Vouraikos gorge

is a famous monastery, Mega Spileo (meaning 'big cave'). The gorge passes through a mountainous area, with Chelmos (see p. 236) just to the south-east and the Panahaiko massif (see p. 248) to the west, giving rise to a spectacular mixture of scenery. In places, there are Aleppo pine forests, with extensive areas of scrub, and cliffs and rocky outcrops. About 5600 ha are considered to be an important area for birds, especially birds of prey. Lesser kestrels breed on the cliffs, and there was a colony of griffon vultures, though these seem to have disappeared. Short-toed eagles still breed, and can often be seen hovering in search of snakes or lizards, while breeding honey buzzards are much more secretive. White-backed and other woodpeckers breed in the forested areas, and crag martins and alpine swifts are common.

Botanically, it is of interest, though not as good as the valley of the Styx further east (see p. 236), and such cliff flowers as do occur are more inaccessible here. The gorge is best seen from the light railway that runs from Kalavrita down to the coast – and the spring flowers can be readily appreciated from the train – but the upper parts can be traversed by road from near Mega Spileo to Kalavrita, which makes it easier to stop where desired. The cliffs around the monastery and nearby are par-ticularly striking, and here you can find clumps of the pinkish-red flowered bedstraw relative *Putoria calabrica*, golden drops such as *Onosma erectum*, a pretty pink woodruff *Asperula arcadiensis*, aubrietas, the scabious *Pterocephalus perennis*, and various other specialist cliff flowers, while lesser kestrels and jackdaws wheel overhead. It is a dramatic place.

SITE 110 Lake Kaiafa

A mosaic of lake, dunes, and limestone hills on the west coast of the Peloponnese.

South of Pirgos, on the west coast of the Peloponnese, there is a long arching bay on the shore of the Kiparissiakos Gulf that supports one of the most unspoilt large beaches in Greece. At the point where the main road almost reaches the beach, just north of Zacharo, there is a conjunction of craggy limestone hills, a large freshwater lake fed by hot springs, extensive sand dunes partly forested with pines, foreshore, and river mouth. It is not a major site, but certainly worth a stop at almost any time of year (though busy in summer).

The waters issuing from the springs on the east side of the lake are clear and unpolluted (though smelling of sulphur!), with a rich invertebrate life, and they are a popular feeding place for bats which probably roost in the caves nearby. The limestone cliffs above the lake support a good range of flowers, including tree spurge, flowery clumps of a bellflower probably best described as *Campanula andrewsii*, the golden drop *Onosma frutescens*, rock alison, the three-leaved form of wild sage, joint-pine, often tumbling down the rock in long curtains, the white-leaved fleabane *Inula verbascifolia*, various rock figworts, ferns such as *Cheilanthes fragrans*, and other cliff-dwellers. The delightful rock nuthatches nest on the cliff, with their loud ringing calls a constant feature of any visit. Black-eared wheatear, blue rock thrush, and warblers such as Sardinian and subalpine breed in the scrub and rocky areas higher up.

The lake consists mainly of open water, with quite a limited reed fringe and very little emergent or floating vegetation. This limits its value to wildlife, though marsh and tree frogs are both abundant, and dragonflies such as red-veined, and

Part of the vast undeveloped sandy beach near Lake Kaiafa

common darters, emperors, and black-lined skimmers are common. Cetti's warblers and a few great reed warblers call from the reeds, and fan-tailed warblers 'ping' monotonously from the surrounding flat grassy areas. On the lake, there are coot, little grebe, great-crested grebe, mallard, and a few other duck in the breeding season, with more in winter. The few muddy areas are well used by waders on passage. Hoopoes breed nearby, and golden orioles often linger on passage but probably do not breed here.

Fan-tailed warbler *Cisticola juncidis*

West of the road and railway line, there is a long line of dunes and a sandy beach. Although the beach becomes busy in summer at the few access points, it is generally remarkably unspoilt. A fine range of dune flowers can be found, and there is some attractive open Aleppo and umbrella pine forest, with serins and other common birds. Dune flowers include sea-holly, sea medick, the prickly umbellifer *Echinophora spinosa*, the luxuriant knapweed *Centaurea sonchifolia* (often supporting small colonies of tree frogs, which hide under its leaves if it is growing near other suitable habitat), asphodels, sea daffodils, the galingale *Cyperus capitatus*, cotton-weed, horned dock, various stocks, including the tiny little *Maresia nana*, and many others.

Where the river emerges, there are terrapins and green toads, and there are sometimes Kentish or little ringed plovers around. Little terns and other terns can be seen offshore, though they probably do not breed. Loggerhead turtles can also turn up, but it is not one of their main breeding beaches (the nearest is a little further north – see p. 252).

This mixture of habitats is reasonably good for butterflies, though mainly more common species: Cleopatras and brimstones, common orange tip, common and scarce swallowtails, southern festoon in small numbers, Bath white, Mediterranean skipper, pygmy skipper, and the usual collection of blues, heaths, and coppers.

The main west coast road passes through the area, and there is a café and parking place at the closest point to the sea. A back road runs around the east side of the lake northwards from Zacharo, giving good access, and tracks run to the lake shore and marshy areas.

Ionian Islands

Ionian islands

Introduction

The Ionian Sea lies between Greece and the southernmost part of Italy, to the south of the Adriatic Sea. Running down the west coast of Greece, from the Albanian border to the northern Peloponnese, there is a series of islands close to the shore that are collectively known as the Ionian islands. In fact, they extend beyond the mainland border of Greece northwards, as half of Corfu is off the Albanian coast, though still part of Greece.

Ecologically and historically, they have links with Italy; they have been colonized by the Italians and other invaders at various times, and have a slight Italian flavour even today, though they are undoubtedly Greek in other ways. In general, they are damper and greener than most of lowland Greece, though not all of the islands have the same rainfall. They form the western bastion of Greece, and receive the first rainfall of the westerly winds. Corfu, in particular, receives much more rainfall as it lies close to a particularly wet region centred around Albania and southern Yugoslavia. The average rainfall for Corfu is about 135 cm, whereas that for Athens is only about 40 cm (Athens is actually one of the drier parts of Greece, as it lies in the rain shadow of several mountain ranges). Zakynthos, the most southerly of the main Ionian islands, has an intermediate rainfall of about 90 cm. So it is not surprising that these islands remain relatively green and lush through the early summer, when other parts of Greece are becoming dry and brown.

All the Ionian islands are composed of limestone, and are effectively the higher parts of a drowned mountain range sitting on the Greek continental shelf, with relatively shallow water between them and the

Cape Arilla, north-west Corfu

Previous page: **Garakas, Zakynthos**

111 Paxos
112 Cephalonia
113 Zakynthos

Corfu:
114 Corfu: North
115 Corfu: Central
116 Corfu: South

mainland, but deeper water immediately to the west. They are all mountainous, with Mt. Pantokrator on Corfu reaching almost 1000 m, though much the highest point of the chain is Mt. Ainos (or Enos) on Cephalonia, which reaches 1628 m and is snow-covered through the winter and into the spring in most years.

Aristolochia rotunda

is worth noting here that many of the smaller and often uninhabited islands are also of interest, though access can be difficult. For example, the Diapontia Islands, including Erikoussa, are known to be an important site for breeding shearwaters and Eleonora's falcons; the Echinades Islands and Atokos off the Messolongi area (see p. 155) are known to be important for wintering eagles and occasional black vultures; and the Strofades Islands, south of Zakynthos, are an important breeding site for both species of shearwater. Such sites, even though they may be inaccessible, contribute greatly to the wildlife of the region. For example, any ferry trip between islands or to the mainland is likely to be accompanied by good views of shearwaters, with the possibility of cetaceans and turtles, too. Zakynthos is easily the best site for breeding loggerhead turtles in the Mediterranean, and they can be sighted offshore when they begin to gather for the breeding season.

The islands are not really isolated enough to have acquired many of their own endemic species, though there are three or four endemic plants on Corfu, and a number of flowers from Mt. Ainos have been separated as distinct species or subspecies, such as the soapwort *Saponaria aenesia*, though generally their affinities to equivalent mainland plants are pretty clear and they have not diverged much. There are other flowers which occur in the islands as a whole, and often parts of the nearby mainland, and Corfu shares a few with Albania.

We have picked out a number of sites of interest on the main islands, though it

The Ionian islands are probably at their best in April and May, with a rather longer spring than in much of lowland Greece thanks to their slightly damper, cooler climate, and the higher areas, especially Mt. Ainos, remain of interest well into summer. September and October are also good, with abundant passage birds, some autumn flowers, and a surprising number of butterflies.

SITE 111 Paxos

A small island lying to the south of Corfu, with a surprisingly rich flora in a quiet and attractive setting.

Paxos (or Paxi), though only small, has ample interest to repay a week's visit, especially in spring. As with other Ionian islands it is greener than many parts of Greece, and remains green through May

and into June. Like most of this area, it is made up mainly of limestone; there are extensive olive groves, and these are the dominant feature of the island, but there are also *garrigue*, cliffs, and other rocky places, and a small amount of woodland. Permanent wet areas are virtually absent, which limits the range of birds and mammals.

The olive groves here are often ancient and, as on Lesvos (see p. 194), they can be worth exploring as if they were open woodland, since the original contours are retained and there is relatively little cultivation or spraying. Plants of interest include the bear's breeches *Acanthus spinosus*, the striking tall alexanders relative *Smyrnium rotundifolium*, tassel hyacinths, crown anemones, the pretty little bellflower *Campanula ramosissima*, the unappealingly named, but rather attractive, lice-bane (one of the wild delphiniums), the purplish-blue, branched broomrape, and large lord's and ladies. Orchids include giant, pyramidal, lesser yellow bee, and sometimes monkey orchid (an uncommon plant in much of Greece), as well as the horned woodcock orchid. In more disturbed parts, there may be wild gladioli, shepherd's needle, and crown daisies, among other flowers. In autumn, you can find the gorgeous yellow *Sternbergia lutea*, pink

Orchis fragrans

Cyclamen hederifolium, and a few meadow saffrons *Colchicum* species. In grassy places and along roadsides, there are bee orchids, tongue orchids, wild pea, asparagus pea, and various clovers. Amongst the tongue orchids, there is an endemic species (found only here, on Corfu, and a few nearby areas) – *Serapias politisii*. It is intermediate between small-flowered tongue orchid and the *S. vomeracea* group, with a narrower petal base than the latter, but larger darker flowers than the former.

The limestone *garrigue* and cliffs probably have the most natural vegetation on Paxos, though they are usually harder to explore than olive groves. Orchids of interest here include bug orchid (in its more fragrant form *Orchis fragrans*), bumble bee, yellow bee, horseshoe orchid, late spider, woodcock, sombre bee, pink butterfly, green-winged orchid (in the *Orchis picta* form), and all the species found in olive groves. There are many attractive shrubs covered with flowers in spring, often making a striking spectacle: Spanish broom, spiny broom, the low-growing *Anthyllis hermanniae*, often covered with pale yellow flowers, myrtle, sage-leaved cistus (white-flowered), and *Cistus creticus* (with large pink flowers), a winter-flowering pink heather *Erica manipuliflora*, together with the usual kermes oak, spiny burnet, mastic tree, and other *garrigue* shrubs. The striking tree spurges grow on warm slopes near the sea.

On limestone slopes and cliffs by the sea, there are masses of the tiny pink *Silene sedoides*, matted sea-lavender, rock samphire, the pretty pink *Putoria calabrica*, stocks such as *Malcolmia maritima*, sand-crocuses *Romulea bulbocodium*, the tiny yellow flax *Linum strictum*, two fumanas *Fumana arabica* (with large yellow flowers), and *F. thymifolia* with narrower leaves and smaller flowers. The tiny silvery rosettes of *Evax pygmaea* grow in bare places (easily missed, but worth close inspection once found), and there is an unusual knapweed with purple flowers and silvery bracts *Centaurea alba* subspecies *deusta*, found on cliffs.

Matted sea-lavender *Limonium bellidifolium*

Birds are abundant here, though not exceptional. Common breeding species include stonechat, blue rock thrush, crag martin and the usual hirundines and swifts, some of which come across from the mainland; black-headed and cirl buntings, woodlark, woodchat shrike, Sardinian and subalpine warblers, and turtle doves. At passage periods, a wide variety of species turns up.

The smaller island of Antipaxos lies just to the south. Although lacking some of the mainland species, it is even more unspoilt. It can be reached by boat from Gaios on Paxos. Paxos itself can be reached by boat from Igoumenitsa or Patra.

SITE 112 Cephalonia

The largest of the Ionian islands, with many unspoilt areas topped by the Mt. Ainos National Park.

Cephalonia is a large and attractive island lying astride the entrance to the Gulf of Patra. It is remarkably unspoilt, and has largely escaped the effects of mass tourism seen on Corfu and Zakynthos, though this is beginning to change now that direct flights from north Europe are more frequent.

The key site on Cephalonia is the Mt. Ainos National Park. This is little known outside Cephalonia (and not very well known on it!) and, like most Greek National Parks, receives little protection, management, or funds. However, it is an important site, well worth a visit. Mt. Ainos rises to 1628 m – a considerable peak, high enough to be snow-covered through winter and into spring. The park, which covers 2240 ha (closer to the size of an average nature reserve than a National Park) was established in 1962 primarily to protect an area of fine old Greek fir forest, for which this is the type location; popular books often suggest that the fir is confined to the National Park, though actually it is a common species through the mountains of Greece, and there are many equally fine forests elsewhere. Towards the summit, the trees become extremely gnarled and windswept, though quite picturesque, and it is a fascinating habitat in its own right. Overall, the mountain area is botanically rich, though it is heavily grazed and most species do not flower in abundance. On the lower slopes, there is a widespread endemic yellow treacle-mustard *Erysimum cephalonicum*, eastern bugle, Gargano dead-nettle, the pretty pink *Putoria calabrica*, the greyish spurge *Euphorbia rigida*, masses of *Anemone blanda*, and a curious little china-blue squill relative *Hyacinthella leucophaea*, amongst others.

Higher up, within the National Park itself, there are many other flowers. The pale yellow spikes of few-flowered orchid (which differs from the similar Provence orchid in that it has unspotted leaves and, sometimes, fewer flowers), four-

Part of the rugged Argostoli Gulf coastline

spotted orchids, yellow bee orchid, stocks *Malcomia* species, alpine squill, *Corydalis densiflora*, the leopard's-bane *Doronicum orientale*, masses of anemones, patches of the pretty *Crocus sieberi* subspecies *sublimis*, flowering as the snow melts, and various other flowers that are common and widespread. Plants that are virtually confined to Mt. Ainos and the surrounding area include a skull-cap *Scutellaria rubicunda* subspecies *cephalonica* in a few high altitude rock crevices, the pansy *Viola cephalonica* (with mauve flowers, flowering in May–June in open grassy areas), and

a soapwort *Saponaria aenesia* (which is rather similar to the more widespread and very pretty *S. calabrica*, differing in having smaller flowers, and more or less spherical fruiting capsules on turned-back stalks) in open limestone habitats, including roadsides. Other unusual plants one might see include the very rare catchfly *Silene ionica*, confined to here and one other mountain, the uncommon *S. ungeri*, a rare sandwort *Arenaria guicciardii* with white flowers in dense terminal clusters, a subspecies of the more widespread Gargano bellflower *Campanula garganica* subspecies *cephalonica*, a fritillary *Fritillaria mutabilis*, and the pinkish-flowered peony *Paeonia russii*. In late autumn, the white crocus *Crocus hadriaticus* can be found, together with autumn-flowering cyclamen.

Bird life is not spectacular, probably limited by the relatively small extent of the mountain area and the heavy grazing. Griffon vultures still occur in small numbers, with short-toed eagles, common kestrel, buzzard, subalpine warblers,

Southern swallowtail *Papilio alexanor*

Ancient Greek fir forest on Mt. Ainos

occasional Rüppell's warblers, Orphean warblers, woodchat shrike, and others. White-backed woodpeckers and other woodpeckers breed in the forests. Part of the area, with surrounding hills, is considered to be an 'important bird area' for 'raptors and a range of passerines associated with a mosaic of forest, scrub and agricultural land'.

The commonest lizard here, and elsewhere on Cephalonia, is the Greek algyroides, a small brownish lizard with darker, white-spotted flanks in males, which occurs mainly in slightly shaded areas and is less conspicuous than most lizards.

There are many other noteworthy habitats on Cephalonia. Some of the olive groves are ancient, such as those near the so-called Lake Avithos (north-west of Poros), and have a variety of micro-habitats including old walls, grassland, shady banks, and scrub. These are good places for Dutchman's pipes *Aristolochia longa* and *A. rotunda*, orchids such as giant,

woodcock, pink butterfly, tongue, and the endemic form of horseshoe orchid *Ophrys gottfriediana*, together with *Iris unguicularis*, *Bellevalia* species, vetches, and many others. Butterflies here include Cleopatra, southern white admiral, southern comma, common orange tip, and skippers such as the orbed red-underside.

On the coast, there are sandy sites such as at Skala, where the dunes and low sandy areas support sea-holly, sea medick, sea daffodil, three-horned stock, the pretty little poppy *Papaver nigrotinctum* with dark-blotched red petals, yellow horned-poppy, Virginia stock, and more. Many places offshore have masses of Neptune-grass which may cause unsightly piles of debris (and the characteristic bristly balls) on beaches, but is a good indication of clean water. Where there are cliffs, the striking purplish-flowered shrubs of *Ptilostemon chamaepeuce* are common, with *Putoria calabrica*, white-flowered *Gagea graeca*, and sometimes masses of tree spurge. The other endemic orchid *Ophrys cephalonica* (a form of early spider orchid) can be found here and there. In hot rocky areas, there are various other butterflies including lattice brown, southern swallowtail and eastern rock grayling.

There are few good wetlands on Cephalonia, though at the head of the Argostoli Gulf (on the west coast) there is a moderately extensive area with grazing marshes, reedbeds, ditches, and a small amount of open water, with a relatively unspoilt sandy beach. At passage periods, especially spring, there are good quantities of birds: masses of little egrets and a few great white egrets, large quantities of grey herons, a few purple heron, squacco heron, little grebe, masses of coot, Cetti's warblers, and many others. Marsh harriers hunt over the area, marsh frogs call from the pools, and tree frogs hide in the denser vegetation. The nearby limestone hills have some good *garrigue* harbouring most of the orchids already mentioned, together with yellow bee and lesser yellow bee, four-spotted, toothed, sawfly, and *Ophrys iricolor*, the

distinctive relative of sombre bee orchid with a strong blue patch on the lip and pink underneath it; peacock anemone, the fritillary *Fritillaria graeca*, and the little *Anchusa cretica*.

Access to Cephalonia is by direct charter flights in summer, local flights from Athens, or by ferry from Killini and Patra. The ferry journeys are worthwhile for the excellent views of shearwaters and other birds, and occasional cetaceans.

Fritillaria graeca

113 Zakynthos

A medium-sized island, best known as home to the largest loggerhead turtle breeding colony in the Mediterranean.

In some ways, Zakynthos is a disappointment. It is an essentially beautiful island, of just over 400 square kilometres, which has suffered from unmerciful, tourist-related development – which is still continuing apace – and agricultural changes. There are still some wild corners and good sites, but if you exclude the internationally important turtle beaches at the southern end, then most other Ionian islands are more rewarding for the naturalist.

Zakynthos supports what is easily the best breeding area in the Mediterranean for loggerhead turtles. Since 1999, a substantial part of the Lagana Bay area has been designated as a marine park, and there are now real hopes that it will be properly protected.

Currently, about 2000 turtles come ashore at Lagana to breed, and the density of nests per kilometre is greater than anywhere else (over 2000 nests were recorded

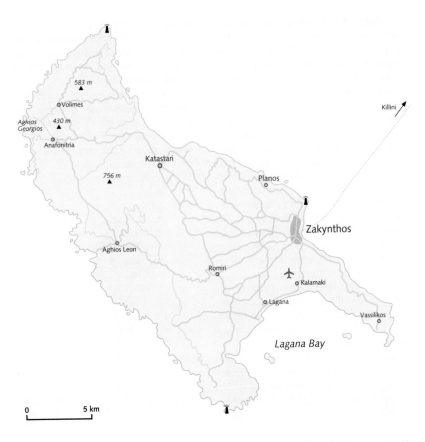

in 1995 over a length of 3.9 km); while this may be partly because the habitat is good, it is largely because of the limited number of suitable sites elsewhere. The combination of extensive off-shore beds of Neptune-grass and good sandy areas above high-water mark suit the loggerhead well. Since 1982, the loggerheads from Greece have been tagged, though it is interesting that new untagged adults continue to turn up on Zakynthos each year.

The loggerhead turtle is primarily a shallow coastal water species, feeding mainly on invertebrate animals such as crustaceans, molluscs, and jellyfish. Adults may reach over a metre in length, though Mediterranean individuals tend to be slightly smaller than this. They spend most of their life at sea, sometimes dispersing over long distances, and since they are

reptiles, they need regularly to come to the surface to breathe. Despite their predominantly marine lifestyle, they have retained their link with the land during the breeding season. From about the end of April, they begin to congregate offshore near the breeding beaches, just relaxing and mating. From late May onwards, the females will start to haul ashore at night, initially for exploratory visits, but eventually to dig a chamber up to 50 cm deep. In these she lays about 120 white eggs, each roughly the size of a table-tennis ball, which are then completely covered with sand. Each female usually makes two or three nests per season, but then will not come back to the site for several years.

The eggs remain in the sand for about 8 weeks, incubated by the heat of the sun, and the temperature inside the nest affects the final ratio of males and females. At this stage, they are vulnerable to typical tourist activities such as digging and over-compaction, but it is when they hatch that their troubles really start. At other Greek sites jackals and foxes may attack the hatchlings, though in Zakynthos their main enemies on the land, apart from humans, tend to be gulls. However, a bigger problem lies in their finely tuned adaptation to their way of life; the young turtles tend to hatch at night to escape predation, and orientate themselves towards the sea because this is the brightest area within their field of view. Unfortunately, the clean sandy beaches favoured by turtles are also favoured by holiday-makers, and the two seasons coincide almost exactly. So on many turtle beaches all around the Mediterranean, the baby turtles are lured in the wrong direction by artificial lights, and fail to survive. On most sites, breeding success plummeted during the twentieth century, and the majority of colonies have become extinct. If you add the problems of damage and death by speed-boats, general disturbance, and deliberate killing, it is obvious why turtles and humans do not go well together in holiday areas.

Problems have continued at Lagana Bay as local people have resisted the idea of limiting development. However, WWF has managed to purchase a substantial section of the main breeding beach, and the final declaration of the marine park, with its additional restrictions, has given cause for greater optimism. Most tourists and locals are aware of the problems and conflicts, and most are interested in trying to help solve them. From the point of view of the naturalist, this inevitably means that there are restrictions on visiting and seeing the turtles, though something can usually be arranged for *bona fide* naturalists through the information centres at Lagana Bay. There is also a centre for rehabilitation of turtles at Glyfada, on the coast just near Athens, where they can be seen.

A flowery olive grove in west Zakynthos

Since 1989, surveys have been carried out on monk seals on Zakynthos, and it has been shown that there is a small but quite stable population, with annual breeding success, associated with the caves along the isolated and largely unpopulated west coast.

Apart from this internationally important mammalian interest, there is much else to see on Zakynthos. The sandy beaches, especially the protected ones, have flowers such as sea daffodils, sea holly, cottonweed, sea medick, an abundance of stocks, and other colourful flowers. On rocky areas, apart from the widespread rock samphire, matted sea-lavender, and tiny *Silene sedoides*, there are great clumps of the striking St. John's-wort *Hypericum aegypticum*, covered in yellow flowers.

In the north-west, near Aghios Georgios, there are some spectacular chalk cliffs (which appear on many postcards, all over Greece), topped with extensive *garrigue*. This is a good area for common *garrigue* plants, but also a few more unusual flowers such as the shrubby *Brassica fruticulosa*, the pretty yellow *Hypericum aegypticum*, blue-flowered, shrubby globularia, pink and white sunroses, and a host of orchids including giant, pink butterfly, and the local endemic *Ophrys cephalonica*. Butterflies such as southern comma, Queen of Spain fritillary, three species of swallowtail – common, scarce and southern – Berger's clouded yellow, Cleopatra, skippers, and many others are common in warm, sheltered areas. In hilly areas, there is a rare grayling, Delattin's grayling, that replaces common grayling in a small area of Albania and adjacent countries; it is inseparable from common grayling in the field (close examination of male genitalia is required!), but the problem is eased by the fact that common grayling occurs no closer than Italy.

In the hilly areas around Anafonitria, there are some unspoilt pastures with fritillaries *Fritillaria messanensis*, snake's-head iris, Barbary nut, peacock anemones, and a variety of orchids including 4-spotted.

A large part of north-western Zakynthos (13 600 ha), extending up to the top of the hill just east of Anafonitria, is considered to be an important bird area, containing 8 of the 21 species that are restricted to the Mediterranean when breeding. Species of interest here include rock partridge, black-eared wheatear, olive tree warbler, subalpine warbler, Cretzschmar's and black-headed buntings, and long-legged buzzard (here at the extreme western edge of its European range). Eleonora's falcons breed in very small numbers (they are much rarer here than in the Aegean), and there are up to 70 pairs of shags. Both Cory's and yelkouan shearwaters can be seen commonly offshore and from ferries, and almost certainly breed nearby.

Access is easy by air from Athens, or direct charter flights from north Europe in the main season. There is a regular (and very pleasant) ferry crossing from Killini, which gives the opportunity to see shearwaters, gulls, cetaceans, and possibly even turtles.

Corfu

Corfu (or Kerkyra) is a rugged and scenic island, noted for its greenness and famous as a popular destination for holidaymakers. It has certainly suffered from the developments of mass tourism, though it is remarkable what has survived, and to a certain extent mass tourism has moved on to other Mediterranean areas in recent years. Geographically, Corfu holds a unique position within Greece; not only is it easily the most northerly of the Adriatic or Ionian islands within Greece, but it is unusual in that most of it lies off the coast of Albania rather than Greece. Climatically, it is rather cooler and damper than other Greek islands, which accounts for its relatively luxuriant vegetation, and ecologically it is undoubtedly influenced to a degree by the proximity of Albania, quite close enough for birds and other mobile species to visit or colonize. As it is such a large and interesting island, we have divided it into three sites.

SITE 114 Corfu: North

The northernmost part of Corfu, which, though busy with tourists,
has many features of interest and contains the highest mountain
on the island.

The expanded 'head' of Corfu is the most mountainous part of the island, rising to 906 m at the summit of Mt. Pantokrator, with hilly areas stretching away to the south-west. The mountains are poorly wooded, with scrub of kermes oak and some pines but little in the way of extensive forest. The summit is mainly bare rock, apart from the nearby monastery and communications mast. The altitude is not great enough for any true mountain species, but there is a good range of interesting flowers here, including the attractive eastern bugle with dark blue flowers hidden amongst hairy grey leaves, a fritillary *Fritillaria graeca* subspecies *thessala* with greenish flowers, blue and white flowers of *Anemone blanda*, peacock anemones in various colours, the deep magenta flowers of *Saponaria calabrica*, alpine rock-cress, sad stock in its brownish form, the grape-hyacinth *Muscari neglectum*, and a number of orchids such as man, giant, Provence, and yellow bee orchids amongst the spiny scrub. In autumn and early winter, there are crocuses such as the white *Crocus boryi* and a form of *C. biflorus*, yellow-flowered *Sternbergia siculus* and the snowdrop *Galanthus reginae-olgae*.

The whole northern area is good for butterflies, especially in the more unspoilt flowery hill habitats. Species of interest include brimstone and Cleopatra (the latter is similar to the former, but a little larger, and with distinct orange wing-tips in the male), the strikingly beautiful two-tailed pasha (one of Europe's largest butterflies, which feeds on strawberry-trees in its larval stages), southern comma, southern white admiral, eastern rock grayling, southern gatekeeper, lattice brown, Grecian copper, various blues, including the pretty little tiger blue, and masses of different skippers, including pygmy, Lulworth, inky, dingy, Oriental marbled, and the orbed red-underside skipper.

There are a few special birds on and around Mt. Pantokrator, including Cretzschmar's buntings at their most westerly regular breeding site, as well as cirl, black-headed and ortolan buntings, rock sparrows, Orphean and subalpine warblers, both rock and blue rock thrushes, rock partridges, black-eared wheatears, red-rumped swallows, and a few birds of prey. The most likely birds of prey are Bonelli's eagles and peregrines, though it is possible that other species such as golden eagle and Egyptian vultures may drift across from nearby Albania.

Eastern bugle *Ajuga orientalis* (Peter Wilson)

Ionian Islands

Cape Arilla (Peter Wilson)

Although the north coast attracts many tourists, it still has some important sites of interest, most notably at Andinioti Lagoon, just west of Aghios Spiridon at the northernmost point of the island. This is a large, shallow saline lagoon, with some reedbeds, saltmarsh, and nearby dunes. Breeding birds here include marsh harriers, little bittern, squacco heron, black-winged stilts, and whiskered terns. At passage periods, there are all sorts of things, including glossy ibis, spoonbills, Temminck's stints, red-footed falcon, and pygmy cormorants. There are often good numbers of wildfowl and other birds in winter including cormorants, great white egrets, ferruginous duck, and the occasional spotted eagle between November and March.

Some of the turf and marshland around the lagoon is of interest for flowers, including orchids such as pink butterfly, horned woodcock, pyramidal, and several tongue orchids, including the rare *Serapias ionica*. Dune flowers include sea medick, sea-holly, cottonweed, and the beautiful white sea daffodil, which flowers in July and August.

The north-west of Corfu, though lacking the key sites of the north-east, is neverthe-

less an attractive and varied area. For example, detailed surveys of the area to the north of Palaeokastritsa have been made over the years by Lance Chilton and Keith Allen (see Further reading), revealing an enormous range of species. Some flowers of interest here include the autumn-flowering bellflower *Campanula versicolor*, several Venus' looking-glass species, the annual rock-rose *Helianthemum aegyptiacum*, cottonweed, several species of stock, the woundwort *Stachys cretica*, 18 species of clover, the large white-flowered saxifrage *Saxifraga chrysosplenifolia*, sea daffodil, common sternbergia, the strange little *Biarum tenuifolium*, *Crocus boryi*, and a number of orchids such as violet limodore, bumble bee, horned woodcock, horseshoe, bug, milky, monkey, four-spotted and loose-flowered, together with the endemic *Serapias ionica*. This is a good area for other things, too, with breeding birds such as red-backed and woodchat shrikes, lesser kestrel, red-rumped swallows, alpine swift, Rüppell's, Dartford and olive-tree warblers, blue rock thrush, black-headed bunting, and many others. Reptiles include Hermann's tortoise, stripe-necked terrapin, Balkan green lizard, Erhard's wall lizard, both Dahl's and Balkan whip snakes, and the striking nose-horned viper. Like the north-east, it is good for butterflies – the combination of relatively luxuriant vegetation and ample warmth seems to suit them, and they do well here. Additional species, not already mentioned above, include southern swallowtail, Balkan clouded

Plain tiger *Danaus chrysippus*

yellow, Amanda's and Chapman's blue, plain tiger, sandy grizzled skipper, and Hungarian skipper, to name but a few. The Troumpeta Pass, on the main road from Sidhari to Corfu town, gives good access to some moderately high country where it crosses the mountain range, and there is good *garrigue* and scrub here, with orchids and other choice flowers.

Sidhari, on the north coast, is a popular area for birdwatchers, with easy access to various sites. The once-good marsh near the town is now all but gone, though there is a small river and wetland east of the town, which still has a few herons, Cetti's warblers, and other aquatic birds. Fireflies (see below) are a common sight at many of the resorts around the Corfu coast.

Fireflies and glow-worms

Many visitors to Greece have their first magical experience of fireflies or glow-worms here, as they emit their eerie green light on warm summer evenings. Both fireflies and glow-worms are actually beetles, not flies nor worms, and of different species, though closely related. Fireflies are perhaps the more exciting, as they are the ones that flash as they fly, often in quite large groups. The flashes come from the male adult beetles, which are flashing to attract the attention of a female; the females are flightless, and sit in the grass, flashing only in response when they see a male, which will then descend to mate. The flashing is the fireflies' way of finding each other in the dark, so they have the advantages of a nocturnal lifestyle (fewer predators) without too many of the drawbacks.

In glow-worms, it is the wingless females that glow, and the winged males seek them out by looking for the light, without flashing themselves. The light from glow-worms is more or less continuous, not flashing, so it is easy to separate the two groups. Glow-worms are widespread through most of the warmer parts of Europe, but fireflies are more eastern, from south-east France eastwards, so many visitors to Greece may not have encountered them before. In Greece, they are quite frequent, especially in rough, grassy flowery places on lime-rich soil. The larvae of both glow-worms and fireflies feed on snails of certain types, so they are commonest where their prey is common.

115 Corfu: Central
SITE

Despite the presence of Corfu town, central Corfu has much of interest.

The central area of Corfu, lying roughly between Corfu town and Palaeokastritsa, is not exceptional, but it is a pleasantly varied stretch of countryside. In olive groves and scrub, there are abundant flowers in spring, including the curious little *Aristolochia rotunda* (one of the food-plants of the eastern festoon butterfly, which occurs here in a few populations), honeywort, the pretty red-flowered woundwort *Stachys cretica*, and a few orchids such as naked man, giant, and

Ionian Islands

Marshland on the Ropa Plain, central Corfu (Peter Wilson)

several tongue orchids. In the central part of the island, between Sgombou and Vatos, including the Ropa Plain, there are remnants of formerly extensive wet areas. It is still possible to find a few wet patches here, and drainage ditches may hold tree and marsh frogs, squacco herons, and the more common waterside warblers, while in marshy areas there are sometimes patches of the striking, reddish-purple, loose-flowered orchids. In spring, Montagu's and marsh harriers, and occa-

Black-headed bunting *Emberiza melanocephala*

sional booted eagles can be seen hunting over the area (though neither breed here), and quails and hoopoe call from the fields. Lesser grey and red-backed shrikes breed around here, black-headed buntings are quite common, and there are masses of red-rumped swallows.

Corfu town has lagoons just south of it, to the west of the airport. These are not outstanding, but can support good numbers of birds on passage, including glossy ibis, many common waders, kingfishers, and occasionally Dalmatian pelicans and pygmy cormorants coming from their breeding sites further east. In the town itself, there are blue rock thrushes nesting around the castle, and serins are common in the parks. The British war cemetery is still a good place to see a range of grassland orchids. Palaeokastritsa is much smaller and quieter, and has cliffs close to the town. Scops owls call frequently at night, and blue rock thrushes, common choughs, and rock nuthatches call from the cliffs. There is plenty of *garrigue* around, which is good for Sardinian and subalpine warblers, and lesser grey and woodchat shrikes nest not far from the town.

SITE
116 Corfu: South

*The long southerly 'tail' of Corfu is relatively undeveloped and has
a number of interesting sites.*

Southwards from Corfu town, the long
narrow tail of Corfu becomes steadily less
developed. Although it is not particularly
rugged, there are a few low mountain
ranges of interest, and a fine large lagoon
at Korission.

The highest hill in the southern part of
the island is Aghios Deka, which rises to
576 m, behind the coastal resort of
Benitses. Although neither high nor extensive in area, it has some good *garrigue* and
patches of pine woodland, and there is a
reasonable range of flowers including
violet limodore, horseshoe orchid,

Adder's tongue spearwort
Ranunculus ophioglossifolius

Violet limodore *Limodorum abortivum*

Provence orchid, giant orchid, *Anemone blanda*, and the green-flowered fritillary *Fritillaria graeca*, amongst other things. Subalpine and Sardinian warblers skulk in the scrub, and black-eared wheatears sing and call from their lookout posts.

Probably the most interesting area in the south is the large coastal lagoon of Lake Korission, on the south-west coast. It is an important bird site, thanks to the combination of large brackish lagoon, salt-marsh, reeds, and sandy areas. It holds water all year, and is particularly interesting at passage periods in both spring and autumn. As with many good wetland sites, the combination of birds changes constantly from day to day – or even as you watch – and it is worth visiting several times in a trip for a variety of species. Regular visitors include purple, grey, and squacco herons, little and great white egrets, glossy ibis, a variety of common waders such as redshank, little stint, and wood sandpiper, masses of hirundines, and a good variety of terns including whiskered, black, gull-billed, and Caspian amongst others. Birds of prey at passage

periods include marsh and Montagu's harriers, red-footed falcons, and Eleonora's falcons (mainly in mid- to late summer). In winter, one might see cormorants, pygmy cormorant, ferruginous duck, and occasional spotted eagles. Breeding birds include occasional black-winged stilts, possible collared pratincoles, little terns, Cetti's and reed warblers, and fan-tailed warblers, the latter soon picked up by their monotonous 'pinging'.

On the dunes and sandy areas to the west of the lake, there are breeding short-toed and crested larks, and tawny pipits. In fact, the sandy bar that separates the lake from the sea (and along which a road runs) is still pretty unspoilt, and holds a good range of coastal habitats, including dunes, foreshore, and pine woodland. It is an interesting area for flowers, with the usual selection of dune species such as sea-holly, sea daffodil, sea spurge, purple spurge, sea knotgrass, sea medick, spiny juniper, and many others. The striking insect *Nemoptera coa* has colonies here; it is related to the lacewings but much larger, and the two hind wings are elongated into long feather-like streamers (see p. 26). In damper areas, there are loose-flowered orchids, and the distinctive little adder's-tongue spearwort with small yellow flowers and leaves like an adder's-tongue fern. Also found here is an orchid now known as *Orchis albanica*, which is related to green-winged orchid but differs in having paler pinkish flowers, a narrow lower lip, and usually a much more open straggly inflorescence. As the name suggests, its centre of distribution is in Albania, though it occurs in adjacent areas.

Further south still, just to the north of Ano Lefkimmi, lie the Alikes saltpans. Like the other wetlands on Corfu, these are particularly attractive for waders and other birds at passage periods. They include similar birds to the other sites, though collared pratincoles are more common here and may breed. The salt-pans can be easily reached by turning left (if coming from the north) in Ano Lefkimmi and heading for the coast at Alikes; access is generally open.

Cretan area

Cretan area

Introduction

Crete is an exceptional place, even in the context of an extraordinary country like Greece. It is the largest Greek island, and the fifth largest in the Mediterranean, with an overall area of almost 9000 square kilometres. It is the southernmost substantial block of land in Greece, or indeed in Europe, and it lies more or less equidistant from the main land masses of Europe, Africa, and Asia – a little over 300 km from each. Not surprisingly, it has something of each continent in it, though it is fair to say that it has most in common with mainland Greece. It is thought to have been isolated as an island for at least several million years, since the mountains uplifted and the Mediterranean Sea became flooded, so it has had time to develop species of its own. It has not been generally glaciated, so many species survived from the Tertiary era and continued to evolve in isolation. This is

most noticeable in the flowers – out of the total native flora of about 1700 species, 171 are believed to be endemic, that is, occurring nowhere else. This is a remarkably high proportion, due not only to the long isolation of Crete, but also to the continued existence of particular habitats, especially gorges and high mountains, where these species have been able to survive. Other groups have not evolved in quite the same way, and there are few known endemic insects (though quite a number of endemic snails), only a couple of broadly endemic mammals, and no endemic birds or reptiles and amphibians.

Climatically, it is broadly the same as other southerly parts of Greece, only more so! It has a Mediterranean climate, with mild damp winters and hot summers, though the summers here – at least in favoured localities – tend to start earlier and end later, and become very hot. There is quite a difference between the north and south coasts – it is by no means uncommon to set off from, say, Chania in poor weather, only to reach the south coast and find it under blazing hot sun. The southern slopes of the White Mountains and other mountains further east are among the hottest and driest places in Europe.

Crete is remarkably mountainous, with peaks as high as almost anything on the mainland of Greece, with the exception of Olympus. High peaks are spread throughout the island, and this gives it a particularly rugged and varied terrain that has much more variety than a lowland island of the same size could possibly have. It has also helped to keep large areas relatively unspoilt, as the mountain terrain is currently unsuitable for intensive agriculture, tourism, or other recreational uses. The high peaks of

Palms on Vai Peninsula

Previous page: **Zakros Gorge**

Cretan area

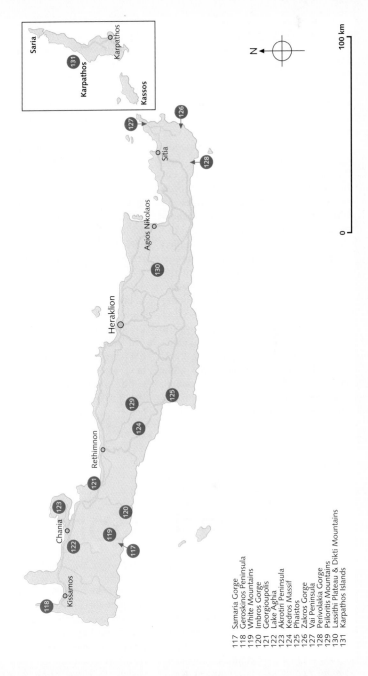

N

100 km

0

117 Samaria Gorge
118 Geroskinos Peninsula
119 White Mountains
120 Imbros Gorge
121 Georgioupolis
122 Lake Aghia
123 Akrotiri Peninsula
124 Kedros Massif
125 Phaistos
126 Zakros Gorge
127 Vai Peninsula
128 Perivolakia Gorge
129 Psiloritis Mountains
130 Lassithi Plateau & Dikti Mountains
131 Karpathos Islands

the island are particularly notable for their variety of species – many of Crete's endemic flowers occur at or close to the

highest altitudes, and these areas are also havens for many of the island's special birds, such as vultures, eagles, choughs, alpine accentors, and citril finches. The other particularly special habitat of Crete for the naturalist is its gorges. There are dozens of these, spread throughout the island, of which the Samaria Gorge is the deepest and most famous, but by no means the only one of interest. One might imagine that all gorges are pretty similar in character, but in fact they vary enormously and no two are anything like the same. They vary according to their altitude, the character of the rock they cut through, their surroundings, their aspect, their depth and length, and much else. In a hot dry place like Crete, the aspect can be particularly important, and the presence of north-facing cliffs which escape virtually all the direct summer sun can make a big difference to the species that survive there. Many of Crete's endemic plants, including a large number of especially impressive species such as Cretan sainfoin, are confined to gorges or similar habitats – they are known generally as chasmophytes.

Crete has changed considerably in the last two decades or so under the combined onslaughts of mass tourism and intensive agriculture, the latter fuelled particularly in recent years by Greece's EU membership. The habitats that have suffered as a result have been, in particular, any soft coastal habitats such as sand dunes and foreshore, and any coastal wetlands. There are very few such habitats of note in Crete now. The olive groves were once flowery, insect-rich places, alive with birds, but most have been converted to irrigated and ploughed, intensively used agricultural land, and Crete is not the place it was to see masses of spring flowers everywhere. This inevitably has knock-on effects, and there is little doubt that many birds and insects are less common now on Crete.

Nevertheless, for the naturalist it remains a dramatic and exciting place to visit. The best time to go is usually April, a little earlier for some of the southern or lowland flowers, or rather later for the mountains and the butterflies. Many of the gorge plants flower a little later, and – in average years – the Samaria Gorge is not open to walkers until 1 May. Autumn is very pleasant, generally warm, with good numbers of passage birds and a few flowers and butterflies, though the landscape is usually dry and brown.

117 Samaria Gorge

Famous gorge with a rich flora and interesting birds, including raptors.

The Samaria Gorge is inextricably linked, both physically and ecologically, with the surrounding White Mountains (see p. 286), from which it drains. However, we have treated it as a separate site because it is so well known in its own right, and visited by so many people who are simply on a day trip with no time for additional exploration. It is undoubtedly one of the most spectacular sites of Europe, dropping steeply from the White Mountains, and narrowing sharply to become a defile between towering limestone cliffs towards the sea.

For the botanist, it is a remarkable place, with many of Crete's special gorge plants to be found. Higher up, in the pine woods, there are clumps of the yellow shrubby flax *Linum arboreum*, silvery mounds of a golden drop *Onosma erecta*, the first of many patches of the endemic

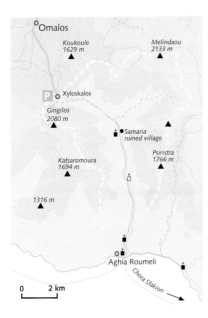

and a fritillary *Fritillaria messanensis* has to be searched for. The trees are worth looking at, too; some of them are the native cypress *Cupressus sempervirens* variety *horizontalis*, confined, in Europe, to just a few southern Greek islands.

Lower down, as the path joins the river, there are fine Oriental planes, some of which are very ancient. The ruined village of Samaria is probably the best place in Crete to see the rare white peony *Paeonia clusii* subspecies *clusii* (confined, in this subspecies, to Crete and Karpathos), and there are many other flowers in clearings at this mid-altitude, such as the cowslip-yellow spikes of few-flowered orchid, the red-purple spikes of four-spotted orchid, and the pale pink flowers of *Cyclamen creticum*, all flowering in spring. As the valley narrows, and the sheer cliffs close in, the number of specialist chasmophytes (gorge-dwellers) increases. Apart from some of the plants already mentioned, this is a good place to see the beautiful endemic Cretan sainfoin, with masses of flowerheads drooping from large silvery bushes; the borage relative *Procopiana* (*Symphytum*) *cretica*, an endemic, yellow-flowered, ever-lasting *Helichrysum heldreichii*, large clumps of the mauve-flowered composite *Ptilostemon chamaepeuce*, the endemic

Cretan wall lettuce (actually a bellflower, from a genus found nowhere else in Europe), and an abundance of the little endemic mouse-ear *Cerastium scaposum*, especially near the top. Most rocks, except in deep shade, have patches of *Aubrieta deltoides*, covered with mauve flowers in spring, while the little white *Gagea graeca* is rather less conspicuous,

Wild goat *Capra aegagrus*

The Samaria Gorge, at its dramatic narrowest point

shrubby composite *Staehelinia arborea*, the rare and endemic dittany *Origanum dictamnus* (related to marjoram, but looking quite different, and whose woolly leaves are the source of a much-prized tea), and masses of the shrubby white-flowered legume *Coronilla globosa*, amongst many others. Binoculars are very useful at this stage for scanning the cliffs, as most of the flowers are out of reach. However, there are many other flowers along the pathsides, including some beautiful orchids such as the spider orchid *Ophrys episcopalis*, and woodcock orchids.

The last part of the walk to the sea is relatively dull, across a gravelly plain, but it is worth looking out for the attractive blue spikes of lice-bane, the native form of oleander, spiny chicory, the woolly labiate *Ballota pseudodictamnus*, and various other flowers that can withstand the harsh heat of this area,

It is a fine place for the birdwatcher, too. In the higher reaches, it is worth scanning the sky for large raptors, particularly lammergeier, griffon vulture, and golden and Bonelli's eagles. Common and alpine choughs and ravens frequently occur as well. It is worth checking around the top of the gorge for alpine accentors which occur here from time to time (but see p. 289 for a more reliable site). In the

Aghia Roumeli from the sea, with the gorge beyond

Coronilla globosa

woods or clearings, there are crossbills, woodlarks, firecrests, and others. In the gorge proper, there are huge numbers of crag martins, which skim by very close, and nest just above the paths. Blue rock thrushes sing from the crags, and grey wagtails and dippers forage along the stream. The mouth of the gorge can be good for migrants in spring.

There *are* mammals in the Samaria Gorge, including badgers, beech martens (in a special Cretan variety), and edible dormouse, though you are not very likely to see them. It is one of the very few places where the rare Cretan wild goat (or kri-kri) can be seen, though very few visitors actually do. The best ways are either to scan all the open mountain slopes across from the top of the gorge with binoculars or telescope, or to be in the gorge in the late afternoon when there is hardly anyone else about, especially in autumn. There is actually quite a substantial population here.

The gorge is also home to a reasonable range of butterflies, a few dragonflies including, surprisingly, the emperor dragonfly, and several amphibians such as the green toad and yellow-bellied toad. Reptiles include the ocellated skink (a

rather curious-looking squat, short-legged lizard, brown speckled with black), Erhard's wall lizard, and the Balkan green lizard, which can all add to the pleasure of a walk here.

The Samaria Gorge is the centre of a National Park, and a relatively strict policy is adopted towards access, partly to protect the environment and partly because a fatal accident occurred a few years ago when tourists were caught in spring floods. The season is usually limited to May to November, although flexible in dry years. The only path begins at the end of the Omalos road, at Xyloskalos, and a well-marked trail descends through the gorge to the sea at Aghia Roumeli. A modest entrance fee is payable at either end. The commonest way to tackle the gorge is as a day excursion – an early morning bus (most hotels and travel agents can help with this) to the top, followed by a relatively fast 14 km walk to the sea, where you catch a boat to Chora Sfakion and a bus back from there. This leaves little time for natural history, and the gorge can be crowded at peak periods. There are hotels at Omalos near the top, and at Aghia Roumeli at the bottom, so it is possible to spend more time there, though you will be largely confined to the path. The gorge is steep and stony in places, and the walk can be very hot, so go prepared. Drinks are usually available about halfway down.

Cichorium spinosum

SITE 118 Geroskinos Peninsula

A wild and mountainous area, away from the tourist route, with special flowers and birds.

Phlomis cretica

At the extreme north-western corner of Crete, there is a long thin finger of land projecting northwards – the Geroskinos (or Gramvousa) Peninsula. It is an un-spoilt, rocky piece of land, rising to 762 m at Geroskinos, with offshore islands and pristine bays. Recently improved access has made it busier, especially around the Tigani headland, but it remains essen-tially unspoilt. Eleonora's falcons breed around it in substantial numbers (up to 100 birds were counted in one survey), with the occasional Bonelli's eagle, kestrel, and raven to be seen. Birds breed-ing in the scrub and rocky areas include black-eared wheatear, blue rock thrush, and subalpine and Sardinian warblers.

The flowers are not exceptional, but include a good range of orchids in the *garrigue,* such as bug, pink butterfly, man, pyramidal, sombre bee, yellow bee, and others; the rare, little spiralled leaved garlic *Allium circinnatum* subspecies *circinnatum,* the only known site on Crete for *Bellevalia dubia,* and white-flowered *Gagea graeca;* in autumn, there are masses of bushes of the pretty heather *Erica manipuliflora,* with bulbs such as autumn squill and sea squill.

Gramvousa Bay

Polyrinia Gorge

At the northern end of the peninsula, on the islands of Gramvousa and Aghia Gramvousa, there is the only population in the world of a mayweed *Anthemis glaberrima*, growing on coastal rocks, with sea lavenders such as *Limonium pigadiense* and *L. frederici*, the little catchfly *Silene sedoides*, and the stonecrop *Sedum litoreum*. Just south of the peninsula, there is one of only two sites in Europe for a striking little winter-flowering bulbous plant *Androcymbium rechingeri*; the other site is on and adjacent to Elafonisi Island (a very beautiful place), at the south-western tip of Crete. Just at the southern end of the peninsula occurs the only Cretan site for a very rare Greek endemic tulip *Tulipa goulimyi* (which also has a few sites on the Peloponnese and intervening islands). The shrubby yellow-flowered *Viola delphinantha* grows nearby on sandy cliffs.

Eastwards lies the other distinctive, finger-like peninsula of this part of Crete: the Rodopos Peninsula. It is generally similar, but it has little in the way of offshore islands, which reduces the possibilities for Eleonora's falcons and shearwaters. Lanner falcon may still be resident, and there is a fine range of rock and crag birds such as black-eared wheatear and blue rock thrush. White-tailed eagles winter here, and large numbers of migrants pass through in spring and autumn. Some 7000 ha of the peninsula are considered to be an important area for birds.

A short way inland, between the villages of Polyrinia (where there is a fine ancient site) and Sirikari, there is a little gorge, rarely visited but full of interest. It has some beautiful cliffs, plenty of *garrigue*, and small areas of other habitats, and can be easily walked in either direction. Flowers of interest on the cliffs (the chas-

Romulea ramiflora

mophytes, for which Crete is so famous) include Cretan blue lettuce (endemic to Crete), an endemic skull-cap *Scutellaria sieberi*, the endemic 'tea' *Origanum dictamnus*, two species of *Staehelinia*, the endemic mullein *Verbascum arcturus*, and more. In *garrigue* and open areas, there are pink *Linum pubescens* and yellow *L. trigynum* flaxes, fringed rue, *Cyclamen creticum*, orchids such as bee, bumble bee, and forms of late spider *Ophrys candica* and *O. episcopalis*, broomrapes, St. John's-worts, including the pretty, fine-leaved shrub *Hypericum empetrifolium*, and even primroses in shady areas, to name but a few. It is a very flowery place in spring (goats permitting). At the ancient site of Polyrinia itself, there is an endemic, pale-flowered pink *Dianthus xylorrhizus* growing on the cliffs with *Ranunculus creticus*. It is confined to here and one other site, near Platanos. Birds of interest include blue rock thrushes, black-eared wheatears, crag martins, and other scrub or cliff birds. Balkan green lizards and Erhard's wall lizards are common; on one occasion, I watched a Balkan whip snake catch a wall lizard here, attempt to swallow it, then drop it as it attempted to slither up a rocky slope away from me; the lizard ran off, apparently unharmed. Butterflies include brimstones and Oberthür's grizzled skipper.

Southwards, the mountain area around Mt. Koutroulis (1071 m) and Aghios Dikaios is an important area for birds, noted especially for species characteristic of Mediterranean scrub, which occurs in large quantities here. The Elos–Plokamiana road runs through the area.

On the south coast, west of the small resort of Palaeochora, there are some reasonably unspoilt beach and coastal habitats harbouring flowers such as *Allium rubrovitatum*, the endemic *Bellevalia brevipedicellata*, which flowers in late winter, the curious little autumn-flowering *Biarum davisii*, the hare's ear *Bupleurum semicompositum*, Cretan palm (see p. 302), a rare catchfly *Silene succulenta* subspecies *succulenta* that is confined to sandy beaches, sand-crocuses such as *Romulea ramiflora*, the striking dragon arum, an endemic love-in-a-mist *Nigella doerfleri*, with greenish flowers, grape-hyacinths such as *Muscari spreizenhoferi*, Cretan blue lettuce, and many more common species. This is a very warm area and it is best to visit early, even in March, to see the uncommon flowers. Although tourist-related development is steadily spreading, it is still a generally unspoilt area, especially in the hills. Westwards from Koundoura beyond the end of the road, around to Elafonisi and beyond, is a particularly beautiful and unspoilt stretch of coast.

SITE 119 White Mountains

An impressive mountain range in western Crete, famed for its rare flowers and special birds.

The White Mountains, or Levka Ori, lie in western Crete towards the south coast, clustered around and to the east of the Samaria Gorge National Park (see p. 280). We treat them separately from the gorge, though they are inti-

mately linked ecologically, because access arrangements are different, and the gorge is usually a self-contained day trip.

The mountains rise to 2453 m at Pachnes and are snow-covered well into

Cretan area

Scilla nana (formerly known as *Chionodoxa cretica*)

spring, though their name derives from the dazzling expanses of white bare limestone everywhere. They cover a considerable expanse, from Chora Sfakion to Sougia on the south coast, stretching northwards half way across the island. There are many plants endemic to the White Mountains, or which have their centre of distribution here. It is impossible to list all of them here (or to see them all in one visit), but the following sites between them present a good selection of species.

From Chania, there is a good road up through Lakki to the Omalos Plateau, lying at about 1000 m. This is one of those intriguing, internally-draining high plateaux that are such a feature of Greek limestone mountains, which have clearly been lakes once but are now dry for most of the year. The Omalos Plateau was once a great botanical site, though it has declined steadily over the past few years. Still, there is plenty to see, and Omalos makes a good base for the Samaria Gorge, the high peaks, and possibly the Aghia Irini Gorge. On rocky slopes around the plateau, there are masses of bushes of pink-flowered *Daphne sericea*, the yellow-flowered barberry *Berberis cretica*, the endemic valerian *Valeriana asarifolia*, spring rock-cress, burnt candytuft, crown anemones in various colour forms, and fine old trees of Cretan maple and wild pear covered with white flowers in spring. In a few places, there are clumps of the rare white endemic peony *Paeonia clusii* subspecies *clusii*, including one clump just near Omalos village, though it is easier to see in the Samaria Gorge (see p. 281). The valley floor has a different range of flowers, including wild tulips, which are now generally classed as the widespread *Tulipa saxatilis* (although until recently they were considered as a separate species *T. bakeri*), a sand-crocus *Romulea bulbocodium*, tassel hyacinths, both lesser

One of the extraordinary ancient cypress trees on Mt. Ginghilos

The upper slopes of the Samaria Gorge, below Mt. Ginghilos

celandines and the lesser celandine look-alike *Ranunculus ficarioides* (with more distinctly lobed leaves), flowery mats of one-flowered clover, snake's head iris, a yellow star-of-Bethlehem *Gagea chrysantha* (formerly *G. amblyopetala*), and others, although the agriculture is intensifying here, and much has been lost. Woodlarks are particularly common, and woodchat shrikes, whinchat, northern and black-eared wheatears, tawny pipits, and cirl and ortolan buntings are frequent. Scops owls live around the village, and Balkan green lizards are as common on the plateau as anywhere, while green toads breed in temporary pools.

On the slopes leading up to the head of the Samaria Gorge, there are other plants of interest, including the very rare, elm-like tree *Zelkova abelicea*, fritillaries *Fritillaria messanensis*, the golden drop *Onosma erecta*, four-spotted orchids, and in autumn the pretty *Crocus laevigatus* and *Colchicum cretense*.

Colchicum cretense

To the east of the road, there is a track into the mountains leading to a refuge, with paths continuing on beyond. However, the best and easiest way to see a range of high-altitude plants, including some endemics, is to walk from the end of the road (passing to the right of the upper café) up towards Mt. Ginghilos. It is hard work, and the initial zig-zag path is a slog, but the rewards in terms of flowers, birds, and views are superb. On average, the best time for the walk is late April to early May, but much depends on the winter snow. On the bare, east-facing slopes, flowers of interest include the little white *Cerastium scaposum*, masses of a large, white-flowered saxifrage *Saxifraga chrysosplenifolia*, and the smaller, rue-leaved saxifrage, beautiful flowery mats of pink-flowered *Prunus prostrata* looking like the ultimate in bonsai almond blossom, clumps of *Aubrieta deltoides*, the endemic sainfoin *Onobrychis sphaciotica*, white-flowered spiny *Astragalus angustifolius* subspecies *angustifolius*, *Anemone heldreichii*, and pretty yellow spikes of few-flowered orchids. As you go higher, there are increasing numbers of remarkable trees of the cypress *Cupressus sempervirens* forma *horizontalis*; many of the trees here are thought to be thousands of years old, and they look it, with gnarled, lightning-sculptured trunks, in a spectacular setting. Closer to the melting snow, there are masses of lovely crocuses *Crocus sieberi* subspecies *sieberi* (an endemic subspecies), the pretty little endemic blue and white *Chionodoxa cretica* (= *Scilla nana*), the little *Corydalis uniflora*, tiny forget-me-nots, and many more. On the upper slopes of the gorge itself, there are mats of the endemic *Anchusa caespitosa* covered in striking blue flowers, with endemic arums *Arum idaeum*, the white-flowered bitter-cress *Cardamine graecum*, and the yellow-flowered endemic *Alyssum sphacioticum*. A little later in the year, there are other endemics here, such as the mullein *Verbascum spinosum*, *Calamintha cretica*, *Scabiosa albocincta*, and *Bupleurum kakiskalae*, known only from around the source of the Samaria River.

This is a superb place for the high-altitude birds of Crete, too, and you can often see them at close quarters. Lammergeiers soar overhead (though you rarely see more than one or two), common (red-billed) and alpine choughs wheel around in flocks, and crag martins are common. There are also several pairs of alpine accentor, which are often very tame around the spring at the source of the river. There is a good chance of seeing both golden and Bonelli's eagles here, as well as blue rock thrush, chukar (one of the main prey items for the eagles), ravens, black-eared wheatears, and others. If you scan the slopes and cliffs on the other side of the valley with binoculars, you can often see groups of the endemic wild goat, kri-kri.

If you have the energy, and the snow has melted, it is worth going on beyond the spring and up to the col, or even the summit of Ginghilos, allowing plenty of time to return. There are other endemic flowers such as the pretty bellflower relative *Trachelium jacquinii*, a semi-parasite *Odontites linkii*, the pink *Dianthus juniperinus*, and many more, not to mention spectacular views. On a good day, this Ginghilos walk is one of the most interesting and exciting anywhere in Europe.

West from Omalos, there is a little-known gorge running down to the sea from the vil-

The Omalos plateau

lages of Aghia Irini and Epanohori, reaching the coast at Sougia. There are masses of interesting plants here, including typical chasmophytes such as Cretan blue lettuce, a large bellflower *Campanula cretica*, a pretty little blue and white annual *Solenopsis minuta* subspecies *minuta*, the endemic asarum-leaved valerian, Cretan sainfoin, a white, shrubby, endemic crown vetch *Coronilla globosa*, the endemic cream-flowered cabbage *Brassica cretica*, and the endemic tea *Origanum dictamnus*, amongst others. Orchids along the way include bug, yellow bee, tongue orchid *Serapias bergonii*, and the late spider orchid forms *Ophrys episcopalis* and *O. candica*.

It is possible to get a boat from Sougia to Aghia Roumeli (at the bottom of the Samaria Gorge) or Chora Sfakion, watching out for dolphins, shearwaters, and some fine unspoilt coastal scenery along the way; there are hotels at all three places, opening up good possibilities for extended circular walks. There is an alternative route into the high White Mountains from the south, starting at Anopoli or Aghios Ioannis, west of Chora Sfakion, accessible by road. This is a long walk, but there are different habitats and species on this hot south side of the mountains, including the very rare *Clematis elisabethae-carolae*, known only from rock crevices in two sites here; it has pretty white flowers that smell of orange blossom! Other species of interest here include the pink *Dianthus sphacioticus*, the white and yellow *Viola fragrans*, a houndstongue *Cynoglossum sphacioticum*, and many of the species previously mentioned.

SITE 120 Imbros Gorge

An impressive gorge with a full range of flowers and birds.

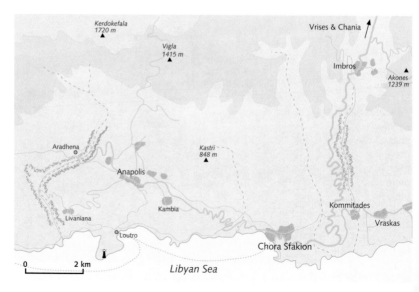

Centaurea raphanina

The Imbros Gorge is much less well known than the Samaria Gorge, and certainly its setting and length are not as spectacular. However, it has the great advantage that there is road access to either end and it is not too long, so it can be dipped into or walked in its entirety. It has many of the more specialized gorge flowers, and some of the birds, though the mountains around it are less high and wild, so the range of possible birds is limited.

Blue rock thrushes sing from high on the crags, black-eared wheatears are common breeders, and crag martins fly close overhead. Alpine swifts can sometimes be seen chattering overhead in groups. Ravens' calls can be heard almost anywhere around here, and there is at least one pair of peregrines, together with kestrels and lesser kestrels. As far as I know, neither Bonelli's eagle nor griffon vulture nests in the gorge, but either is likely to be seen soaring high overhead.

Around the top of the gorge, there are notable flowers such as the tight rosettes of *Centaurea raphanina* subspecies *raphanina*, widow iris, white *Saxifraga chrysosplenifolia*, spiny spurge, sun-roses, pheasant's eye, and *Gagea graeca*. As you go down into the gorge, and the gap between the cliffs narrows, the flowers become more specialized: clumps of the endemic pink-flowered Cretan sainfoin, the pretty endemic mullein *Verbascum arcturus*, the endemic blue rock lettuce, an endemic skull-cap *Scutellaria sieberi*, a rock-hugging bellflower *Campanula tubulosa*, the comfrey relative *Procopiania cretica*, white-flowered shrubs of *Coronilla globosa*,

clumps of the shrubby yellow flax *Linum arboreum*, spiny chicory, the pink-flowered cress *Ricotia cretica*, with unexpectedly divided leaves, and succulents such as the pinkish-red flowered *Rosularia serrata* and a pennywort *Umbilicus parviflorus*. A rare tree *Celtis tournefortii* grows here, closely related to the more widespread nettle tree, but differing in its more rounded leaf-teeth, and yellowish-brown fruits (not black), though in most places it is either heavily grazed or out of reach.

There are many other special flowers here, too numerous to describe in detail, but including *Erysimum raulii*, *Sanguisorba cretica*, *Calamintha cretica*, *Verbascum spinosum*, *Staehelinia arborea* (a rather striking gorge-side shrub with big silvery leaves and purplish-pink flowers), and a little garlic *Allium callimischon* subspecies *haemostictum*.

The land around the base of the gorge is hot and dry, dominated in places by massed spikes of yellow asphodel and hummocks of spiny spurge. It can be good for migrant birds in spring.

A few miles to the west of the base of the gorge, beyond Chora Sfakion, the small road climbs vertiginously on to the village of Anapolis. There is a fine gorge here at Arahova, which runs down to the coast between closely spaced vertical cliffs. There is a beautiful old zig-zag track, which may even be of Minoan origin, that begins on the east side and

Turban buttercup *Ranunculus asiaticus*

can be easily walked to climb up to Aradhena (now more or less deserted) on the west side. There is a range of gorge and scrub birds and flowers here, including many of the same species found in the Imbros Gorge, with a few extras such as the striking cut-leaved bellflower, which grows in clumps towards the mouth of the gorge. There is a reasonable range of orchids in *garrigue* and limestone rubble,

such as yellow bee, pyramidal, bug, and four-spotted, and rock tulips can be found, though they are usually over by April here. The rare red variant of turban buttercup grows at this site.

There is a reasonable path down the gorge from where the ancient track crosses it, or it can be admired with its abundant crag martins from the high bridge just by Arahova.

SITE 121 Georgioupolis

One of the few wetlands of any significance in Crete, with good birds and coastal flowers.

Georgioupolis is a little seaside town devoted mainly to tourism. However, immediately to the west of it a river issues from the rock in a series of springs which form a modest lake before flowing into the nearby sea. It is not a major site, but very attractive (especially on a hot day), and

easily approached from the main east–west road. There are small areas of reedbed and other marginal vegetation. In spring or autumn, it attracts good numbers of migrants, and almost anything can turn up. Likely species include little egrets, purple and squacco herons, little bittern,

The spring-fed year-round lake at Georgioupolis

Little crake *Porzana parva*

little and spotted crakes, black tern and white-winged black tern, yellow wagtail, marsh harrier and possibly other large birds of prey, cuckoos, nightingales, shrikes, and others. Cetti's warblers, little grebes, white wagtails, coot and other birds seem to be resident. It is worth also checking the nearby beach, scrub and headland, at passage periods, too. There

are a few dragonflies, such as emperor, but in general flowing calcareous water does not suit many species.

The marsh and open water is best viewed from the minor road that skirts it, just west of the town.

Away from the developed parts of Georgioupolis (which are steadily spreading), there is a reasonable range of sand and dune flowers such as sea medick, round-headed club-rush, the pretty red catchfly *Silene colorata*, and several stocks in abundance, providing a marvellous wash of colour. Here and there in damper areas to the east, there are loose-flowered orchids, and tongue orchids in damp turf.

A few miles inland lies Lake Kournas. This could be an excellent site, but is usually disappointing due to disturbance. However, there is a good total list which includes regular black-necked grebe, ferruginous duck, and garganey. It is best visited in autumn, winter, or early spring, before the tourist season.

SITE 122 Lake Aghia

An old reservoir, which is now the best wetland in Crete for birds, amphibians, and dragonflies.

A few miles south-west of Chania, immediately north of the little village of Aghia (or Agia), there is a small lake, of artificial origin but with a reasonable amount of marginal and aquatic vegetation, and secluded surroundings. Despite an almost complete lack of management, and some disturbance, it positively teems with life, and is an indication of just how good a real wetland reserve could be in Crete.

Birds are perhaps the most obvious attraction, especially in spring, and to a lesser extent in autumn. Hirundines can pass through in clouds, with the balance of species constantly changing – at first pri-

Little gull *Larus minutus*

Lesser red-eyed damselfly *Erythromma viridulum*

birds in the air include whiskered tern, black tern, white-winged black tern, little gull and other gulls, and marsh harriers. Around the margins, and in the reeds, there are little and spotted crakes, night, purple, grey, and squacco herons, little egret, Cetti's, reed, great reed, and sedge warblers, and yellow wagtails, including blue-headed. On several occasions, we have had very close views of little bittern in spring. Spanish sparrow, woodchat and lesser grey shrikes, and other birds can be seen round about. Waders such as black-winged stilt, wood and common sandpiper, collared pratincole, and others can be seen around the margins. In autumn, there can be a similar range, and kingfishers seem especially common.

It is also a good place for amphibians and reptiles. Tree frogs are abundant along the margins (best found by looking at reeds or at the base of the large white-veined leaves of milk thistle), green toads and marsh frogs breed here, and dice snakes and grass snakes can be seen swimming in the water looking for tadpoles and young frogs. Stripe-necked terrapins are abundant, though not as tame as in some sites, and usually difficult

marily common swallows, then suddenly mainly sand martins, then house martins, with red-rumped swallows mixed in. Swifts and alpine swifts pass overhead. Other

Lake Aghia

to approach. Erhard's wall lizards are common in drier places. It is a good place to see dragonflies, though they tend to be hard to approach; common species include emperor and lesser emperor, a skimmer that looks like black-lined but is actually *Orthetrum albistylum*, longer and thinner, with distinct white appendages at the end of the 'tail', keeled skimmer, and darters including the striking pink *Crocothemis erythraea* and the red-veined. Damselflies include the lesser red-eyed damselfly (common red-eyed does not occur here), blue-tailed, and the banded demoiselle. Butterflies are common in the flowery areas near the lake, including eastern festoon, common and scarce swallowtails, clouded yellows, long-tailed blues, brimstones, and many more.

It is not a great place for flowers, but worth a quick look. Species of interest include loose-flowered orchid, three tongue orchids – common, small-flowered tongue orchid and *Serapias bergonii* – small-flowered catchfly, a lord's and ladies *Arum concinnatum*, milk thistle, yellow iris, saw sedge, and yellow bartsia.

Not far away to the south-east lies a fine gorge with a rich flora. A road, running southwards from the western edge of Chania up a valley to a village called Therisos, passes through the gorge, so making it very accessible, though parking places are limited. Flowers of interest here include the endemic *Coronilla globosa*, the evergreen dutchman's pipes (or climbing birthwort), lice-bane, the borage relative *Procopiania cretica*, the endemic 'tea' *Origanum dictamnus* with its white-felted leaves and red-purple flowers, both spring and autumn-flowering cyclamen, Cretan blue lettuce, saxifrages such as the tiny *Saxifraga hederacea*, tree spurge, myrtle, french lavender, and many more. Orchids in more open areas include four-spotted, late spider, sombre bee, yellow bee, and man.

It is quite a good locality for butterflies. Recent records include Gruner's orange tip, dappled white, Bath white, Cleopatra, powdered brimstone, eastern festoon, southern comma, and common blue, amongst others. I have seen Balkan whip snakes on several visits, so they are probably common.

123 Akrotiri Peninsula

A rugged limestone peninsula to the north-east of Chania, particularly rich in flowers.

The Akrotiri Peninsula juts northwards from Chania like a leaning cauliflower. The southern part is busy and rather messy, with military sites and the civil airport, although even here it is noticeable how flowery the remaining patches of *garrigue* or pasture are. However, the north-eastern part is composed of rugged limestone hills, with several monasteries, and one particularly good site for flowers.

Head towards Aghia Triada Monastery, then on to Gouverneto Monastery, where

Cretan area

Anthemis rigida

the road ends. On the way, there are fine olive groves, *garrigue*, and pastures with beautiful dragon arums, up to a metre high and smelling strongly of dead animals, pheasant's-eye, giant fennel, large Mediterranean spurge, wild love-in-a-mist, French lavender, the blue-flowered stork's-bill *Erodium gruinum*, three species of sun-rose, and many other good flowers.

Gouverneto Monastery is worth a visit, and if you look over the wall into the grassy grounds, you may often get a good view of hoopoes feeding. Areas of scrub, both here and at Aghia Triada, are likely to be good for migrants including pied flycatchers, wryneck, quite large parties of golden orioles, redstarts, and others. Drinking troughs often attract birds as there is very little water on Akrotiri.

There is a car park at the monastery, and a path leads down the hill to the ruins of the Catholic monastery, and eventually down a modest gorge to the sea. Around the car park, there is a rare little endemic garlic *Allium circinnatum* subspecies *circinnatum* with tightly spiralled leaves, and a yellow, mat-forming

rayless mayweed *Anthemis rigida*. In March, there are Cretan tulips in flower here, long finished by the time most people come. Along the path, there are masses of clumps of a spiny, yellow-flowered greenweed *Genista acanthoclada*, a pretty bindweed *Convolvulus oleifolius*, horned dock, Cretan sorrel, Cretan blue lettuce, rough marsh mallow (anywhere less like a marsh is hard to imagine!), the little yellow flax *Linum trigynum*, lots of the iris relative barbary nut, often so dwarfed here that they resemble the African species *Gynandiris monophylla* (which is recorded from a few places in Crete), and various orchids including pyramidal, sombre bee, and yellow bee. Around the cave chapel, there are rock-dwelling species such as wall pennywort and wall pellitory, little robin, and the pretty little blue-flowered spring rock-cress. After the cave, the path begins to drop down the south side of a small gorge towards the picturesque Catholic monastery ruins, which include a fine bridge across the gorge covered with the rosettes of the winter-flowering *Ranunculus*

Hypericum perfoliatum

Cretan tulip *Tulipa cretica*

Verbascum arcturus

bullatus. There are many more flowers here, including the endemic mullein *Verbascum arcturus* in abundance, the pretty purple-flowered clover *Trifolium speciosum*, the endemic yarrow *Achillea cretica*, the endemic skull-cap *Scutellaria sieberi*, great clumps of Cretan sainfoin, covered in pink spikes of flowers, annual red valerian, an annual bellflower *Campanula erinus*, the endemic *Origanum dictamnus*, the borage relative *Procopiania cretica*, and many others. It is possible to walk on beyond the monastery down the gorge to the sea, where there are similar species, with much more Cretan sainfoin, dragon arum, wild Cretan tulips, a tiny little daisy relative *Bellium minutum* in rock crevices, and the pretty bellflower *Campanula tubulosa*.

Blue rock thrushes are common, with black-eared wheatears, stonechats, chukars, hoopoes, and Sardinian warblers. Butterflies are not abundant, though southern comma and Cretan grayling are not uncommon. Cretan grayling looks just like common grayling, differing in minor anatomical details, but here replaces common grayling.

While on Akrotiri, or directly from Chania, it is worth visiting the British war cemetery at Souda Bay, which is noted for its orchids in the hay meadow beyond the low wall at the seaward end. It can also be good for birds, especially at passage periods. It is an interesting and moving place to visit, and has imaginative garden plantings.

SITE 124 Kedros Massif

A rugged range of limestone hills, particularly good for orchids and other flowers.

The Kedros Mountains are a little-known range to the east of Spili. They rise to 1776 m but are often overlooked in favour of higher nearby peaks. There are two areas which have particularly interesting flowers.

At the western end, a newish road climbs north-eastwards from Spili, sign-posted to Gerakari. At about 800 m, it crosses a plateau with a few cultivated fields and a building. These fields are one of the few sites for the endemic red tulip *Tulipa doerfleri*, which used to colour them red in April, and, although they have steadily declined, are still quite common. There are also crown anemones (often the same colour as the tulips), bluish *Anemone heldreichii*, corn marigolds, turban buttercups, tassel hyacinths, both yellow and white stars-of-Bethlehem, and other flowers in the field. On the low hills across the stream, there is a startling collection of orchids, with about 25 species in flower at the same time, often in great abundance. Highlights include Bory's

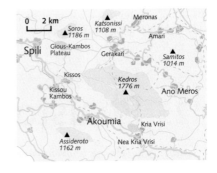

orchid, which is the same reddish-purple as several other species but opens its flowers from the top downwards, so its upside-down conical shape gives it away instantly; few-flowered orchid, the striking relative of woodcock orchid *Ophrys heldreichii*, the endemic *O. cretica*, late spider orchid forms such as *O. candica*, Anatolian orchid, naked man orchid, toothed orchid, four-spotted orchid, various tongue orchids, and many more. There are also some fine stands of

Tulipa doerfleri

widow iris, lots of clumps of *Iris unguicu-laris* subspecies *cretensis* (not as pretty as the Peloponnese ones, but attractive nonetheless), sand-crocuses, *Viola cretica* by the stream, fritillaries *Fritillaria messa-nensis*, cyclamens, *Gagea graeca*, and stands of tulips *Tulipa saxatilis* on top of the hill. Daffodils *Narcissus tazetta* are common, but they flower here in March. There are also fine old Oriental planes along the stream, and old trees of wild pear and wild cherry.

It is a good place to see Balkan green lizards, which are abundant, and Erhard's wall lizard. There is a colony of tree frogs along the stream, at an unusually high altitude.

Griffon vultures are a common sight overhead, and Bonelli's or golden eagles are occasionally seen. Other species include woodlark, corn bunting, stonechat, raven, hooded crow, and black-eared wheatear.

At the south-east end of the massif, above the village of Nea Kria Vrisi, there is an extensive area of degraded limestone *maquis* that is particularly good for orchids, though it needs thorough searching to find them all. In fact, it is probable that large areas of this mountain range will prove to be of interest, but much of it has barely been explored. The *garrigue* is dominated by spiny burnet, spiny spurge, spiny broom, both yellow and white asphodels, and vari-ous other plants that resist grazing by one means or another. Hidden amongst them are about 30 species of orchids, including four-spotted, pink butterfly, sombre bee, yellow bee, sawfly, pyramidal, late spider, *Ophrys cretica*, *O. spruneri*, and others, including hybrids. There are also some nice clumps of barbary nut here, and the strik-ing, tall yellow spikes of Cretan arum are frequent along the roadside. Griffon vul-tures are often overhead.

Access to the first site is easy via the new Spili–Gerakari road (not shown on many maps yet), in the Amari valley. The second site can be reached by following the old (upper) main road at Nea Kria Vrisi and parking at the sharp hairpin bend.

125 Phaistos

SITE

A beautifully flowery area between two ancient sites.

The ancient site of Phaistos (or Festos) lies south-east of Timbaki near the central southern coast of Crete. About two miles to the north-west lies the site of Aghia Triada, and the road between the two traverses an area of soft limestone hills, particularly rich in orchids and other flowers.

On the warm, sunny hillsides, there are masses of orchids including various forms of *Ophrys cretica*, yellow bee orchid, early spider, naked man, monkey, dense-flowered, pyramidal, at least three species of tongue orchids, and *Ophrys mammosa*, *O. iricolor*, *O. omegaifera* and *O. gortynia*. The last-named is an endemic Cretan form of early spider, named after the ancient capital at Gortyn, which usually has a yellow margin to the base of the lip, narrow green petals, and distinct pale-topped swellings on either side of the lip. Along the roadsides, there are tassel hyacinths, bladder vetch, the

Cretan area

Ophrys cretica

Cretan sainfoin *Ebenus cretica*

shrubby composite *Phagnalon rupestre*, pitch trefoil, smelling characteristically of tar, the pretty pink bindweed *Convolvulus althaeoides*, turban buttercups, bright blue 'summer forget-me-nots' *Anchusa italica*, asparagus peas, wild gladioli, several broomrapes, and others. At a few points, there are clumps of Cretan sainfoin, in flower here by early April. Other flowers in the area include the distinctive 'strawberries and cream' blooms of a semi-parasite *Bellardia trixago*, giant orchids, southern bug orchids, mandrake (the autumn-flowering form), Jerusalem

sage, the shrubby, semi-parasitic, sandalwood relative *Osyris alba* with greenish-yellow flowers and red berries, Narbonne star-of-Bethlehem, tree medick, both yellow and red horned-poppies, white mignonette, and many more – a lovely mixture, with fine views to the south adding to the spectacle. In cultivated areas, there are tall spikes of *Allium nigrum*, smaller white *A. subhirsutum*, crown daisies, annual bellflower, and the purplish cress *Erucaria hispanica*, with dragon arums scattered here and there.

Birds are not exceptional here, but it is a good place to watch birds of prey, and some of the larger migrant birds such as grey herons (a group of 27 were seen on a recent visit), and possibly storks and cranes. Chukar partridges call from the hills nearby.

SITE
126 Zakros Gorge

The finest gorge in eastern Crete, with a marvellous selection of flowers and other wildlife.

This special gorge runs from the small isolated village of Zakros down to the sea at Kato Zakros, where there is also an ancient site being excavated. Although one might think that all these Cretan

gorges are very similar, they are all quite distinct scenically, and these far eastern ones have a distinctly different flora.

Above Zakros village, the stream (harbouring freshwater crabs) issues from a

Cretan area

narrow valley with springs and old plane trees, with the impressive broomrape *Orobanche pubescens* growing below them. Other flowers of interest here include the endemic valerian *Valeriana asarifolia*, the endemic, yellow-flowered scorpion-grass *Scorzonera cretica*, Cretan buttercup, turban buttercup and the little copper-coloured *Ranunculus cupreus*, the endemic Jerusalem sage *Phlomis lanatus*, the pretty *Cyclamen creticum*, ferns such as rusty-back, *Cheilanthes maderensis*, and maidenhair, the club-moss *Selaginella denticulata*, and an endemic bellflower *Campanula pelvi-formis* on the cliffs. Birds of interest in this upper area include blue rock thrush, Spanish sparrow, Cetti's, Sardinian, and subalpine warblers, nightingale, serin, hooded crow and raven. Cretzschmar's buntings are quite common. Tree frogs chatter excitedly at night from anywhere with tall vegetation near water.

Below Zakros, the upper part of the gorge is relatively open, with *garrigue* and rocky areas. Here there are pink *Cistus creticus* and white *C. salvifolius*, yellow

Fumana arabica, the winter-flowering *Erica manipuliflora*, spiny broom, wild spiny pear, turban buttercups, an everlasting *Helichrysum conglobatum*, the shrubby St. John's-wort *Hypericum empetrifolium*, wild pea, crown anemones and *Anemone heldreichii*, and various orchids such as pink butterfly, pyramidal, late spider, yellow bee, tongue orchids, early spider, bumble bee, *Ophrys cretica*, and *O. iricolor*. As the gorge narrows, there are more specialized plants such as the endemic *Ricotia cretica* on stony rubble, the pretty endemic shrubby St. John's-wort *Hypericum amblycalyx*, confined to eastern Crete, and masses of the extraordinary, endemic Dutchman's pipes *Aristolochia cretica*, with its large dark furry flowers. Also growing here is a little bulbous plant that is being named as a new species of the genus *Bellevalia*, endemic to east Crete. Other plants of interest in the lower part of the gorge include the borage relative *Procopiania cretica*, with thin blue or white petals, the endemic *Nepeta melissifolia*, wild oleander, virgin's bower, hoary stock, a rather undistinguished catchfly *Silene behen*, and many other flowers. In autumn, the curious little *Biarum davisii* flowers here, at about the same time as clumps of the composite *Staehelina fruticosa* on the cliffs.

Green toads come to the lower reaches of the river in quantity to mate and lay their long strings of eggs, and there are snakes here, including cat snake and Balkan whip snake. It is an excellent place for birds, with a good mixture of residents, summer visitors, and migrants. Breeding birds include blue rock thrush,

Aristolochia cretica

Zakros Gorge

peregrine, kestrel, raven, occasional griffon vultures, rock dove, turtle dove, crag martin, Cetti's warbler, black-eared wheatear, woodlark, chukar, and woodchat shrike. Other birds that one might see include grey and purple herons, honey buzzard, lesser kestrel, hoopoe, little egret, and scops owl. Towards the mouth of the river, there is a slightly more extensive wet area, especially in late winter, and here there can be little bittern, glossy ibis, squacco heron, wood sandpiper, and occasional little crakes.

It is also a good place to see butterflies, including eastern festoon, southern comma, holly blue, Bath white, Cleopatra, two-tailed pasha, Cretan grayling (see p. 297), Oriental meadow brown, Cretan small heath, and the southern form of speckled wood.

There is good road access to the top or bottom of the gorge, and a well-made path which emerges half-way down and joins the road, so various walks are possible. Zakros makes a sensible base, with hotels.

127 Vai Peninsula
SITE

A rocky peninsula in north-east Crete, most famous for its palm groves, and with an interesting coastal flora.

The Vai Peninsula forms the north-eastern point of Crete, northwards from the village of Vai. Its principal claim to fame is

the presence of an extensive forest of native Cretan palms. They are not confined to Crete, as they also occur in

Viola scorpiuroides

large clumps of a pretty shrubby violet *Viola scorpiuroides* covered with fragrant yellow flowers dotted with black; it is quite common in parts of north-eastern Crete, and has a few sites in western Crete, but is otherwise a north African species. On the sun-roses here, the little parasite *Cytinus hypocystis* is quite common, the Cretan tulip flowers very early, and there are spotted rock-rose, yellow forget-me-nots *Neatostema apulum*, the rosettes of *Centaurea raphanina*, hummocks of *Teucrium brevifolium*, and various other attractive flowers, with baton blue butter-flies plying between them.

south-west Turkey, and here and there in the islands, but are not common and are the only tree palm native to Europe. Their closest relative is the date palm, from which they differ in that Cretan palm tends to be shorter and multi-stemmed, and does not bear edible dates. The main locality where they occur is classed as a protected 'aesthetic forest', actually a very attractive place, especially where the palms grow right down on the beach.

Apart from the palms, there are other features of interest on the peninsula. On the rocky coastal outcrops, there are many

At Itanos, a few kilometres to the north, the normal road ends. There is extensive *garrigue* and grassland here (drying out by late spring), with wild cliffs, making an unusual landscape. Noteworthy flowers include annual bellflowers, slender cen-taury, a sea-heath *Frankenia hirsuta*, the native *Mesembryanthemum nodiflorum*, and a blue legume *Biserrula pelecinus* with extraordinary fruits like a double-edged saw. There is an unusual endemic woodruff *Asperula crassula*, with white flowers and woolly leaves; it only occurs over a couple of hectares, and nowhere else in the world. This is an unspoilt and little-known area, though there are plans afoot to cover it with tourist developments and a golf course,

Palms *Phoenix theophrasti* on Vai Peninsula

and parts of the beach have become popular with sun-worshippers.

The offshore islands have a few endemic plants such as *Carlina dia*, and the striking parasite *Cistanche phelypaea* (otherwise just known from south Spain and Portugal). They are also home to one of the strongest populations of Eleonora's falcons anywhere in the world and a sizeable breeding colony of Cory's shearwaters.

SITE 128 Perivolakia Gorge

A coastal gorge with good flowers and a spectacular monastery, with a nearby flowery, ancient site on an inland hilltop.

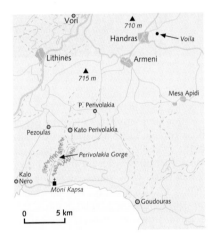

weed *Centaurea argentea*, the woodruff *Asperula tournefortii*, and the shrubby, grey-leaved, white-flowered labiate *Thymbra calostachya* which grows only here and in one neighbouring gorge. Nearby, there are bushes of the local relative of Jerusalem sage *Phlomis lanatus*.

Around the base of the gorge, green toads breed in quantity (though they

The extreme south-east of Crete, from Makrigialos round to Kato Zakros, is wonderfully unspoilt and little known. It is highly likely that there is much more to be discovered here, especially botanically.

On the south coast, sheltered by the mountains and baked by the sun, there is a fine monastery – Moni Kapsa – at the mouth of a gorge which runs inland to Perivolakia. It is worth a visit for the scenery, but it is also of interest botanically. Whilst not as rich as the very best gorges, there is a range of typical chasmophytes here, and one that occurs nowhere else in the world. Clumps of Cretan sainfoin hang down from the cliffs, with Cretan cabbage, *Staehelinia fruticosa*, a striking knap-

Arum creticum

The Kapsa monastery at the mouth of the Perivolakia gorge

finish early here in this warm spot, and have usually dispersed by late March), and there are eastern festoons, Cretan small heaths, southern speckled wood, wall browns, Bath whites, and holly blue butterflies. On the cliffs above, crag martins, blue rock thrushes and house martins nest, and chukars call from the nearby slopes.

There is a road along the south coast to the monastery, and it is possible to visit the bottom of the gorge from here, or there is access higher up via the tiny village of Kato Perivolakia.

A few kilometres inland as the raven flies (though quite a distance by road) is the ancient, hilltop ruined town of Voila, just above present-day Handras (Chandras). It is a fascinating spot, remote and little visited, with spectacular views, interesting Venetian ruins, and a good range of flowers and other wildlife. There are masses of crown anemones and pink hawksbeard, jostling on the terraces with grape-hyacinths *Muscari commutatum* and naked man orchids. There is an interesting mixture of *Orchis* species, with four-spotted,

Geranium tuberosum

Green toad *Bufo viridis* (Peter Wilson)

Crag martin *Ptyonoprogne rupestris*

Anatolian, and the rare endemic *O. siti-aca* growing close together, with some looking suspiciously intermediate in character. Tall yellow spathes of *Arum creticum* grow from rocky grassland (it is one of the most elegant of the arums), and the little saxifrage *Saxifraga heder-acea* grows on shady rocks. On field margins one can find *Geranium tubero-sum*, together with several *Ophrys* orchids. There are tree frogs around the spring at the southern end of the village.

It is a good place to watch birds from. Few species breed here, but many pass through or over. Flycatchers such as col-lared flycatcher gather in the nearby trees, with common and black redstart, shrikes, warblers, and regular golden orioles. Corn buntings are resident, sub-alpine warblers sing from the scrub, and hoopoes call in the distance. Overhead, there is usually some activity, such as ravens and buzzards, a group of grey herons purposefully heading north, and the occasional eagle. In good weather in spring it is a marvellous place.

Purple orchids

There are quite a number of purple orchids on Crete, two of which are endemic and several of which are rare. One of Crete's many endemic plants is an attractive purplish orchid which might easily be passed over, at first sight, as a four-spotted orchid or similar. A distinctive feature, however, is the patch of green at the centre of each concave sepal, which separates it from *Orchis anatolica* or four-spotted orchid; this is *O. sitiaca*, confined to the mountains of eastern Crete. It has a pale lip, spotted and edged with red, and a slender, slightly up-curved spur. *O. anatolica* is similar generally, but darker in colour and lacking the green on the sepals. Four-spotted orchid has a broad, open flower, with 2–6 small spots at the centre, and a very slender horizontal spur.

There is one other confusingly similar orchid, though it is confined to just a few mountains. This is the endemic *O. prisca*, which has the green-centred sepals of *O. sitiaca* but a more deeply and evenly purplish lip, and a short, blunt down-curved spur. See also Bory's orchid, on p. 297.

See also Bory's orchid, on p. 297.

SITE
129 Psiloritis Mountains

A large range of mountains containing the highest peak in Crete,
with endemic flowers and good birds.

Mt. Psiloritis (or Mt. Ida) is the highest point in Crete, at 2456 m, just higher than the highest peak in the White Mountains. Although there is plenty to see here, the Psiloritis Mountains somehow lack the charm and variety of the

Psiloritis Mountains (Peter Wilson)

White Mountains, and it is much harder to find interesting species. In the high areas, there is a mixture of snow-edge species similar to Ginghilos (p. 288), with *Crocus sieberi*, *Corydalis uniflora*, *Scilla nana*, and yellow stars-of-Bethlehem such as *Gagea chrysantha* and the endemic yellow alison *Alyssum idaeum*. Around the summit itself, later in the summer, there are some interesting endemics and rarities, including the scabious *Scabiosa sphaciotica*, the whitlow-grass *Draba cretica*, the endemic mayweed *Anthemis abrotanifolia*, and various others, though it is not a striking flora.

The high parts of the range are good for birds of prey, breeding on the cliffs and in gorges. There is usually at least one pair each of golden eagles and lammergeiers, and good numbers of griffon vultures, together with common choughs in the higher areas. Chukars breed throughout (the main food of the eagles, probably),

and Rüppell's warblers are quite common in scrub areas.

On the lower slopes of the mountains, especially to the south, there are some interesting flowers, such as the endemic white helleborine orchid *Cephalanthera cucullata*, growing in open pine and oak woods, in the same sort of habitat as the endemic *Epipactis cretica*, and yet another endemic orchid *Orchis prisca* (see p. 305). There is a very beautiful endemic St. John's-wort *Hypericum jovis*, which grows in flower-covered hummocks on cliffs around the mountain.

It is not exceptional for butterflies, though the endemic Cretan argus is locally abundant, just here and in the Dikti Mountains.

Mt. Psiloritis can be approached on a reasonable trail from Fourfouras to the west (though it is less clear than the maps imply), or by road southwards from Anogia on the north side onto the Nidha Plain and up to the end of the road at 1420 m.

130 Lassithi Plateau and Dikti Mountains

The easternmost block of high mountains in Crete, with a rich flora and fauna.

The Lassithi Plateau lies on the north side of the Dikti Mountains. It is rather similar to the Omalos Plateau of western Crete

(see p. 287), but has become famous for its windmills, originally ancient, though now mainly replaced by electric pumps. However, it is much more intensively cultivated than Omalos, and has lost much of its original botanical interest; the best areas are now on the surrounding slopes and up into the hills.

Around the rugged pass where the road from the north-west via Krasi comes onto the plateau, there are good areas for higher-altitude scrub birds such as black-eared wheatear, stonechat, woodchat shrike, and chukar. It is a good place to watch for some of the birds of prey that

Lassithi Plain (Peter Wilson)

breed up in the mountains, including lammergeier, peregrine, golden and Bonelli's eagles, and griffon vultures. Flowers of interest around here include the pink-flowered *Daphne sericea*, Cretan iris, and orchids such as four-spotted, toothed, milky, few-flowered, and pink butterfly. This locale is also one of the strongholds of the recently described endemic *Sternbergia greuteriana*, which flowers in autumn and looks like a golden autumn crocus, though actually it is more closely related to daffodils. The more widespread *S. sicula* also occurs here.

The famous Psichro Cave is on the south-west side of the plateau, with fabulous views, and it makes a good starting point for walks higher into the mountains. There are also choughs and crag martins around here. Flowers of note in the stony *garrigue* on the slopes includes the endemic arum *Arum idaeum*, *Anemone heldreichii*, sand-crocuses, Cretan cyclamen, and spiny chicory, with similar orchids to those on the pass. On the higher slopes and cliffs, there are choice flowers such as *Crocus sieberi*, *Scilla nana*, the endemic alison *Alyssum lassiticum*, the whitlow-grass *Draba cretica*, and the endemic, late-autumn flowering, bluish-lilac *Crocus oreocreticus*. Some remarkably fine trees of dwarf oak also grow here.

Sternbergia sicula

On the eastern side of the massif, there is one site for Crete's rarest plant, a pretty, silver-leaved bindweed *Convolvulus argyrothamnos*. It is known only from six plants on a cliff at about 450 m altitude.

Butterflies include the endemic Cretan argus.

131 Karpathos Islands

A group of little-known islands lying to the north-east of Crete, with a rich flora and interesting birds.

The Karpathos group of islands, comprising Karpathos, Kassos, and Saria, lies roughly midway between Crete and Rhodes. Botanically, it is treated as being on the extreme edge of Europe (Rhodes is considered to be in Asia, botanically), and its flora reflects this. Karpathos is much the largest island of the group, almost 50 km long, with a significant human population, though all the islands are quiet and undeveloped. The islands are all rugged, reaching 1215 m at Mt. Kalilimni in the centre of Karpathos, 630 m on Saria, and 583 m on Kassos. They are made up predominantly of limestone so there is little surface water, though Karpathos is still quite well wooded –

mainly with Aleppo pines – and has a generally green appearance.

The flora is not exceptionally rich, but it is of particular interest as there are a number of endemics, and the links with Crete and Turkey are obvious. Some predominantly Asian species, such as the

Cymbalaria longipes

woad *Isatis lusitanica*, reach their most westerly site here, and plants such as *Rosularia serrata* and the shrubby borage relative *Lithodora hispidula* are typical of the east Aegean. Out of the total native flora of about 900 species, 10 are endemic to the Karpathos group alone, and a further 22 are endemic to Crete and Karpathos. The central mountain areas of Karpathos, especially around Mt. Kalilimni and Mt. Kollas, are particularly rich in rare or endemic species. These include the delicate, pink-flowered marjoram relative *Origanum vetteri* (closely related to the better-known *O. dictamnus* of Crete), known only from a few populations on shady calcareous rocks at 1000–1200 m in this area, and nowhere else in the world. There is a little, pink-flowered cress *Ricotia isatioides*, related to the Cretan *R. cretica*, which just occurs in a few areas of mobile scree in these mountains, where hardly anything else can grow. Other endemics include two bellflowers: *Campanula carpatha*, which grows on shady cliffs, and the annual *C. pinatzii* (formerly known as *C. drabifolia* subspecies *pinatzii*), which grows on bare limestone cliffs; two catchflies: *Silene insularis* and *S. ammophila* subspecies *carpathae*, which grows on a few coastal sandy areas in the south of

Karpathos and on Kassos. *Carthamus rechingeri* is a relative of the safflower, which grows in calcareous scrubby areas only on Karpathos, and *Phlomis pichleri* is related to the widespread Jerusalem sage, but grows only in the Karpathos group, mainly in limestone scrub and river valleys.

Karpathos is an excellent region for orchids, with around 40 species recorded for quite a small area. It shares a number of species with both Crete and Rhodes, as well as having many more widespread species. Common species include violet limodore and Provence orchid in the pinewoods, numerous *Ophrys* species including *O. aegaea*, *O. bilunulata*, *O. episcopalis* (a large-flowered form of late spider orchid), horseshoe orchid, sombre bee orchid, *O. heldreichii*, *O. mammosa*, and *O. rhodia*, which it shares as an endemic with Rhodes, and many others. Other flowers of interest to be found on the Karpathos Islands include the pretty tulip *Tulipa saxatilis*, the south-eastern Aegean endemic grape-hyacinth *Muscari weissii*, the autumn-flowering *Colchicum pusillum*, common sternbergia, and the endemic *Sternbergia greuteriana*; sea daffodil on the dunes, two crocuses *Crocus biflorus* subspecies *nubigena* and *C. tournefortii*, both confined to the south Aegean area, and a rare gladiolus *Gladiolus anatolicus*.

About 9000 ha of northern Karpathos and associated islands are considered to be particularly important for birds, with abundant blue rock thrushes, and breeding Bonelli's eagle, Audouin's gull, and Eleonora's falcons. Kassos is an important area for breeding seabirds such as shearwaters and Audouin's gull, and at least 50 pairs of Eleonora's falcon breed here. The scattered uninhabited islets to the west of Karpathos, in the Karpathos Sea, are collectively of enormous value for the same species, and it is estimated that at least 125 pairs of Eleonora's falcons nest there.

There are airstrips on Karpathos and Kassos, and flights or ferries from Rhodes town or Sitia, in north-east Crete.

Lithodora hispidula

Further reading and useful addresses

Further reading

Brooks, R. (1995). *Birding in Lesbos.*
Brookside Publishing, Fakenham,
Norfolk.

Heath, M. and Evans, M. (2000).
Important bird areas in Europe. Vol. 2:
Southern Europe. Birdlife International,
Cambridge.

Kremezi-Margaritouli, A. (1995).
*CARETTA: the loggerhead sea turtle in
Greece.* Erevnites, Athens.

Polunin, O. (1980). *Flowers of Greece and
the Balkans.* Oxford University Press.

Sfikas, G. (1999). *The mountains of Greece*
(2nd edn). Efstathiadis, Athens.

Snow, D. W. and Perrins, C. M. (ed.)
(1998). *The Birds of the Western Palearctic*
(concise edn). Oxford University Press.

Tolman, T. (2001). *Photographic guide to
the butterflies of Britain and Europe.*
Oxford University Press.

Useful addresses

**Anthophoros (Center for the Protection
of the Greek Flora),** 2 Vyzanliou Street,
Argyroupolis, 16 452, Athens.

Elstead Maps, PO Box 52, Elstead,
Godalming, Surrey GU8 6JJ. Tel: 01252
703472. Suppliers of maps.

**Hellenic Federation of Mountaineering
Clubs,** 7 Karageorgi Servias, 105 63
Athens. Fax: (01) 3237666.

Hellenic Ornithological Society, 53 Em.
Benaki Str, 106 81, Athens. Tel/fax: (01)
3811271.

**Hellenic Society for the Protection of
Nature,** 24 Nikis Str, 105 57, Athens. Fax:
(01) 3225285.

Marengo Publications (Lance Chilton), 17
Bernard Crescent, Hunstanton, PE36 6ER.
Tel/fax: 01485 532710. Publishers of
booklets on walks and flowers in various
Greek sites, including a series of checklists.

Road Editions, 41 Ilia Iliou Street, GR 117
43, Athens. Fax: (01) 9296492. Publishers
of the best generally available maps.

Sea Turtle Protection Society of Greece,
Solomou 35, GR-106 82, Athens. Tel/fax:
(01) 3844146.

World Wide Fund for Nature, Greece, 14
Asklipiou Str, 106 80, Athens. Fax: (01)
3623342.

Geographical Index

KEY TO SITE MAP SYMBOLS

National border		National park
River, stream or canal		Reserve or area of interest
Torrent		Information point
Road		Parking
Dual carriageway		Hide or observation point
Path or track		Shelter
Railway		Peak, height in metres
Ferry		Land above 1000 metres
Airport, airfield		Land above 1500 metres
Lighthouse		Land above 2000 metres
Castle or tower		Marsh
Ecclesiastical building, disused		Cliff or crag